ALSO BY THOMAS KESSNER

*Fiorello LaGuardia and the Making of Modern New York*

*Today's Immigrants, Their Stories: A New Look
at the Newest Americans* (with Betty Caroli)

*The Golden Door: Italian and Jewish Immigrant Mobility
in New York City, 1880–1915*

# CAPITAL CITY

NEW YORK CITY AND THE MEN BEHIND
AMERICA'S RISE TO ECONOMIC DOMINANCE,
1860–1900

## THOMAS KESSNER

*SIMON & SCHUSTER*

NEW YORK LONDON TORONTO SYDNEY SINGAPORE

SIMON & SCHUSTER
Rockefeller Center
1230 Avenue of the Americas
New York, NY 10020

For information regarding special discounts for bulk purchases,
please contact Simon & Schuster Special Sales:
1-800-456-6798 or business@simonandschuster.com

Manufactured in the United States of America

1   3   5   7   9   10   8   6   4   2

Library of Congress Cataloging-in-Publication Data

Kessner, Thomas.
Capital city : New York City and the men behind America's rise to economic dominance,
1860–1900 / Thomas Kessner.
p.   cm.
Includes bibliographical references and index.
1. New York (N.Y.)—Economic conditions—19th century. 2. Corporations—New York (State)—
History—19th century. 3. Capitalism—New York (State)—History—19th century. 4. Capitalists
and financiers—New York (State)—New York. 5. New York (N.Y.)—History—19th century. I. Title:
New York City and the men behind America's rise to economic dominance, 1860–1900. II. Title.

HC108.N7 K47 2003
330.9747'1041—dc21
2002036699

ISBN 0-684-81351-3

# ACKNOWLEDGMENTS

I am indebted to a great many people whose contributions have enriched this book. Those whose work bears directly on my themes are cited in the notes. But there are many more individuals who have shaped my thinking, and while I cannot thank them all here, I do want to single out Kenneth T. Jackson, whose writing and research have been an ongoing influence since the days when he was my mentor at Columbia University more than a few years ago.

I have also benefited from colleagues at the Graduate Center, the City University of New York, whose generosity of spirit and willingness to share are part of the joys of academic life. I am especially indebted to Abe Ascher, Carol Berkin, and Kathleen McCarthy for their incisive critiques of several chapters. I want also to thank David Nasaw, Jim Oakes, Nicholas Papayanis, Mike Wallace, and Richard Wolin for their advice and suggestions. So many curators, librarians, and archivists have been characteristically generous that I am reduced to a blanket thank you, but Madeline Kent of the Seymour Durst Old York Library deserves special mention. As I slogged through piles of historic photos she was lavish with her time and assistance.

It is also a pleasure to thank a number of my students. Cindy Lobel, Matthew Cotter, and Megan Elias assisted me with some of the research. Angelo Angelis and Julie Miller made helpful comments on several draft chapters, and Luke Waltzer helped me with preparing the images.

My literary agent, Heide Lange, has supplied me with endless encouragement and boundless good cheer. It is with great affection and warmth that we both recall her colleague and my original agent, the late Diane Cleaver. My editor, Bob Bender, has been an unflagging supporter of this book. It is very much a part of his consummate craft that the extent of his contribution is evident to me alone.

To my wife, Rachel, and to my family, who contribute to my work in so many ways, I owe a special debt.

*B'EZRAS HASHEM*

IN DEDICATION TO

LIVIA KESSNER,

ABE AND ESTHER ROTH

AND THE MEMORY OF YEHUDA KESSNER, A. H.

# CONTENTS

# INTRODUCTION

*In everything New York is the city that is different. When considering*
*Boston, Philadelphia, Chicago, or San Francisco it is customary to speak*
*of what their people think or are or do, but no one ever speaks thus of*
*the people of New York, but only of the city itself. For the city is so much*
*greater than its people! With New York the city makes the people; else-*
*where the people make the city.*[1]
        —ROBERT SHACKLETON, *The Book of New York*

BETWEEN THE END of the Civil War and the last years of the
nineteenth century, America's vast western domain, ripening industrial system, and eastern money market joined in spectacular
fashion to transform a small nation of scattered farms into the
world's leading economic power. This transformation uprooted an
economy built on measured growth and small-scale proprietary capitalism and replaced it with a new economy of audacious investment
and global scope.

New York City kindled this crucible stage of American capitalism.
Wielding an influence unmatched in any other city, Manhattan's financial houses shaped all of American banking. Its stock and bond
markets dominated the trade in securities; its banks stored most of the
nation's cash reserves; and its investors controlled the massive new
railroad corporations. Around the world Wall Street became a synonym for money power. New York's unique business environment attracted to the city the leading capitalists of the age and with them
platoons of lawyers, accountants, insurance experts, and corporate
managers, a modern infrastructure for the new order of business. So
defining was New York's role in this economic transformation that
even today America's economy remains largely the invention of
Gotham's Gilded Age.

In the searing shadow of September 11, 2001, it is clear that after the passing of more than a century, New York remains the capital of capitalism; to people around the world, in other metropolises as well as in the caves of Afghanistan, Gotham is the most potent and inviting symbol of America's prosperity.

---

From early in the nineteenth century, Manhattan with its magnificent waterways and the best natural harbor on the continent was the leading port city in the hemisphere. To its docks came the high-masted sailing ships bringing goods from around the world for distribution to a growing hinterland. New York's merchants expanded this trade into a system of exchange with wide ramifications that came to anchor national economic activity. Thanks to the profitable mercantile business, money accumulated more rapidly in New York than anywhere else on the globe. When the South seceded, New York alone of all Union cities had the resources to finance the Civil War. In the colossal economic boom that followed the peace, Gotham's investment houses and freewheeling speculators financed an economic expansion unparalleled in U.S. history.

These were the years when, in Henry Adams's words, New York "exploded its wrapper" to become America's technological showplace, its communications and information capital, its financial center, ushering in a "prosperity never before imagined." New York boasted America's most audacious and most driven businessmen, men like John Jacob Astor, America's wealthiest real estate mogul; Jay Gould and Cornelius Vanderbilt, its most influential railroad strategists and speculators; Moses Taylor and A. T. Stewart, who developed their local commercial baronies into multinational empires; Andrew Carnegie, the world's leading industrialist; John D. Rockefeller, whose pioneering oil trust set the pattern for global cartels; and the most feared financial power of them all, J. P. Morgan. These New Yorkers and their colleagues forged a fresh business culture of daring investment, converting a proliferation of markets based on the local exchange of real goods to a consolidated commerce in virtual property signified by stocks, bonds, and assorted certificates. This step, which New York's role as the nation's money market made possible, dramatically expanded the economy. It magnified the volume of trade, accelerated the flow of profits, and fostered immense projects like the railroad system. In the last years of the century, the equities market promoted the most intense wave of business mergers in history, furnishing America with titanic new corporations.

Although we often think about the technological revolution, the explosive growth of industry, the rise of big business, and the ascendancy of the city as an entwined cluster of inescapable forces, the new economy was crafted by individuals whose decisions shaped the evolving system of corporate capitalism. "All New York was demanding new men," Henry Adams recalled in his *Education*, "all the new forces condensed into corporations, were demanding a new type of man,—a man with ten times the endurance, energy, will and mind of the old types. . . ."[2]

These fascinating "new men" were very much products of their times, even as they extended its possibilities. They adopted the imperative to build wealth far beyond any individual's ability to consume it. Many of the more captivating figures in this story were ruthless in exploiting the land, the markets, the political system, and their own workers. In another time or a more fastidious atmosphere, some would no doubt have viewed the world from behind bars. But in an era when powerful men pursued their own dreams amid the least government possible, there was little to temper those dreams or make them altruistic. And although Jay Gould, Cornelius Vanderbilt, Andrew Carnegie, John D. Rockefeller, et al. did not set out to build corporate America, their speculations and pursuit of the main chance so entwined with the larger forces of economic growth and expansion concentrated in New York that their personal story is crucial to understanding this economic transformation.

In the span of less than forty years, these capitalists mobilized the financial, entrepreneurial, and managerial resources to lay out a powerful new basis for American business and fix a course for the future. No succeeding generation enjoyed the economic power, the open political atmosphere, and the shaping influence available to this group of capitalists. When John Pierpont Morgan first came to Wall Street, not a single industrial concern was listed on the New York Stock Exchange. By the time he had completed the U.S. Steel consolidation in 1901, the NYSE listed more than one thousand companies, including the cornerstone businesses of the twentieth-century economy.

That was what the *New York World* meant when it wrote upon Morgan's death that he "was the last for his line. Never again will conditions . . . make it possible for any financier to bestride the country like a Colossus." "He could have done what he did," the *Herald Tribune* wrote similarly of Rockefeller, "in no other setting. . . . A great expression of a great age." Moreover, these men not only shaped business but also the city that came to be its headquarters, recasting the physical environment, influencing its politics, and setting the pace for cultural change and social refinement.[3]

During the past thirty years, scholars of the city and urban life have studied the impact of metropolitan experience on child rearing, household relations, gender roles, labor, and politics. They have written revealingly about the ordinary lives of ordinary people and have minutely explored the sway of such great variables as race, class, ethnicity, and gender. Their new histories have given a historical voice to lives that previous histories have marginalized. But if traditional histories focused excessively on heroes constructed around favored racial and gender assumptions and excluded too much of the quotidian, the more recent work has too often held the lens to the excessively parochial, the particular, and the ordinary, offering brilliant fragments instead of a grand mirror to the past.

I am sensitive to the new approaches, but a group of elite white men dominates this story of a profoundly altered economy because these men steered the action and their influence was seminal. The best-known individuals of their times, their stories took on mythical significance. Their experiences were inscribed on the collective consciousness of New York, creating expectations and molding behaviors. Countless Gilded Age New Yorkers framed their perceptions of "rags to riches" opportunity on accounts of Jay Gould, Andrew Carnegie, and John D. Rockefeller. And a great many Americans looked to these men not only for economic inspiration and philanthropic assistance, but for their views on religion, society, and politics. Not only were their business decisions carefully analyzed, but their homes, their art, their social clubs, and their society functions were all avidly observed and followed.

Their worship of economic growth suffused the country. Not long before, Americans defined the national mission in religious terms. Now Americans measured progress in tons of steel produced, telephones installed, and businesses consolidated. Other societies honored the intellectual, the warrior, the leader of men, the artist, but the New York hero was the self-made corporate mogul. Success was assayed in units of stock. Fundamental political concepts like liberty and equality were applied not to issues of personal freedom and economic justice, but to debates on the tariff and laissez-faire economic policy.

Commercial Gotham had been a city scaled to human dimension. New Yorkers born in the decades before the Civil War remembered growing up in a compact, pedestrian city. Its warehouse district, political center, cultural institutions, and residential neighborhoods lay in proximity, all within easy walking distance of one another. Church spires dominated the sky. This modest vista made way before a differentiated landscape of capital that boasted a strutting new skyline and the grand signatures of a world metropolis. French historian Bernard Fay would write later that New York was "the only city in the world rich enough in money, vitality and men" to build itself anew; "the only city sufficiently wealthy to be modern." Gotham, he continued, "is constructed to the scale of the United States. . . ." Its structures were not mere homes, "they are the Eiffel Tower cathedrals which shelter Mr. Rockefeller, the Emperor of Petroleum, or Mr. Morgan, the Czar of Gold. . . ."[4]

Herald of twentieth-century modernity, fin de siècle New York catapulted the United States to the center of international capitalism. Its political figures drawn from the business community and allied professions contended for high national office and set the terms of political discourse. Its bankers and industrialists guided America's economic reorganization, and its disparate immigrant population, drawn from the eclipsed lands of Europe, cast the mold for national diversity. Before the end of the century, Gotham annexed its neighboring municipalities to form a metropolis that stretched over 359 square miles, holding more inhabitants than all but six states. In the entire world, only London was more populous, but no city matched New York's reach in ambition and influence.

What proved especially remarkable was New York's irrepressible ability to master the changes that so swiftly reshaped the American economy. Other cities passed from importance as their role in the national economy changed, but New York, putting to great advantage the momentum of its mighty commercial system, never relinquished its dominance. It remained the world's most active port, even as it developed into the center of national banking, information, and manufacture. And then it went on to become the world's corporate center. In each successive iteration, from commercial hub, to investment center, to hemispheric money market, and to corporate headquarters, New York initiated the most innovative techniques, attracted the most talented experts, boasted the most venturesome entrepreneurs.

Other cities might organize the economy of a state or region, but Gotham was the central nervous system for the entire system of cities in the United States. Here the other cities bought their goods, sold their own merchandise overseas, took their labor forces, came to find funding for their large undertakings, banked their surpluses, traded their securities, and managed their corporations. In the process, Wall Street converted an economic system theoretically committed to laissez-faire to a market dominated by corporate conglomerates. Absorbing competitors and swallowing up suppliers of raw materials, as well as producers and distributors, these giant monopolies supplanted the competitive market to control production, set prices, and cast industrial policy.

The sweeping restructuring of the economy posed real threats to the rights and independence of smaller businesses and citizens, consumers, and workers. Bristling with authoritarian and even tyrannical possibilities, the new corporations wielded broad sway over the market, profits, jobs, and politics. Yet this change of vast scope proceeded peacefully, in contrast, for example, to the way the struggle over slavery played out.

In the contest over slavery, both sides embraced their exclusive certainties and marched off to war. But corporate capitalism developed in the tempering environment of New York City, where it was forced to address an increasingly outspoken press, New York's substantial labor unions, and the varied formulas proposed by Gotham reformers for modifying the free market. For New York was more than just a center for business and business leaders. It was also the center for social reform, unions of every stripe, intellectual radicalism, elite philanthropy, the social gospel movement, and a freewheeling municipal politics that empowered the working class. Even as the bankers and the industrialists went about consolidating corporate capital, New York's diverse metropolitan interest worked its checks into the new system, helping save it from some of its own excesses.

Even New York's conservative "best men" argued that the large corporations needed to be restrained. Andrew Green, the real estate attorney and urban planner nonpareil, pulled no punches in staking his case for a greater, stronger city on the need to bridle the corporation. Mere Manhattan with its twenty-three miles and ragged force of low-end politicians could not regulate and police against the "exactions of colossal and all pervading monopoly," he declared. Monopolies were moving "in concert upon fixed plans to definite purpose," exerting control over foods, necessities, jobs, and utilities. Green's successful campaign to consolidate the metropolitan region into Greater New York was based at least in part on the need to counterpose the colossal city to "the organized forces of relentless and absentee capitalism," the "lawless enterprises," and the illicit "leagues, guilds, combinations, federations, monopolies, pools and trusts."[5]

Moreover, while Morgan, Carnegie, and Rockefeller shaped the new capitalism with their investments and initiatives, they often did not agree. New York's internally diverse business class included not only the new banking and securities sector and corporate enterprise, but also long established trade and commercial houses, many different fields of manufacture, the information industries, retail business and real estate. This eclectic business community subdued some of corporate capital's more extreme possibilities, even as it ultimately rendered it more pliant and durable.

From this process came a tough but ideologically flexible capitalism, the product not of a single line of development, but of many. This rise of the corporate movement represented the most peaceful change of such vast scope in American history. Yet its adversaries never managed to mount a sustained or meaningful opposition. One may dispute the ultimate result, but the fact that corporate capitalism emerged from a richly diverse New York gave it a resilience and a complexity that helped account for its wide acceptance.

For it was widely accepted. In 1900, the majority of Americans still lived on farms and in rural communities. Many of them had more than a few reservations about Wall Street, and they comprehended the process that had reshaped the national economy only imperfectly at best, but in election after election they ratified its effects. Even urban workers were impressed with the greater stability in employment, better wages, and cornucopia of consumer goods that a new prosperity had wrought. That, and the possibility of advancement, if not for themselves, then for their children. They ratified the great changes at the polls, and in the first election of the new century, they elected a bully New Yorker to the White House.

That same year, Henry Adams returned to New York after a long absence. As the bay came into view, "more striking than ever—wonderful—unlike anything man had ever seen," he was struck by what he confronted. "The cylinder had exploded, and thrown great masses of stone and steam against the sky. The city had the air and movement of hysteria. . . . Prosperity never before imagined, power never yet wielded by man, speed never reached by anything but a meteor. . . ."[6]

Let us turn to that story.

# CHAPTER 1

# Foundations

## Licking Up the Cream of Commerce and Finance of a Continent

*The unequal distribution of wealth we believe to be not only an unalterable consequence of the nature of man, and the state of being in which he is placed, but also the only system by which his happiness and improvement can be promoted in this state of being. . . . Once touch the rights of property, let it be felt that men are imperiled and harassed in their efforts to obtain it, that its possession is insecure, and that portions of it may be taken from them, . . . and you immediately stop enterprise, and with enterprise the progress of knowledge, and with the progress of knowledge that also of virtue—and then where is the happiness of such a community?[1]*
—REVEREND JONATHAN MAYHEW WAINWRIGHT, 1856

*Every man [in New York] seems to feel that he has got the duty of two lifetimes to accomplish in one, and so he rushes, rushes, rushes, and never has the time to be companionable—never has any time at his disposal to fool away on matters which do not involve dollars and duty and business.[2]*
—MARK TWAIN, 1867

TURN OF NINETEENTH-CENTURY Manhattan was a rising city of some fifty thousand, occupying the water's edge of an overwhelmingly agricultural America. In a national economy dominated by the trade in staples, New York City lacked anything to compare with the great cash crops of tobacco, cotton, wheat, or rice. Its citizens worked the margins of the land-based economy, buying agricultural surplus, exchanging it for myriad finished goods, and squeezing a profit out of the difference. But, unlike Charleston, for example, whose merchants lived off the staple crops in their vicinity, or Philadelphia, with its fertile Piedmont, New York lacked a natural hinterland of much consequence. Manhattan's traders had to venture farther and work harder for their business. The Manhattan economy was more competitive, the product of larger risks; its public was more varied, more unsettled; and its society was disproportionately filled with upstarts who lacked the polished grace and cultivated learning manifested by other urban elites. Even the streets were less orderly. Visitors noted the absence of the elegant touches they found in America's other principal cities. British travelers compared New York to second-tier Liverpool. Philadelphia was America's London.[3]

Not for long. In 1816 a visiting Frenchman, Baron de Montlezun, conceded the Quaker City's settled splendor and dignity, but he closed his observations on the early national cities with the prediction that the American city "destined to become the most frequented port and most flourishing city of the New World" was the narrow isle on the Hudson. That a single informant might express such expectations for Manhattan provokes scant astonishment, even in the face of claims blithe and colossal; but that such a prediction should before long become the conventional wisdom, trumpeted by every observer and foreign traveler, testifies to the triumph of serendipity and shrewdness over experience and planning.[4]

New York did boast one extraordinary advantage. Natural geography had provided Manhattan with the best harbor in the Western Hemisphere. Ample, well sheltered, and deep enough to accommodate even the large draft vessels that came into use for the cargo trade late in the eighteenth century, New York Bay was still shallow enough to facilitate convenient anchorage. Wharves and shipyards nestled easily in its protected waters. And fanning out from the inlet were hundreds of miles of water channels providing direct access to the sea. From the Narrows, the mile-wide breech separating Upper New York Bay from the Atlantic, ran the main sea lane to Europe and the routes to the southern and Caribbean ports. Alternatively, ships headed for the Great West could course up the Hudson, while those destined for New England traveled the East River around the turbulent Hell Gate and past Long Island.[5]

New York's harbor had advantages over the harbors of other cities. The huge brigs and ocean liners coming into use for transatlantic shipping in the early nineteenth century could not easily dock at ports that were tucked deeper inland. Philadelphia, wrote the French statesman Talleyrand, was "too buried in the land" to comfortably accommodate these deep draft vessels, except during high tide. But, he added, New York's deep, "good and convenient harbor which is never closed by ice [and] its central position" allowed these large ocean craft direct access.[6]

Orders cascaded in from around the globe, sending Manhattan's merchants deeper and deeper inland to gather the farm goods, meats, leather, lumber, and raw products for which Europe and its colonies clamored. More than twenty years of on and off conflict between England and France had also forced many of Europe's merchant ships out of commercial service and into war, expanding Manhattan's carrying business. Between its revived merchant marine and its mounting share of commerce, writes Robert Albion, the distinguished historian of Early American business, New York effectively diverted the "channels of trade with Europe . . . [away from] Philadelphia or Boston."[7]

Cities are profoundly plastic environments, shaped by inspiration and will, and in New York the focus on commerce, on building trade, led the state and the city to promote a ramifying system of new canals, bridges, roads, and turnpikes, extending Manhattan's reach far into the interior. Unlike Boston, for example, where city fathers hesitated to invest in expensive public construction projects, Manhattan was prepared to build for business. City Hall erected a new seawall, extended the New York shoreline, and sank landfill to create new streets and lengthen the business district. Beyond the city limits, New York State pursued the most ambitious program in the Union for building roads and turnpikes, carving new paths to the burgeoning communities that kept extending the frontier line westward.[8] These new regions increasingly relied on New York to sell their surplus and bring them their necessities.

This thickening hinterland spread south as well. For years southern tobacco planters sold and shipped their product through New York. But the cotton trade proved still more important in making New York the primary broker for southern staples. Soon after the introduction of the ginning machine in 1793, Manhattan dominated the phenomenally popular trade in cotton and, as demand increased, Manhattan's brokers, insurance companies, shippers, and exporters laid claim to an immodest share of the slave regime's cotton profits.[9]

Inlanders might dismiss city merchants as percent men who lived off commissions and profits squeezed from the honest work of real yeomen, but farmers and planters needed New York more than they were willing to acknowledge. Gotham merchants advanced the credit that made it possible for them to pay their bills—for food, seed, implements, new land, and everything else they needed—while they waited for the harvest to come in. And once it did come in, they needed brokers and factors to arrange for shipping and marketing their produce. And they needed insurance. They also needed to have their notes discounted and their bills of exchange cashed. They needed the entire system of trade and transport that Manhattan's middlemen had erected in order to convert agricultural surplus into market commodities. And they needed the goods that New York's merchants brought back, the coffee from South America, fine calicoes from England, quality furniture from Paris, rum from Jamaica, tea from Canton, and pepper from Sumatra.[10]

Between 1790 and 1807, as the United States built its economy out from under Britain's control, the volume of its international trade multiplied sevenfold. In these years New York, making capital of the opportunities provided by her great port, continental turmoil, and the cotton gin, pulled together the most productive hinterland in the hemisphere, surpassing Philadelphia to become the young nation's chief entrepôt and principal link to global markets.[11]

Not all of the fruits of this success were welcome. In a theme that would echo repeatedly throughout Gotham's history, there were New Yorkers who feared that the pursuit of wealth had become too consuming, that just a few years after the Revolution, mammon and its tempting gifts threatened the republican virtues of "plainness and simplicity." But New Yorkers were exhibiting less interest than ever before in pious austerity. John Lambert, a Canadian travel writer, recounted in 1807: "The port was filled . . . with commodities of every description. . . . The merchants and their clerks were busily engaged in their counting houses. . . . The Tontine coffee-house was filled with underwriters, brokers, merchants, traders, and politicians, selling, purchasing, trafficking, or insuring. . . . Everything was in motion; all was life, bustle, and activity." In the first two decades of the century, difficult years that involved trade embargoes and war, per capita income for New Yorkers increased fourfold.[12]

Already observers said of New York that its merchants worked harder and longer than counterparts elsewhere. An English visitor marveled at their energy and indefatigability. In the morning they hastened to the countinghouse to sort the mail and dictate responses about prices, goods, and deliveries. Then they were off to the docks, "flying about as dirty and as diligent as porters" to "roll hogsheads of rum and molasses" in their aprons. Thereafter they rushed to the Merchant's Exchange to drum up new business before dashing back to the wharves to arrange for day workers to make their deliveries. All the while they kept an ear open for the latest information from arriving sailors and visitors about overseas conditions, prices, and any political intelligence that might hint at the market's future. "What a day's work this would have been for a Carolinian," exclaimed the bedazzled observer.

But the day was only half-done as these dynamic businessmen prepared to party as hard as they worked. Upon arriving home after four, they changed into dinner clothing, then enjoyed a meal followed often by a visit to the theater. Once the play was over, they were off again at eleven "to supper with a crew of lusty Bacchanals," followed by a round of smoking, drinking, and singing, sometimes till three in the morning. The New York merchant, the visitor concluded, "enjoy[ed] his span of being, to the full stretch of the tether."[13]

Descriptions of the New York market, like the men who molded it, convey the sense that whether it had to do with the swift recovery after the Revolution or a competitive streak that went back to the Dutch, business was more intense here. Ideology and tradition counted for less, and a hard-driving pragmatism for much more, than in Philadelphia or Boston. There was less ambivalence or reticence about doing what had to be done to make money. Immediately upon the heels of the peace treaty that ended America's War of 1812 with Britain, for example, New York seized its chance to snatch a favored position in the restored European order. While merchants in Boston and Philadelphia, considering it unseemly to cooperate with so recent and so despised a foe, refused to distribute Britain's surplus war inventories, New York went right ahead. Its Pearl Street auction houses fed the pent-up demand for textiles, iron products, and a miscellany of bargain-price luxury items, turning the heavily discounted goods into quick fortunes. Before long Pearl Street had cornered the market for British imports.[14]

The explosive growth of these auctions forced New York's more conventional merchants to make improvements by offering new services and wider selections. Meanwhile, the popular auction houses continued to expand the market, as more of Europe's producers sent their excess goods to Pearl Street, where twice a year, in the fall and spring, shopkeepers and wholesale distributors ("jobbers") would descend by packet and steamer to lay in the season's stocks. These jobbers linked New York's traders to a widening locus of general stores, plantations, and villages. Less than a year after the peace was concluded, New York was collecting more import excises on tea, crockery, hardware, and textiles than Philadelphia and Boston combined. When these and other ports made belated overtures to win this "dumping" trade, New York's auction community pressed a sympathetic legislature to slash import taxes, securing Pearl Street's continued advantage.[15]

Gotham's pursuit of the main chance led to another crucial breakthrough, the introduction of Manhattan's transatlantic shuttle in 1818. Before, merchants were forced to rely for their overseas shipments on sea tramps that made the rounds of American ports to pick up cargo and set off for sail only after they managed to fill their holds. The only other option, aside from commissioning a ship, was to secure space on a private vessel run by the large traders who generally sailed twice a year. The owners would load their goods on these liners and then take on extra freight as space permitted. Neither option offered the midsize merchant much of a chance to ship on a consistent or reliable basis.

The initiation of New York's regularly scheduled monthly shuttle to Liverpool changed this, releasing merchants from the mercy of uncertain transport. Traders who borrowed to assemble their exports and to insure this cargo could now pay off these loans more quickly and more cheaply, while the quicker turnaround on investment drove up trade volume and stepped up the pace of the economy. The shuttle's five-week one-way course from England also brought the speediest tidings of war, overseas prices, and news of the European market, no small dividend in these years before the transatlantic wire. Weeks ahead of rivals in other ports, Manhattan's businessmen learned the latest intelligence on overseas cotton prices or the vote on English tariff.[16]

In 1825, New York State opened its long-awaited Erie Canal. Seven years before, New York City mayor De Witt Clinton pushed through the state legislature a bill committing the state to a 363-mile system of inland canals. Critics had derided the investment as foolhardy, dismissing the project as "Clinton's ditch." At $7 million, the project *was* expensive, more costly than any improvement project in history. It was also audacious, involving the excavation of hundreds of miles of hard land, much of it by hand; and it was visionary imagining a vast unbroken corridor of linked roads and water connections between Albany and Lake Erie. It did not take long for the canal to prove the critics wrong. Enormously successful (within ten years it repaid the entire cost of its construction), it demonstrated for all New York's commitment to speeding commercial progress.

More important, the Erie Canal system provided western farmers with a superior outlet to the Atlantic. Before, the rich grain regions of the West and the wharves and mills of the great inland lakes that sought to use water transport were forced to ship along frontier waterways to New Orleans. Now, Manhattan was opened to them. And back along the same new traffic line came the riches of New York's import trade, filling the many new country stores that dotted the interior with finished products, fabrics, and foods from overseas. From 218,000 tons in its first year, canal traffic rose to 1.4 million tons by 1840. Even before the canal opened, New York City was the principal axis for north-south trade. Now, its merchants claimed an increasing share of the trade passing between east and west.[17]

Gotham's commercial activity was concentrated on three streets at the southern tip of Manhattan. Pearl Street held the auction houses, dry goods merchants, and wholesalers of some sixty different lines of merchandise. Wall Street, originally a neighborhood of fine single-level colonial residences, came to be dominated by the three- and four-story Greek Revival stone fronts favored by banks and insurance companies. In 1836, it welcomed a massive new Merchant's Exchange, where traders gathered to broker deals and learn the latest prices. But if New York took on "the air of a town sacrificed to trade," it was the doing of South Street's more than four hundred countinghouses. Here multifloor buildings occupying the landfill that had been added to New York's southern shoreline formed the bustling hub of mercantile New York. The upper levels of the squat structures were devoted to warehousing merchandise, while the lower section was divided between a showroom and a counting room, where a battery of male clerks, errand boys, and "copyists" tallied wares, packaged goods, filed data, copied bills, translated overseas communications, and processed manifests and bills of lading.[18]

The privileged Knickerbocker elite, secure in their landed wealth and inherited status, by and large shunned the stormy fortunes of commerce, leaving the exchange in goods to others. As a result, as New York's merchant population multiplied rapidly in the years after 1815, Manhattan's trading class, including its most successful tier, came to be composed largely of "new men," immigrants and others who had parted with their past to seek new futures. More open, more turbulent ("About seven in the hundred" among traders were successful, observed an experienced old merchant. "All the rest . . . have been bankrupts"), and less fixed in its class makeup, New York appealed to men who had more to offer than pedigree or inheritance. It offered men like John Jacob Astor and Alexander Stewart the opportunity to try to make their fortunes in trade, if they dared.[19]

John Jacob Astor arrived from Waldorf, Germany, in 1783 at the age of twenty. He had no friends, money, or education and turned to street peddling to earn a meager livelihood. With his small savings he opened a shop selling toys, only to begin purchasing fur hides, which soon enough he was shipping overseas. Within ten years of his landing in the city, John Astor was its most important fur trader, dealing in otter and beaver pelts gathered from America's rich forests. These furs he processed in his Manhattan warehouses and distributed to the distant corners of the earth. His first shipload of animal skins bound for Canton (together with immense quantities of an herb that promised among other cures to restore male sexual vigor) left in 1800, and before long, Astor had the China import trade virtually for himself.[20]

Astor displayed a genius for trade prodigiously leavened by a special New York business audacity. He vaulted barriers of language and culture, and even the embargo that President Thomas Jefferson placed on American shipping in 1808 designed to avoid entanglement with Europe's warring powers. The widely damned embargo decimated American trade, shuttering more than 120 businesses in New York alone. "Not a box, bale, cask, barrel, or package," mourned a visitor to the city, "was to be seen upon the wharves," except that is, Astor's *Beaver*, which won a rare exemption to carry home a notable "Mandarin" stranded in the United States. Astor filled his ship with $200,000 in skins, placed the dignified Asian in a conspicuous berth, and sent the carrier off for Canton. Later the man turned out to be a less than distinguished debt collector whom Astor had dressed well.[21]

In exchange for the animal skins, Astor brought back teas, porcelain chinaware, and silks, becoming America's first millionaire. In his most brilliant stroke he invested his profits in a liberal reading of New York's future, buying title to vast slices of Manhattan property. (In this he grasped a piquant secret of New York economic life: The more its businessmen and laborers sweated, invested, and profited, the higher they sent land values, furnishing real estate with an immense passive dividend.) When he died in March of 1848, Astor was the richest man in the country, with an estate estimated at $30 million, a fortune very close to that of the wealthiest Rothschild and second to no one else in the world. This fortune owed nothing to family, but a great deal to an environment that generously rewarded the speculative spirit. The old trader voiced but one regret upon his deathbed, that he had not invested his every penny to buy much more of Manhattan when he had had the chance.[22]

Newcomers of foreign background like Astor and the successful traders Archibald Gracie and Robert Lenox built some of Gotham's most successful trading houses. Jeremiah Thompson, another immigrant, originated the transatlantic shuttle and helped establish the triangular trade in southern cotton that brought New York an extraordinary share of cotton profits. Even more familiar in the counting-houses were the New Englanders who dominated South Street for the first half of the century. "They," writes Robert Albion, "built and commanded most of the ships," and they, recalled a contemporary, with their "long legs, hatchet face, skin and bones, slight, pokey and keen as a briar," became the leading shipowners and merchants. The point was not that you had to be from out of town to succeed, but that on South Street an openness to unanticipated possibility counted for far more than genealogy and inherited status. In this open atmosphere apprenticeship in the countinghouses not infrequently set sharp clerks on the path to independent enterprise.[23]

In 1821, Moses Taylor, the son of one of John J. Astor's general agents, went to work for G.G.&S.S. Howlands, a South Street shipping house that specialized in the Latin American trade. The fifteen-year-old Taylor began as an apprentice, opening mail and transcribing prices. Accompanying the senior clerks on their rounds, he familiarized himself with the specialized world of the busy port and the particular needs of foreign merchants. In time Taylor moved up to making trades on his own responsibility, collecting his own commissions. Taylor's adroit business skills so impressed Cuba's leading shipper, the Drake Brothers, that they encouraged him, while still in his mid-twenties, to set out on his own. With savings of some $15,000 and excellent references from the Howlands, Taylor struck out on his own in 1832. Like many others who set their eyes on a piece of Gotham's trade, he had no family business behind him and no kin network to advise him or to smooth connections on his behalf. He announced his availability to the business community as a commission merchant, promising "any business in my charge . . . the best attention that industry and dispatch can give it."[24]

Taylor moved to Cuba for a while where he specialized in developing sugar accounts and then returned to South Street, where by the age of thirty-two he was the leading American importer of Cuban sugar. These were years of fevered business growth. President Andrew Jackson's veto of the charter for the Second Bank of the United States removed the tamping influence of the national bank and released a huge wave of unregulated credit. The resulting inflation stepped up the level of business activity, sending prices higher and confidence in the New York market higher still. During these heady years it seemed impossible to go wrong on a business investment. The number of business failures dropped to historic lows, as in all of 1834 there were no more than thirty bankruptcies in New York. Taylor read the times perfectly, completing his climb from apprentice clerk to prominent New York merchant with a personal fortune of $200,000 and a spacious home in Manhattan's fashionable Washington Square. As a mark of his success, Taylor joined the New York State Chamber of Commerce, then a circle of fewer than a hundred leading merchants who advanced commercial interests before city authorities and the U.S. Congress.[25]

Even more spectacular was the rise of Alexander Turney Stewart (1803–1876), who arrived as a teenager from Belfast around 1820. He filled various jobs before returning to Ireland to claim a modest inheritance, which he used to buy Irish laces and cloth. These he brought back with him and opened a small retail stall on Broadway above City Hall Park in 1823, restocking his inventory from the Pearl Street auctions. Local merchants and producers, hurt by the cheap British imports, sought to unite against the sale of dumped goods, but Stewart ignored their protests. Instead he built a clientele from among the expanding company of middle-class and working women who developed a taste for bargain-priced imported textiles. Within a few years he opened a succession of larger shops retailing fine fabrics.[26]

As urban life moved ever further from home-churned butter and homespun self-sufficiency, the potential for the finished goods market swelled; but most families were not yet acclimated to purchasing in stores items that their mothers used to make at home. And proprietors were slow to encourage them. The typical outlet was either a dingy street-level shop at the bottom of a dwelling or a drab corner in a brick warehouse building. These cluttered shops featured a single line of merchandise amid an atmosphere of joyless utility. A clerk took orders, retrieved the goods from a shelf or cabinet, measured the required length of material, and haggled out a price.[27]

Few clerks took the initiative to recommend items that had not been requested. And even fewer customers took the time to look at more than the item they came to buy. Little if any space was devoted to display. Most of the energy and artifice surrounding a purchase went into bargaining over price. In short, the act of purchasing was entirely utilitarian. It offered no escape, no appeal to the imagination, no delight in *shopping*. Stores reflected little personality, little of the urban exuberance and new wealth that marked the new homes along upper Broadway. For all one could tell, the exchange counter could have been located in a rural general store.

Stewart recast retailing, making it respectable and desirable. Before him, most retailers were known as mongers, with the more reputable term *merchant* being reserved for shipowners and importers. He applied new approaches to selling, appealing to New York's expanding population and its developing tastes with enticing window displays and graceful ads placed in genteel ladies' magazines. He priced his goods competitively and assembled the widest array of goods under one roof, churning profit through high volume. "Although I realize only a small profit on each sale," he told a colleague, "the enlarged area of business makes possible large accumulations of capital and assures the future." Systematizing retailing, he adopted policies that stand to this day: accepting returns and exchanges on retail purchases; advertising end-of-season markdowns; and establishing a single price (putting an end to haggling), uniform policies, and centralized buying. He organized his staff in a hierarchy, assigning distinct responsibilities to buyers, managers, and floor sellers. By 1840, the onetime rag peddler from Belfast was renowned as the premier dry goods merchant of New York and one of its few millionaires.[28]

Then in 1846 Stewart opened a store that gave retailing a new face and did New York proud. "A few years ago," marveled one booster, "when a man returned from Europe" with memories of luxurious architecture, "our cities seemed insignificant and mean." Stewart put an end to that. He built an immense Italianate structure characterized by an enthralled observer as "a key-note, a model . . . stately and simple . . . [rising] out of the sea green foliage in the [City Hall] Park, a white marble cliff, sharply drawn against the sky." Philip Hone, the urbane city diarist, was equally impressed: "Nothing in London or Paris . . . compare[s] with this dry goods palace." Clad in striking white Tuckahoe marble, Stewart's emporium rose eventually to five stories, towering over the entire block on Broadway between Reade and Chambers Streets. Its lavish features included a spectacular domed atrium, ceiling and sidewall frescoes by Bragaldi of Italy, and huge mirrored panels that doubled the size of everything. A ladies' gallery overlooked the opulent rotunda. One of the few stores to feature rest rooms, the "marble palace" converted the simple comfort station into a captivating ladies' parlor, with graceful full-length Parisian mirrors. Everything was designed to make shopping pleasurable to women.[29]

Stewart sectioned the building into more than a score of main departments and filled it with $600,000 in merchandise. Fifteen huge display windows invited the attention of passing pedestrians onto a genteel bazaar of fabrics from all over the world, furs, upholstery, carpets, linoleum, and a variety of household items. Garments for the entire family, including the latest in Paris fashions, were arrayed amid dramatic store furnishings of rich mahogany, sweeping staircases, and exquisite carved glass chandeliers. Each class of goods got its own counter. "Mr. Stewart," reported the *Herald*, "has paid the ladies of this city a high compliment in giving them such a beautiful resort in which to while away their leisure hours. . . ." Scores of handsome young sales clerks tactfully stood by, ready to be of assistance. "A grand magazine of everything," raved a bedazzled contemporary. And no one ever had to sheepishly ask a price. Everything, from the most exquisite of Belfast laces, to Paris designed silk gowns and $1,000 camel-hair shawls, was clearly marked.[30]

Those who have studied consumer markets disagree about which was the first true department store and whether it was a French or American innovation. What is beyond dispute is that Stewart's was one of the first, and perhaps the most important, of these new-style emporiums to mold mass tastes from the selling floor. Of all spectacles offered up by the new urban capitalism, none, writes Alan Trachtenberg, surpassed the department store, where "the citizen met a new world of goods; not goods alone, but a *world* of goods. . . . Thus the department store stood as a prime urban artifact of the age, a place of learning as well as buying: a pedagogy of modernity." Immersing the shopper in a surfeit of goods, Stewart's five stories of merchandise, set in grace and beauty, projected a metropolis of achievable urban dreams. Stewart, *Harper's Bazaar* editor Gail Hamilton once wrote, taught "that we ought to enjoy wealth"; to "cease our idle carping against money."[31]

Months after opening in 1846, Stewart was taking in $10,000 a day. By the eve of the Civil War the figure was more than double that, a total of $9 million a year, making his the largest dry goods retail establishment in the world. His success spurred imitators like Arnold Constable and Lord & Taylor and others that opened around the country in fostering the new consumer culture of fulfillment through material acquisition.[32]

Stewart had by now outgrown the Pearl Street auctions that he had relied upon to stock his inventories. He established his own buying organization, with agents in Europe to select goods for his counters and for distribution to other retailers. By the late 1850s, Stewart had purchasing offices in each of the principal producing centers on the continent. Branching out into manufacturing, he opened textile mills in Manchester, Belfast, and Nottingham and others in the States. Initially developed to supply the marble palace, Stewart's multinational operation grew into the largest distributor of dry goods in the Americas. By the Civil War, Stewart was the nation's largest importer, and in a comment that applied to countless other New Yorkers, a contemporary remarked: "He is a slave to business. . . . His happiness is in his accounts and profits. . . ."[33]

More important than this single climb from rags to riches, a story whose many echoes made it a New York cliché, was the impact that this superb merchandiser had on advancing the appetite for fashion and finery, projecting a culture of consumption to city dwellers in particular. Stewart promoted the new leisure pursuit of *shopping;* of going to the store not with a specific acquisition in mind, but rather to be titillated into consumption by tempting displays and graceful presentations; of allowing elaborate merchandise tableaus to shape new tastes and styles; of stores that encouraged purchases not exclusively for their utility, but also for the visceral satisfaction that *buying and having* gave to the purchaser; of suggesting that a joy in accumulation was an index not of coarse vulgarity, but of success and good taste.[34]

Importing merchandise of every type and origin, merchants like Astor, Taylor, and Stewart made New York into America's assembly point for hemispheric trade, its grand commercial showcase. On its wharves, laborers and dockworkers bundled the vast produce of America's verdant forests, rich mines, and fertile fields for shipment to Latin America, Europe, and Asia and by way of the same trade network brought back a global assortment of finished merchandise for distribution far inland to isolated communities from Michigan to Arkansas. Through this expanding commercial authority, New York integrated a set of internally dynamic and wayward regions into an emerging national economy and advanced southern cotton to global dominance.[35]

In the remarkably short time that it took for cotton to become the "grand prize of American commerce," accounting by 1820 for 40 percent of all American exports, South Street seized control over its distribution. Critics decried the "Manhattan premium" (at the height of the cotton market, southerners complained that forty cents of every cotton dollar found its way into New York pockets). Why should the cotton carriers have to haul the astoundingly popular white filament hundreds of extra miles to New York? "The South," ran a common protest, "stands in the attitude of feeding from its own bosom a vast population of merchants, shipowners, capitalists and others who . . . drink up the life blood of her trade." But all efforts at avoiding New York failed because the planters could find no replacement for Yankee credit, commercial experience, and shipping tonnage. Manhattan's access to early information on English price fluctuations was alone worth millions. And Manhattan held the key to the coveted output of Europe's factories. "All other cities of the United States are centres of local business," declared *DeBow's Review* in 1848. "New York, however, is the centre of national capital and trade." So powerful had the New York market become that not a tree was felled in all the land, went one popular saying, that did not in some way increase the wealth and power of New York City.[36]

During this golden age of New York commerce, the mercantile elite controlled the city's government, ran its philanthropic and cultural institutions, and set the pace for its spectacular expansion. Representing some 70 percent of Gotham's wealthy, they built and carefully nurtured long-term relationships with British and continental capital, controlled the city's financial institutions, and banked so much of the profit that they were in a position to fund the new ventures that propelled the economy into modernity.[37]

---

Moses Taylor, the large importer of Cuban sugar, had once promised clients and investors the kind of singular attention that had built the old countinghouses. He promised to make the essential decisions about what to buy and at what price; how and when to sell; and whom to trust with merchandise. But the New York business environment had grown more complex, offering many new opportunities since the time he had begun importing from South America.

As late as 1815, on the eve of New York's commercial boom, finance and credit were limited to face-to-face transactions among merchants who knew and trusted one another. And credit itself was still viewed as an expedient best used sparingly. A merchant who made excessive use of credit was regarded with suspicion, and defaulting on a debt was seen as a moral, not a business, failure. That is why it was considered appropriate to punish indebtedness with prison. The larger business perspective was framed by what has been called a moral economy, where a businessman was expected to charge not the most profitable, but rather the "just" price (based on cost plus a modest profit), and to accept limits on how he made, borrowed, and used his money. He was expected to place pursuit of the general good ahead of his own profits, and those profits that he did earn were to be used in a manner that comported with the community's needs and standards.[38]

The greatly accelerated pace of commerce and its widening reach following peace with England in 1815 wore away the strict constraints of this moral economy. Economic relations based on communitarian ideals yielded before a capitalist urge that focused on profits ahead of other considerations. The impersonal market, with its system of supply and demand, competition and the profit motive, replaced moral criteria as the switching system for the economy.

The new market perspective led to corresponding changes in borrowing. The limited credit market of the moral economy had restricted loans to kin and trusted business clients. One loaned money to trusted acquaintances, and even then only sparingly. But the larger, more active, more dispersed markets after 1815 required an expansion of currency beyond the amount on hand if economic growth was to be sustained. This broad demand for new currency placed pressure on merchants and others in business to extend more loans in order to keep their businesses growing. Without enough hard cash in circulation, only borrowed money could provide the capital for large-ticket modernization, for transforming an agricultural nation into a modern system. Only the fiat money created between lender and borrower could pay for new transport, manufacturing, and trade.

The intense demand for credit (expressed in part through the high rates that loans commanded) loosened habitual hesitations. Borrowing and indebtedness came to be viewed not as a personal failing, but as a way of doing business. Within perhaps a decade, New York's leading businessmen internalized the new notion that debt was a constructive and necessary feature of modern economic growth and that as long as the economy was sound and business healthy, it was possible to create new currency without undue risk and even a high assurance of profit. The law, too, made credit less risky by treating debt and default more leniently, adopting liberalized bankruptcy statutes and ending the policy of jailing debtors who failed to repay their loans.[39]

Moses Taylor had initially declined to advance credit to his clients. He preferred to use his cash for his own business needs rather than to lend it out to others. But Taylor was too keen a businessman to ignore the novel turns of a modernizing economy. Despite his earlier demurrals, by the late 1830s he was discounting notes and procuring bills of exchange for foreign clients.[40]

Taylor learned another important lesson about credit. In the past, when a merchant loaned money to a client, it was a service meant to bolster his own business. If he made money from the loan, it was incidental to his main purpose, which was trade. But as businessmen exchanged pieces of paper obliging them to pay or collect monies with a confidence that only a few years back had been reserved for gold, debt became the primary means for financing business, investment, and speculation. The *business of credit*—of providing loans and other debt—changed from being incidental to becoming itself a business that offered handsome returns. Taylor, for example, found that making loans brought him even better profits than Cuban sugar, so he turned more and more of his attention to the credit business, purchasing shares in the New York City Bank and becoming a director in 1837. According to a man who was himself an experienced banker in these years, directors were chosen for their "wealth, commercial experience and influence in attracting a good class" of borrowers. Clearly, Taylor, who had made his first fortune in the well-tracked paths of hemispheric trade, was pursuing new possibilities that extended well beyond sugar.[41]

As he found that he earned higher profits from renting out capital than from keeping it tied up for months at a time in seafaring cargoes, Taylor handed over direction of his countinghouse to a partner and turned to investing and manipulating capital. The man who had earlier resolved to focus on his sugar business, to avoid speculation and protect his integrity, now spent his days evaluating investment ventures and assessing the projections of entrepreneurs seeking loans for new businesses. Entrepreneurs took him into their confidence, asked for his advice, and appointed him to their boards. Others offered partnerships ("& Co." in a firm name signified one or more silent partners) in return for funding. By the 1840s his earnings, once derived exclusively from trade, came largely from interest and dividend income, as Taylor helped lead the transition between the age of South Street's hands-on commerce and the Wall Street era of investment banking and venture capitalism.[42]

The primary source of credit for major undertakings was still in England and continental Europe, but as the United States consolidated its indigenous credit resources, New York's merchants and financiers took the lead in issuing notes, releasing bonds, and injecting capital. From one bank in 1790, the city had twelve in 1825; and by midcentury Wall Street and its environs had become the nation's banking capital and credit had itself become a big business. Notes from its twenty-five banks were widely regarded as superior to all other commercial paper. Merchants around the country willingly paid a premium for "New York Exchange" (Manhattan banknotes)—with its universal recognition and easy bankability. Reassured by the sheer volume of New York's money supply and set at ease by a newly established safety fund for Manhattan financial houses, banks from all sections of the country, and from Canada and Europe as well, shipped their balances to the metropolis. Of an estimated seven hundred incorporated banks in the United States in 1850, nearly six hundred deposited their reserves in Manhattan, which held more than 85 percent of the nation's bank balances.[43]

This flood of cash brought rapid expansion (in just two years between 1851 and 1853, forty new banks opened in the city, as over the next four years foreign and domestic deposits jumped by 70 percent) and sharper competition. Banks vying with each other for this new business threw off the musty traditions that had cosseted banking for centuries. The more venturesome introduced interest on deposits and to pay for this innovation initiated what came to be known as the "call market."[44]

In the past, deposits were commonly treated as idle funds that were stored for safekeeping. Now these funds were put to work, to earn money by being loaned out "on call"—that is, for an indeterminate period, payable when the bank "called" in the funds. This innovation meant doing risky business with other people's money, but New York banks happily broke with habit and custom to make new business. As a result, the nation's reserves, which in the past had occupied nothing more productive than vault space, were converted through the call loan market into active capital, funding investment locally and economic growth across the nation.[45]

With its rudimentary central government, Washington was in no position to exert any oversight over these activities or to restrain the more reckless among the financial institutions. On their own, Gotham's banks took the initiative to tighten banking practices, but the most consequential product of their collaboration was the New York Clearing House (NYCH). Its origins lie in an effort to solve a rather mundane problem: The soaring volume of business transactions in Manhattan meant that a proliferation of banknotes drawn on local banks were regularly presented for payment to their sister institutions. These notes would then have to be physically transferred to the issuing bank for redemption in gold. These transfers took place at the week's end, which meant that for a few hours each Friday, lower Manhattan's narrow canyons turned into a bedlam of clerks dashing with notes and stressed porters rushing gold to the banks to meet the rain of checks coming their way. Crowds of messengers converged on harried bank tellers, who hastened to complete the transactions while keeping track of the tally. Business slowed to a crawl, and the loan markets spiked each Friday as financial houses competed for funds to make their reconciliations.[46]

The process was primitive, disorganized, and fraught with error. To correct this, the city's leading banks formed the New York Clearing House, a bank for bankers. Initially it was limited to settling the interbank accounts in an orderly fashion (by 1857 the NYCH had put an end to the weekly scramble for funds and was settling accounts of as much as $20 million daily), but this consortium grew into a larger role than anticipated. Through its criteria for membership, the Clearing House enforced reserve requirements. It also served as lender of last resort, tiding members over short-term difficulties. Given its location and the fact that its members were the most powerful financial institutions in the nation, the NYCH came to function as an unofficial central bank, providing more than a modicum of control over banking practices. During the national crisis of the Civil War, the New York Clearing House coordinated the purchase of hundreds of millions of dollars of government securities on behalf of the Union.[47]

This control over much of the discretionary capital in the nation represented an expanded role for New York. As men like Astor, Taylor, and Stewart built phenomenally successful businesses, Gotham's merchant capital and the deposits from around the country with which it was mingled created a national money market that seeded new business growth across the nation. Nowhere was this process of new investment pursued more actively than on New York's market in corporate securities.[48]

The corporation was initially a form of business organization designed to attract financial backing for local and state projects that could not be funded through taxes. These quasi-public corporations built roads, supplied water, erected bridges, and ran ports. In order to make these projects attractive to private investors, state and municipal governments granted them extraordinary privileges. Individual corporations received exclusive rights of way, tax exemptions, powers of eminent domain, and the exceptional protection that limited the liability of investors so that they could not be held personally responsible for corporate debts. Over the years legislatures, eager to promote development, extended the use of corporations, granting its precious exemptions to projects for developing new territories, fortifying outlying districts, chartering universities, and expanding trade. These corporations were not designed with profits in mind, and in fact New York's Erie Canal Company was one of the first transport-related corporations to turn a profit. Its example proved riveting, encouraging the development of transportation corporations around the United States after the 1830s.[49]

The next step in the evolution of corporations came with the first large industrial corporations, the railroads. While some of these companies did involve partnerships with local governments, most railroads were funded by private sources. The rationale for awarding them the prized corporate charters lay in their immense impact on the common economic environment. And there was no denying that impact, as the iron horse compressed space by slashing travel time. Before the railroad, writes Arthur Hadley, "the expense of cartage was such that wheat had to be consumed within two hundred miles of where it was grown." In 1830, with no more than twenty-three miles of track in the entire country, it took three weeks to travel overland from Chicago to New York. Over the next thirty years, rail companies laid thirty thousand miles of track into the wilderness, linking cities, villages, and farms across the land, greatly extending the trading circle. By then the trip from Chicago to New York took just three days.[50]

Many of the larger rail projects were too ambitious for an individual or a set of individual owners to undertake. Such a railroad might form a joint stock company that raised money by selling shares of ownership to investors on the securities markets. The largest of these markets was originally in Philadelphia. But the panic following Andrew Jackson's veto of the charter for the Second Bank of the United States (also headquartered in Philadelphia) ultimately cost the Quaker City its hold on this market in the late 1830s. For a brief moment, Boston, awash with textile and shipbuilding money, stepped into the void, underwriting large business investments. But the Brahmins proved too cautious for this market. "Our rule of action," William Sturgis wrote characteristically, "always is to *earn* money . . . & to let corporations *get out of debt & keep out of debt.*" Boston's tightly organized commercial elite formed a circle of conservative men who were more concerned with avoiding loss than venturing for gain.[51]

In the 1840s, textile mills were still the most ambitious investments, and they were capitalized at not much more than around $1 million; Boston's capitalists could handle that level of financing. But as railroads grew into regional carriers and then into entire systems, like the New York Central and the Pennsylvania, capitalization ran into tens of millions. This proved too rich for Boston's tightfisted financiers. Their overcautious business approach and the financial crisis of 1847, which forced a number of Brahmin investment houses to close, put an end to Boston's brief reign as America's investment capital. In 1845, when Moses Taylor sought capitalization for expanding one of his companies, he arranged a bond issue for $100,000 in Boston; by the 1850s, Taylor raised funds for his companies almost exclusively in New York.[52]

Awash in cash, home of the nation's bank reserves and the call loan market, New York took over the leadership of the securities market. In its early days, members of the New York Stock Exchange would come together twice daily in staid surroundings to offer bids as an approved list of securities in municipal bonds and public corporations was read off. On one March day in 1830, thirty-one shares were exchanged; by mid-1850, investors from all over bid in chaotic cacophony on hundreds of thousands of shares of railroad stock, bank securities, and municipal bonds each day.[53]

The Gotham market had proven itself, and in these volatile years of failed European revolutions and ensuing political unrest, it attracted new capital from London, Paris, Geneva, Frankfurt, and Bremen, as investors searched the globe for reliable outlets to invest their speculative capital. On the eve of the great railway boom, the Erie, the New York Central, the Hudson River, the Harlem, the

New Jersey Central, and the Reading all turned to the New York money market for their funding. Southern and western roads, which for more than a decade had raised cash in Boston, now issued their securities from New York. There was another change. In the past, bonds had been issued in sterling denominations or made payable in London. Now their principal and interest was payable in New York dollars.[54]

Experienced in executing trades, serviced by a pride of lawyers, accountants, and lenders, boldly innovating such new speculative devices as call loans and margin loans, New York's fertile business environment funded and built the new railroad corporations. Here, Henry Varnum Poor and his editors published the authoritative *American Railroad Journal.* Gathering information from all over the globe, the journal promoted common standards, dispensed new industry information, and kept an eye on shoddy practices and financial improprieties. Here, also, the Winslow, Lanier Bank established the first specialty house, catering exclusively to the railway industry. Far-flung roads depended on the bank to purchase their rails and locomotives, supervise their finances, and provide management services; for smaller lines the bank even set business strategy. And here in Manhattan were to be found the supercontractors with the expertise and the capital needed to carry out the complex railroad construction projects. (These same firms went on to build America's urban infrastructure, laying sewer systems, erecting waterworks, paving miles of streets, and building public schools across the country.)[55]

By midcentury, Moses Taylor stood at the center of this world of investment and new industry. Enlightened, urbane, well-informed about the imperatives of American business growth, the erstwhile importer of Cuban sugar rode the wave of change in New York's business scene. In the years after he relinquished day-to-day control over his mercantile business Taylor assembled a portfolio that included investment loans, mortgage bonds, real estate, insurance shares, and bank stocks, as well as some businesses that fell to him through loan defaults. His work as director of First City Bank and his investments brought him in excess of $100,000 a year. He had not much altered his modest lifestyle even as his profits kept mounting, so he had a growing cache of discretionary income for which he sought a productive use. This capital he now invested in industries, three in particular that formed the core of the emerging industrial economy: coal and iron mines; the Atlantic Cable telegraph; and the glamour industry of the age, railroads. As an acquaintance remarked, Taylor was a master not only of striking "when the iron was hot, but, when need required, struck the iron until it became hot." In 1856, Taylor assumed the presidency of First City Bank, greatly extending his opportunity to make irons hot.[56]

While an increasing number of Taylor's investments were located far from Manhattan, these dispersed properties were controlled from New York. Taylor's large anthracite coal and iron holdings in Pennsylvania led him to invest in the Delaware, Lackawanna and Western Railroad and to become one of the new road's directors. Initially, this road was to link Scranton, Pennsylvania, with the Erie railroad, but the Taylor-dominated board adjusted these plans to forge a direct connection between the Wyoming valley and New York City. Company founders had followed a policy of maximizing immediate dividends. This too Taylor altered in favor of a more conservative policy that set aside 13 percent of the road's net earnings for a depreciation allowance. Taylor installed handpicked associates to direct daily operations, hire personnel, and upgrade services. Financing and fiscal control was transferred to his own bank.[57]

It did not take long for mine operators in Pennsylvania or railroaders in the Wyoming valley to learn that they had sold more than their debt on the New York market. Accustomed to serving local needs and objectives, these businesses found themselves tethered to a golden yoke of distant capital, with New Yorkers taking over their books, their board meetings, and their business strategies. It was far from all bad, as the New York aegis replaced processes both bewildering and random with rational order and established solid business traditions. Still, this control by remote financiers significantly altered the business calculus of the companies involved, supplanting priorities like local need, regional economic considerations, the preferences of workers, and even the interest of the firm itself in favor of broader corporate priorities.[58]

Taylor, for example, had his coal, iron, gas, and railroad interests patronize one another (rather than local businesses) and work collectively on larger projects. When a number of his coal companies (which extended as far as Chicago) suffered heavy losses during a period of fierce industrial warfare, Taylor ordered these companies to consolidate. He then carved up the territories into competition-free zones, closing up some of the franchises, with painful local effects. The removed reckoning of New York investors with their broad plans and diverse portfolios replaced the narrower contexts of the local economy and the private owner.[59]

Local investors had misgivings about these trade-offs, but the allure of New York's cash overrode these hesitations. This is clear from this letter from a Pennsylvanian, pleading with Taylor to invest in the Lehigh and Lackawanna Railway:

> For several years I have worked earnestly and unselfishly for developing the state interest . . . , but you with one word . . . can now do in a few months what it would take us years to do. . . . We have met with the usual fate of Pioneers—have been able to do nothing except what our limited capital could do. But when it comes to completing 40 miles of Railroad . . . it will all depend on you as to what is done.[60]

For more and more localities, "what is done" came to depend upon New York–based investors like Taylor.

Why New York? What made New York so different from its principal urban counterparts? If structural attributes provided Manhattan with commercial and financial advantages, they also gave rise to a unique business environment. Charles Latrobe, a perceptive Englishman, compared American cities in the 1830s. Philadelphia, the first city of the new nation before the turn of the century, he found the most elegant and well laid out, but New York was the most "bustling." Even earlier, the British consul had reported that Philadelphia's trade was "on the decline in all its branches. . . . Commercial men here seem to have lost all their accustomed enterprise."[61]

There was no shortage of enterprise in Manhattan. Its merchants exploited every advantage, bent every effort, and sought every opportunity to pursue investment, expansion, and profit. Few who passed through Manhattan missed its uncommon speculative elan, its venturesomeness, and its distinctive egalitarianism. Here new wealth competed with old on equal ground. In this town money was the great equalizer. It dominated discussions, served as sport and culture, and stirred an incomparable competitive environment. Anthony Trollope, visiting in 1862, observed: "Every man worships the dollar, and is down before his shrine from morning to night." "Here," added essayist James D. McCabe, "as in no other place in the country, men *struggle* for wealth. They toil, they suffer privations, [and] they plan and scheme and execute with persistence that often wins the success they covet." Elsewhere poverty was a misfortune; in New York it was an enemy to be defeated. Aside from its superior initiative, energy, zeal, and inventiveness, wrote one Philadelphian, New York attracted the most ambitious and talented from all over. By 1855, Manhattan held close to 630,000 inhabitants, more than ten times the population at the beginning of the century, and the volume of its exports and imports shot up at an even more remarkable pace.[62]

Like New York, Boston too had a magnificent harbor, and a Baring Brothers correspondent comparing commercial firms in the two cities preferred Boston's. They were "entirely safe," careful, and predictable. Boston's leading maritime families had achieved local prominence back before the Revolution and never relinquished it. Held fast by an integument of kin and tradition, their narrow group of Peabodys, Crowninshields, Saltonstalls, Derbys, and perhaps fifty more interrelated families formed a business circle closed around pedigree and the rules of gentlemanly behavior. Among these elite Bostonians, family was stressed above business considerations. When "strangers . . . connect themselves in business," wrote Thomas Handasyd Perkins to brother James, "great uneasiness" and "low suspicions" often result. The family firm did bolster dynastic stability, but it also sheltered weak members who might otherwise have fallen from the privileged order. Moreover, it disposed Boston's elite to focus on conserving family fortunes rather than venturing to make them grow. Tormented by fear that the patrimony might be frittered away in unwise investments, Brahmins limited heirs to living off trust account dividends, while sheltering the principal.[63]

In contrast, Gotham nourished a disdain for precedent, for the past's confining influence. New Yorkers placed no Brahmin-type restraints on their bequests, and while many of their successful men came from comfortable backgrounds, many more than elsewhere made it on their own, as did Astor, Stewart, and Taylor. Anson Phelps, America's leading metal importer, began as a poor orphan; millionaire merchant Thomas Tileston's origins were as a penniless printer's apprentice; civic and business leader Philip Hone started at the bottom. New York's wealthy class was fresher, more upstart, and more audacious. Outsiders who rose to the top of the city's commercial houses—many of them New Englanders and immigrants—imparted to the city a hybrid energy, a blend of experiences and pasts, a stir of backgrounds less deferential to any one tradition or collection of customs. Henry Adams once remarked about Boston: "The painful truth is that all of my New England generation, counting the half century, 1820–1870, were in actual fact only one mind and nature; the individual was a facet of Boston." There was no single New Yorker—indeed, no single New York.[64]

Boston emphasized order, preserving capital, and striking a proper balance between commerce and family, profit and culture, scruple and cashbook. Conservatism and prudence signal Brahmin virtues, curbed adventurousness, innovation, and boldness. Boston's leading merchants fashioned their Athenaeum to foster both commercial interest *and* literary pursuits. No such ambivalence restrained New York's Chamber of Commerce, whose goal was unequivocal: to promote the commercial prosperity of its members. In New York, Henry Varnum Poor observed, the man of action and business supplanted the figure of intellect and religion. The city's modest cultural attainments were respected as ornaments upon worldly success rather than for their own importance.[65]

Every once in a while Gotham offered a sop to learning, as when the Mercantile Society of New York announced a series of distinguished lectures by "Mr. Longfellow, the poet," Horace Mann on education, and "R. W. Emerson, an impressive speaker possessing a peculiar style and mode of thinking," on the philosophy of history. But no New Yorker, no matter how boastful, dared echo Oliver Wendell Holmes's claim about his cherished Boston, that it "is . . . the thinking center of the continent and therefore the planet. . . ." For all of their superior airs, however, Bostonians bowed before New York's economic power. The same Oliver Wendell Holmes for whom beloved Boston occupied the center of the universe was forced to confess that New York was becoming the "tongue that is licking up the cream of commerce and finance of a continent," while Charles Eliot Norton lamented to James Russell Lowell: "We are provincials, with a very little city of our own. . . . A few years hence and Boston will be a place of the past, with a good history no doubt, but New York will be alive."[66]

America's tragic Civil War lends this last statement a retrospective irony. For by the early 1860s, it was unclear whether the Union itself would remain alive, and New York's business health, so robust before the conflict, was profoundly jeopardized by the cleaving of America.

By 1860, New York stood at the axis of a wide-ranging trade system, gathering the products of America's farms, mines, and small manufacturers and relaying them to the remote corners of the earth. South Street merchants brought back and distributed a cornucopia of industrial products and desirable commodities, knitting America's disparate markets into an incipient national economy. Yet for all its economic puissance, not Gotham's banks nor its merchants, not its millionaires nor its commercial giants, could hold back the forces of political sectionalism dividing the nation. Crossroads of domestic and foreign trade, the largest manufacturing city in the nation and "the fastest growing large industrial area in the world," America's principal money market and proudest commercial achievement, New York proved helpless before the single most profound political challenge of the times.[67]

If any place in the nation had an interest in keeping the states together, it was New York. While holding no brief for slavery, metropolitan merchants cared less about the southern labor system than about its cotton. The Empire City's single largest export by far, King Cotton reigned as absolutely in Manhattan as in Charleston. Cotton profits underwrote southern purchases, which in turn filled the pockets of New York merchants, bankers, lawyers, brokers, shipowners, insurance agents, and wage workers. New York's leading textile houses operated branches in the South; others held investments in southern plantations, mines, railroads, and even slaves.[68]

New York merchants feared that secession would sever commercial links and lead to war taxes, perhaps even to the confiscation of northern-owned properties and the repudiation of hundreds of millions in debt. Before this alarming possibility, the commercial-manufacturing-financial capital of the nation stood as if dazed, desperate to prevent a terminal breach, but incapable of anything more constructive than opposing Abraham Lincoln's candidacy. After Lincoln won the presidency despite them, metropolitan spokesmen were reduced to beseeching the South to remain in the Union while pressing for northern concessions. Paralyzed by its conflicted interests and by its huge stake in peace, the rich and powerful city, the "hinge of the Union," offered timid guidance. New York's politics lacked the kind of verve and command displayed by its markets. Perhaps some merchants calculated that they might profit from war, but few urged battle, and fewer still, in the wake of the disruption of northern trade following the Confederate attack upon Fort Sumter, looked to the future with equanimity.[69]

Scholars interpreting the economic effects of the Civil War have sometimes read a thought-out design into the war's effects, a transfiguring postwar boom. While it is true that the exigencies of war helped anneal a modern urban economy, it is another thing entirely to suggest that those who ultimately benefited had the prescience or the ability to bring it about. Only the foolhardy would predict the war's course in 1861, much less its duration. Had the war been as brief as initially conjectured, the economic results would have been vastly different. But it was a long, destructive, costly, and transforming conflict.[70]

In rapid succession, the Confederacy invented itself, declared its independence, cut off trade with the North, and made it a criminal offense to pay any part of the debt owed to Union merchants, bankers, and brokers. Manhattan firms placed the losses due to repudiation at $160 million. New York's rich cotton trade dwindled down to those hardy souls willing to carry contraband, and in the first months of the conflict about 5 percent of the city's businesses went under. Ocean shipping was restricted, and railroad construction came to a virtual standstill. In August 1862, the *New York Tribune* rued "our paralyzed industry, obstructed commerce, our over-laden finances, and our mangled railroads."[71]

But hostilities shook New York businessmen from their torpor. Cornelius Vanderbilt offered his ships to the war effort. The Astors donated $15,000. J. F. D. Lanier of the Winslow, Lanier Bank raised $400,000 from the investment community, and volunteers formed the Union Defense Committee, underwriting troops, workers, and equipment, while offering stipends for soldiers' families. In the first months of conflict, the New York Chamber of Commerce poured close to $100,000 into the mobilization, while the municipality itself committed another $1 million in public funds to the Union Defense Committee.[72]

The conflict proved much more costly than anything ever undertaken by the American government in the past. With little in the national treasury, the North had to amass a war chest, and rapidly. Unwilling at first to increase taxes on the commercial classes in the thick of a "flagitious rebellion [that] had deranged their business and temporarily deranged their incomes," Secretary of the Treasury Salmon Chase looked to New York's banking community to guarantee federal bonds. Moses Taylor assembled a consortium in Manhattan that pledged a total of $150 million in loans in August 1861. These funds were quickly exhausted, leading the government to suspend specie payments and issue legal tender notes (backed not by gold, but by a simple promise to pay), soon known as greenbacks. Still the demand for funds continued. In fiscal 1862 the Union spent $475 million, and by 1865 it was spending $4 million a day—in two and a half weeks the entire budget of 1861.[73]

Spiraling expenditures forced Washington to seek more loans, but the traditional source for such funding, Europe's *haute banques*, had dried up. Unsettled by the uncertainties of war, European investors had scaled back purchases of American paper from $400 million in 1860 to virtually zero three years later. As their hasty departure left a gaping capital void, Wall Street's banks rose to the challenge, serving virtually alone as the financial brace of the Union. When the Treasury released a large bond issue in the fall of 1862, Wall Street investors absorbed more than 80 percent of the securities. For the next six years, New York absorbed two-thirds of all federal debt issues sold *in the entire country*. When Washington turned to Jay Cooke and Company to market securities to the general public, Cooke associates plastered New York with ads, distributing bonds in denominations as low as $50 through a network of retail outlets that attracted laborers and common folk who had never bought a security before. So successful was the Cooke drive that for the first time since the beginning of the war, the Treasury was able to step back from the brink of bankruptcy.[74]

New York's role as the financial mainstay of the Union was further secured by the National Banking Law, passed in 1863. Going into the Civil War, American banking consisted of a congeries of state-chartered banks that included New York's highly reliable commercial banks, but also inland institutions that historian Irwin Unger has described as "little more than legal counterfeiting shops." This collection of unregulated "banks" distributed a total of twelve thousand different loan notes, promoting a troubling confusion on the market. The new law replaced the dizzying array of monies with a uniform and reliable national currency, eliminating state banknotes entirely. It also designated New York as the nation's central reserve city, resting America's credit structure exclusively upon its deposits, while acknowledging its critical role in safeguarding and managing the flow of American capital.[75]

Early in the conflict there had been talk among New York's merchants of declaring New York a noninvolved free city in order to preserve its neutrality and allow it to trade with both sides. But with New York holding much of a national debt that climbed from $64 million in 1860 to $2.7 billion by war's end, its support for the North was ensured by the fact that only a victorious North would redeem these bonds. Or as the New York Chamber of Commerce observed in 1863, failure to put down the southern rebellion threatened the North's "vast pecuniary obligation." This, and Gotham's privileged role in the Union economy, lashed New York unambiguously to its side. The debt worked with perverse efficiency to sustain the Union war effort, expand the responsibilities of the central government, foster large business, and bind debt-holding New York to the Union cause.[76]

This enormously expensive and tragically destructive war also concentrated the collective economic resources, inventiveness, and energies of the Union. The secession itself materially altered the balance of America's political economy. The Republican coalition of industrialists, western farmers, and labor, all from the North, advocated a program of vigorous, centrally catalyzed, economic development. It supported federally financed roads and canals, western expansion, and the fostering of American industry. With the agrarian South in rebellion, the departure of the states' rights caucus removed the single largest constraint on this mercantilist agenda.[77]

While Lincoln prosecuted the war, the Republican Congress proceeded with this economic program. The war Congress approved the construction of two transcontinental railways through northern and central United States, providing as much as $60 million in loans and lavish subsidies. The franchise issued to the Union Pacific was the first *national* charter granted since 1816. New York's investing class, including such business leaders as New York mayor George Opdyke, New York Chamber of Commerce president Abiel A. Low, and industrialist William A. Dodge, all bought shares in the new road. To promote economic growth, the Republican Congress gave away millions of acres of the national patrimony in the form of land subsidies to railway companies, colleges, and the states themselves. Banks and investors provided the capital to clear the land, build the farms, and pay for new agricultural machinery, converting, in the anguished plaint of Wisconsin senator Timothy O. Howe, the "whole Northwest and the whole West [into] but little more than a province of New York."[78]

The doleful early months of war that had brought manufacturing and trade to a virtual standstill made way now for economic recovery, greatly aided by the fortunes of war. American cereal growers, enjoying a bumper yield, sought to sell overseas and avoid flooding the American market. Because hostilities had closed the Mississippi, eliminating New Orleans as a serious overseas transporter, they piled the crop on boats and railcars and shipped it east, where only New York had the capacity to handle this trade. A fortuitous failure of the European crop sent overseas demand for wheat to levels even higher than those for prewar cotton. Eleven Gotham steamship companies ran lines to Europe, sending grain exports up from twenty million bushels before the war to sixty million in the year after Sumter. New York's waterways swelled with traffic. "All the canals of the state," writes E. D. Fite, "delivered at tidewater in 1862, two hundred per cent more wheat than in any year before 1860."[79]

Southerners had boasted before the secession that the loss of King Cotton would cause New York's economy to collapse. But wheat more than filled the void. There is evidence that Great Britain might have granted the Confederacy official recognition, but for fear of losing its critical shipments of northern grain.[80]

Gotham hummed with other new business as well. Freshly opened workshops and refineries processed payloads of crops, sugar, petroleum, lumber, and cattle for export and war supply. Manhattan's two hundred–odd abattoirs slaughtered more cattle than Chicago: two million heads a year by 1864. City shipbuilding revived from its prewar doldrums, while iron foundries, rubber works, and manufacturers of every description expanded production to meet the orders that came flooding in from the battlefields. Every type of war-related business, from medical supply to armaments and carriages, to horses and copper rolling mills, prospered. Faced with the challenge of clothing its rapidly mobilized troops, the army initially ordered uniforms from London's East End garment factories. In 1863, when domestic capacity finally caught up with demand, Congress switched to New York's sweatshops and erected a high tariff wall around these manufacturers to seal them off from all foreign competition. By then the volume of Manhattan's factories alone almost outstripped the industrial output of the entire Confederacy.[81]

Army and navy purchase orders for more than a million dollars' worth of uniforms and other garments poured in to Seligman Brothers (later the famed J&W Seligman & Co. investment banking house) and to A. T. Stewart's. With business flourishing, Stewart surmounted war shortages and labor interruptions to complete a new headquarters for his worldwide operations in 1862, on Broadway between 9th and 10th Streets. Fronted in fashionable cast iron, the block-long emporium became an immediate landmark, so well-known that it went without an identifying nameplate. Stewart's kept a stable of forty horses and five full-time grooms busy making hourly wagon deliveries to customers avid to convert war profits into consumer goods.[82]

By 1865, total sales from Stewart's combined retail, wholesale, and manufacturing divisions exceeded $50 million. At the head of a vast international merchandising organization, Stewart's carried the largest payroll of any commercial house in the nation. Nineteen department superintendents, 25 bookkeepers, 200 cash boys, 320 clerks, and 900 seamstresses made up the bulk of a 2,200-person operation, the likes of which, gushed a contemporary, "were never known before in the trade of a single house." "Next to the President," confided an English guidebook, Stewart was "the best known man in America. For dry goods are a surer road to fame than politics and legislation." His origin, raved an overseas visitor, "was of the humblest and today his wealth and political and social influence are paramount." The prince of dry goods brought in a yearly income of $1.85 million.[83]

In New York years, Stewart was old wealth. The war had forged new wealth overnight, especially on the financial markets. Bond investors, brokers, and bankers all profited prodigiously. Wall Street balances swelled with deposits from the national banking system and from border states that sought to protect their holdings from the insecurities of war. Deposits climbed from $80 million to $224 million, almost tripling bank profits. The insurance industry, buoyed by war, sold more than 250,000 life insurance policies, boosting total policy values from $141 million to $865 million. New York agents wrote more policies than the three next largest markets combined, while the marine insurance specialist Atlantic Mutual declared a dividend of 40 percent for one war year.[84]

Bank holdings and insurance deposits formed immense pools of capital in search of new investment outlets, sending security values up by some $200 million. In Manhattan alone, the *New York Independent* found "several hundred men worth $1,000,000 and some worth

$20,000,000, while some five years back there had not been five men in the whole United States worth as much as $5,000,000 and not twenty worth over $1,000,000."[85]

Just before the end of the conflict, the *New York Sun* reflected on the war's course and its impact. The South had boasted in the early days of the war that "grass would grow in the streets of New York." But New York had rapidly filled the void left by southern secession with robust growth. "There never was a time in the history of New York," the newspaper declared, "when business prosperity was more general, when the demand for goods was greater, and payments more prompt than within the last two or three years. . . . New York . . . to-day . . . stands more prosperous in every way than at the outbreak of the rebellion."[86]

The erratic and uncertain war economy, affected by factors ranging from the fortunes of battle to the unfolding of politics, rewarded risk takers extremely well, but it had not necessarily made them good. Exploiters of every advantage, they included those who knew that buying the telegraph clerk and his access to information was often a surer investment than buying gold itself. Commentators took note of the unappealing underside of war prosperity. Urgency had rewarded innovation and speed and greed. Unscrupulous manufacturers substituted "shoddy" (rags mashed into a pulp and reprocessed) for wool, resulting in uniforms that came apart on the battlefield. So pervasive did this supply problem become that "shoddy" became a popular term for all sorts of flimsy government issue, ranging from slipshod shoes to haphazard artillery.[87]

Corruption pervaded Congress. The Union Pacific, it was said, dispensed close to half a million dollars to push through a revision of its charter. Rampant graft, conflict of interest, the sale of influence, traffic in contraband, draft dodging, and war profiteering all mocked the high purposes of the warriors and the statesmen.[88]

There was no shortage of travesty. The *London Times* correspondent was appalled by the unrestrained indulgence that he witnessed in New York. In the midst of a "grievous national calamity," the people seemed mired in nonchalance—indeed, a "high glee" permitted "every variety of pleasure, luxury and extravagance." Newly wealthy New Yorkers, "sybarites of shoddy," kept up a regular schedule of opera, theater, recitals, circuses, prizefighting, and yacht regattas. A metropolitan culture of lavish display flourished, heedless of escalating death on the battlefields. Self-absorbed prodigals, having exhausted the established avenues of expenditure, invented ingenious new ones. "The men," *Harper's* reported, "button their waistcoats with diamonds . . . and the women powder their hair with gold and silver dust." "The world has seen its iron age, its silver age, its golden age and its brazen age. This," the *New York Herald* declared in disgust, "is the age of shoddy."[89]

This "age of shoddy" badly skewed war's rewards: soldiers who braved the fields of combat and lived to recall the terror were coming home empty-handed and not always whole, while plungers who risked nothing more than their savings and their reputations stacked staggering profits. But then war is no more just in its distribution of profits than the market, and it has seldom rewarded fidelity ahead of exigency. Nor can any moral critique blur the fact that it was New York credit and commerce that enabled a nation with limited resources to stamp out a rebellious slaveocracy.

Moreover, the circuit of change brought on by the war went well beyond the issue of equitable reward. Before the war, New York represented the most powerful center of finance in the United States. It must, however, be confessed that this meant less than it would seem. Antebellum America was largely an agricultural nation with a tributary relationship to Europe's more sophisticated economy. Remarkably well situated to manage the international exchange of goods and capital, New York essentially processed and delivered the transfers between Europe's cities and America's farms, building a money market of national reach from the profits, albeit one that until the war depended for its vigor upon massive infusions of English capital. In sum, prewar New York was a satellite of London's financial system; its commercial economy was dependent upon foreign capital and external markets.

But after the attack on Fort Sumter, foreign investment closed

down. The nation had no choice but to satisfy the war's insistent demand for credit and battle goods from its own resources. Thirteen
billion dollars in war expenditures force-fed the transformation of
the American market, forging a more self-reliant and resourceful
economy. The larger, more engaged state that emerged fostered industry, established a national monetary and banking structure, advanced transportation through subsidies and loans, promoted
internal markets, and sheltered them with a ring of tariffs. Prying
the nation loose from its agrarian and commercial moorings, the war
Congress set in place the scaffolding for a new economic departure.[90]

In this new order, the influence of New York loomed large. No
longer did it depend so heavily upon Europeans to buy the bonds it
sold or to underwrite its most attractive investments. No longer did
so much of its prosperity hinge upon the trade in southern staples
and goods brought in from foreign ports. No longer did the merchant princes of South Street command the metropolitan economy
or its priorities. Fifty years before, observed New York State Chamber of Commerce president Pelatiah Perit, the great merchants
"held a prominence which at the present time is not accorded to
those of the same position." With so much else, the touch of aristocracy had, he feared, "become obliterated."[91]

The weakening influence of the merchant elite also signaled
changes in an economy that had favored small, stable, prudent businesses. In an environment that was nothing if not speculative, the
war had raised investors, bankers, brokers, and industrialists to new
importance. Those who ventured to advance loans and to develop
industry and expand production in the teeth of war uncertainty, to
plunge their fortunes into circumstances both treacherous and futile
to predict, not infrequently claimed bold rewards. One manufacturer
reported making $2,000 a day in the early days of the war. He was
not unique in a war economy where factories and mills reported dividends as high as 40 percent a year. "I am in no hurry for peace," allowed another manufacturer. William E. Dodge, the New York
metals mogul, wrote a friend in the spring of 1863:

Things here in the north are in a great state of prosperity. . . .
The large amount expended by the government has given activity to everything and but for the daily news from the War in the
papers and the crowds of soldiers you see about the streets you
would have no idea of war. Our streets are crowded, hotels full,
the railroads, and manufacturers of all kinds except cotton were
never doing so well and business generally is active.[92]

Responding to the pressure for swift production, innovative technology, and mass outputs, businessmen built larger and better-
organized plants than ever before. The replacement of ferries with
bridges, the laying of double tracks to allow the running of trains to
and fro simultaneously, the increased use of grain elevators and of a
single uniform gauge for rail width, all fostered expansion. Over the
course of the war, Western Union pulled together through its own
efforts and a policy of federally assisted acquisition more than fifty
thousand miles of telegraph line. In 1866, it succeeded in bringing
its major competitors under one management, giving it control over
seventy-five thousand miles of instantaneous communication. John
D. Rockefeller too was busy creating the early foundations of his petroleum empire, bringing together five refineries, "to unite our skill
and capital in order to carry on a business of some magnitude and
importance in place of the small business that each separately had
heretofore carried on."[93]

The very expensive (and frequently corrupt) competition for war
contracts also favored size and wealth. In industries as disparate as
communications, munitions, iron production, mining, food distribution, and ready-made clothing, observers reported seeing larger
firms than ever before. The trend to larger scale was unmistakable.
Smaller businesses were absorbed by larger competitors. The *Commercial and Financial Chronicle* reported that "the power accumulating in the moneyed classes from the concentration of capital in large
masses is attracting the attention of the close observers of the money
market. It is one of the signs of the time and will probably exert no

small influence over the future growth of our industrial and commercial enterprise."[94]

Two wars frame the trajectory of New York's progress in the years between the founding of the nation and Robert E. Lee's surrender at Appomattox. The first was really a series of wars between England and France that ultimately involved the United States in hostilities with Britain. This era of continental conflict dominated by the Napoleonic Wars roiled established trade relationships, unlocking Europe and its colonies to New York's merchants and shippers. From a port city with a limited hinterland, New York formed itself into the major port of the new nation and the mercantile center of the American hemisphere. Its magnificent deepwater harbor, its aggressive pursuit of trade, its liberal commitment of public resources to roads, docks, and waterways, its willingness to hazard private capital to run an Atlantic shuttle full or empty, in good weather or treacherous, and on time, all helped make Gotham the nonpareil trading city of the New World. Upon these powerful advantages New York heaped others: large auction houses, well-endowed banks, maritime insurers, numerous shipping lines, an expanding labor pool, jobbers who broke up the larger parcels arriving from England for resale inland, and an expanding volume of shipping that by mid-century exceeded in tonnage every city in the world but London.[95]

From this cocoon of commerce, New York formed the vast concentrations of capital, broad expertise, and innovative strategies that developed the mechanisms for nineteenth-century finance. It consolidated the reserves of the developing banking system and through its innovative call loan market gave these reserves an invaluable second life, activating millions of dollars in the service of new economic growth. Gotham emerged richer and significantly changed, but also with a new blueprint for national economic progress.[96]

The Civil War greatly accelerated these changes. Forced to meet staggering costs and supply needs over the long season of war, the federal government relied on New York for its credit, for its war goods, and for underwriting the Republican program of expansion in railroads and western development. The volume of spending called forth by the war boomed the economy. But more significant, it greatly advanced the shift in economic focus from the farms to the cities, from trade to domestic production, from modest small scale to big business. In all of this, Manhattan's money market and investment community were now destined for roles far more audacious than ever before.

CHAPTER 2

# New York's Napoleon

*The splendor, picturesqueness and oceanic amplitude and rush . . . the
unsurpassed situation, rivers and bay . . . costly and lofty new buildings,
facades of marble and iron, of original grandeur and elegance of design,
with the masses of gay color, the preponderance of white and blue, the
flags flying, the endless ships, the tumultuous streets, Broadway, the
heavy, low, musical roar, hardly ever intermitted, even at night; the
jobbers' houses, the rich shops, the wharves, the great Central Park . . .
these I say . . . completely satisfy my sense of power . . . and give me
through such senses and appetites, . . . a continuous exaltation and absolute fulfillment. . . .*[1]
— WALT WHITMAN, *Democratic Vistas*, 1870

*We cannot dream visions of greatness fast enough.*[2]
— *Architectural Review*, 1869

FOLLOWING THE CIVIL WAR, New York's merchant establishment
confronted a vexatious social scene. The war had raised a new class
to importance. Gotham's "genuine aristocracy," reported Mark
Twain, "find themselves supplanted by upstart princes of Shoddy,
vulgar with unknown grandfathers. Their incomes, which were
something for the common herd to gape and gossip about once, are
mere livelihoods now—would not pay Shoddy's house rent. They
move into remote new streets uptown." Shoddy industrialists, upstart bankers, and opportunistic financiers had ascended to prominence. "Not a few of the ladies who were driving in the most

sumptuous turn-outs, with liveried servants," observed the diarist George T. Strong, "looked as if they might have been cooks or chambermaids a very few years ago." The concern went deeper. The war had only intensified an already highly competitive economy that more than ever rewarded fast talking over deliberation, display over substance, speculation and boldness over achievement.[3]

Moses Taylor was close to sixty now. His style of doing business had been molded in the old traditions of merchant moderation and prudence. As he looked out upon the economy and its new masters, he longed for the old days before the war. To tell the truth, he would rather deal with southerners. Hoping to salve the wounds of war and recover the sundered past, Taylor and his colleagues at the Chamber of Commerce called for a policy of moderate reconstruction, promising both "magnanimity and clemency" for the former Confederacy. The South had been purged of slavery, declared chamber president William Dodge in 1865, and it was ready for the "enterprise of the North." Eager to demonstrate their goodwill, the merchants sent a shipment of supplies to Savannah, Georgia, to relieve those who had been burned out during General Sherman's march to the sea.[4]

Taylor and his class of elite New York businessmen championed President Andrew Johnson's efforts to restore a prewar America, with its Atlantic-dominated trade economy. They supported his policy of easy forgiveness for the rebellious states, even as Johnson sedulously resisted congressional efforts to protect the freed slaves and lost the backing of much of the nation. Republicans in Congress, led by representatives from Boston and Philadelphia, formed an anti-Johnson bloc that set out to impeach the unpopular president. In New York, Taylor and his stalwarts rallied to Johnson's side, honoring the embattled president with an opulent banquet at Delmonico's.[5]

Swift restoration for the rebellious states proved fanciful and ultimately quixotic, however. New York's merchants dispatched Thomas Conway, a Freedmen's Bureau commissioner, to assess the sentiment in the secessionist regions and make recommendations for the "money in vast quantities" that they wanted to invest there. He came to the defeated regions expecting to find remorse and a humbled spirit. Instead, he encountered a corrosive bitterness. The South, he reported, was no more penitent than Congress could compel it to be. Large portions of the old Confederacy were committed to undermining emancipation through terror and subjugation. Northerners, Conway concluded, were not safe there, and as far as he could tell, neither was their money.[6]

A handful of merchants disregarded the warnings. They hastened to resurrect the cotton trade, while others built businesses in the South, even acquiring plantations. Moses Taylor and William Dodge financed southern railroads. But despite sporadic southern overtures to Yankee capital, the old trade-based nexus between New York and the southern agricultural system was beyond retrieval. Postwar prosperity and the boom in investment speeded an economic turnover toward industrialization that was pointing the nation in a different direction.[7]

In the four years following Appomattox, rail and canal corporations attracted about $500 million in new investment and laid thirty-five thousand miles of track (including the transcontinental railway), a figure exceeding the entire rail network in 1860. In addition to funding the new road system, Gotham's investors opened the trans-Mississippi West to mining, lumbering, ranching, and commercial farming, helping develop the region into a global breadbasket and abbatoir. Growth spurred the demand for new products and new labor, attracting three million immigrants to American shores between 1865 and 1873. Foreigners—mostly men in their working years—formed a large pool of inexpensive labor, while also expanding the demand for foodstuffs, textiles, housing, and all types of consumer goods. In these eight years, investment in mechanization, new production techniques, and labor efficiencies drove up national industrial output by an astonishing 75 percent. "The loyal states," Senator Henry Wilson of Massachusetts observed, "have accumulated more capital, have added more to their wealth, than during any previous seven years in the history of the country." New York State senator Cheney Ames had little doubt about who would reap the benefits of this success: "New York will absorb it all; and . . . with [London] will dispute the title of the commercial metropolis of the world."[8]

Three major rail thoroughfares now led from the American interior to New York, while six regional telegraph networks, newly consolidated by Western Union, brought Gotham into direct conversation with the rest of the country. Manhattan's Park Row enhanced its already formidable stranglehold on the transmission of news and commercial information when the two communications titans, the Associated Press and Western Union, formed an exclusive compact in 1865 to gather and relay news copy across the land. As early as 1858, an even more ambitious project joining New York and London by transatlantic cable (Moses Taylor was a major investor) was completed, only to break down within less than two months. With the support of the New York Chamber of Commerce, the link was successfully rebuilt in 1866, bringing the two financial centers into almost instantaneous communication.[9]

These advances accelerated deeper changes in the New York economy. Easier transport and rapid wire-borne communication allowed smaller trading houses to compete for distant business, something they were not able to do on their own before. Moreover, Gotham's open loan market made it possible for even moderate-size merchants to qualify for credit, eliminating another advantage from the large commercial houses. Although merchants still accounted for the largest wedge of New York's business class and the volume of trade continued to expand, the great old figures of American commerce, the venerable merchant/financiers of South Street who funded the emerging businesses of old, no longer steered the metropolitan economy.[10]

Manufacturing was the next largest sector of New York's business community. Well before the war, New York had already become the most rapidly expanding industrial metropolis in the world. Over the course of the 1860s, as cutting-edge technologies stimulated new industry, the number of manufacturing concerns based in Gotham rose from 4,400 to more than 7,600. But even as investment dollars doubled, and the number of factory workers rose from 90,000 to 130,000, Manhattan's industrial potential was reaching its limits. It simply cost too much for large plants to locate on the costliest and most highly congested terrain in the hemisphere, remote from prairies, ranches, and mines. The number of large-profit heavy processing industries actually declined in these years while New York manufacturers focused increasingly on light industry consumer goods, such as the production of clothing.[11]

The most dynamic sector of the economy, the one driving the postwar economic rush and reaping its largest rewards, was financing. Already it accounted for one in ten New Yorkers with substantial assets. One-fourth of all the banking resources *in the United States* could be found within the radius of one Manhattan mile. The wartime legislation that had made New York into the national depository, writes financial historian Margaret Myers, placed "virtual control of the whole credit structure" in Gotham, driving an extensive expansion of its banking business. The expansion had been lightning fast. Of the ten top banks in the city in 1870, five had not even been in existence a decade before.[12]

Government had accounted for a huge volume of bank business during the war years. The experience had taught the banks a great deal about working together to raise large sums. It had also whetted their appetite for extraordinary rewards on such investment. Now, with Washington no longer borrowing, what remained was a much expanded credit market, with a large craving for speculative profits. Moreover, the prosperity era had promoted a pervasive boom psychology in which it seemed that every investment was assured great returns. The combination of war profits, debt repayments, and the release of pent-up energies fed a speculative frenzy in business securities. By 1868, Wall Street, with more than $10 billion in total security sales, commanded "a bull market," that urban scholar David Scobey concludes, "managed with almost lunatic persistency . . . to keep credit easy, prices buoyant and the influx of money at flood-tide." Soaring security sales prompted the New York Stock Exchange to install a telegraph ticker, making continuous trading feasible. The Wall Street exchange also annexed rival exchanges and tightened discipline on its members, reinforcing the NYSE's position as the central securities market in the nation.[13]

The buoyant economy—Gotham historian Sven Beckert calls these New York's "seven years of plenty"—brought great immediate advantage to Manhattan's real estate industry. Gotham acreage had long been a commodity prized more for its potential resale value than for anything that could be built upon it or extracted from underneath. "Overturn, overturn, overturn! Is the maxim of New York," former mayor Philip Hone had written in his diary. The fevered land market led the industry to launch its own journal in 1868, the *Real Estate Record and Builder's Guide*, to report on weekly lot transactions, mortgage rates, and building costs. Nothing seemed so clear, the journal declared in one of its early numbers, as the imperative to develop land until every square foot of Manhattan was covered, and Brooklyn, too.[14]

More important, this market led to a wholesale reordering of the city landscape, remaking the downtown and pushing development rapidly northward. Not long before, much of what was important in New York could be found in several concentrated acres on lower Manhattan. Business, religious, and political institutions shared the undifferentiated "walking city" with citizens of all classes. Workers and entrepreneurs, municipal officials and scavenging cave dwellers, all inhabited a collective mile not far from the shadow of the high-masted sailing ships crowding the piers. It was a city scaled to human dimension. Trinity Church, Castle Garden, the Customs House, the Merchant's Exchange, and City Hall all formed a unified city center, dominated by Trinity's spire reaching majestically 290 feet into the heavens.[15]

This concentrated city did not endure for long. Already in 1836 Philip Hone reluctantly sold his home across from City Hall on Broadway ("I have turned myself out of doors; but $60,000 is a great deal of money"), predicting that "all the dwelling houses [on Broadway] are to be converted into stores . . . and all the downtown burgomasters who have fixed to one spot all their lives, will be . . . marching reluctantly north to pitch their tents in places which in their time, were orchards, cornfields or morasses." He was correct, though even he did not foresee the speed with which these changes would overtake the city. By the 1860s, James Parton commented ruefully on the passing of compact, unified Gotham, concluding his study of Manhattan's elite cathedrals with the observation, "The old . . . Christian church, as the one place where all sorts and conditions of men came together to dwell upon considerations interesting to all equally, is not adapted to modern society. . . . It may be that never again . . . will ignorant and learned, master and servant, rich and poor feel themselves at home in the same church." Or the same New York neighborhood.[16]

One of the city's oldest churches, Trinity, standing at the corner of Wall Street and Broadway, offers a fine précis of the city's expansion and the real estate market's role in disaggregating even long-held parish properties. Chartered in the seventeenth century and awarded a patent of thirty-two acres of land west of Broadway, Trinity went on to become the Northeast's grand sanctuary for Episcopalian worship. Over the years, purchases and bequests swelled church holdings so that by 1800 Trinity controlled an immense urban estate of close to a thousand Manhattan lots that it leased out for homes and work spaces.[17]

One of its most attractive properties was situated in St. John's Park, just south of Canal Street and not far from the Hudson River. An exclusive neighborhood of redbrick Federal-style houses amid lovely old shade trees and carefully manicured lawns, these houses were leased by Trinity to only the most fastidious of wealthy Protestant New Yorkers. Many of the residents wanted to buy their homes, but the church refused to sell. Even when it pleaded that deficits forced cutbacks on its missionary services to the impoverished, Trinity, the second largest landholder in the city, refused to part with any of its property.[18]

Perhaps church authorities thought that its immense temporal dominion would allow it to withstand the swiftly running currents of New York life. But not even this venerable sanctuary could hold back the forces of the market. Around midcentury, when Trinity objected to a new street extension planned to run through its ancient cemetery, city officials rejected the claim of hallowed prerogatives. Even Trinity had no right to exclude "a large and growingly important section, in the very heart of commerce . . . from its natural and just share in the commerce of the city." By 1860 the last traces of residential Wall Street had disappeared, depriving the exquisite Gothic cathedral of its elite parishioners. It stood anomalously, in what had become the nation's financial hub, amid rushing clerks and votaries of the market, surrounded by tall buildings that, wrote James Gordon Bennett's *Herald*, were "scheming, magnificent and full of all kinds of roguery."[19]

Through all these shifts, Trinity continued to cling to its properties with a feudal resolve, refusing to sell off any land. But the press of trade along the Hudson's docks and the laying of West Side tracks for Cornelius Vanderbilt's Hudson River Railroad transformed the neighborhood. Businesses attracted by the new facilities outbid residents for nearby properties, creating a new commercial corridor. Once pleasant tree-lined streets were now filled with traffic and the noise of careless moneymaking. St. John's wealthy leaseholders fled the area for finer homes in less expensive areas farther uptown. By the late 1860s, the once proud section housed a strip of raunchy boardinghouses set among warehouses and storefronts.

Trinity had fiercely held on to its domain for centuries. But as the market displaced its genteel leaseholders, even as it drove up the value of these downtown properties, Trinity's resistance was worn away. Nothing better reflected the mutability of New York space and its profound commercialization than the transfer of prized church lands to Cornelius Vanderbilt, for $1 million. New York's profane traffic master demolished St. John's Square and replaced it with a modern transport complex replete with switching yards, grain depots, stockyards, and an immense foul-smelling slaughterhouse.

The dislodging of Trinity and the leveling of the once exclusive square to make way for the Vanderbilt yards augured even more far-reaching changes in the city's landscape.[20] Towering above the busy scene rose a new altar of sorts, a three-story frieze depicting the heroic life of the earthy Admiral Vanderbilt in its various stations.

"[He is] the railway king of New York," wrote a British journal. Profane, illiterate, a man of coarse habits and fiery temperament, Cornelius Vanderbilt, the report continued, was "a favorite type of the kind of [New York] success which the average American has constantly before his eyes."[21]

The handsome, sandy-haired Vanderbilt was brought up in a family of fourteen children on a farm in Staten Island's Dutch community. Before the age of sixteen, he opened a ferry to Manhattan that within a few years he managed to build into a fleet of profitable sailing vessels. When swift new steamships began to appear on the run, the young mariner sold his sluggish brigs and wind-driven skiffs and hired himself out as a steamboat captain to apprentice in the new technology. Grasping the critical role of quick and dependable transportation in forming a national network of trade, Vanderbilt mastered the sleek steam vessels and struck out on his own again. Fierce in competition, he pared costs and slashed fares, successfully capturing a large share of New York's coastal trade along the Hudson. The slope-shouldered seafarer emerged from the 1840s with his favorite title "Commodore" and a shipping fleet, one of the largest in the nation, worth an estimated $1.2 million.[22]

New York port historian Robert Albion calls Vanderbilt "the greatest transportation genius of them all." Brilliant he may have been, but nothing matched his iron will and fortitude. When waves of beguiled forty-niners sought quick passage to California gold,

Vanderbilt determined to win this traffic for his ships by finding a shorter, quicker, cheaper route to the West Coast. He hastened to Nicaragua, where he wheedled rights of passage for his company. Then he put crews to work deepening the San Juan River and hacking through rough jungle terrain. Finally, in a path that took them past rushing rapids and around nests of pirates and revolutionaries, his ships pioneered a new passage to the gold. "Artificer of his own fortunes," in the words of the *New York Herald*, Vanderbilt emerged from the 1849 gold rush earning $1 million a year.[23]

The time had come to seek a larger stage. The lavishly impatient Commodore erected a substantial Manhattan residence on Washington Place, off Broadway. When his wife objected that she had not been consulted and that she did not want to move, Vanderbilt had the mother of his thirteen children committed to an asylum, giving her "several months in which to reflect." With little pretense to faithfulness, Vanderbilt insatiably pursued young women, hard liquor, and fast horses deep into old age. He brought this same unquenchable zest to his business enthusiasms. Steamships had made him rich, but it was railroads that turned the irascible mariner, with a penchant for imposing his will on men and landscapes, into the wealthiest investor in America. He had refused to buy steamships until he had become familiar with them firsthand, and he had also refused to become involved in early schemes for local rail lines. But in time the railroad's grand possibilities captivated this New Yorker.[24]

Trade goods, the basis for so much of New York's prosperity, had for the longest time arrived largely through the port. But the run-down East River wharves, ramshackle when they were first clapped together from planks of wood in the 1850s, had decayed badly, failing to keep pace with mercantile development. Periodically the unsafe docks would collapse, merchandise and whatever else happened to be on the rickety boards plunging into the water. The overcrowding was just as bad. Ships filled with western grain, the most important of the city's trade commodities, spent as much as a week clotting the pier, clustered around Coenties Slip, dozens abreast, before they got to unload their cargoes. Pilferage was rampant. A million dollars in goods were stolen from the poorly guarded docks each year. And the filth! Pier waters were fouled with sewage that in the summer literally boiled gases off into the fetid atmosphere. "Filth," read one harbor report, "lies frothing like yeast, setting free offensive and pernicious gases. . . ." And once cargoes were finally unloaded, they had to be hauled across the busy streets to warehouses and terminals across town. "It is preposterous," griped the *Real Estate Record*, "that our merchants [are] compelled to pay as much for the removal of a load from Courtlandt to Canal Street as is required to bring it from Chicago to New York."[25]

The thickening net of railroad connections offered a flexible alternative to water transport. Both the Erie and Pennsylvania rail trunks had established large freight and passenger terminals in neighboring New Jersey, but Vanderbilt's immense St. John's Square freight terminal, with depots, stockyards, and storage tanks all in one place, brought shipments right into the city. So powerful was their lure that these new yards drew South Street's long established East River countinghouses to the new West Side terminal. Like so many filings arranging themselves around a charged horseshoe, scores of cast-iron warehouses rose up alongside the new Hudson freight yards. Dozens of secondary businesses devoted to processing, packaging, and distributing the goods that came coursing through the Vanderbilt complex followed. By the mid-1870s, rows of these stately neo-Renaissance buildings with their distinctive outer columns lined the blocks above City Hall, from Duane Street to Canal, forming a fresh riverside mercantile district.[26]

The volume of postwar trade expanded so rapidly that in 1869, Vanderbilt, who by now controlled all of the railroads coming into the city, broke ground for a new terminal at 42nd Street and Fourth Avenue. The "Grand Central" station would bring together in one facility the commuter and long haul traffic of the Harlem, New York Central, and New Haven lines. Two more years and $3 million brought New York an imposing twelve-track brick-and-granite depot, the largest on the continent and second largest in the world. Here was essentially a rail terminal and train shed that Vanderbilt had dressed up into a showplace offering New Yorkers a monument to size, speed, and technological achievement, an example of ambitious "New York scale."[27]

Transit improvements not only promoted commerce, they also demolished the boundaries of what was left of the peripatetic city. Municipal transit freed New Yorkers, particularly those of the middle class, from the need to live within walking distance of the necessities of urban life. It made wide swaths of new uptown space accessible for residence, while clearing the city core for more intensive business use. In 1866, twenty-nine omnibus lines sent out horse-drawn passenger carriages for ten daily rounds about the city. An additional fourteen lines ran their horse- or mule-drawn carriages along rails as far north as 59th Street. By 1873, streetcar lines were ferrying 150 million passengers a year and Manhattan's area of significant settlement already had climbed as far as 42nd Street.[28]

If the real estate market made property liquid and the railroad promoted an expansion of the city and the formation of a new commercial zone, other, even more comprehensive shifts led to the emergence of the complex segmented metropolis. Eric Hobsbawm has called this period, roughly the third quarter of the nineteenth century, when global developments in transportation, communication, and credit converged in a central market for commodity exchange and investment, "the age of capital." In this age of capital, as the modern economy took on a deeper complexity, it inscribed corresponding changes on the urban landscape where these changes originated.[29]

As Hobsbawm suggests, these changes reflected more than simple "modernization." The breakup of the communal city into specialized sectors with new commercial districts, "streetcar communities" (within commuting distance from the city center), and the rise of central business districts were part of a larger pattern of urban trans-

formation on both sides of the Atlantic. In these years, London's
Metropolitan Board of Works began a long awaited overhaul and
consolidation of the city. Vienna inaugurated its acclaimed
Ringstrasse road system, which was soon copied in Budapest and
elsewhere. In France, Napoleon III installed the driven and visionary Baron Georges Eugène Haussmann as prefect of the Seine in
1853 and gave him an unfettered hand to remake Paris. On this side
of the ocean, a modern Chicago rose from the devastating fire of
1871, and grand new urban parks were planted in Brooklyn,
Philadelphia, Baltimore, San Francisco, and other major cities. In
Boston, Philadelphia, and Cincinnati, the self-contained municipality, with its religious, commercial, business, and governmental functions arrayed within walking distance, was extended and partitioned
into a differentiated landscape. New York too was dramatically recast.[30]

For urban planners, Second Empire Paris, the Paris of Napoleon's
Haussmann, quickly became the model for systematic urban reform.
Sweeping aside political opposition and fiscal restraints, Baron
Haussmann tore down a filthy and medieval Paris, ill equipped to accommodate its expanding population, and in its place raised a grand
metropolis with broad boulevards, one hundred thousand new
apartments, and modern amenities. "The Attila of the straight line,"
as Victor Fournel called him, brought the narrow, winding, and often unconnected streets of the old municipality into a unified, orderly system that featured scenic thoroughfares, strategic avenues,
and a belt railway girdling the city perimeter. He replaced Paris's festering waste canals with hundreds of miles of modern underground
sewers; erected a fresh, protected water supply; illuminated the
streets with gas lighting; and planted a lavish network of picturesque
parks. He added graceful touches that included artificial lakes on the
Bois de Boulogne and glass and metal stands at les Halles. Applying
the magisterial powers that Napoleon had granted him, the Baron
ripped out decrepit slums, relocated the worker populations, erected
large central markets, and added the magnificent signatures of Paris

life: the Louvre, a new Opera House, a grand hotel, and pedestrian bridges, all planned down to the smallest detail.[31]

"The . . . imposing palaces, the broad avenues and boulevards, the splendid and artistic views . . . ," reported an admiring, if somewhat daunted, *New York Herald,*

> were not the spontaneous work of the tastes and desires of the people; not the work of the natural growth of the city. It was by the order of the government that narrow streets, lanes and alleyways were widened, that blocks of dingy dwellings extending for miles and dating their origin back to past centuries of history, were demolished and that rows of modern, luxurious and costly palaces were erected in their places. . . . Th[is] work was one of the *Idées Napoleoniennes,* and was carried out with that resistless energy and power which have characterized the present imperial government in all of its relations with the French people.[32]

The Emperor permitted no conventional limits to hamper Haussmann as the grand builder moved from commission to commission, condemning properties and launching new operations with breezy insouciance. For funding, the Baron at first relied on his charmed ability to juggle contracts and loans and, ultimately, he relied upon the Emperor. In an age when Paris's annual expenditures ran to 55 million francs, Napoleon lavished 2.5 *billion* francs on the seventeen-year-long reconstruction. "There is no power in France today," declared a Parliamentary deputy in 1864, "that can control the omnipotence of the Prefect of the Seine."[33]

"Make no little plans. They have no magic to stir men's blood," the American architect and city designer Daniel Burnham was fond of saying, and Haussmann's dramatic remaking of Paris was stamped with just such audacity and monumental aspiration. The Second Empire cast a new Paris that was more efficient, more secure, better protected from disease; a grand city made modern and rational in one integrated plan.[34]

Chicago was also rebuilt in these years, but in her case as a result of the greatest natural disaster to that time in American history. At great human cost, the 1871 fire cleared away the city's old downtown and razed much of its wooden residential housing stock. Within days a modern Chicago began to rise from the burn. Barely a year after the fire, downtown land values stood well above prefire levels, leading many to ask, "Was not the Great Fire a blessing in disguise?" And within another year the city discharged thousands of tons of fire debris into the waters, creating a new lakefront upon which it erected a Crystal Palace Exposition Hall. The fire modernized the city. New safety legislation proscribed wood construction and banned fire-prone industries from the city center, promoting Chicago's first masonry-clad iron and steel skyscrapers. The real estate market did the rest, driving the cost of central city property too high for worker housing. As a result, poorer citizens were forced from the city core. Specialized manufacturing was also squeezed out to the periphery. By 1893, Chicago boasted "the busiest and most modern downtown in the country," with a dozen of "the highest buildings ever constructed." In these skyscrapers, an expanding business and professional class worked by day and in the evenings rode the commuter railroads out to a ring of new suburbs. Sectoring a city in this fashion was taken as the highest form of advance, of specialization inscribed on the very landscape of urban life.[35]

New York had no Napoleon and suffered no transforming conflagration. What it had was Andrew Haswell Green, and over the forty-year period following the Civil War, no New Yorker gave more serious or more systematic thought to the direction of urban development than he did. The fields of battle had barely cooled when Green leveled his critique at "the lamentable results of the want of largeness of ideas" in trying to meet the needs "of a great people." Deeply informed about technical innovations in city design, troubled by the inadequacies of Gotham's infrastructure and layout, inspired by a growing sense of the metropolis's importance and its want of refinement, Green called upon his fellow citizens to seize control of unguided urban expansion to shape New York into a grand city.[36]

Born in 1820 to a well-to-do New England family, Green traced his lineage back to colonial Massachusetts. He was raised on a picturesque estate near Worcester, and though he never lost his affection for the soothing landscapes of ancestral Green Hill, in 1835, at the age of fifteen, he moved to New York to pursue a future in commerce. Green landed a job in one of Manhattan's leading dry goods concerns. Often putting in fourteen or more hours a day, the bright, honest, and frugal New Englander moved ahead rapidly.[37]

He pursued a demanding regimen of self-improvement. He once caught his own bookkeeping error of ten cents and earnestly resolved that it would never happen again. Upon learning that his older sister had said that he would not amount to much because of his aversion to books, he scribbled in his diary that he must "apply myself . . . night and day that I might not merit what she has said," adopting a corrective course of reading in biography, history, and the Greek classics. At other times he taxed himself for his inadequate memory, his primitive style in making an argument, and his faulty knowledge of history. "I feel a great desire to be a good writer, but do not deem myself at all competent to write even a decent paragraph." To add a patina of continental refinement, he decided to attend a church where the services were in French, only to chastise himself for making profane use of what was meant to be sacred. Religious issues lapped at his teenage conscience until he decided, finally, that he must accept his faith anew and be born again.[38]

Only word from his dearest friend, Samuel G. Arnold, was able to melt the grave and introspective demeanor. "Inexpressable, unbounded, unheard of, inconceivable emotions of joy and delight," he wrote upon receiving Arnold's "beautiful, delightful, exquisite, intense . . . epistle." In the late thirties, when the economy took a plunge, he went off to Trinidad for work as an assistant overseer on a plantation. But in 1843 he returned to New York for good, determined to pursue a career in law.[39]

Green sought out the acquaintance of Samuel J. Tilden, six years his senior and already a respected business attorney. Tilden brought the younger man into his firm as a law associate and the two became fast friends, working together on real estate business and promoting rail mergers throughout the Northeast. Green became Tilden's law partner in 1852 and, though he complained that Tilden was "surrounded with political hangers-on," he helped launch his colleague's budding career in elective government, while Tilden furnished Green with a web of important business and civic connections. While he could be tartly cynical about politics, Green admired the influential Tilden, who went on to become New York's governor and the Democratic candidate for president in 1876.

The two life-long bachelors remained intimate comrades until Tilden's death in 1886. Though a Democrat like Tilden, Green kept a guarded distance from Tammany, establishing a record for independence and integrity in civic affairs. While his patron Tilden pursued elective office, Green spent much of the rest of his life engaged in promoting an agenda to fit Manhattan for its role as "the metropolis of the Western World."[40]

Cold, austere (a few glasses of wine were enough to last him a year, and even after he became a millionaire his house remained very simple), and endlessly suspicious, Andrew Green established a record of thorough devotion to public service and civic improvement. He represented a type of citizen who, though avid to make a living, thought that greed was wrong, that merely making money was not enough to fulfill a life. Self-righteous in the extreme, he kept few friends while gaining many admirers for his versatile skills in municipal planning and his undoubted integrity. Severe, demanding, caustic in debate, with a reputation for cantankerousness, he could be very persuasive in person and even more so in his writing, which had greatly improved over the years.[41]

Two rules guided his public priorities. The first was to hold on to every penny of public money as if it were an only child ("extravagantly penurious" wrote the *Times*). Incongruously, his second rule was to cast New York as an expansive, efficiently designed, and majestically arranged commercial metropolis. For the rest of the century he led the forces who conceived the metropolis as a central place for organizing the regional economy, fostering national wealth, molding a refined civic culture, and setting a standard for municipal grandeur. His political and commercial connections and engagement with leading cultural and charitable institutions gave him a role in virtually all of the major decisions regarding public works and city growth in the decades following the Civil War.[42]

In 1857, Green, by now a successful lawyer and president of the Board of Education, won appointment to the state-designated Central Park Commission. The CPC brought together intellectuals and urbanists around the larger question of how to nestle a scenic park with open space and generous woods in the middle of kinetic Manhattan. Green was the leading voice on the commission and he swayed its members to support the "Greensward Plan" drafted by Frederick Law Olmsted and his partner Calvert Vaux. The two landscape designers conceived a 700-acre pleasure ground filled with soothing lawns, artfully created waters, and rustic patches. Planted in Gotham's midsection, this undulating greenspace would provide respite from the corrosive, congested city and its unvarying linear layout. Endeavoring to change more than the landscape, Olmsted and Vaux thought that tranquil greens and rolling meadows would exert a therapeutic influence on the rushed city, producing calmer, more wholesome citizens and healthier children.

Green, who had grown up surrounded by the natural beauty and generous slopes of Green Hill, shared the park designers' respect for the anodyne powers of rustic space. He was as troubled as they by the wholesale felling of America's virgin woodlands, voicing concern for the "forests of the country, with their magnificent beauties, the growth of centuries . . . swept away rapidly and wastefully and the beasts and the birds that live in their shelter . . . becoming extinct for want of an intelligent appreciation of their value both to the present and the coming generations." Through his influence Olmsted was appointed the Park's superintendent so that it would be built to reflect this vision. And while he soon grew disillusioned with Olmsted, especially over the landscape architect's unbridled spending, he never backed away from the idea that responsibility for the urban landscape and its environment must not be left to the free market alone.[43]

The creation of Central Park formed Green's apprenticeship in city planning. He mastered its every detail as well as the larger vision. For the ten years that he presided over the Central Park Commission, Green set aside his other work to give the project his full attention. He was the commission's workhorse and its most forceful member. "No one but Green knows," Olmsted wrote of his sometime adversary, "or will take the trouble to inform himself, of the facts bearing on any question of policy sufficiently to argue on it effectually." Green would show up unannounced at work sites to check on tasks and demand greater productivity. "Not a dollar, not a cent, is got from under his paw," Olmsted would complain regarding his prickly nemesis, "that is not wet with his blood & sweat."[44]

His work on the commission placed Green in a position to think broadly about the city and its development. He read widely and studied what other cities had done, incorporating their experience into a series of remarkably farsighted reports. He did not allow the Civil War and its many shortages to sidetrack the work of city building. "In . . . war and pestilence," he declared, "those great works that render . . . [New York City] the convenient abode of masses of men and attract to its shores the industry and capital that determine its metropolitan character, should in anticipation of its brilliant future, not only not be abandoned, but should be steadily prosecuted."[45]

With Central Park a much-heralded success, Green continued to press for a larger, more generously endowed New York. The vastly detailed and expensive park project had proved that Gotham could focus its energies and resources to carry out important public undertakings. But grand amenities, even on the scale of the park, were only a hint of what Green had in mind. If city leaders could be mobilized to secure more than 700 acres of Manhattan land; if Gotham's wealthy merchants and landowners could be enlisted in the costly endeavor of creating uplifting leisure space; if more than 20,000 laborers could be assembled to blast and slash and rearrange a daunting swath of city wilderness while removing more than 1,600 individuals from the "path of progress," then larger possibilities, especially in this age of Haussmann, beckoned. He aimed to plant in and around the Park a new cultural-educational complex where scientific, educational, and artistic institutions would blossom. As early as 1860 he proposed establishing a meteorological observatory, zoological and botanical gardens, and museums of art and natural history. Turning his thoughts to the larger issue of New York's uncharted growth, Green drew a new layout for the city's undeveloped north end as well as lower Westchester and he projected bridges for the Harlem River and Spuyten Duyvil Creek.[46]

The respected journalist and civic leader William Cullen Bryant wrote in 1868 that in order for New York to live up to its destiny as the "first city of Christendom" it must "improve in plan still more rapidly than it grows in size." *The New York Times* joined the call: "The daily experience of New York, and of most American cities," the paper declared wistfully, "leads to the wish that some Haus[s]man[n] had presided at their planning." The *Real Estate Record* agreed, pleading for "a Haussmann who will do for New York what that great reconstructor did for Paris." Busily penning report after report—the latest of which called for Manhattan to consolidate the metropolitan region into a unified Greater New York—Green signaled his willingness to assume the responsibility.[47]

Under normal circumstances, once a commission completes its work it is thanked, more or less profusely, and eased into retirement. But the Central Park Commission was not prepared to go out of existence. New York's one agency with some responsibility for thinking systematically about city growth and its possibilities, the CPC insisted that there was much more still left to do. Settlement was pushing uptown into new districts more swiftly than streets could be laid out and a rational structure imposed on the rapidly receding wilderness. Meanwhile the old downtown, which just a few years before represented all of settled Manhattan, was becoming something new again: a central business district for a booming and highly differentiated city. But it was all proceeding without apparent design or plan and—except for the park—without the benefit of major public funding. The *Times* thought it knew why: City authorities are "incapable of entertaining any conception of the necessities of this great Metropolis, and incapable of taking any view of its affairs apart from their own personal pecuniary interests."[48]

Politics intruded as well. State legislators, largely Republicans from rural districts, were less concerned about the city's planless growth than about trusting city Democrats to channel its development. To prevent this, upstate Republicans had meddled shamelessly in the city's affairs, appointing a Metropolitan Police Force and a Board of Health that were run from Albany. Now, as the legislators took up what the *Evening Post* described as "how to plan and how to build a city so as best to accommodate business and promote health," Green lobbied the legislature to assign his Central Park Commission this responsibility. The commission had won wide public respect for having successfully built a "fragment of utopia." Its commissioners had thought deeply and less contentiously than most such bodies about the efficient allocation of space and resources, and the business community admired Green's hectoring patrol of the Central Park budget. Green also had the real estate industry's trust. "In this career," a local journal wrote about Green, "by universal consent he has no compeer." With little appreciation for what this authority might mean, Albany handed responsibility for supervising Gotham's uptown development to the Central Park Commission and appointed Green its chairman.[49]

Green savored the task of shaping the CPC into an agency for rationalizing Gotham's postwar municipal growth. Able to speak knowledgeably about the history of ancient cities as well as the details of Paris's recent modernization, this student of urban life was as familiar with the unique rock formations of northern Manhattan as he was expert in the relative merits of different pavement materials, sewer pipes, and street systems. His years in politics, civic work, and the real estate industry equipped him with hard experience in city building and a supple wisdom in navigating municipal politics. His studies and specialized reports laying out a comprehensive plan for the upper city are models of intelligent analysis, informed by a practiced understanding of the physical layout of the city and a deft reading of relevant experience from ancient Rome, Athens, and Corinth, as well as contemporary Paris, London, and Chicago. From these cities he took his basic principles in planning: cities must seek a balance between freedom and safety, between cost and necessity, and ultimately between what makes city life more secure and what allows it to soar with unscripted possibility. A planner, he understood, must design for the future without trampling the legitimate expectations of those who live in the present. Planning of this sort would involve more government than city dwellers had ever imagined, but it also promised to surmount "the process of gradual irregular expansion" to bring a more even, more sensible, and more fully realized process of urban development.[50]

In the sweep of his planning vision and the long season of his influence, Green has been compared with New York's powerful twentieth-century planner Robert Moses. Moses, however, worked on a city that had already been built, while Green worked on a nearly empty canvas. New York's notorious nineteenth-century political bosses may have controlled the daily activities of the municipal government, but in shaping the long-term development of the city, propertied and wealthy men of Green's station took the initiative to sketch bold plans with, it is worth noting, remarkably little scrutiny. Green differs from Moses in yet another important respect. Moses never pursued a private career. But Green ran a successful law practice for large property holders and railroad companies, both of whom had a not insignificant interest in city planning. Yet neither Green nor his detractors thought it remarkable that at the same time that he participated in every major civic and public project in New

York between the Civil War and the end of the century, he earned handsome fees servicing the city's propertied elite.

Admittedly, Green, reflecting the priorities of society's "best men," thought that it was more important in planning modern New York to look back to classical cities than to study, for example, the needs of a diverse, multiplying, and propertyless working class. One can shine a modern searchlight on Green's thinking and identify more traps and snares. But concentrating on these limitations threatens to cripple our understanding even more than it did his. It is all too common to assume that objective circumstances fix individual goals and interests; that a member of the middle class is hard-wired with a bourgeois mentality. Yes, Green did think of the city as a place of commerce, but so, it must be said, did the hundreds of thousands of immigrant workers who poured in during good times and avoided the city in bad times. And yes, he shared with the Chamber of Commerce and its bevy of wealthy traders the aim of moving merchandise swiftly and safely through unobstructed streets. But he also placed New York in the tradition of the world's grand cities, challenging its citizens to meet that standard, not only with its sewers and pavements, but also with institutions committed to refinement, learning, and uplift.

Derided as a railroad attorney and a "spokesman for the city's property owners," he nourished a broader notion of what a city is and what its future demanded. He did not hesitate to criticize property owners or to excoriate the very railroad industry that the Tilden firm serviced, as an industry "where pecuniary interests are likely to be promoted by facile representatives, . . . to the injury of those who pay rents and taxes, as is instanced in the case of railroads occupying streets that have been graded and prepared as it were, for and without expense to them, without any compensation for franchises worth millions. . . ."[51]

What made such men as Moses and Green important in the end was not their conflicted interests, or even their personal shortcomings. Their importance lies in their profound impact on reimagining the city. Green may have been a railroad and real estate attorney, but finding a town that could accommodate a population of one hundred thousand, in the earlier decades of the century, he made it into a metropolis of capital and refinement for more than a million souls.

The city had been laid out in 1811 as a spare grid of lengthwise streets crossed by perpendicular avenues. All the way up beyond Harlem, the planners had mapped out straight streets and easy grades, making optimal use of land. Following this plan, the municipality leveled rugged patches, blasted rock formations, poured landfill into intruding ponds, swamps, and marshes, and filled in sections of the waterfront, apportioning property in uniform lot sizes to make exchange easy and practical. The march of progress uptown followed the unvarying grid. In the 1840s, Edgar Allan Poe, looking into the future of the scattered uptown villas and mansions, declared their impending doom. "The spirit of improvement has withered them with its acrid breath. Streets are already 'mapped' through them and they are no longer suburban residences, but 'town lots.' In some thirty years every noble cliff will be a pier, and the whole island will be desecrated by buildings of brick, with portentous facades of brownstone." Making no concession to natural formations, forgoing whimsy, and avoiding the distinctive curves, plazas, and boulevards that made other cities memorable, the grid promoted Procrustean utility over inspiration and flair. By extending the "radically simple" and strictly predictable rectilinear lattice into the uptown frontier, the plan assured that New York evolved without much new thought about circulation or land use or opportunity for a tailoring hand.[52]

In the half century after 1811, the city had changed far more than any of the early planners had imagined or allowed for. The plan made no provisions for new street uses, for rapid transit, for the huge expansion of the population, or for the new economy. The simple and clean grid stood as a testament to the modest, pedestrian city that New York no longer was. In 1866 lower Broadway alone carried an estimated eighteen thousand vehicles a day. It was sheer hyperbole to refer to the clogged horde as traffic. The pandemonium and recurring battles over rights of way on the clotted streets resulted in an unconscionable waste of time and often posed real dangers to life and limb, not to say to productive labor.[53]

No one proposed tearing out the settled downtown and replacing it with a fresh layout, but Green and his colleagues did override the grid at Gotham's north end. It would have taken an incredible amount of money to blast through the stone heights of upper Manhattan and to bring its undulating natural topography to a uniform grade. The expense would have delayed development there indefinitely. Instead, Green's commission proceeded with the swift development of upper Manhattan, displaying a flair for scenic beauty that was new to the city. The commission designed plans for tree-filled squares, grand boulevards, and ample riding trails. It launched new parks and picturesque bridges, an imposing "Grand Circle" entrance to the southwest opening of Central Park (later named after Christopher Columbus), and a graceful waterfront. Departing from the "utmost private-use planning" of the past, Green withdrew from the market wedges of property along the unspoiled bluffs of the Hudson valley to create a series of terraced drives for recreational use. Beyond the creation of striking public spaces, he planed for the coordinated development of the Upper West Side, Washington Heights, and the northern riverfront along the Harlem River and Spuyten Duyvil.[54]

For all the respect that he had for Olmsted as an urban visionary, Green had long before lost patience with the architect's fondness for larding costly flourishes onto Central Park. Green dismissed these touches as precious, "fanciful," and a waste, clamping firm fiscal restraints on Olmsted. Frugal by disposition, he was also a realist who understood that taxpayers would quickly lose patience with a project that kept driving up nonessential expenditures. More important was his objection to reserving Central Park for pastoral space. He had no intention of limiting the vast privileged domain, the first American undertaking of such size and scope, to reflecting gardens and passive spaces for rustic respite.[55]

Even more than rolling landscapes and bucolic tranquillity, he believed that great cities needed cultural institutions that engaged citizens in enlightenment and uplift. Green set out to furnish New York with a public culture that matched its position as the nation's "acknowledged seat of wealth and moral power." Over Olmsted's objections he planned a cluster of institutions devoted to the stimulation of thought, moral improvement, and delight around this grand urban amenity. He invited high cultural institutions to locate in the park, forging a national center for modern metropolitan refinement far from the old city center.[56]

For years the New-York Historical Society had talked of erecting a "Museum of History, Antiquities and Art," going so far as to commission Richard Morris Hunt to design a Louvre-style museum. But after the society withdrew from the project, the idea languished until after the war, when it emerged as the Metropolitan Museum of Art. Despite its grandiose title, the museum's founders rejected the European model of august galleries filled with original masterpieces. They wanted no "mere cabinet of curiosities which should serve to kill time for the idle." The museum's charter, adopted in 1870, identified its purpose as, in addition to encouraging the fine arts, "the application of arts to manufacture and practical life, advancing the general knowledge of kindred subjects, and to that end furnishing popular instruction and recreation." The founders intended to fill the museum with objects of beauty and pleasure, but also with lessons in technology and industry for "the working millions." Together, the Boston Museum of Fine Arts; the Corcoran in Washington, D.C.; and the Metropolitan (all incorporated in 1870) represented the first major art museums in the country.[57]

Ten years later, in March 1880, the Metropolitan completed its move from the temporary quarters that it had occupied since 1870 into its new Central Park home. President Rutherford B. Hayes officiated at the installation ceremony, where the dedicatory speaker boldly addressed New York's industrial elite: "Think of it ye millionaires of many markets—what glory may yet be yours," the lecturer exhorted, "if you only listen to our advice to convert pork into porcelain, grain and produce into priceless pottery, the rude ores of commerce into sculptured marble and railroad shares and mining stocks into . . . the glorified canvas of the world's masters . . . [O]urs is the higher ambition to convert your useless gold into things of living beauty that shall be a joy to a whole people for a thousand years."[58]

Convinced that an "urban menagerie" would be a splendid supplement to the city's free educational system, Green helped bring a touch of exotic nature to the concrete city. No American city had its own zoo, but New York had long before stopped looking to its American neighbors for inspiration. Increasingly, Gotham took as its models the grand overseas metropolises, patterning the Central Park Zoo after Paris's Jardin des Plantes and the London Zoological Garden. At first no more than an assortment of cast-off children's pets and abandoned animals, the zoo continued to grow and ultimately assembled a fine zoological collection that became one of Central Park's most popular attractions.[59]

Green's commission also won the authorization to "erect, establish, conduct and maintain in the Central Park . . . a meteorological and astronomical observatory, and a museum of natural history. . . ." An expanding list of elite supporters from the "upper ten thousand," including the importer Theodore Roosevelt Sr. (father of the future president), J. Pierpont Morgan, A. T. Stewart, and half a dozen bankers, underwrote the American Museum of Natural History. The founders aimed for something more accessible than Harvard's Museum of Comparative Zoology (which primarily served the scientific community), to enrich what the *Times* called "the culture and good habits of the masses." The closest thing New York had to something of this sort was the eclectic blend of scientific wonders, valued artifacts, and bizarre oddities with which showman P. T. Barnum filled his "American Museum" on Broadway and Spring Street. The popular downtown storefront lived off its admissions, combining its "wonderful and miraculous . . . mysteries of the past," with humbug-laced displays like the "feejee Mermaid" and Tom Thumb.[60]

For many this combination of legitimate knowledge with spurious knockoffs and counterfeit curiosities was suspect. "Private efforts for the mere purposes of profit can never accomplish anything in the right direction," admonished the *Herald*. Individuals "may get up a show," the daily added, "but a museum to be of any sterling value, must be a public institution." When Barnum's burned to the ground in 1868 (and Phineas T. went on to found America's first three-ring circus), the Natural History Museum's trustees resolved to separate authentic knowledge and high culture from low commercialization.[61]

Like the other new cultural institutions, the museum was ensconced in uptown legitimacy and was also public, in the limited sense of being noncommercial, adhering to objective professional standards, and opening its doors to the masses; public in that it fostered a civic realm for intellectual endeavor, artistic cultivation, and refined inquiry. But both Green, who vividly recalled the open wrangling that marred the early history of Central Park, and the trustees, who were determined to safeguard cultural activities from the rough stewardship of partisan politics (as in "greedy, corrupt, and treacherous *politicians*"), agreed that the institution would be funded by private donors with intermittent state and local subscriptions. Green arranged for the city to pay for the buildings and maintenance, while private sources funded the art and specimen collections. Responsibility for administrative policy was placed in the hands of "intelligent citizens, men of leisure & scientific men," that is to say individuals appointed by the private trustees. This public/private model governed the city's relationship with elite cultural institutions well into the future.[62]

A host of other public projects followed, including a magnificent eighty-five-thousand-book collection in the Richard Morris Hunt–designed James Lenox Library for scholars at Fifth Avenue and 71st Street, furnishing New York with a cultural infrastructure that projected a bold new authority—older elite institutions had taken names like the New-York Historical Society, newer ones were the

American or Metropolitan—not only in economics, but in refinement as well.[63]

For Green and the trustees of urban gentility, these institutions represented an escape from the clamorous and unrefined city streets far more profound and transforming than Olmsted's sylvan pastures. They took very seriously, though admittedly in a far more hard-nosed spirit than the words seem to convey, the mission to "humanize, to educate, to refine, a practical and laborious people." In 1870, when the Metropolitan Museum was first established, *New York Post* editor William Cullen Bryant explained that a booming Gotham had attracted men, some of them eminent and able, but also a good many who were "most dextrous in villainy" and "most foul in guilt." It was therefore critical to "encounter the temptations of vice in this great and too rapidly growing capital by attractive entertainments of an innocent and improving character." Or as a museum official put it: "Art is a luxury for the rich but a necessity for the poor."[64]

In the annual reports of the 1870s, the Met's trustees made a point of how many "mechanics and artisans" the museum attracted, boasting in 1876 that "the Museum today is not surpassed as an educational power among the people by any university, college or seminary of learning in the metropolis." The museum ran art and vocational classes for craftsmen and made serious efforts to teach the common man, though this commitment later ebbed as Europeans, fallen on hard times, turned to stripping their walls of fine art in return for New York dollars and the trustees became entranced with collecting Old Masters. (Finally in 1908 the trustees formally deleted from the museum's 1870 mission statement the phrase identifying its purpose as "furnishing popular instruction and recreations.")[65]

In this age of rising cities, Green and his commission succeeded in giving New York an uptown landscape of pleasure drives, boulevards, and scenic riverfronts. They designed a park system of generous green spaces and raised a complex of world-class cultural institutions. "Mr. Green is more to New York," crowed the *New York*

*World*, "than the Baron Haussmann to Paris. . . ." But comparisons with Paris overlooked the gorilla in the room, the not trivial matter of the French capital's authoritarian aegis. Green could plan only for unoccupied New York. He could plan streets and run sewers under them and parkways alongside them and museums upon them, but he could not remake New York. He studied with envy the newly widened thoroughfares in Paris. "It has been well said," Green wrote, "that, next to the genial influence of the seasons, upon which the regular supply of our wants and a great portion of our comforts so much depend, there is perhaps no circumstance more interesting to men in a civilized state than the perfection of the means of interior communication." But for all he accomplished uptown, Manhattan's problems with core circulation and the increasing congestion of its southern districts stood outside his shaping influence.[66]

Lower Manhattan's problems had only grown more intense with time. Between 1840 and 1870, Manhattan's population tripled from 312,710 to almost a million. Another half million lived in the surrounding suburb communities, "all," Green wrote in a report to the park commission, "drawing sustenance from the commerce of New York." At the same time that the population was growing and urban reformers were building parks and metropolitan cultural institutions, business was expanding into new warehouses, banks, railroad terminals, and office buildings. "The Imperial City of the American continent," Daniel Webster had called New York City. Gotham's financial influence easily leaped over political and geographic boundaries to dominate the regional—indeed, the national—economy, but for all the work of the Central Park Commission, New York had made no comparable strides in rationalizing the municipal landscape. A metropolis of hemispheric reach and international impact was conceiving projects, Green complained, on "too narrow and limited a scale."[67]

New York urban reformers like Olmsted embraced the concept of a "city of many rooms," a city where the work of business would be concentrated in an ever more efficient downtown, while new residential districts of "undisturbed seclusion" were built uptown, connected by a midtown section of retail trade and amusement. "The separation of business from domestic life," Olmsted wrote, was one of the marks of "civilized progress":

A business man during his working hours, has no occasion for domestic luxuries, but . . . wants to be near a bank . . . , or near the Stock Exchange, or to shipping, or to a certain class of shops. . . . On the other hand, when not engaged in business, he had no occasion to be near his working place, but demands as much of the luxuries of free air, space, and abundant vegetation as, without loss of town-privileges, [he] can . . . secure.[68]

A Central Park Commission, no matter how imaginative its leadership, could not carry out this sort of rearrangement. Lacking the power to make zoning decisions, to clear property, to move families and tear down festering old buildings—lacking the authority to pay for any of the improvements it might advocate—the CPC could play no role in the wholesale rearrangement of the downtown into a landscape of capital.

Chaotic, unfettered Manhattan had no emperor, not even effective local government. Projects of even modest scope were forced to pass a gauntlet of parochial jurisdictions. When New York's worker population spilled over into lower Westchester, for example, there was a clamor for new transit facilities, ferries, and bridges. This involved negotiating with five different townships, each further divided into several villages, all with their own regulations, local priorities, and preening officials and all very tight with a dollar. Urbane, prosperous, and with an ever expanding sense of its own importance, New York was often reduced to frustrating turf skirmishes with local villages and their satraps.[69]

Planning a new New York required a substitute for Napoleon. The state had denied City Hall self-rule as just reward for its repeated fits of brazen corruption. Manhattan's destiny rested with a legislature dominated by upstate lawmakers, and Albany was at best distrustful and envious of the most famous city in the hemisphere. Green's solution was to recast the city, bulking it up by amalgamating a number of neighboring municipalities under its metropolitan aegis. The result would be to expand New York's municipal responsibilities and give it the power to seize back authority over its own affairs.

Reformers had periodically called for joint efforts among the local counties, generally in order to ease transportation, make regional improvements, or improve the waterfront. But Green had more profound changes in mind than the building of an East River bridge or the development of roads leading to Westchester. He proposed consolidating Manhattan, Brooklyn, Queens, Richmond (Staten Island), and lower Westchester into the largest, most populous, wealthiest, most colossal city in the hemisphere. "All progress points toward eventual consolidation," he wrote in his annual report of 1868, describing these communities as "striving by all material methods that the skill of man can devise to become one. . . ." A unified, centrally directed, greater New York would create a grand canvas with a vast tax and population base. It would also provide the needed breadth and power for planning an integrated landscape that could offer its citizens generous services, coordinated traffic systems, and massive public works.[70]

The possibility of so powerful a metropolis intrigued Green and a small band of New Yorkers, but for the while New York remained only Manhattan, a place without the power or concerted will to exert or tolerate a rationalizing hand. One force alone was powerful enough to stir a wholesale rearrangement of Manhattan's landscape, and that was the real estate market with its furiously churning turnover in properties. "Business," the perceptive reform journalist Jacob Riis wrote, "has been New York's real Napoleon III, from whose decree there was no appeal." The market galvanized the forces of change, reorganizing the walking city into a differentiated, modern metropolis. Unlike Haussmann's work, this one followed no plan more intelligent than the profit motive.[71]

With population mushrooming, businesses multiplying, and savings banks and life insurance companies funneling cash into the mortgage market, all of Manhattan turned into one large bull market in land. In the five years after 1868, close to twenty-three thousand plans were filed for new construction, reflecting an unprecedented 15 percent rate of growth *per year.* Land values skyrocketed. The price commanded by uptown lots multiplied tenfold in a decade, while in one year newly desirable properties around Central Park doubled in value. Two blocks between 66th and 68th Streets on the West Side went for $200,000 in 1868; four weeks later, one of the blocks brought $172,000. The YMCA purchased a corner lot on 23rd Street for $75,000 in 1868. Almost immediately after the closing it was offered $125,000 to sell. Streets that only a short while before had been covered with shanties now boasted blocks of fine new homes. The booming real estate market broke up long-held dynastic lands. The scion of an old and established New York merchant family, James Lenox, sold off $3 million in assorted parcels carved out of the East Side estate his father had put together earlier in the century. And in the downtown business district, where available space was at a premium, assessments leapt 50 percent.[72]

In New York, wrote *Harper's Weekly,* "everything which has lived its life and played its part is held to be dead, and is buried and over it grows a new world." At the heart of this new world pumped a real estate market that encouraged the most efficient use, that is to say the highest return value on land. In an earlier competition for prime space, commercial users—for whom downtown location offered such multiple dividends as proximity to shipping, warehouses, local transport, workers, politicians, the money market, law firms, and insurance offices, as well as advertising and newspapers—bid the price of land up so high that homeowners limited to simple residential use of the land sold out and moved uptown. Now the wholesalers and warehousers were in turn ousted by the new money market as it recast lower Gotham. This dynamic market covered the land with high-rise offices and lofted railroads above the streets creating new traffic lanes in the air. It threw a spectacularly engineered bridge across the East River and catapulted development out toward Harlem and Brooklyn.[73]

In the middle distance, north of Canal Street rose new residential areas, retail shops, hotels, and a diverse string of entertainment locales. Around Washington Square between 4th and 8th Streets, in Stuyvesant Square at 16th Street and Second Avenue, and along lower Fifth Avenue, developers laid out fashionable districts for New York's "upper ten thousand." Middle-class housing filled Greenwich Village between Canal and 14th Streets and in pockets west of Broadway all the way up to 34th Street. Lower-middle-class and worker families moved into the areas below Houston Street, toward the East Side. Farther uptown, above 42nd Street to Central Park and its environs, appeared a fresh realm of genteel residences, elite clubs, civic institutions, and select houses of worship.[74]

The downtown underwent the most spectacular makeover, giving rise to a new central business district with well-defined areas for finance, shipping, warehousing, retailing, publishing, and city government. Lower Manhattan rapidly became the highly specialized headquarters for national capital. Banks, brokers, merchants, and the many related artisans and service providers who administered and financed America's new businesses drove out longer-settled residents, sending them to brownstone affluence farther uptown. At the outset of the postwar boom, 170 bankers and brokers serviced Gotham's investors. Less than five years later in 1870, the number had shot up to 1,800. In just a few years, rents around Broadway and City Hall climbed as much as 1,000 percent. The changeover proceeded unevenly, leaving behind pockets of housing "in spots and gaps" unsuited for commerce. These were filled with worker housing for the poor who could not afford to move so far from their jobs and their ethnic social networks. The more desperate erected shacks and shanties on vacant ground, edging the rivers, in a day when the urban waterfront was viewed as unfit for decent family life.[75]

The old countinghouses and retail establishments had been de-

signed to attract pedestrian traffic and facilitate street-level exchange. The new financial offices, however, had nothing to show the
street. The swelling corps of corporate personnel could carry out
their work recording transactions, tracking inventory, logging property exchanges, and keeping payroll ledgers in a secluded world.
Older commercial structures, pitched to human scale, made way for
a new regime of elongated architecture, as the competitive real estate market pressed property holders to "sweat" the land by intensi-
fying its use. Construction breakthroughs involving the use of iron
shell framing and improved load-bearing supports made it struc-
turally feasible to build higher, while such innovations as the passenger lift or elevator made tall buildings practical. The result ushered
in not only a new skyline, but a change in urban scale described by
one wag later in the century: "When they find themselves a little
crowded, they simply tilt a street on end and call it a skyscraper."[76]

The high buildings towered over the pedestrian, standing in monumental relation to the citizen. These overbearing, larger-than-life
headquarters with the names of their corporate owners emblazoned
on the front and huge statues molded onto their facades easily overshadowed everything else, symbolizing in their substantiality the
outsized power of capital itself.[77]

New York's leading newspapers were among the first to put up
prestige headquarters around City Hall, even before the war. *The
New York Times*, utilizing the latest in iron construction to create
large work spaces uninterrupted by support beams, erected an imposing building on Park Row featuring tall arches and exterior
columns with two-story arcades. Its elegant facade was decorated
with medallions and the company logo. Gotham's other dailies soon
raised their own ornate buildings. Five went up after the war, each
named eponymously, on what came to be called Printing House
Square. Richard Morris Hunt designed the most striking of these,
the ten-story New York Tribune Building, which was begun in 1873.
When completed, the dark red-and-black building with its contrast-
ing light granite trim and its elaborately encased watchtower stood

taller than any building in the city. The structure was forced to devote a large part of its lower floor space to broad wall foundations that tapered as they went up the building in order to support its height. The interior was finished with a profusion of imported marbles, detailed stone decorations, and distinctive wainscoting. A portion of the offices in the building was prepared for rental, although one journal predicted that "tenants would never be found to risk their lives in" this too tall "piece of folly." When the top floors were in fact the first to be rented, and the building proved a financial success, high construction received a strong vote of confidence.[78]

Whether New York's first skyscraper was the Tribune Building or one of the other pioneering efforts at tall construction, most agree that the Equitable Co. headquarters played a critical role in raising the skyline. Organized in 1859 with a capital investment of around $100,000, the Equitable Assurance Company rode the wave of war-induced insurance prosperity to accumulate assets in excess of $11 million by 1870, tracking premiums and filling claims in rented space along lower Broadway. In 1864, Equitable's directors approved plans for a heavily ornamented gray granite structure in the Second Empire style, to be erected on Broadway and Cedar Street. The building made extensive use of internal iron and placed over the entrance portico a marble bust of "Protection" shielding widows and orphans. The building committee had opposed tall construction, but given the personal guarantee of supervising engineer George B. Post that the top floors would be rented, Equitable's founder, Henry Baldwin Hyde, overruled the committee and approved an eight-story office tower.[79]

The lowest floors were leased to bank and corporate renters. Equitable took the next two levels for its public business, while the less desirable middle floors supported back-office operations. The elevator-serviced upper floors, touted for "pure air," isolation from street noise, and spectacular panoramic views, were quickly leased to high-end law firms. Total rentals, which amounted to $136,000 annually in 1871, more than covered the building's costs, giving the company a commanding corporate center rent-free. It did not take long for others to break the traditional six-story barrier. Vertical expansion captured New Yorkers' imagination, extending the city's dominion into the sky, fashioning new giants from steel frame construction.[80]

If the Equitable and the Tribune structures signaled the advent of the skyscraper, the Western Union Building marked its full arrival. In 1872, not far from Printing House Square, Equitable architect George Post designed an even more monumental signature building for America's telegraph monopoly, creating the tallest corporate headquarters in the city. Reaching 230 feet above the ground on the corner of Broadway and Dey, on property bought from the deposed Louis Napoleon himself for the unprecedented sum of $840,000, the structure with its striped facade, rococo design, and ornate mansard roof gave the appearance of a whimsical castle perched above a massive lower block. High above street level, inside the seventh-floor ceiling, coursed the nerve center of Western Hemisphere wire operations. And on the unobstructed twenty-three-foot-high eighth floor, scores of telegraphers arrayed in long neat rows conveyed news, market prices, and business intelligence to the world. The structure, thought to be fireproof, boasted its own firefighting apparatus, with an emergency sprinkler system connected to private wells, allowing its owners to dispense with fire insurance. In an added flourish, Western Union graced its "Telegraph Palace" with full-size bronzes of Benjamin Franklin and Samuel F. B. Morse. Like the other corporate landlords, the wire monopoly earned a handsome rental income from its imposing headquarters.[81]

High construction maximized central land use, concentrating an extraordinary volume of professional, administrative, and expert services on modest property lots. The densely occupied tall structures consolidated the chief lines of American information, transportation, trade, capital, and communication in one tightly packed corner of Gotham. But while Andrew Green applied an informed, cultured urban vision to uptown development, neither he nor anyone else could discipline the downtown transformation. Property holders built as high as technology and architectural imagination permitted, ignoring the effect of such dense use. Resulting congestion and the need for new municipal services were not addressed, either by the municipal government or by the property holders. The reconfiguring of downtown resulted in a radically unbalanced use between day (intensive) and night (slight), when this important part of the city was largely abandoned. These consequences were not thought out, or even much considered. No zoning rules, no codes, and no local guidelines hemmed in the changes for the benefit of the broader public. "The ascendancy of dollars," wrote the British novelist Anthony Trollope, was "written on every paving stone along Fifth Avenue, down Broadway, and up Wall Street."[82]

City leaders learned about new construction the same way as everyone else, from the appearance of work crews and tons of fresh debris on the streets. Gotham's municipal government had no more to say about the reshaping of its domain into a landscape of capital than did the rudest Parisian about Napoleon's initiatives. In a manner that paralleled the government's studied forbearance in guiding the economy, the remaking of lower New York proceeded free of constraining plans or policies. Each of the new buildings was designed in splendid isolation from its neighbor, resulting in a jumble of aesthetic styles. And nothing was done to bring order to the large crowds that daily converged on these offices or to provide a reliable system of transit to serve the needs of both commerce and pedestrians.

Municipal authorities displayed a similar disengagement from the growing number of tenement houses that filled the interstitial spaces between elite work and well-to-do residences. Scores of new five- and six-story tenements went up in these years to replace the shanties, caves, and haphazardly subdivided houses that passed for worker housing in the first half of the century. The high concentrations in these dwellings formed incredibly congested slums, all without a guiding design or policy. "It is shameful," wrote George Templeton Strong, "that men, women and children should be permitted to live in such holes." The cholera outbreak that swept through these "holes" in 1866, he was certain, was a judgment on the poor for their bad habits and on the rich for tolerating these vices. But for those who preferred to ignore the question, the process of differentiation provided luxurious insulation from the city's nastier streets. They could do business in the city and go to homes located far from the disagreeable tenements. This process too had been left to the Napoleon of invisible hands.[83]

By the end of the decade, it had become obvious to many New Yorkers that the economics of competitive land use had dramatically intensified the city's divergences and embedded class differences in the land. "Her narrow streets, frightful tenements, and filthy markets yet remain in vivid contrast," the superintendent of New York's buildings reported, "to her Broadway, 5th Avenue and Central Park." A visiting Scotsman found a metropolis of "colossal wealth and haggard poverty . . . all that is best and all that is worst in America." None who passed through the city missed the painful incongruities between the majestic facades that dressed the new railroad stations, department stores, and office buildings and the decaying housing, decrepit storefronts, and rutted streets in the slums. She is a "lady in a ball gown with diamonds in her ears," wrote the author of *Baedeker's Handbook to the United States*, while "her toes were out at her boots." A "whole country [is] tributary to its power . . . [as] the centre of science, art and wealth, . . . [a] pinnacle of commercial imperium, grandeur and glory," concluded the Citizens' Association, while Gotham lacked control over its own landscape.[84]

The unimpeded market in land, the visiting Scotsman predicted, would "soon convert the whole island into one huge hive of industry" and make bedroom communities of her neighboring cities. No planner could, or did, dictate that Brooklyn, the third largest city in the nation, should become what a visiting Charles Dickens called "a kind of sleeping-place for New York." But the same market that cleared out lower Manhattan for business promoted the East River

Bridge project to knit the two cities together and make Brooklyn a catch basin for Manhattan's overflow, "a place," in the words of Olmsted and Vaux, "for the tranquil habitation of those whom the business of the world requires should reside within the convenient access of the waters of New York harbor."[85]

The same forces of capital fostered an imperial conception of the metropolis, as a center not simply of wealth and enterprise, but of resplendence as well. It was not simply that the office towers were strikingly tall, they were also extravagantly decorated with ornamental watchtowers, arches, arcades, balconies, cupolas, statues, and roof exhibits, all styled to project imperial excess. Their conspicuous disregard for cost communicated a swaggering new confidence, a sense of endless abundance. "The Venice of the New World," asserted the *New York Daily Graphic*, "ought to be a city of business palaces, inviting as well as accommodating the commerce of all nations."[86]

The buildings were important symbols, spectacles of capital, and all of the grand things new capital could do. Talk about shoddy quickly faded in the face of such striking imperium. It may have been Jay Gould who took over Western Union, but even his reputation for low dealing could not diminish the authority proclaimed by the company's headquarters. Businessmen could speak of democracy and even participate in building a commonly accessible public culture; but their buildings conveyed supremacy and domination. They did not have to assert their own power and privileged status or demand deference. The monumental buildings did it for them in an idiom designed to awe the onlooker. Architecture critic Montgomery Schuyler, reading the new landscape, concluded that it ceded dominance to capital; "comity," he wrote of the skyscrapers, "is defied."[87]

In addition to celebrating the companies whose names they so sturdily emblazoned on the city skyline, the striking scale of Stewart's Marble Palace, the Tribune Tower, and the Western Union Building provided a public dividend, as it were. New Yorkers, not just capitalists, but common citizens as well, took pride in these buildings as great civic achievements. They may not have had anything to do with creating these citadels, and the buildings were assuredly not public in any sense other than that they stood on the street, but ordinary New Yorkers basked in the glow of an enriched common landscape nevertheless. Moreover, displays like Vanderbilt's terminals, replete with the monument to his rise, or Stewart's palatial emporiums gave concrete form to the ascent of rags-to-riches capital. Grand construction—the sweeping parks, the towering elevated railways, the culture palaces, and the planned East River Bridge—glorified the capitalist urge, inscribing upon the landscape a new imperial standard. Like King Ozymandias in his days of triumph, Gotham proclaimed: If you wish to see my glory, my strength, my grandeur, look around you. "Who will deny," declared *Leslie's Illustrated Weekly* in 1875, "that New York . . . may yet become the grandest city on the face of the globe."[88]

Fifth Avenue was already one of the globe's grandest streets. Wealthy New Yorkers kept moving northward along this majestic lane, replacing shacks, garbage dumps, and hog pens with zones of tasteful luxury that stretched, by 1870, all the way up to the 59th Street entrance to Central Park. Nearby rose new churches, elite men's clubs, and restaurants. Lots north of 42nd Street that had sold for $4,000 in the mid-1850s boasted homes costing upward of $135,000. Even the plain-faced town houses featured "string courses, pediments, rustications," and the ornate accents that bespoke refinement and Parisian style. In these fancy homes the parlors were turned into centers of display, overfilled with rich wood tables, gilt mirrors, opulent frames, expensive art, plush upholstery, and marble hearths.[89]

The superficiality of it all led visiting English novelist Anthony Trollope to dismiss the Fifth Avenue arriviste with British disdain. "I know of no great man, no celebrated statesman, no philanthropist of note," he sniffed, "who has lived on Fifth Avenue. That gentleman on the right made a million dollars by inventing a shirt collar;

this one on the left electrified the world by a lotion; as to the gentle-man at the corner there—there are rumours about him and the Cuban slave trade, but my informant by no means knows that they are true. Such are the aristocracy of Fifth Avenue. I can only say that if I could make a million dollars by a lotion, I should certainly be right to live in such a house as one of these." He was correct. This was not the center of Gotham's intellectual life; it was where newly rich men and women chose to dwell at arm's length from their places of work. And here they built the most expensive show homes in the nation.[90]

In 1869, when Junius Henri Browne published *The Great Metropolis*, he included a profile of dry goods king Alexander Turney Stewart. "More than anyone else in America probably," Browne wrote, "Alexander T. Stewart is the embodiment of business. He is emphatically a man of money, thinks money; makes money; lives money. Money is the aim and end of his existence. . . ." One of New York's most affluent men, Stewart had for many years lived on a modest terrace block on Bleecker Street. But in 1864 he yielded to the growing spirit of conspicuous construction, erecting a new $2 million home on Fifth Avenue and 34th Street. It took seven years to complete, but when it was done Stewart's massive three-story French-style marble mansion, with full exterior detailing on all sides (the neighboring Astor homes were embellished only on the surface that faced the avenue), set a new standard for opulence.[91]

The rooms on the first two floors were of commanding proportion, each well over eighteen feet high, with sculptural details and a cascade of marble framing the windows, running down the walls, and draping the Corinthian columns and the staircase, while also assuming lovely shape in monumental sculptures by Italian and American artists. An exquisite Cornu clock stood in an immense silver figure fourteen feet high. "Furniture and hangings," declared *Artistic Houses*, "seem to have been obtained without care for cost; or, rather, only the most costly seem to have been selected. Money flowed abundantly . . . and in exchange for it came magnificence, splendor, luxury." The house featured an eighty-foot-long by thirty-foot-wide art gallery that *The New York Times* thought "far surpassed in importance and value any other in this country." The gallery displayed prominent American artists like Daniel Huntington, Frederick Church, Albert Bierstadt, and Charles Loring Elliot, as well as contemporary French painters like Rosa Bonheur, Hippolyte Paul Delaroche, and Jean Louis Meissonier.[92]

Professional architects dismissed the mansion as "simply the most ostentatious and pretending and the most ugly house in New York City." *The American Builder* described it as "a profusion of ornament, bad of its kind and ill-chosen." Others, including architects Richard Morris Hunt and Peter Wight, thought that the palace was out of proportion with its surroundings. But journalists, not disinclined to heap praise on the man with the most munificent advertising budget in the nation, lauded the show house. The *New York Sun* praised Stewart's "public spirit" in gracing New York with such a house. *Harper's Weekly* went even further, exulting that New York finally had "one edifice . . . that, if not swallowed up by an earth-quake, will stand as long as the city remains, and will ever be pointed to as a monument of individual enterprise, of far seeing judgment, and of disinterested philanthropy. There is nothing like it in the world, not even among the palaces of the European nobility." "Palatial" was the word favored in newspaper descriptions.[93]

Stewart's palace captured well the temper of an era that conflated pretension with magnificence. A host of imitators soon sprang up along upper Fifth Avenue. These mansions, the colossal new office towers, the grand parks, the ambitious thoroughfares, and the vaulting bridges all trumpeted a common pride in capital accumulation. One does not fully comprehend the place of the East River Bridge (later the Brooklyn Bridge) in Gotham's imagination without an appreciation of its reach for grandiosity, its grandiloquent syntax of metropolitan venture, its New York triumphalism. The old values of quiet functionalism, of virtuous plainness and understatement, no longer served. "From Brooklyn Bridge to genteel parlors to uptown promenades," writes David Scobey, New York's new scale "testified to the shift in bourgeois values: a diminishing of the antebellum virtues of republican austerity and entrepreneurial self-discipline; an embrace of gentility and cultural hierarchy, of consumerism and material display."[94]

Many things contributed to remaking New York. No single intelligence, no planning commission, and no Chamber of Commerce piloted this transformation. City Hall did not review property transfers or enforce guidelines for use, design, or safety. No public authority made its own plans for the city estate. Unchecked, the New York property market remolded the city landscape to the multiform needs of its high bidders, lower Manhattan's powerful new companies. This is not to say that economic decisions governed the process entirely. Few who have studied real estate transactions have failed to come across examples where sentiment or gall got in the way of profitable transfers. Nor can the proliferation of expensive architectural accents and details be understood on the basis of profit considerations alone. Nor was the market always successful in achieving rational results. The filth and congestion for which lower Manhattan was so well-known made no sense to anybody. And the market's response to the calls for adequate worker housing and expeditious mass transportation failed to meet the need.

What New York capital did manage to do extraordinarily well was to project the city as the center of wealth and business. "The entire result of the country's labor seems to seek New York by inevitable channels," a contemporary observed in 1865, lauding the city as a "capital of broad congenialities and infinite resources . . . widely diffused comfort, luxury and taste." Other great cities had their hanging gardens, their viaducts, their royal roads, their immense theaters. New York captured the imagination with its conspicuous wealth, the intensity of its materialism, and the rapidity with which it created a commanding landscape of accumulation and accomplishment.[95]

The national fascination with Gotham resulted in a glut of magazine pieces, dime novels, and sensational exposés as well as illustrations and photographs. Representations of the Manhattan landscape were staples of this emerging industry. Images of the metropolis hung on parlor walls and graced reading tables throughout the country. Earlier in the century, these lithographs depicted Manhattan's storied harbor with the high-masted ships in the foreground. Beyond stood a set of busy streets leading to City Hall. From the city's natural geography flowed all else. By 1876, the new metropolis of the lithographs is dense with activity all the way up to the new Central Park. The waterfront has receded in importance, and the focus is on the city, not the water, a city of colossal dimension, dominated by soaring man-made structures in the form of elevated trains, tall corporate buildings, and the towers of the uncompleted Brooklyn Bridge.[96]

This modern Manhattan of the last quarter century is a quintessentially urban landscape, shaped by men and women, pursuing what this city was already famous for: profit. And while such single-minded and prosaic motivation might have embarrassed an earlier generation, in this new age inspired poets wrote hymns to Gotham's visible emblems of power and success. "The lofty new buildings," Walt Whitman wrote in 1870 in *Democratic Vistas*, "facades of marble and iron, of original grandeur and elegance of design . . . the rich shops . . . the great Central Park . . . these I say, and the like of these completely satisfy my senses of power, fullness, motion &c., and give me, through such senses . . . a continued exaltation and absolute fulfillment." They brought him to a metropolitan epiphany, an appreciation of man's power to shape his environment to his own design: "I realize . . . that not nature alone is great in her fields of freedom and the open air, in her storms, the shows of night and day, the mountains, forests, seas—but in the artificial, the work of man too is equally great . . . in these ingenuities, streets, goods, houses, ships—these hurrying, feverish, electric crowds of men, their complicated business genius, (not the least among the geniuses,) and all this mighty many-threaded wealth and industry concentrated here."[97]

Bertolt Brecht has reminded us that throughout history it was not the "kings who hauled the craggy blocks of stone" to erect the world's wonders and that the masons never got to live in the palaces that too many of them died to build. Study the exquisite achievements, analyze the great wars, say the critics, and precious few of those who did the hard work got to dance at the victory ball.[98]

We cannot avoid these questions even if we cannot address them or their implications here. Families were displaced from their homes, and unemployment and insecurity lapped at the workers who built these grand buildings. Side by side with the grandeur existed a large population for whom hunger was common, disease a present danger, and suicide a too oft employed resolution to life's tragic frustrations. The rewards in this period of economic boom were as skewed and capricious as a free market is prone to make them. Exploitation both conscious and structural accompanied New York's changeover, and while these issues have left no grand emblems or monuments, we cannot efface them, for they are the underside of the unfettered magnificence and accomplishment of these years.

New York's Napoleon made no plans to address these problems, but then with all of the power at his disposal, neither did Paris's. He simply moved the poor out of sight. Successful New Yorkers suggested that the same economy that enriched them would ultimately reward the deserving poor, though frankly they did not give much thought to these matters. What did impress them was the fact that New York's transformation had been effected under a system that rejected the efficiencies of brute force in favor of private initiative and free enterprise. "Look at the immense number of new buildings now being erected," exclaimed the *New York Herald*, "some of which are of gigantic dimensions and some surpassed nowhere in beauty of design and solidity of construction. . . . The thrift of republican New York has outstripped the capital of France, and the individual enterprise of our citizens has done more than all the vaunted powers of modern Caesarism."[99]

The process proceeded with characteristic unevenness, but in a remarkably short time the free market had converted the compact port city into a differentiated metropolis of capital. For all of its disorder, New York's business resources consolidated into an enormously powerful financial and business center that shifted the economic axis of the entire nation.

# CHAPTER 3

# The Rottenness in New York Will Ultimately Destroy It

*The railroads and the river boats, . . . are witnesses to an energy and a luminous sagacity which before now have bought whole legislatures, debauched courts, crushed out rivals, richer or poorer, as the unmoral, unsentimental forces of nature grind down whatever opposes their blind force. . . . In short, . . . [Cornelius Vanderbilt] may have been illiterate indeed; and . . . not humanitarian; and not finished in his morals; and not, for his manners, the delight of the refined society of his neighborhood; nor yet beloved by his dependents; but [he] knew how to take advantage of lines of travel; [he] had a keen eye for roads, and had the heart and hand to levy contributions on all who passed his way.[1]*
—E. L. GODKIN, "THE VANDERBILT MEMORIAL" (DESCRIBING THE BRONZE FRIEZE MEMORIALIZING CORNELIUS VANDERBILT'S LIFE), 1869

*The curtain rose on the American era that began with the civil war. It was an era of individualism uncurbed, of complete adherence to the Adam Smith philosophy. Rockefeller did not make that era. No more did Fisk and Gould, Hill and Harriman, Carnegie and Frick, Commodore Vanderbilt and Pierpont Morgan. The era made them in the sense it gave them opportunity.[2]*
—*New York World-Telegram,* 1934

RETROSPECT AND ARTFUL NARRATIVE have lent the corporate economy that rose out of those large downtown skyscrapers an air of inevitability, of a privileged history guided by outsized forces. After the fact, the puzzle pieces fit together neatly with thematic grace and elegance. But in fact, the process by which the new forces of corporate capital supplanted the individual scale economy of merchant relations was characterized by disarray, by the undermining of old customs and rules before the wisdom required to cast new ones allowed their orderly replacement.

In his insightful study of Gilded Age New York, nothing so impressed historian Seymour Mandelbaum as its spirit of disorder. Not only were the streets undergoing a constant "tearing up and pulling down," but side by side with the prosperous and settled merchant economy a new economy was rising. Its harbinger was a bold new investment market that raised an unfamiliar class of capitalists to importance even as it greatly extended Gotham's influence throughout the nation. Clearly an investment market was going to be edgy, more risk laden, but it was equally clear that ultimately the new system that emerged would have to win the trust of the larger society into which it was set. Postwar New York's blend of capital and opportunity attracted the most venturesome figures of the age, men who could not be more different from the solid, respected merchants of prewar Gotham's business establishment. Many of these new men came from modest circumstances. They had little learning and less polish. Instead they relied on native qualities of immense cunning and colossal resolve, and a vast hunger for profit, qualities that they sharpened upon Gotham's competitive investment exchanges, where the foundation institutions of American corporate capital were cast.[3]

In 1841, the celebrated New England minister William Ellery Channing described the impact of the new railroads on American life. He ignored the wondrous feats of complex engineering and the scores of secondary industries that the chugging locomotives had fostered. He disregarded the railroad's ability to free transport from customary limits and to link villages, towns, and countrysides. He was struck by something else. The railroads, he said, had injected a new tone in American society, "stirring up fierce competition, a wild spirit of speculation, a feverish, insatiable cupidity, under which fraud, bankruptcy, distrust, and distress are fearfully multiplied. . . ."[4]

Over the next thirty years, the cupidity, speculation, fraud, and distress all intensified, but it was the benefits of the new system of transport, the benefits that Channing had disregarded, that captured the American imagination. In Europe, the railroad had a more limited impact. Railroad tracks were laid atop well-established roads, inscribing a new technology on the entrenched routes.

In the United States the railroad did not simply upgrade the existing transportation system; it opened a vast new territory to intensive settlement. "American culture *began*," wrote Max Weber in 1882, "what European culture completed with [the railroads]. . . . In Europe the railroad system facilitates traffic; in America it *creates* it." From less than nine thousand miles of track in 1850, the American railroad system expanded by 1873 to cover the nation with an overland transportation network of seventy thousand miles. It "seemed to create new spaces," writes the urban scholar Alan Trachtenberg, "new regions of comprehension and economic value, and finally to incorporate a prehistoric geological terrain into historical time." In the last third of the nineteenth century, the heyday of the railroad era, close to half a billion acres, a territory only somewhat less than the entire expanse of Europe, were added to the cultivated area of the nation.[5]

To Americans across the land, the speeding locomotives, faster, larger, and mightier than anything they had ever seen, evoked progress, modern technology's power to expand human dominion over space and time. Implacably, the roads changed the way space was conceived, from miles to days or even hours. Ultimately "land navigation" reset America's clocks. Marking time by the traditional measure of sun movement meant innumerable clock adjustments as the locomotives traversed the land, resulting in a chaotic dance between time and space. These endless minor adjustments of time wreaked havoc on railroad scheduling and safety, until finally the roads established a national system of four administratively determined "time zones." Nothing else could compare with the iron horse's ability to collapse space, bend time, link communities, tame the American wilderness, and spur the economy. "The railroad," writes economic historian William Roy, "is to American imagery," in these years, "what the church was to Europe . . . in the Middle Ages."[6]

The railroads not only fostered myriad new businesses, including such basic industries as iron, steel, coal, lumber, leather, and glass, they also became the largest employer in the land, with brigades of construction workers, maintenance men, operations specialists, and clerical staff. To supervise and direct these vast armies, the railroads developed new techniques of organization and management as they covered American prairies and unsettled territories with track.

These railroads molded the early history of corporate America. Indeed, the railroads *were* the early history of corporate America. Until the last decade of the century, these carriers were virtually the only large corporations run as private businesses. For a quarter century, nearly all of the corporate securities traded on the stock exchanges were railroad-related securities. The budding field of corporate law was in large part railroad law. The advances made in accounting and business organization were dictated by the need to keep track of increasingly scattered and complex rail activities. Railroad men were the first business leaders to influence national policy regarding corporations and monopolies. "In short," concludes the scholar of the modern American corporation, "the corporate institutional structure *was* the railroad institutional structure."[7]

As railway construction extended westward, beginning with the river centers and later moving to new frontiers beyond the Mississippi, settlers filling in the regions from east to west transformed the frontier West into a global breadbasket and cattle farm. More than any other industry, or even group of industries, the railroad stimulated America's economic consolidation, knitting together what had been a series of discrete and isolated small-size economies into a larger fabric of national exchange and investment. In bringing America's varied markets into intimate and direct relationship, the railroad redefined the parameters of trade and the nature of exchange itself.

Take the case of wheat. It used to be shipped in individual sacks on ships, dependent on uncertain water transport. As a result, farm settlement favored the river valleys, from where the cereal crops were sent to grain merchants who came to know each farmer's wheat intimately—its type, quality, and cleanliness. With the tracking of the West, agriculture fanned out along the new railroad corridors, immensely increasing output. Rail transport made it much cheaper to ship by large volume than by individual farm. Before long farmers no longer sent grain in individual sacks bearing their markings. Instead, when Farmer Jones brought his produce to the railroad, he had it weighed and graded and received a receipt for it. His grain was then dumped into the railcars with tons of grain of the same grade and shipped to modern distribution hubs like Chicago and New York, with their steam-powered grain warehouses and processing terminals. As a market pitched to the "minute and endless diversity" of the different farms came to an end, Farmer Jones's grain was no longer separable from that of thousands of other producers. What he had for it was a receipt.[8]

The seemingly small and prosaic step of putting an end to the individually sacked grains brought significant consequences. The receipt that Farmer Jones held did not, of course, entitle him to his own wheat, which was no longer distinguishable in the high-capacity storage bins where it had been merged with the produce of scores of other farmers. He had turned in the physical wheat in return for a piece of paper that created an obligation for an equal measure of similar grain or its value. His slip of paper entitled him to the *exchange value* of his wheat. His property in wheat had been converted into market-friendly, fungible paper *rights* to wheat. This step freed the grain market from the cumbersome concerns of Lilliputian scale and the idiosyncrasies of individual sellers and buyers.

The new system amalgamated the endless variety of grains into several uniform categories and standard grades, making the goods readily transferable. Separating the value of the wheat from its clumsy, hard-to-handle physical reality and creating paper proxies for these cereals brought wheat into the orbit of capital. No longer confined to its physical form, grain could be easily sold and transferred in a new economic world where railroads and the telegraph brought together goods, buyer, and seller in a virtual market of shared information and instantaneous exchange. Grain became a paper commodity, bid upon, traded, and speculated over.

From this point it was a short step to "futures." By completing the process of abstraction of value from corporeal reality and converting what had been one of America's most real and necessary resources into paper notes, the new market opened fresh opportunities for speculation. Farmers could sell their produce (in the form of note obligations) "to arrive" even before it was harvested. As historian William Cronon makes fascinatingly clear, this market "was not a market in grain, but in the *price* of grain." In this way the railroad fostered a new commodities trade in New York, where speculators who had never held up a handful of kernels for inspection and did not know the difference between spring and winter wheat bought and sold certificates exchanging the wealth of America's prairies.[9]

A similar process of separating value from the physical product and embedding it in paper had large consequences for the railroad itself. By abstracting the worth of the railroad from its land, locomotives, and terminals and placing it in security certificates, investors could segment a road's value into shares. Instead of buying an entire railroad or becoming a fully responsible partner, one could buy portions of a company—not actual pieces of the cars or the tracks, but shares in the total value of the corporation. This made the business of property transfers simple and quick. A road interested in buying a competitor or a related business did not have to negotiate with the owners and go through the time-consuming legal steps of drawing up a contract for the deal, exchanging deeds and so forth. The stock market in business shares made it possible to buy corporate securities anonymously, without dealing with the owner—indeed, without his consent or even his knowledge. This process made it possible to combine disparate local roads into an integrated railroad system from an office on Wall Street.

In Europe, the leading industrial nations did not leave such development to the unregulated market. There the state underwrote railroad construction, laid out the routes, and set the rates. Although it was never intended to involve this level of state control in the United States, the corporation was initially a special business category that brought government and business into partnership. Early corporations were often state-chartered public improvement companies like canals or turnpikes. And in return for their corporate privileges, they carried special public responsibilities. Had corporations remained confined in this way to the status of quasi-public agencies, Wall Street's influence would have been more limited.[10]

But the corporation changed. After a series of financial disasters, including the default of five different states on their public investment bonds in the first half of the century, many critics argued that government was too clumsy and too politically compromised to run businesses effectively. New York and other states passed legislation prohibiting the investment of public funds in private businesses and corporations. Together with the subsequent enactment of general incorporation laws that encouraged the widespread use of the corporate form, this restriction on public investment brought to a close the era of state-sponsored public-private partnerships. The state ratified the laissez-faire spirit of the age, stepping back from any regulatory involvement while making corporate privilege widely available and far less publicly accountable than before. Concludes legal historian James Hurst: "Men . . . [were to] enjoy the privilege of incorporating for their ordinary purposes at their own initiative, while the state played a generally passive, ministerial role implementing their decisions."[11]

At the federal level, the Republican Congress that came to power with the Civil War extended the powers of the government to end slavery. Would the activist Republican Congress establish a national trade and transportation policy and lay plans for a coordinated national railroad system? Would it nationalize the railroad industry, cap profits, fix rates, and oversee the sale and trade of corporate securities?

During the war, Washington did push railroads toward greater efficiencies. Federal superintendents integrated rail operations to speed mail, transport soldiers, and deliver munitions. Under the threat of federal intervention, the roads connected their terminals and adopted a single-standard track to replace the eleven incompatible gauges they were using. Rail companies also pooled their resources to bridge major waterways and cluster proprietary roads into a rudimentary system. But while the war, in the words of historian Edward Kirkland, helped the road companies "shed their local chrysalis" and revealed the large possibilities for integrating the dispersed roads into a more efficient and more profitable system, it did not lead to federal control. Congress limited its intervention to awarding the railroad companies immense land subsidies—one-fifth of the territory of the states of Wisconsin, Iowa, Kansas, North Dakota, and Montana, and vast stretches of land in Washington, Minnesota, Nebraska, California, and Louisiana—to spur new projects. But aside from delivering a generous portion of the national domain and stalking the Indians on their behalf, the federal government laid the lightest possible hand on the railroads.[12]

Amid the uncertainties of Reconstruction, Washington made clear that the federal government did not intend to interfere with private economic prerogatives. This demonstration of respect for free enterprise braced investors—that, and gross industry revenues that grew from roughly $110 million in 1860 to about $375 million in 1867. From 1867 to 1869, the twenty leading railroads brought in $114 million in dividends. The Erie alone declared dividends of $32 million, while the figure for the New York Central was $25 million. These roads were the largest prizes in the American economy, dwarfing all other business projects. The most expensive canal, the Erie, had been built for about $7 million, while the New York Central, the Erie, and the Baltimore and Ohio Railroads were valued each at more than $20 million.[13]

No one individual or group of individuals could finance these railroads. Instead, corporate-scale projects were funded through the release of stock shares to a growing investment community. This investment activity required a well-developed money market to underwrite and trade the securities, tap the domestic and overseas investment markets, and broker the sales. With Washington benignly removed from operating or funding the roads, Wall Street seized the initiative. Its call loan market provided investors with access to America's capital reserves on deposit in its financial institutions. Its securities exchanges, the largest in the hemisphere, processed the escalating trade in securities that undergirded corporate financing. And its investment brokers won back the overseas investors who had withdrawn their investments during the war.

Gotham's investment bankers reinstated critical links with London, Paris, and the other leading capitals where investors were seeking outlets for their surplus capital. Overseas rail securities, for example, the state-run railroads in France, Germany, and Belgium, could not compete with the high returns that New York brokers brought them on American rail stock. Moreover, in a turnabout that Americans relished, the age of European expansion began to fade as the continent confronted an era of political uncertainty and economic instability, just as the United State made a stunning economic recovery from its war. Rattled investors seeking safer opportunities for their funds poured more than $240 million into American rail-road shares in 1869, much of it through New York. By then the New York Stock Exchange was trading $3 billion in securities a year, with perhaps four times this amount exchanging hands in other deals. It was one of the two or three most active investment markets in the world, concentrating the levers of corporate investment and enter-prise in Gotham.[14]

New York not only capitalized "the great line of connection with the West and the South," it also consolidated the ramifying road sys-tem. Removed from the concerns and responsibilities of local mer-chants and politicians, supported by teams of expert accountants, insurers, lawyers, bankers, and construction specialists, Wall Street investors merged, annexed, and extended the individual roads into regional systems of transport. "Expert," in the acid words of a con-temporary, "at amassing wealth without labor," Gotham welded to-gether America's scattered railroad companies into a national lattice of transport, credit, and investment.[15]

To bring the roads under unified and integrated control, Wall Street developed advanced systems of management. Running iron behemoths powered by steam on narrow tracks demanded a degree of precision previously unknown. Two ships going in opposite direc-tions can maneuver around each other, but rails are unforgiving, es-pecially when virtually all roads ran their cars, coming and going, on a single track. A rash of disastrous collisions, some of them head-on, made painfully plain that the new scope of operations required very careful coordination. Schedules, maintenance, construction, and per-sonnel training all had to be precisely meshed. From Manhattan's tall new office buildings, white-collar armies systematically collected and analyzed the data critical to organizing and managing the railroads. The larger roads transmitted telegraph reports hourly, giving train locations and updated traffic information while managers gathered weekly and monthly data on breakdowns, traffic density, and costs per mile in order to plan and coordinate their extensive operations.[16]

These large dispersed businesses challenged management to innovate. For just one example, conventional double-entry bookkeeping could not amalgamate the numerous daily transactions from the dozens and even hundreds of different accounts handled by these railroads. The roads needed more sophisticated systems of accounting to make informed business decisions for their far-flung systems. In order to tell them if they were running at a loss or profit, if they should expand or cut back on a particular stretch of road, they needed systems of accounting that were far more revealing and more powerful than the simple bottom line. These roads developed a new accounting that considered amortization, capital depreciation, and other more refined categories for financial analysis. With the nation's leading accounting houses concentrated in the vicinity, Wall Street developed the intricate new accounting systems that allowed the industry to measure productivity and performance. By the 1860s, the railroads employed more auditors and accountants than the federal government.[17]

The rail corporations also turned to New York's high-powered law firms to handle the growing volume of legal work. In addition to safeguarding their interest in contracts, these lawyers developed innovative business models and lobbied state and federal legislators to enact favorable legislation. So powerful did these attorneys become that they were (less than admiringly) referred to as a third house of Congress. Granted easy access to government officials, they helped write the legislation that defined corporate law.[18]

In this dense investment environment, where the most audacious of New York's investors stood before large interstate maps, planning private strategies to knit together individual railroad lines into regional systems of transport, men who were by and large outsiders, men on the make like Cornelius Vanderbilt, Jay Gould, and Andrew Carnegie, stalked New York's rags-to-riches opportunities. Skirting the divisive politics of the Civil War, they focused unremittingly on private gain, displaying a colossal self-confidence and a sure sense of maneuver for navigating the turbulent economic environment. Strong willed, steel nerved, and extraordinarily cunning, these men pursued Gotham's dreams of limitless wealth and economic power, each becoming an icon for this new age.

Of all possible train routes, the most coveted were those that connected the Northeast's rail arteries with New York City. No road would be more powerful or more profitable than the one that dominated this transport corridor. In 1863, at age sixty-nine, Commodore Cornelius Vanderbilt, the most successful shipping magnate in the Americas, turned to this purpose.[19]

Already a millionaire ten times over, he was as familiar as any American with the nation's generous expanse and with the potential for bringing its disparate segments into profitable convergence. In 1863 he bought control of the New York and Harlem, a road that had begun as a local line from lower Manhattan, and extended it as far north as Brewster, New York. The road hauled milk and farm products to the city. In addition to its direct access to the single most attractive destination in the hemisphere, the Harlem's charter also made it eligible for streetcar franchises to service Gotham's commuter trade.[20]

It did not take long for the Commodore to understand why years back Philip Hone had called "stock jobbing a most profligate and ruinous system of gambling; infinitely worse than any of which the laws take cognizance." In the spring of 1863, amid complex municipal tensions that would soon erupt in the infamous Draft Riots, the New York Common Council turned its thoughts to Wall Street— not to regulate the chaotic market, but rather in the hopes of making some quick money for the honorables. Daniel Drew, a notoriously crafty colleague of Vanderbilt's and a fellow director of the Harlem road, sold council members on a scheme to "short" Harlem—that is, agreeing to sell the stock for delivery to the buyer on a future date, but at the price current on the day of sale. The short seller expects that by the time of the delivery date the market price will have dropped and he will be able to fulfill the contract with stock that is much cheaper. If he is right, he will walk away with the difference between the price initially agreed upon and the stock's price at time of delivery. Speculators in shorts anticipate a decline in a stock's value, and the council had good reason to expect such a drop. Its authorization of the Harlem's Broadway commuter franchise on May 19 sent the stock climbing nearly sixfold in value, to over 116. After contracting to sell the stock at that high current value, the council would now rescind the franchise, sending the price tumbling. Not for nothing did this elite body come to be known fondly as the "forty thieves."[21]

But Vanderbilt, whose will, it was said, was iron and whose temper sulfuric, had gotten wind of the plan, and he began secretly buying all the Harlem that he and his surrogates could get their hands on. The price reacted to the shortage of stock by starting to climb. The councilmen now faced the cheerless likelihood that they would have to buy the stock from Vanderbilt to meet their contract obligations, at prices he dictated. Known as a "corner," this powerful expedient led the distraught legislators to revisit the issue of the Harlem commuter franchise once again. They withdrew their termination of the franchise, and Vanderbilt repaid their statecraft by relaxing his iron grip on Harlem shares.[22]

The next year, Vanderbilt acquired the Hudson River line, which connected the principal cities along that waterway. The courts had, in the interim, ruled that authority over the Harlem's Broadway franchise did not belong with the Common Council after all. The matter passed to the New York State Legislature. Undaunted by his earlier failure, Drew recycled his scheme to manipulate Harlem stock (which had by now reached 140), this time assembling a ring of state legislators to short Harlem and then depress its price by depriving the road of its Broadway franchise. Once again lawmakers sold the stock for future delivery in the hopes of making its price drop, and once again Vanderbilt went on a buying spree, this time sending Harlem shares above 224 at one point. This corner cost the foxy

Drew more than $1 million. How much it cost the grasping legisla-
tors is hard to say, as they were understandably reticent to disclose
the extent of their damage. Vanderbilt, his admiring friend and
sometime partner Russell Sage once said, "was to finance what
Shakespeare was to poetry and Michelangelo to art."[23]

The Commodore had succeeded in punishing those who had tried
to outsmart him and he had garnered millions, but Vanderbilt did
not assay a new railroad career at the age of sixty-nine without a
larger goal. He had mastered the undisciplined securities market,
blending the skillful release of information with shrewdly camou-
flaged "corners." "Never," the elusive commodore instructed his
would-be emulators, "tell what you are going to do till you have
done it." The passionate cardplayer had taught the market to respect
him, leaving his adversaries stunned and depleted. But he wanted to
be America's railroad king.[24]

With control of the Harlem and the Hudson well in hand, he
bought a large holding in the best-equipped and most efficient road
of the time, the New York Central, which serviced the prosperous
cities along the Erie Canal route. The New York Central enjoyed
the heaviest local business of any road in the nation, and by 1867 it
was a Vanderbilt property, as he joined with Edward Cunard, John
Jacob Astor III, and other principal stockholders to form a controlling majority of its board of directors.[25]

Intending to put an end to the competitive rate wars that threatened stability and profits, Vanderbilt sought an understanding to fix
prices and divide territory among the Pennsylvania, the New York
Central, and the Erie, the three rail lines that fanned out westward
from the Northeast. The Pennsylvania could be trusted, but the
Erie, under the influence of its wily treasurer Daniel Drew, could
not. Instead of negotiating with the Erie, Vanderbilt began buying
enough of its stock to make his plan secure. A panicked Daniel Drew
now turned his rare powers of ingratiation on the Commodore. He
convinced Vanderbilt, who by now owned a considerable bloc of
Erie shares, not to oppose his reelection to the board of directors.

The same election that returned Drew as treasurer also brought onto the board two rather obscure traders—"nobodies," the *New York Herald* called them—whom Drew had favored. They were Jay Gould and James Fisk, Jr.[26]

Having trumped the slippery Drew's shorts with chastening corners, Vanderbilt believed that he had tamed the aging speculator. Few doubted that Vanderbilt's plot to weave a regional monopoly had been advanced by his alliance with the dextrous Drew. "Vanderbilt," wrote the patrician critic Charles Francis Adams, "is but the precursor of a class of men who will wield within the state a power created by the state, but too great for its control. . . . [He] has introduced Caesarism into corporate life."[27]

Between Vanderbilt's plans and their success stood someone far more adept than the fading Drew, someone Joseph Pulitzer later described as "one of the most sinister figures that has ever flitted bat-like across the vision of the American people." Sickly and sallow complexioned, Jay Gould had been painfully withdrawn as a boy. The diminutive Gould grew up in a life marked by poverty and vulnerability, yet he became the model for the new capitalist man, the unscrupulous, power-hungry New York robber baron, whose gladiator's approach to business helped give the age its clouded reputation. "It is scarcely necessary to say," the genteel intellectual Henry Adams added, "that he had not a conception of a moral principle."[28]

Born on May 27, 1836, on a small farm in Delaware County's Catskill Mountain region, Gould contrived from early in life to escape the farm. He took a job in a general store, working sixteen hours a day. In his spare time he studied land surveying. Not yet sixteen, he did some map work on the Pennsylvania hinterlands, supplementing his earnings by writing speeches and letters and working as a surveyor (he turned one of his studies into a history of Delaware County). Surveying exposed the bright teenager to some of the most successful men in the region, including Zadock Pratt, who took Gould as a partner in a leather tanning business. Headstrong, Gould fell to feuding with the venerable Pratt, putting a quick end to the partnership, but Gould got the better part of the division, and by 1859—but not before another tempestuous venture, this one involving a suicide and a shootout—he was running a large leather business on 39 Spruce Street in New York City. Behind him lay a string of bitter partners, spoiled lives, and mounds of lawsuits. But Gould had learned that the law—with its high bar of verification—proved a wonderful refuge for what a biographer described euphemistically as his "unveiled contempt for harassing conventions."[29]

"The moralist and philosopher," wrote William Fowler in his nineteenth-century history of Wall Street, "look upon it as a gambling den . . . an abomination where men drive a horrible trade, fattening and battening on the substance of their friends and neighbors— . . . a kind of modern Coliseum where gladiatorial combats are joined, and bulls, bears and other ferocious beasts gore and tear each other for the public amusements." In this arena marked by crafty scheming and economic adventure, where the most audacious entrepreneurs of the age speculated in gold, traded in possibilities, and bought and sold businesses, the astringent, full-bearded Gould, not yet twenty-five, cast his métier.[30]

The war opened new opportunities for him, not on the field of battle, for which the sickly speculator, like many of his peers, secured a draft replacement for $300, but in investments, where those who dared were snatching bargains. He bought bonds in a small undervalued railroad, the Rutland and Washington, and helped turn the road into a success.

He had by now befriended one of the most colorful figures of the day, James B. Fisk Jr. As good-natured and rollicking as Gould was dour and withdrawn, Fisk displayed a "love of notoriety so extravagant that he preferred to be insulted than ignored." He too managed to avoid army service, by making himself important as a supplier of scarce southern cotton to northern clothing contractors, who turned it into uniforms for Mr. Lincoln's army. It was not always possible to follow the quick hands, but Fisk generally managed to deliver the goods. He emerged from the war as one of the band of "shoddy rich" and sought out the closest thing he could find to the charged atmosphere of the supply business, landing on Wall Street, where in time he married, took a mistress, and joined Drew, Gould, and Vanderbilt on the Erie board of directors.[31]

It did not take Vanderbilt long to realize that he had made a mistake in trusting Drew. He learned that Drew was surreptitiously negotiating to expand Erie's line west, threatening Vanderbilt's own New York Central. Vanderbilt had bought Erie shares primarily in order to bring the road into a cooperative pool with the Pennsylvania and the New York Central lines. He was stunned when Drew and his executive committee, wielding authority in the name of Erie's stockholders, killed this plan. The Commodore responded by pulling together his allies and setting out to purchase enough Erie stock to assemble a controlling interest and dump the Drew claque.[32]

Drew, Gould, Fisk, and their committee determined to make that impossible. They began issuing more shares of Erie—literally printing more stock and issuing it—making it hopeless for Vanderbilt to acquire a majority of the stock. Not without resources, the Commodore called upon Judge George Barnard, described by a contemporary as "a Tammany helot numbered among the Vanderbilt properties," and had him issue an injunction to halt the issue of new stock. Drew and Gould responded by using their own friendly judge to stay the injunction. Amid this crossfire of judicial decrees, the executive board continued to print stock, ultimately sending Erie's capitalization up from $34 million to $57 million, glutting the market and foiling Vanderbilt's efforts.[33]

In March 1868, Drew, Gould, and Fisk (with mistress in tow) crossed the Hudson to the safety of Jersey City to avoid arrest on charges of contempt for having violated Justice Barnard's injunctions. They were said to be carrying $7 million in folding money and most of Erie's official documents. To those left behind, the peripatetic directors explained that their flight was intended to protect New York from Vanderbilt's designs on monopolizing the carrying trade. Vanderbilt did in fact have monopolistic designs, and this helped muddy the issue for many New Yorkers, though it remained unclear how a railroad worth many tens of millions had so easily become a plaything of a pack of speculators or why Gotham's citizens were better served by an Erie controlled by Drew and Gould rather than Vanderbilt.[34]

It did not take Erie's executive committee, or at least its operating nucleus of Gould, Fisk, and Drew, long to tire of Jersey City's charms. The haven lacked the lawyers, bankers, and accountants needed to operate this business. To clear their path back to Gotham, the transplanted directors sought the protection of the New York State Legislature. The *New York Herald* reflected with some glee that the bill offering relief to the displaced Gould crew arrived just in time for "the hungry legislators and lobbymen, who have had up to this time such a beggarly session that their board bills and whiskey bills are all in arrears and their washerwomen and bootblacks are becoming insubordinate." The journal added "that Vanderbilt is determined to defeat the bill and fabulous sums are mentioned as having been 'put up' for that purpose." Charles Francis Adams, who wrote a classic account of the Erie wars, reported reading that some of the solons had sold their votes for $1,000, only to be ridiculed as pikers by their much more expensive brothers. He concluded that "probably no representative bodies were ever more thoroughly venal, more shamelessly corrupt, or more hopelessly beyond the reach of public opinion." Erie's titanic mudslinging match threatened to eclipse even the national agony over presidential impeachment.[35]

Both sides exhausted themselves over this expensive contest until finally, having bought enough judges, journalists, and state senators to form two contending governments, they acknowledged the stalemate and cobbled together a $9 million settlement that assured that no bad deed went unrewarded. To spare Vanderbilt any losses from having misplayed his high-stakes strategy, the Erie treasury bought back his depressed stock at inflated prices. Drew was permitted to resign with but a small obligation. No one was charged with offering or accepting bribes. (Months later, an investigating committee asked

Jay Gould, who as part of the concluding agreement ascended to the Erie presidency, how much he had paid out to politicians during the Erie war. "There was so much of it; it had been so extensive that I have no details now to refresh my mind," he replied.) The ever colorful Fisk became Erie's comptroller. And Albany, now limited to the mundane business of passing laws for which it could not extort any extra money, passed a bill prohibiting any individual from owning both the New York Central and the Erie Railroads, protecting New Yorkers from the evils of railroad monopoly.[36]

Nothing, however, protected the Erie from its wayward directors. With Vanderbilt out of the way, Gould and Fisk, who could not bring Erie profits, nonetheless gave it some style. They privately bought the once fashionable Pike's Opera House on West 23rd Street and leased it to the Erie for $75,000 a year. For an additional $250,000, or ten times the road's profits in the previous year, they converted the space into a garish urban palace, setting up Erie officials in a phalanx of offices that featured gilt balustrades, crystal partitions, and trompe l'oeil walls and ceilings. A few doors down, Fisk (the "Prince of Erie" in the beguiled press) installed his mistress, Josie Mansfield, who held parties and hosted card games for city politicians. On the next block, Fisk built a suite of fancy stables for his horses.[37]

Its offices may have been the most lavish corporate headquarters in the world, but the Erie was in dismal shape. Its roads, laid out over irregular terrain were hazardous and ramshackle. Its finances were precarious. Its employees were the cheapest foreign labor that could be had, and its reputation was deeply tarnished. The road's iron rails were so worn down and rotted that car speed had to be drastically reduced, resulting in a loss of roughly two to five hours on each trip. Of Erie's 371 engines, at least 70 were of little or no use. The carrier suffered twenty-six passenger fatalities in 1868. Its finances were equally ravaged. Already burdened with immense debt, the Erie's recent debacle added $9 million more on top of many millions in new convertible bonds that had to be issued for construction and repairs. Twenty-one million dollars had been added to Erie's outstanding stock since 1866, and despite the booming economy, its share value tumbled from $70 in April 1868 to below $45 in late August.[38]

By early November, Erie's price stood at under $40 and appeared hopeless. A sloth of bears, including the Wall Street eminence August Belmont (who represented the Rothschild interests in the United States) and the still frisky Drew, made the mistake of assuming that things were as they appeared. They bought Erie short, betting on the stock's continued decline, only to have Gould and Fisk spring a "bear trap." The two directors spiked trade in the stock just before the date for delivery of its shorted shares. The price went to $61 and cost Daniel Drew and the other bears as much as $20 for each share that they had shorted. The *Herald* reported with a mixture of awe and reproach that "speculations . . . as were never equaled before on Wall Street . . . make the . . . public gape with astonishment at the boldness of the operators." The once proud Erie became "the Scarlet Woman of Wall Street," while Drew, outmaneuvered on familiar territory, was moved to say of his much younger nemesis that Gould's touch "is death."[39]

Gould and Fisk had thwarted Vanderbilt and won Wall Street's attention. Erie's stockholders were not pleased, however, by the cavalier use to which their company had been put. They wanted to remove the men who had played so disturbingly with their fortunes, but they soon learned that while they owned the railroad in law, they could exert very little control in fact. The corporate setup concentrated power in the board of directors, and that board included, in addition to Fisk, Gould, and Gould's brother-in-law, two of Tammany Hall's favorite sons, Grand Sachem William M. Tweed (who collected over $100,000 for "legal services" from the road) and City Chamberlain Peter Barr Sweeny (who was paid $150,000 in Erie funds to serve as a "receiver," though no one could figure out what beyond his fee he was to receive). Utilizing the services of the best lawyers (including for a while Samuel J. Tilden) and the worst Tammany judges, this board managed to erect a protective moat around itself, adopting a policy that required stockholders to be present at meetings in order to vote.

The ban on proxy voting effectively disempowered the majority of stockholders, many of whom were overseas investors.[40]

The Erie debacle provided an unnerving glimpse into New York's new financial world. "Nothing," lamented the authoritative *Commercial Advertiser,* "in the history of this or any other country . . . begins to compare to this unblushing scoundrelism. . . ." The shocking spectacle of a wasteful, corrupt, and singularly self-absorbed conflict over control of a multimillion-dollar railroad made obvious that the economy of modest scale and personal accountability had gone the way of the three-story South Street countinghouse. While Gould, Fisk, et al. were no doubt astonished by what they had managed to pull off, no one stopped them from wasting millions of other people's money on a personal power struggle. Corporate officers had mocked their fiduciary responsibilities, printed reams of depreciated stock, undermined equity values, and frittered away the company treasure on personal caprice. And along the way they had managed to tempt even respected judges into rascality, while laying waste to any notions of legislative integrity.[41]

Gould had burst on the scene by boldly outmaneuvering Vanderbilt and taking over one of the nation's largest railroads. He moved with such lupine stealth that—while still a young man—he was feared as no other adversary on this street of feral competitors. His most audacious move, the one for which he would be best remembered, came within months of his capture of Erie.

"Of all financial operations," wrote Henry Adams in his account of Gould's gold scheme, "cornering gold is the most brilliant and most dangerous, and possibly the very hazard and splendor of the attempt were the reasons for the fascination to Mr. Jay Gould." Poor Adams lacked the practical imagination to appreciate the allure to Gould's serpentine intelligence of a corner on the metal that undergirded world currency, without investing it with transgressive allure. Perhaps poets and disillusioned intellectuals like him needed drama and adventure to explain a gold corner. For Jay Gould the hot potential for great profit was cause enough. The possibility did exist that the scheme might fail, especially because the federal government had the resources to break a gold corner, but as Jim Fisk later testified, one could always repudiate one's contracts, losing in Diamond Jim's immortal words "nothing . . . but honor."[42]

Superior to legal tender for many reasons, not the least of which was its recognition the world over, gold had been traded at a premium during the war. Reports of northern setbacks would send greenbacked paper money into free fall, sending the price of gold soaring. Speculators, wagering on the fortunes of war and the ebb and flow of gold supply, tried every which way, short of fixing battles, to gain an advantage in this treacherous market. John Pierpont Morgan, just beginning a career that would catapult him to the crest of American finance, participated in one of these ventures, which netted a quick $132,000 on gold speculation for himself and his partners. This sort of speculation, bound up as it was with issues of blood and loyalty, offended even the hardened traders of the New York Stock Exchange, who banished gold traders from their floors.[43]

New York was the center of the nation's gold market. On a typical day in the late 1860s, $15 million to $20 million in gold circulated through the city, largely for use by importers who had to pay for foreign goods in gold. Gould set out to gain control over as much of this gold as he could, hoping to do nothing less than corner the metallic base of the American money supply. In April of 1869, Gould tested his scheme. He instructed his brokers to purchase millions in gold, sending the price of the metal up from $132 to $140 in one week. Then he cashed in the metal. The return of so large a volume of gold sent the price skidding back down, as he had expected.[44]

Having developed a taste for this high-stakes game, he went for a talk with his friend Fisk. Gould was confident that they could tie up much of the gold circulating in New York by buying on margin. They would receive certificates for rights to millions of dollars of the metal and then loan out these gold receipts on the call market. At the right time, they would call in all the gold, draining the market of the metal in order to create an artificial scarcity, sending the price rocketing. There remained one catch. With more than $100 million of the precious metal in the Sub-Treasury Building at the head of Broad Street, the U.S. Treasury could release millions in gold reserves to undermine a corner.[45]

Gould and Fisk had pulled off the Erie maneuvers with the aid of a pliant judiciary and a solicitous legislature. For the gold corner, the schemers set out to recruit the president of the United States.[46]

Ulysses S. Grant was one of the great heroes to emerge from the War Between the States. He had also demonstrated an appreciation for wealthy businesspeople, who showered him with expensive gifts. This proved fortunate for Grant's marriage, because his wife, Julia, had an abiding desire for the first-class life she believed her husband's service entitled them to, even on an officer's salary. A group from Philadelphia presented the Grants with a fully furnished mansion. Not to be outdone, the citizens of Galena, Illinois, made the couple a gift of a second house. Fifty solid citizens of Boston contributed a $75,000 library. But it fell to the more practical men of New York to put cash on the table. "In accordance with the request of many citizens of New York, whose names are herewith transmitted," the lawyer Daniel Butterfield wrote to Grant, he was honored to transmit payment of the mortgage on Grant's Washington home, a selection of high-rated bonds, and also some cash, a gift package comprising a total of $105,000, as a proper (if the term may be used) "testimony of their gratitude." Although it was not unusual for public officials to accept gifts, the scale of these gratuities was very generous even by the standards of the day. Grant thanked Butterfield for "the substantial token of the friendship of the citizens named in your letter" and promised to "always appreciate their generosity towards me and endeavor to pursue a course . . . as will meet with their approval."[47]

In November 1868, Americans made this "rags to riches" general, who so fit the acquisitive mood of the times, their president.

For Jay Gould, Ulysses S. Grant's election proved to be welcome. Gould did not know or understand the impeached president Andrew Johnson, but Grant was another story. Grant was not obsessed with the South. He adopted the economic policies of the Republican Party, with its emphasis on full-throttle economic growth. Post–Civil War America was still a developing nation, and Grant was more interested in fostering business than in reining it in. Confronted with schemers bearing proposals, his administration invited them in. Experienced in the purchase of aldermen, judges, and state senators, Gould set out to win the president to his plan for cornering gold.

Gould recruited the urbane and well-traveled Abel Rathbone Corbin to smooth the way. Abel Corbin had worked himself up from the St. Louis frontier to editing a newspaper and finally to working for the Congressional Committee on Claims in prewar Washington. When he was dismissed from the committee for peddling privileged information, Corbin was less embarrassed than momentarily discomfited. He moved on to a less assailable means of trading in access, marrying in 1869, at the age of sixty-one, General Grant's shy, withdrawn, thirty-seven-year old sister, Virginia Paine Grant, and settling down in New York. Jennie Grant Corbin may have been ignored before, but her new home, an elegant West 27th Street brownstone, became a very popular place indeed, especially when the president came to New York. Jay Gould befriended Corbin and soon enough began preaching to him the gospel of gold inflation (that is, have the federal government keep gold scarce). It would, Jay lectured the First Brother-in-law, raise farm profits, enrich the railroads, and, not incidentally, Gould pointed out, make Corbin a fortune.[48]

To cement Corbin's enthusiasm for the secret project, Gould (who ordered some $7 million in gold for himself) advanced payment for the purchase of $1.5 million in gold in Mrs. Corbin's name. When the price climbed high enough, the Corbins could sell, pay Gould back, and keep the difference; if it went down—well, no one expected that to happen. Meanwhile, every time the price of gold went up by a dime, the First In-laws stood to gain $1,500, without having advanced a penny.[49]

Gould needed a reliable confederate in the Treasury office, and he got Corbin to recommend Daniel Butterfield (the same Butterfield who had put together the New York subscription for Grant) to his brother-in-law, who dutifully appointed Butterfield as the New York–based assistant treasurer. Within two days of occupying his office, Butterfield received a $10,000 check. Butterfield later characterized this "benefaction" as an interest-free real estate loan that Gould (who until this time had not demonstrated a penchant for donations to impecunious bureaucrats) advanced to him after learning that Butterfield needed some money.

As late as March 1870, when a disconcerted Butterfield was hauled before a congressional committee to testify about the deeper meaning of this benefaction, it had not been repaid. Butterfield, whose annual salary was $8,000, continued to insist that the loan had nothing to do with gold. This, despite the fact that soon after he took office he purchased and sold gold in the amount of $750,000, a transaction that brought him $35,000 in profit. From his New York office, Butterfield was privy to any Treasury plans to release gold into the market, which could undermine the Gould scheme. And clearly he could be used.[50]

On June 15, 1869, Grant was introduced to Gould by the Corbins. Gould engaged the president in conversation, leading the discussion to his theory that keeping gold scarce and expensive was a key to national prosperity. The president seemed to disagree, suggesting that gold had already risen above its true price, and the bubble might as well be punctured by releasing reserves. Unnerved, Gould objected that such a step would produce great distress and "almost lead to Civil War," closing businesses, setting off labor strikes, and shuttering factories. Grant's attitude, Jim Fisk would recollect, "struck across us like cold water."[51]

Gould met with Grant several more times before the end of September (once as the president was frantically rushing back to Washington to a dear friend's deathbed) to make the case for restraint in the release of government gold. Meanwhile, he proceeded with his plan, buying some gold in Secretary Butterfield's name, paying for editorials that supported gold inflation in the *The New York Times,* and in August depositing a check for $100,000 in Corbin's account, while directly handing over another check in the amount of $25,000. A congressional investigating committee later concluded: "Gould seems to have left no means untried to . . . buy or conciliate all possible influence and aid. . . ." The campaign apparently succeeded in changing Grant's mind, for the Treasury made no gold sales, and Corbin assured Gould that there would be no release of federally held gold.[52]

In September 1869, with gold selling at $135 ($135 in greenbacks for $100 in gold) and both Fisk and Gould convinced that they had tied down the Treasury, the pair accelerated their secret gold purchases. After checking in with Corbin, Gould decided to add some more insurance, sending the president's close confidant and secretary, General Horace Porter, a telegram advising that he had opened a $500,000 gold account in Porter's name. The general refused the offer. Less clear is the nature of Mrs. Grant's involvement. It is possible, if Jim Fisk is to be believed, that she earned more than $25,000 on gold investments handled for her by Gould.[53]

With an abundant harvest of western crops beginning to attract gold from around the world, and with American mines adding regularly to supplies, gold prices should have been going down. But the Gould consortium continued to sweep the market clean of surplus. Close to $15 million was gathered up, propping up the price. Merchants unnerved by gold's high price hesitated to close deals. More could be gained or lost by changes in the value of the medium of exchange than in the deal itself. Markets slowed considerably. Pressed by concerned merchants, Treasury Secretary George S. Boutwell ordered the Treasury to begin selling reserves, only to receive a letter from President Grant (then in New York) that "it was undesirable to force down the price of gold." Boutwell later testified that the president thought (in words remarkably similar to those Gould had planted in his head) "that if the gold should fall, the West would suffer and the movement of the crops would be retarded." Boutwell canceled his order.[54]

Gould continued buying, dipping into Erie's treasury to pay for some of the purchases. Gould also used his controlling interest in the Tenth National Bank to have the bank issue certified checks. When a bank certified a check, it meant that there was cash in the account to cover the face value of the note, or at least this is what it meant in other banks, but the Tenth National issued millions in certified checks on Gould's word, extending to him a fiat credit, multiplying his buying power on the gold market.[55]

With the Treasury seemingly neutralized and the price of gold climbing—*The New York Times* described the level of intense trading in gold by Wednesday, September 22, as "at white heat"—the scheme advanced as planned. In the past, gold price fluctuations of a few cents had created unease. On this day, gold shot up from $137 to $141. Traders, urged on by rumors of a gold scheme that had the highest political backing, placed bets on the side, wagering that the price would climb to $145. Speculators with short contracts to deliver gold rushed in panic to buy before the price went even higher.[56]

On the following day, Thursday, the price rose to $144. Business on the Produce Exchange slowed, and international trade stopped entirely. Fear for its currency system gripped the nation. In page one coverage, the *Times* described a scene with "torments worse than any Dante ever witnessed in hell" on the exchange floor. Its editorial denouncing the gold conspirators reported in blunt terms rumors of a political conspiracy reaching perhaps even as high as the White House. Allowing the price of gold to continue its calamitous ascent, added the paper, would only fuel the suspicions.[57]

The editorial unsettled Gould. He feared that it would force the president's hand to release gold. He hurried over to Abel Corbin's home and had Corbin compose a letter that he hustled off by courier to his vacationing brother-in-law in Pennsylvania. The urgent delivery and the agitated tone of the letter demanding that the government not sell gold from its reserves finally opened the president's eyes. Julia Grant composed the reply. In a frosty tone, she warned the Corbins to end their speculations immediately. As soon as he got the letter, a shaken Corbin raced over to Gould, who was no less disturbed by the terse message. He dismissed Corbin, warning him to keep everything secret. Then he turned to considering his next course of action.[58]

The new economy that dealt in virtual commodities represented by paper had made it possible for Gould to carry through his plan. He had once explained that someone with good credit could acquire $1 million of gold with no more than $50,000 "at the outside." Had each sale required a physical transfer, the level of trading that was possible would have been limited by the amount of actual gold in circulation, because it could be held by only one person at any one time. But in the new economy purchases did not necessarily involve actual transfers. Traded on paper, one measure of gold could be sold to B for delivery by A. Then even before its delivery date, the certificate could be sold to C, who could sell it short to D, and so forth, all based on the same single quantity of gold. Much like bank checks, which in passing from hand to hand expand the currency, the gold market supported a volume of exchange greatly in excess of the amount of gold that actually existed. This way of doing business put Gould's ring in control of rights to tens of millions in gold.[59]

That Thursday, September 23, the Gold Exchange cleared $239 million, more than three times the usual daily volume. On Thursday night, Treasury Secretary Boutwell told President Grant that the stampeding gold market threatened the nation's economic stability. The secretary also reported the suspicious behavior of the Tenth National Bank, which had issued $8 million in certified checks to Gould, who had no more than $300,000 on deposit at the time. According to later testimony before Congress, the gold ring had gathered the rights to call in as much as $100 million in gold. With no more than a fraction of that amount actually available, these contracts threatened an enormous squeeze that would convulse the economy. Confronted by evidence of serious economic hazard and a conspiracy that implicated his brother-in-law, as well as some of the wealthiest investors in the land, Grant permitted the Treasury to act.[60]

Meanwhile, Gould had taken the letter from Mrs. Julia Grant to heart. He began quietly unloading his holdings. He did not inform Fisk or any of the others. The gold market was still soaring.

On Friday, September 24, the gold room opened to pandemonium. "In the history of Wall Street since the gold market first became an institution . . . there has never been such a day," began the next day's *Times* report. In the first hour, speculators, scrambling to buy, drove the price of gold to $150. The floor was rife with rumors that the ring was determined to go to $200 before letting up. Gold climbed above $155. Those with obligations to deliver at prices around the low $130s saw in each point rise another degree of ruin, of hopes blasted and careers sunk. The National Guard was ordered to stand by. Fisk and the gold claque, oblivious to Jay Gould's change of direction, continued buying. Shouts to buy mixed with screams of maniacal emotion at the terrible but irresistible scenes unfolding in the gold room. All, reported next day's *Herald*, were crying, "Gold, Gold, Gold." The overtaxed telegraph sending the information out to the rest of the country went dead. As its wires melted, gold hit $158.[61]

It went to $160, and for a moment even higher. The gold ring stood to make fortunes, but the bonanza could easily evaporate once the astronomical prices began attracting gold from all over. All were afraid of what might happen next, but the roller coaster could not stop itself.

Finally, at 11:57 A.M. a telegram arrived from Washington ordering Assistant Secretary Butterfield to release $4 million in government gold. The ring had already learned about this, either by tapping the telegraph wires or directly from Butterfield himself. The price of gold, $164, just two minutes before, tumbled 20 percent in a moment. Fortunes evaporated in minutes. Fisk, still unaware of Gould's concealed sales, had directed his broker, Albert Speyers, to bid gold up to $160 and take all he could get at the price. Seconds after the Treasury's announcement sent prices plummeting to below $140, Speyers, "craz[ed] as a loon," in Fisk's account, continued to shout orders for "any part of $5,000,000 at 160." Temporarily crazed Speyers may have been, but after the panic was over, Jim Fisk wanted very much to see him. Diamond Jim was working on retrospectively piecing his story together, and Speyers knew how much gold had been bought, at whose behest, and at what price. Fisk did not want this information to get out as he prepared to renege on his orders, and he intimated that a very selective recollection could be worth a small fortune to his broker. "That is all nonsense talk to me," responded the man slandered by Clarence Stedman in his scathing poem "Israel Freyer" as a mendacious Hebrew clown. He turned his back on the hush money.[62]

The gold room became a bedlam. Men facing ruin were thrown together with those who had led them to the precipice. The crazed wailing and terrified yells created a fearsome chorus of panic. It was impossible, the papers wrote, to exaggerate the grotesqueness of the scene, reeking as it did with the awful stink of failed greed and sheer fright. The conspirators, reported the *Times*, "lay prone beside their victims." It "was each man drag out his own corpse," said Jim Fisk. Fisk himself was less than safe. Those not yet ready to shoot him advocated the suspension of punishment for anyone who did.[63]

A cascade of unfilled contracts descended upon the financial district. Thursday's clearings were not yet registered, much less the avalanche of orders that came on Black Friday. The total exceeded "one thousand millions of dollars" for the two days. Many dealers failed. Jim Fisk's brokers had bought on his oral command. Now the Prince of Erie repudiated the purchases, seeking refuge behind friendly judges. It remains unclear whether even Gould came out ahead. One ruined broker shot himself to death.[64]

Commodity prices plunged, bringing calamity to western farmers. Sales volume declined by as much as a third from the year before. Having little to do with the traditional determinants of farm profits—hard work, good earth, sufficient rain, and plentiful sun—the ebb in their earnings provided a sure sign of the transfer of control over their own fortunes from their hands and Nature's to a distant constellation of market forces that would lead the western yeomen increasingly to blame their distress on eastern speculators. The failed corner also ruined scores of commercial firms, as importers, especially, absorbed heavy losses. The speculative orgy had diverted millions from trade and industry into a ruinous search for quick profits. A congressional committee closed its investigation of the affair by recommending the passage of a law that would make it a crime to conspire "against the credit of the United States and the business of the people."[65]

Black Friday demonstrated how extensively Wall Street, with the speculative trade in virtual property that it now stood for, had changed American business. It was no longer possible for serious observers to say that this new market was of concern only to the speculator, that all solid conservative entrepreneurs had to do to protect themselves was to avoid the temptation for quick profits. It was possible perhaps to say that about the Erie wars. The only ones directly affected were security holders. But the gold corner was no distant spectacle. The gold manipulations directly affected American agriculture, commerce, and the national currency, and Gould had aimed to compromise the president. The gold corner with all of its repercussions demonstrated the concentration of wealth and the centralization of national financial markets in lower Manhattan and the enormous influence of this market.

That, and the indulgent business environment that the Gotham markets had fostered. Calling yourself an investor, suggested the *Herald*, raised deceptive dealings and underhanded business practices to the level of a profession. Foreign observers were struck by the unregulated climate of insouciant greed and the disavowal of responsibility, as if the limited liability statutes had exempted the corporations from honesty. Business failures and defalcations had become routine, with companies casually repudiating debts through bankruptcy. "Congress has no power over them," complained the *London Spectator*. "The State legislatures can scarcely touch them . . . the judiciary is in their pay, and even if they stepped beyond the law . . . juries could not be found to convict them." (The London press had good reason for its bitter tone. English investors held more than half of Erie's heavily manipulated stock, yet they found it impossible to control Gould or secure justice. An Albany assemblyman salted the wounds when he remarked that things might have been different if the agent representing the British stockholders "had brought $20,000 [to Albany] to smooth the way.") The congressional committee that investigated the gold corner did not implicate any individual, but its conclusion could not have been more damning: "The foundations of business morality were broken."[66]

A vigorous, brash corporate capitalism had taken root in the metropolitan markets. Neither Gould nor Fisk nor Vanderbilt nor Drew had any idea at the outset of the extent to which the new economy eased their sway over other people's money. With few rules and little precedent, they kept pushing back the margins of restraint, and the barriers kept falling. A man arrested for stealing an item from a store would be prosecuted, but a Gould, who compromised the U.S. Treasury, conspired to influence the president, had a bank on whose board he served falsely certify millions in notes, and went on to disrupt the entire economy and hurt countless numbers of Americans, faced no reproof.

---

Moses Taylor was an old man now. He had seen business evolve from the commercial trade of his youth to the emerging world of corporate America. He had begun in the back rooms of the South Street countinghouses, opened his own import firm, and achieved substantial success as a banker, investor, and utilities mogul. As investor and banker he advanced the growth of big business, venturing capital in transportation, utilities, mining, banking, and communications. As a corporate director he established the practice of long-distance management for widely dispersed companies from the metropolis.[67]

He could still remember a market based on individual relationships and personal exchange held fast by practice and custom in ways that did not require judges or legislators, a market based on the familiar reputations of its entrepreneurs. In his youth, a business culture of gentlemanly trade ruled the commodity and securities marts. Merchants met during fixed hours at the Merchant's Exchange, while investors attended twice-a-day sessions at the New York Stock and Exchange Board to bid on stocks that were read off a list. Misbehaving during the formal reading of the stock list resulted in fines—interruptions cost twenty-five cents, cigar smoking brought a $5 punishment, while standing on the furniture to make oneself heard set back the offender by $10. Convention and ethics were enough to keep the small commercial elite within these well-established business rituals. Even the courts followed the English tradition of common law that rooted the law in local custom and practice, as opposed to the more formal statute law that was applied in France and Germany.[68]

As the number and complexity of business interactions increased, however, and the business community itself became less homogeneous, simple custom, with its reliance on voluntary behavior and scruple, proved inadequate. When brokers reached the end of the formal trading day, they were supposed to close up shop, but in the booming economy many of them just continued dealing on the street. When securities brokers expelled gold traders from the NYSE for their excessive speculation, the gold traders just went around the corner and opened their own exchange. Old routine provided scant guidance or control as the postwar economy turned more complex, abstract, and anonymous.[69]

American law too became more formal, adopting systematic statute-based law to define what was permissible and what was not. Business decisions came to turn less on what was right or good than on what was strictly legal. Leagues of eager Wall Street attorneys assumed a growing role in corporate decisions, devoting extraordinary efforts to discovering what the formal law permitted, even if inadvertently. Unconventional and often unprincipled behavior found legitimacy in loopholes, in the failure of the law to anticipate a particular twist of interpretation or to foreclose an unexpected course of action. By its nature, statute law could prohibit only what it could identify or envision. Little wonder that the law proved a rigid and clumsy tool against the lithe operators now drawn to the corporate economy. In all the misery caused by the gold corner, *The New York Times* exclaimed in amazement shortly after Black Friday, not a single law was violated, reflecting not the innocence of the conspirators, but a system in which keen lawyers "chopped logic," to prove in the face of ample misbehavior that none had misbehaved.[70]

Moses Taylor represented an older business generation. He lived a socially modest life in which his goals extended significantly beyond assembling as much money as possible. His name often stood at the head of endeavors ranging from civic reform to public improvement, but he shied away from public attention and conspicuous display. Even when his yearly income ran into the millions, his annual living expenses never exceeded $100,000, including taxes. He decried the new spirit of money worship. "The great aim of life is not to buy cheap and sell dear," said an editorial that reflected this outlook, "but is to organize society that it shall perfect the bodily and spiritual welfare of the race and insure comfort and happiness to men." When he died in 1882, leaving an estimated $50 million fortune, leading journals and newspapers emphasized Taylor's "soundness." His projects, one journal wrote, "were intended to be permanent investments; they were not speculations from which he might snatch a hasty profit."[71]

Snatching hasty profits aptly defined Jay Gould's approach to business. He suffered no tempering regard for honor or community standards of the sort that shaped Moses Taylor's dealings. He developed a new specialty, that of a stock speculator who bought and sold companies. Less concerned with building the long-term health and prosperity of a business than with making quick profits from manipulating its securities, he specialized in weak companies that he dressed up for market. He took great pleasure in the feints and strat-

agems that separated men from their money. "Proper men," writes
biographer Maury Klein, "regarded him as a speculative roué" who
recognized no constraints but the naked statute.[72]

Who but the senseless and the foolhardy would be drawn to this
new money market with its collapsing ethical boundaries? Yet despite stock gyrations of huge and unpredictable amplitude, New
York continued to attract entrepreneurs, investors, and financiers
from all over. Charles Francis Adams's attribution of this anomaly to
a "strange fatuity" on the part of these investors explains nothing.
For how could business ignore the chaotic environment reflected in
the Erie wars and the gold corner? How could business countenance
a climate where even Cornelius Vanderbilt, the wealthiest industrialist in the country, could not count on a judge, once having been paid
for, to remain bought? Who in his right mind would pursue big
business in a community described in the *American Law Review* as
"not apparently unaccustomed to seeing one justice of its Supreme
Court enjoining another on the ground that his respected associate
has entered into a conspiracy to use his judicial power in a stock jobbing operation"?[73]

"The rottenness that is in . . . [New York]," the *Cincinnati Gazette*
warned, "will ultimately destroy it. . . . [I]ts influence is of the worst
character, and . . . the people of the country should set their faces
against it." "Something," *Harper's Weekly* admonished, "must be
done" if New York were to continue to attract foreign capital and
maintain its position as the leading commercial metropolis, or else,
as George Templeton Strong wrote in his diary, "capital will flee to
safer quarters."[74]

It did not. Indeed, it kept seeking out this unique, mysterious metropolis. Why?

Jay Gould's story is one key. He had come to Erie a little known
upstart, with a reputation for prickly dealing, and in a remarkably
brief time he managed to wrestle with the likes of Vanderbilt and
Drew and the Pennsylvania Railroad's Edgar Thomson. Businesses
could certainly find more stable settings, but no other place com-

pared with Gotham for its stimulating investment environment where it was possible to rocket from obscure poverty to wealthy notoriety. And its resilient economy was irrepressible. A few weeks after the gold panic, its investors were pursuing profit again, scouting new investments, and taking new risks.[75]

Those afraid of what the metropolis might do to them had good reason to find Gotham terrifying. For those, however, who aimed to seize opportunity and squeeze from it every prospect, it provided the single most exhilarating and most rewarding arena. Ignoring the warnings, the tales of business menace and cunning, driven, ambitious men sought out the challenge. Just one year before Black Friday, another of the legendary rags-to-riches business figures, Andrew Carnegie, had returned from a grand tour of Europe and was taken in by the lure of this difficult and undisciplined city.

Carnegie had encountered the burnished high culture of the continent, the great music, venerable art, and rarefied conversation of its moral philosophers. But the depleted old lands that he saw were played out. His mother country, Scotland, was too small for him or his dreams. As for the French, he thought they were dead. Even Haussmann's improvements could not overcome their habitual lethargy. Only "grim, overcrowded London" had the ambition and enterprise to be modern, but even London he found too beholden to its past.[76]

Gotham was different. New York was not a national political center. Its aesthetic was entirely derivative and provincial, and it could not compare with the high culture of London, Paris, or Berlin. Unlike these cities, it made no bows to its own history. On the contrary, the past was less salient here. New York was the champion of the modern, of unceremoniously dispatching the unserviceable past, of making history instead of worshiping it. This city excelled at one thing: generating capital and making profits. Other cities embraced the warrior, the intellectual, the leader of men, the artist. Their heroes had pursued good and shaped social ideals with their examples of courage and sacrifice. New York's heroes were crafted in its own spirit: the businessman as artist, leader, sage, and, above all, symbol of prosperity. Sons and daughters of farmers, small-town merchants, failed bankers and gold miners, successful entrepreneurs, and penniless immigrants cast aside warnings about indecency, corruption, and chicanery and flocked to the new metropolis.

Determined to accelerate an already exceedingly fast-paced career, Carnegie in the summer of 1867 moved with his elderly mother from Pittsburgh to the fashionable six-story St. Nicholas Hotel on lower Broadway. History has left us with memories of an altruistic Carnegie, whose overriding ambition was to distribute as much of his fortune as possible before his death, but in the booming 1860s Andrew Carnegie was a young man of buccaneering nerve whose own flexible morality led him to the one metropolis that matched his tropism toward risk and accumulation.[77]

His father had been a weaver of fine linen cloth in Dunfermline, Scotland, whom famine and economic stagnation chased from a way of life preserved in the amber of artisanal tradition. Unable to make peace with his new environment, Will Carnegie died in 1855, only seven years after coming to the United States, at the age of fifty, a melancholy and broken man. Andrew, meanwhile, moved briskly through a succession of factory jobs. He would work for twelve hours and then attend classes, advancing rapidly from shop to office to telegraph work within a year. Impressed with the bright teenager who "read" a telegraph by ear right off the wire, Thomas A. Scott, superintendent for the western division of the Pennsylvania Railroad, hired him as his personal telegrapher and secretary.[78]

As Tom Scott's deputy, young Carnegie apprenticed with the best-organized and largest privately owned company in the world. In 1859, the twenty-four-year-old took over as superintendent of the road's Pittsburgh division. He also experienced his capitalist epiphany. With money borrowed from Scott, he bought some express company stocks and received his first dividend check: "I opened the envelope. . . . I shall remember that [$10] check as long as I live . . . , revenue on capital—something that I had not worked for with the sweat of my brow. 'Eureka!' I cried. 'Here's the goose that lays the golden eggs.'" Within a few years, the $600 that he had borrowed and invested was bringing him $1,440 a year *in dividends*. Privy to the Pennsylvania's plans to order sleeping cars, he bought securities in the company that produced them, as well as in an oil company and in the Western Union Telegraph Company. By the end of 1863, his investments alone were bringing him close to $50,000 annually. "I'm rich. I'm rich," the twenty-eight-year-old Carnegie exulted.[79]

When the army summoned him to service, the immigrant son who loved America and hated slavery did not think long about what to do. Exploiting the indulgence offered to men of means, Carnegie paid an agent $850 to secure a recent Irish immigrant who went off to battle in his stead. The war occupied little of his thinking. He was focused on himself. "Whatever I engage in I must push inordinately," he once wrote.[80] He decided to press ahead on his own, declining a promotion to general superintendent of the railroad and turning all his efforts to maximizing the Eureka moments that brought profits "not worked for with the sweat of my brow." He took his grand tour and came to New York.[81]

Years later, Carnegie condemned speculators who traded companies instead of building them, but the young man who settled in New York in these boom years played the securities markets with great aplomb. The $817.50 that he had borrowed several years before had turned into investments in sixteen companies. He held assets of $400,000.[82]

Carnegie's focus on the main chance brought him into contact with George Pullman, and he was dazzled. He, Tom Scott, and Pennsylvania president J. Edgar Thomson (the latter two hiding their conflicted interest by putting everything in Carnegie's name) had acquired a large share in CTC, a company that outfitted railroad cars with sleeping berths, but Carnegie became convinced that it was George Pullman who represented the "lion" in this industry. He proceeded, in the words of his biographer, to "deliver [CTC] over to Pullman" in return for a quarter share for him and his partners in the Pullman Palace Car Company.[83]

He displayed a similar craftiness in his telegraph acquisitions. In the early days, someone with little more than a crude wire and some poles could tap out messages, but in April 1856 Western Union Telegraph Co. combined a host of smaller start-ups into a $500,000 telegraph business. Its March 1863 return to investors was a dividend of 100 percent. Just nine months later, it declared another 33 percent dividend. Over the next six years, its stock value zoomed from $3 million to $41 million. A traveler, upon seeing telegraph wire crossing the Mississippi River, remarked: "It seemed like the nervous system of the nation, conveying . . . the pulsations of the heart to the farthest extremity; and by these wires stretched across the Mississippi, I could hear the sharp, quick beating of the great heart of New York." Carnegie coveted a serious part of this "sharp, quick beating of the great heart of New York."[84]

In 1867, Carnegie, Thomson, and Scott, taking advantage of their railroad connections, formed a company to run telegraph lines along the extensive Pennsylvania Railroad route. Soon after filing the corporate papers, they sold out in return for a one-third interest in Pacific and Atlantic Telegraph, a Western Union competitor. When Western Union responded to the new threat by slashing its prices, Carnegie denounced the wire monopoly for its cruel tactics. At the same time he secretly arranged to sell out his (and his partners') interest to Western Union for a share in the monopoly and a fat profit, leaving behind an eviscerated P&A that soon enough became little more than worthless paper.[85]

Focused on erecting an investment empire around America's transportation-communication system, Carnegie also acquired the Keystone Bridge Company, which specialized in building iron railroad bridges. When the firm won the contract for the dramatic St. Louis Bridge, consisting of three vaulting arches across the Mississippi River that were sunk into bedrock nearly one hundred feet below the water's surface, Carnegie went to London and secured financing for the $4 million project from the banking house headed by Junius S. Morgan. It had taken Carnegie a full year to earn

$50,000 in 1863; and in another of those moments of joyous discovery, he learned that it was possible to earn that much on this one bond transaction alone.[86]

With more cunning than honor, Carnegie had learned to swim in the swift currents of New York finance. He had built a tangle of interlocking business interests, from railroads to sleeping cars, to bridges and telegraph companies, to the foundries that produced and processed iron. Using his connections to arrange loans for strapped roads, he would demand in return a place on their boards. Then he would use his influence to bring their business to his bridge and iron companies. His stealth was legendary, and for a brief moment he captured the prize coveted by the boldest rail speculators.[87]

The Union Pacific (UP) had been the largest and costliest American construction project in its time. It represented the extensive middle link of the transcontinental railroad, between the eastern railroads and the California-based Central Pacific. Like so many roads in this period of high-risk capitalism, the UP was loaded down with debt, and Carnegie was able to offer the strapped road a crucial $600,000 loan. He was again acting as a front man for Thomson and Scott, who were eager to expand the Pennsylvania's lines to the Midwest while blocking Jay Gould's plans for a rail empire. Carnegie accepted $3 million in UP stock certificates as collateral for the loan. The agreement placed both Carnegie and his partner Pullman on the UP board and made Scott president. "You see," Carnegie wrote gleefully to an associate, "we have Union Pacific. I go on the Executive Committee in March." In February 1871 the *Railroad Gazette* predicted that with this new addition, the Pennsylvania would "control transcontinental traffic for many years to come."[88]

Actually, as it turned out, the reign lasted for just about a moment. For the same greed and hunger for personal profit that drove the deal toppled it.

With new cash and the respected Scott at the helm, UP stock climbed in value. Carnegie and his partners had planted an option in their agreement allowing them to purchase any part of the $3 million in securities, which they held as collateral, for the depressed stock price prevailing at the time of the loan. This they now turned into a very substantial profit by exercising their option to sell the collateral. The move reeked with greed and with a breach of their responsibilities as directors. Appalled, the Union Pacific board dumped Carnegie and ousted Scott from the presidency, costing the pair "our party['s] . . . splendid position . . . in connection with the Union Pacific" and dashing hopes for the Pennsylvania's extension into the far West. Brought in to replace the discredited Scott was Cornelius Vanderbilt's son-in-law, H. F. Clark. Carnegie was left with handsome profit but no transcontinental.[89]

Years before, he had questioned his own greed. "Thirty three and an income of $50,000 per annum," he wrote on Hotel St. Nicholas stationery. He did not need more money. He could pursue a "thorough education" at Oxford and learn to speak in public and form a circle of bright, informed "literary men." He understood his own nature and that whatever goal he chose he would drive himself relentlessly. Therefore, he wrote, he must choose a goal worthy of his efforts, a goal that would elevate him. To remain chained to the pursuit of wealth "must degrade me beyond hope of permanent recovery." In two years, he pledged, he would "cast aside business forever."[90]

At the end of 1872, the much reviled Jay Gould made Carnegie an offer. He was prepared to buy the Pennsylvania and place Carnegie at its head in a push for domination of the rail industry. "The whole speculative field was laid out before me in its most seductive guise," Carnegie recalled. He had already been thinking about the meaning of his success and the sinful profits he took from his deals; he was sufficiently introspective to fear a life enslaved to chasing money, but his promise to leave business could not stand up to the allure of New York's economic environment, where so much was possible and restraints were so few. Gould's offer was a revelation. It gave him a chilling insight into what had become of his promises. He was living the life that had earlier made him tremble; deeply involved in squeezing superfluous profits out of half a dozen businesses, he had made no progress on his refinement. And the widely detested Jay Gould wanted him as a partner.[91]

---

Focused on national reconstruction and lacking an effective model for government regulation or economic planning, Washington followed a policy of strict reticence in economic policy. With the federal government removed from the scene, the possibility of strong city controls took on a new reality as Gotham, in the half-decade following the Civil War, took back its home rule authority from the state, and passed a charter that aggressively asserted its metropolitan prerogatives. It replaced the state-run commissions with its own mayoral departments and seized control over the growth agenda pioneered by Andrew Green and the Central Park Commission. With its governing coalition of businessmen, reformers, ethnic groups, and workers, this newly energized urban regime built new city institutions and revamped old ones. It fashioned a powerful, independent urban government that could serve as a countervailing force to the aggressive business elements and regulate the way the new corporate sector did its business. For a moment, business and political leaders joined behind a municipal growth agenda that gave New York a taste of great metropolitan accomplishment and authority. Then, as swiftly as it had risen, this new departure in hands-on urban governance came crashing down, resulting in a long decade of municipal inaction.

New York's local politics had largely been limited to aldermen naming streets after dead people and collecting bribes to avoid harassing the live ones. Compared to Paris, to London, to any of the world-class cities, New York's most striking feature—aside from its disposable wealth and insatiable appetite for more—was its scruffy inelegance and a politics that offered little promise of better. It was busy elsewhere. "[T]he general corruption in respect of the local funds," Charles Dickens wrote during a visit in 1867, "is stupendous."[92]

The city was booming. Yet prosperous, glittering, postwar Gotham may well have been the most primitive and ill-served major city in the modern world. Its docks were unsafe and rotting. The streets were filthy and poorly maintained. Ceaseless construction added to the noise and dirt. Its sewers were primitive and overtaxed. And "for several hours each day," lamented the *Commercial and Financial Chronicle*, the "section . . . below City Hall is so crowded that passengers on the sidewalk find it embarrassing to get forward, and the blockade of vehicles is complete. Pedestrians attempt to cross the street at the risk to life and limb." A French visitor called Manhattan "repulsive and vulgar," while a Scottish minister observed more deeply that "the condition of the streets seems to be only a picture of the municipal government generally."[93]

Local officials had made scant efforts to expand city services, much less to imagine Manhattan as a modern metropolis. Steeped in the penny-pinching spirit of the old merchant elite, they kept expenses low and accomplishments modest. "We are," declared *The New York Times* late in 1868, "under the domination of municipal authorities incapable of entertaining any conception of this great metropolis, and incapable of taking any [large] view of its affairs. . . ." What local government did exist, writes urban historian Alexander Callow, was a "thing of shreds and patches," a crazy quilt of uncoordinated petty sovereignties. Sixteen independent departments, some with as many as eighteen bureaus, divided the work of city government. Each of the separate departments had its own budget and negotiated directly with the state legislature for its finances.[94]

The municipal government, which the local honorables had demonstrated a vast unfitness to manage, had been stripped of the authority to rule itself by the Albany legislature. Executive powers were lodged in state commissions. Albany commissions directed the municipal police, fire and health departments, Central Park, local charities, the corrections department, city education, and local taxes. Few of these commissions (Green's Central Park Commission being a singular exception) were experienced in urban governance. The metropolis, home to the nation's largest corporations and most powerful citizens, was reduced to sending its representatives trekking hat in hand to lobby rural legislators for the meanest of services, for the smallest of reforms, while local politicians committed their best thinking to concocting excuses for not doing something. The Union League Committee on Municipal Reform described New York as one of the worst-governed cities in the world, "a national disgrace and shame."[95]

The postwar city with its many new businesses and capital markets cried out for more municipal attention. Reformers were demanding more rational, more effective government. The growing population and its extension into new neighborhoods exerted additional pressure for more and better services, while France's remaking of Paris raised expectations, stimulating New Yorkers to think in more ambitious terms for their own city. Reformers had long been crying for greater municipal responsibility. Now the city, its businesses, and its workers all seemed ready for more government. And William M. Tweed, who spied hidden possibilities in a broad urban agenda, made ready to take up the challenge of bringing it to them.[96]

Our image of William M. Tweed is colored by the piquant Thomas Nast cartoons of the bearded, beady-eyed man, whose small head, giant diamond stickpin, and massive girth projected a figure entirely abandoned to vile and corrupt appetites. The Nast caricatures were brilliantly subversive, drawn to pierce the public image and chop down a man rich and poor New Yorkers admired, but they obscure Tweed's popularity and power. His project for making New York into a grand liberal metropolis inspired a great many principled men and women who enthusiastically backed his reforms. Three hundred pounds of avuncular charm, with a girdle of suet that bespoke much good food and fine wine, he was "an immensely likeable man" who laughed easily and loved simple stories. He was generous and giving. In 1869 he delivered to the commissioner of public charities and correction a personal check in the amount of $10,000, and in the bitter winter of 1870 he donated $50,000 in groceries and coal for the poor. Between 1866 and 1873, Tweed distributed close to $300,000 of his own money to charities.[97]

Bright and amiable, the physically imposing Tweed managed to be both intimidating and well liked. He followed simple rules for popular success: avoiding airs, doing good, giving charity, loving his kids, and weeping at the ritual pieties of Fourth of July speech makers. And while he did not forswear the occasional favors of a mistress, he was loyal to his wife after a fashion, and to his friends without stint. His word, all agreed, though often coarse, was solid. A born genius at organization, he molded the ragged band of Tammany hacks and ward heelers into one of the most successful voting machines in history and forged the local political club into the instrument of his awesome ascent.[98]

Command over Tammany Hall, his party, and half a dozen state and city posts gave Tweed unchallenged authority over Gotham politics. He and his ring of followers achieved their greatest influence in 1869, when voters placed Democrats in control of both the Albany statehouse and City Hall. The governor was an ally, and the mayor, "elegant A. Oakey Hall," a precious dandy who captivated New Yorkers with his erudite speeches, polished insouciance, and outrageous affectations, was a sworn vassal. Hall's social connections and Harvard education gave the ring a patina of grace (if, gibed the *Tribune*, one was prepared to overlook his one major defect, "a lack of ability"). With Albany friendly, the mayor a disciple, and the comptroller, the police, the city aldermen, and countless key officials all taking careful direction, Tweed honeycombed the municipal service with twelve thousand of his loyalists, placing them in every corner of city government.[99]

In addition to his city posts, Tweed was also a state senator in Albany, where his men dominated the most important legislative committees. Under his influence, the state approved a fourfold increase in allocations to Gotham. The Tweed machine adopted as its own the goals of the environmental reformers, who had campaigned for a progressive city. Working with expert engineers and architects, the

Tweed forces pushed through a vastly ambitious plan for urban modernization and municipal improvement. They extended the Croton waterworks, paved miles of new streets, installed gas lines, added parks, and commissioned a new network of vitrified pipe sewers. The bossed city developed ambitious plans to repair its dilapidated piers and to build new access roads. Tweedmen rapidly built up the East Side of Manhattan into an appealing and exclusive residential community. And the metropolis inaugurated truly remarkable projects, including elevated rapid transit and the Great Bridge ("[T]his structure," Chief Engineer John Augustus Roebling promised, "will forever testify to the energy, enterprise and wealth of that community which shall secure its erection"). Broadway was widened, Columbus Circle constructed, and Central Park expanded. At Tweed's benign direction, money poured out of Albany into orphanages, almshouses, hospitals, and public baths. Elite causes, upper-class cultural programs, Catholic charities and parochial schools, Jewish institutions, and Protestant organizations all received state assistance.[100]

With Democrats in control of both the New York State Senate and Assembly, Tweed launched a campaign for charter reform aimed at reclaiming home rule for the metropolis. The *Herald* praised Tweed's imperial vision. Corporate leaders, labor groups, investors, bankers, reformers, and a host of commercial interests, as well as religious and philanthropic organizations, all joined in backing the progressive Tweed charter. Even such longtime Tammany foes as *The New York Times* and the Citizens' Association supported the changes. The few who opposed the revision—Samuel Tilden criticized it as a design for despotism, and Andrew Green feared that it would just mean more patronage—were tartly dismissed by the papers as "silk stocking magnates of the *debonair* democracy." Most New Yorkers, including such "Best Men" as the "morally irreproachable" Peter Cooper, the respected banker James Brown, John Jacob Astor III, Moses Taylor, and others of their ilk, all championed the new compact. William Martin of the West Side Association (WSA), representing the elite real estate interests, threw in his support as well.[101]

Tweed invested as much as $600,000 of his own money to guarantee the passage of the new charter, but which successful man in this age was not willing to front some money for good opportunities? Passed by an overwhelming margin, the new city charter put an end to state commissions, returned the city's government to its elected officials, and gave New York City control over its own finances. Executive departments were streamlined, redundancies eliminated, and departmental jurisdictions tightly drawn.[102]

The machine filled these niches with a cohesive, politically focused municipal workforce and proceeded to commit millions to a stylish modernization. The *Real Estate Record and Builder's Guide* later limned the machine's accomplishments: "[F]rom One Hundred and Tenth Street to Harlem river, from St. Nicholas avenue to the East river, the Boulevards and cross-streets are laid out and improved in the highest style of Tammany Art—opened, regulated, curbed, guttered and sewered, gas and water mains laid, with miles and miles of Telford-McAdam pavement, streets and avenues brilliantly lighted by fancy lamp posts." The *Herald* marveled at the talent and refinement of the new regime, which was concerned not only with improving the city, but also with rousing its soul with works of art, elegant architecture, and graceful parks. In these grand projects, the delighted editorialist reported, one could discern the metropolitan spirit that had remade Paris. It was Tweed and his cohorts who provided the resources to make Andrew Green's plans into a reality.[103]

Many of the city's leading businessmen also had reason to cheer. Tweed-influenced government proved adept at calming class tensions. Just a few years back, Manhattan's crisscrossed ethnic, class, racial, and cultural antagonisms had raised the terrifying specter of urban disorder in the Draft Riots. Tweed was a master at calming the disaffected with inexpensive tokens: Tammany turkeys at Christmastime and judicial indulgences year-round. In the burgeoning immigrant neighborhoods, the machine speeded naturalization, intervened with judges to go easy on ghetto criminals, and distributed other party favors; and it won over organized labor with its support for the eight-hour workday.[104]

Tweed's troops plied the working classes with circuses, offering them political rallies, parades and festive picnics, and identity politics. Important city posts were filled with Irish appointees, and on St. Patrick's Day Mayor Oakey Hall reviewed the parade resplendent in a green suit, with a hat, tie, and spats to match, captivating a community that had only recently been denounced for its rioting and disloyalty. Most important of all, the Democratic administration provided poor relief and employed thousands in a system of ambitious public works and citizen assistance that was unmatched until the La Guardia years of the 1930s. The Great Bridge project alone gave work to one thousand men.[105]

There was less talk these days of violence or labor threats. But business took other benefits from active government as well, claiming a hefty share of the millions that the machine committed to the growth agenda. Tweed's own men worked closely with contractors to develop large-ticket items. Then they ran these bills up to Albany, where Tammany's battalion of loyalists did what they had become expert in doing to secure approval. The decisive Tweedmen had an enchanting ability to get things done. And cost seemed to present no obstacle. In the past, local property owners lobbied against street improvements because they were billed for these projects. Mayor Hall discarded this approach. An audacious, grand city, he asserted, cannot have its street plans obstructed by "rich old men who cannot realize that New York is no longer a series of straggling villages." Declaring that the municipality and not its citizens was the master of its public spaces, City Hall accepted responsibility for half the improvement costs for the area above 14th Street, and full costs in the more extensively developed sections of lower Manhattan. The Board of Public Works (president: William M. Tweed), which replaced the Central Park Commission, inaugurated the most expensive building program in history. A separate Department of Parks, chaired by

Tammany's statesman and strategist Peter B. Sweeny, was extremely generous with its allocations. Over the fourteen years in which Central Park *was being built*, the CPC had spent about $425,000 a year. In the less than two years after Tammany took over, the Parks Department approved $2.25 million in expenditures for "improvements."[106]

This raised the interesting question of where all this money was coming from.

The proliferation of public projects should have sent taxes rocketing, affecting every property owner in the city and no doubt diminishing somewhat the luster of both the growth agenda and the Tweed government. But in fact, in this age of virtual value, when stock certificates were being printed to fund titanic battles among railroad moguls, expenses were less of a problem than might appear. While New York feasted on a banquet of expensive projects, the spending regime found a way to keep the tax bill to about one-third the cost of the expenditures. The rest was paid for by an assortment of artfully contrived sources that masked the tab for growth.[107]

The Tweed machine took a lesson from Wall Street's lawyers, brokers, and accountants, creating imaginative techniques for capitalizing debt. Instead of funding the new projects with taxes, Gotham paid with bonds that were released on the Wall Street money market. By this method, the machine freed city spending from the limits imposed by its tax base and linked its dramatically mounting expenditures to the high-flying securities market. Investors who had gone one time too many around the fast track of railroad stocks and gold ventures were only too happy to turn from Goulded securities to high-yield municipal bonds that were underwritten by Rothschild associate August Belmont and other respected bankers. London, Frankfurt, and Paris snapped up the bonds, advancing generous allowances for Gotham's new streets, sewers, and bridges. It all seemed so painless, as Tweed kept initiating new projects while charging the bill to the morrow. The more fastidious complained that capitalizing anticipated growth (or mortgaging New York's future) was a fancy term for stock watering, but good times muffled the message.[108]

The prodigal's bargain allowed Tammany to actually lower city taxes to 2 percent of assessed property value. With New York's banks doing a marvelous job of selling the securities, city debt doubled to $90 million in just two years between 1869 and 1871. Thus was profligate government underwritten by many of the same securities dealers and investment companies that had brokered the high-flying market in railroad securities.[109]

To quiet the timorous, who questioned whether a city could rebuild itself, create monumental signatures of empire, hand out generous sums to charities and churches, and at the same time cut taxes, the city administration, weeks before the 1870 election, asked six of the wealthiest and most influential New Yorkers, including John Jacob Astor III and Moses Taylor, to inspect the city's books.[110]

The all-too-gray eminences skimmed the figures with rose glasses. Too experienced to miss the hazard in so much debt, too practiced to disregard the peril of massively expanding carrying charges, they relied on the comfortable, if unfounded, assumption that the Tammany growth program would ultimately generate enough new wealth to cover its debts. They issued a strong vote of confidence, reporting that the "account books . . . are faithfully kept. . . . [W]e have personally examined the securities . . . and found them correct. We . . . certify that the financial affairs of the city . . . are administered in a correct and faithful manner."[111]

Of course, their cursory review of the books missed the largest discrepancies in city history. An outraged *New York Times* attacked the report as "a manifestation . . . of the selfishness and unscrupulousness . . . building up the great jobbing corporations, which are corrupting the Legislature and the courts." It accused the venerable Taylor (who was part of the underwriting consortium that sold city bonds overseas and also owned two Gotham utility companies) of unseemly conflict of interest in issuing the whitewash. An early opponent of the ring, the *Times* denounced Taylor as one of the "Honest Democrats" who were covering up a corrupt government.[112]

The paper was right. New York's best men had bought into the ambitious growth policies. And they were not alone. Under the machine's unbridled spending program, bankers, bond dealers, and investors reaped large profits from municipal loans and securities. Religious and philanthropic organizations claimed an unprecedented share of the city budget. Property owners saw their land values appreciate. Contractors took in more business. City contracts for advertising and printing stilled the curiosity of book, journal, and newspaper publishers. Immigrants and laborers got some jobs and some free coal and a friendlier face in City Hall. There was something for everybody in the torrent of municipal spending, and many voiced pride in New York's robust development.

So thoroughly had the Tweed outlook wormed its way into the city consciousness that honorable citizens stared at the city's cooked books and reported nothing untoward. Even Samuel Tilden, whose quixotic opposition to the Tweed charter reflected some independence, had a cordial and cooperative relationship with the Boss. Tilden was chairman of the Democratic Party since 1866, so he knew the schemes that Tammany used to pay for its gifts.[113]

Earlier in the decade, reformers had articulated a generous vision of New York and its possibilities. They had laid out a design for the future inscribed with grand metropolitan flourishes. Theirs were civic goals inspired by a desire to make city life easier, more secure, more grand. They hoped to place Gotham in the historical tradition of great metropolises both past and present; to match its powerful markets with a dramatic program of self-improvement. Civic refinement was key.

The Tweedmen took the goals of making the city better, brighter, more attractive, and gave the citizens even more than the reformers had promised—a larger, better-equipped city and a modern charter that made it possible to reimagine municipal government and grant more power to those groups that had been denied access in the past. And they did all of this while lowering taxes. Here was a powerful municipal government capable of controlling the new corporations.

But Tweed had profoundly corrupted the agenda for activist reform government. The most vigorous of the growth coalitionists, the West Side Association, boldly proclaimed the quid pro quo that underlay the city's new dynamism. William R. Martin, WSA president, declared in 1870 that the new administration had been brought into office "by our aid" and "are well paid, and paid in advance. . . . They hold certain prominent pieces of property which stand out, as one walks uptown, as so many 'Receipts of payment.'" In another era, this complaisant tolerance for bought government might have raised hackles, but in this age of falling restraints, of disappearing standards, the expectation of civic virtue had been worn down.[114]

When Alfred Beach, publisher of the *Scientific American*, proposed an underground subway in 1868, Tweed feared that the wondrous plan might pose a threat to the ring's lucrative arrangement with the existing transit franchises. By 1870, Beach, working in secrecy, had developed a prototype of the Beach Pneumatic Subway and asked the legislature for the rights to build a $5 million strip of subway up to Central Park, at no cost to the city or state. The ring countered with its own plan to erect viaducts the length of Manhattan and run trains some forty feet above the ground at an initial cost to the city of $60 million. The Astors, Horace Greeley, Peter Cooper, August Belmont, Levi Morton, and James Gordon Bennett, men not known for their cupidity, all fell in behind the Tweed plan. Clearly New Yorkers had been acclimated to think big, scorn bottom line considerations, and leave to Tweed the last word on whether something was practical or not. "You may not be aware," Washington Roebling wrote to explain why his father became disillusioned with the Great Bridge project and was preparing to retire from it shortly before he died, "that this bridge was started by the infamous 'Boss Tweed Ring' for the sole purpose of using it as a means to rob the cities [of Manhattan and Brooklyn]."[115]

It is an exaggeration. But Boss Tweed, who was one of the six members (Peter Sweeny was another) of the bridge company's executive committee, did ask for around $65,000 to pass the bill authorizing the bridge. Tweed later testified that this pittance was not meant for him. And we may believe him, for his expectations were more ambitious. The two cities, Brooklyn and New York, invested $4.5 million in the project, but Tweed's influence in Albany lodged actual control over the bridge in the hands of its private stockholders, and Tweed together with two of his closest confederates formed the single largest bloc of shareholders in the bridge company. In addition to the dividends that he expected to collect, Tweed explained later to official interrogators, he "expected to get employment for a great many laborers and . . . money for the different articles required to build the bridge."[116]

The Boss and his cohorts filled in the city's open spaces through their deals and special treatments, and in the process Tammany took the project of civic improvement and turned it inside out. "This," David Scobey writes, "was the dirty little secret" of New York's reformers. The ring adopted their plans and laced the projects with patronage and boodle, "feasting on every public undertaking."[117]

Not everything repaid the ring's interest, and when it did not, no matter how important to the future of the city, it was ignored. All agreed that Manhattan's harbor was badly in need of repair. Merchants feared that other ports would bite into their trade unless the docks were improved. They united behind a state plan to create a regional policy for the New York and Brooklyn waterways. But Tweed would not cede so important a source of patronage and contracts to Albany. He placed a strong centralized municipal Dock Department with a comprehensive harbor plan in his charter. But when pressure from the mercantile interests prevented Tammany from making the Dock Department into a patronage trough of any value, he allowed dock reform to languish.[118]

And for all the hoopla and gifts of coal that went to the working class, their "deep connection" to Tammany brought few improvements to the streets, sewers, and lights in their slum districts. The model Tenement House Act, which mandated construction and maintenance standards, required fire escapes and ventilation in bedrooms, and mandated a minimum number of privies, shut down as many as ten thousand cellar units as unsafe. It was allowed to fall into disuse under the ring. The substantial benefits that made life easier and more enjoyable were reserved for the wealthier areas.[119]

The program to give New York new parks, parkways and boulevards, new streets and utilities, new access to rapid transit, and a bridge over the East River was led by a ragtag band of mendacious clubhousemen who executed a broad parody of the grand project of urban reconstruction. Like a surrealist painting, they drew a familiar outline of metropolitan modernization but twisted it around the warped axis of graft, payoffs, and patronage. The large undertakings were distorted by a perverse motivation to spend as much public money as possible in order to yield more jobs for the machine and more graft for the Tweed forces.

When the city decided to build on a piece of property, a ring member would often buy it first and then resell it at a tremendous premium. Friendly judges helped them collect compensation for city "damages" to their property. Damages? Ring properties, many of them on the Upper East Side, were the first to be improved with streets, sewers, and other benefits, generally within months of purchase. These improvements often resulted in trumped-up lawsuits against the city, claiming botched work or collateral damages, which drained the treasury of quite remarkable sums, sometimes even exceeding the price of the land. To assure their East Side properties a competitive advantage on the real estate market, the deputy street commissioner and head of the Department of Public Works (Tweed in both instances) saw to it that West Side development proceeded much more slowly. By 1870, Tweed's real estate investments made him the city's third largest landowner.[120]

Olmsted, Vaux, and Andrew Green had envisioned a disinterested program of city betterment; Tweed made it a function of party. Green had fought with Olmsted over costs for Central Park, but both recognized that there was a limit to how much could be spent. The fear of overspending kept Green hammering at Olmsted, but Tammany dispensed money as if budgets did not matter. It led the city to the edge of bankruptcy and drove up the interest it paid on financial paper. The elite urbanists pushed efficiency; they imagined projects that stood as monuments not only to design but also to execution: solid work done under exacting supervision. Green sought for each penny paid from the city treasury a penny's worth of work. But for Tammany the quality of work was less significant than jobs, graft, and influence to get more jobs and even more graft. Even more startling than the payoffs in the infamous Tweed courthouse (a $250,000 project that ended up costing the city more than $13 million, of which the ring pocketed 65 percent), were the *repairs*—repairs that were ordered *before* the building was even opened for use; plaster repairs of over $1 million, and repair to the woodwork running to $800,000. In 1857, Tweed earned a salary of $3,600. In 1871, after fourteen years in public service, his personal fortune exceeded $6 million.[121]

A fine example of the Tweed style was his purchase of some three hundred surplus benches owned by the city, for $5 apiece. After selling seventeen of them at cost, he sold the rest back to the city for use in armories at $600 apiece. Tweed chaired the Committee on Armories. This deal cost the people of New York close to $170,000 and seventeen chairs.[122]

The ring took over the supply of stationery, printing, advertising, and office goods for the city. For six reams of notepaper, twenty-four pen holders, four ink bottles, a dozen sponges, and thirty-six boxes of rubber bands, one ring company bill came to $10,000. The city's new interest in such projects as compiling municipal records from 1675 to 1776, printed at a cost of $300,000, sent profits skyrocketing. On a capital stock of $10,000, the ring-owned New York Printing Company paid a dividend of $50,000 to $75,000 to each of its stockholders. After Tweed, Sweeny, and Connolly bought a small newspaper called the *Transcript*, it received assignments for printing a full list of the fifty thousand persons liable to serve in the army, official records of the courts, statistical reports, new ordinances, and much more. Never selling more than one hundred copies, the paper took in more than $800,000 in city contracts. Of the city's ink-stained brotherhood, twenty-six dailies and forty-four weeklies enjoyed ring-directed city advertising, and sometimes received payments outright to bury articles. The boss also bought favorable coverage in national journals and important newspapers. He passed out gifts to reporters for Christmas and gave others as much as $2,500 to use discretion in what they printed.[123]

As for the hope that a strong metropolis would take a hand to business and patrol its rougher precincts, the Boss had no such thing in mind, of course. Tweed guided city government toward a mutually rewarding relationship with the new speculating elite. After his good and valuable friend Judge George Barnard admitted him to the bar, Tweed became a very pricey part-time advocate. The Erie Railroad alone handed him a retainer of $100,000 per annum for his services, and he made many thousands more in stock profits. He served as a "consultant" to Jay Gould during the battle with Cornelius Vanderbilt, putting his judges to work helping Gould avoid prison. Few who were familiar with the extent of the cooperation between the machine and its corporate retainers would challenge Trumbull White's judgment that "the two were really one," with "the Gould-Fisk ring . . . sucking the life-blood of the Erie, [and] the Tweed-Sweeny ring . . . plundering the city of New York."[124]

When Gould's gold scheme failed, it was rumored that city money had been removed from its repository and placed in the Tenth National Bank (Directors: Gould, Fisk, Tweed, Connolly, and Mayor Hall) to save it from faltering. This was the bank that arranged Gould's $100,000 gift to President Grant's brother-in-law, Abel Corbin, and later certified $8 million in checks for Gould without adequate security. When outraged creditors pursued Gould in court, a faithful Tweed liege shielded him from their suits, for which the Boss was rewarded with a seat on the Erie board of directors. But Tweed did not discriminate. When city officials demanded that Gould nemesis Cornelius Vanderbilt cover the New York and Harlem tracks that ran along Fourth Avenue, Tweed worked out a deal for the Commodore that had the city pick up half the tab for a more modest solution.[125]

On July 22, 1871, George Jones, the crusading publisher of *The New York Times*, cracked open the scandal. His disclosures, based on pilfered secret city documents, described in great detail the ring's swindles, duplicity, and payoffs. Clearly corruption went beyond a few dollars here and there. A thoroughly venal municipal gang had sacked the city treasury and dispensed vast portions of the government to the highest bidders. Boss government did not come cheap. Estimates on the boodle acquired in this unique form of government run as high as $300 million (or roughly $3.74 billion in year 2000 dollars). The ring did steal from the rich and give to the poor, but it also profoundly cheated the poor, leaving them unprotected against abuse and privilege, denying them the benefit of fair, prudent, and rational government. By September, an aroused citizenry coalesced around a campaign to rout the rogues.[126]

---

Two separate reconstructions led from the Civil War. The one, well-known for its bitter controversies over the aftermath of slavery, the tragic loss of Lincoln's steadying hand, the rise of the Ku Klux Klan, and the impeachment of Andrew Johnson, is a story of thwarted hopes, pinched visions, timid idealists, and bold scoundrels. Pitting radicals and freedmen against redeemers and bourbons, filled with tales of scalawags and carpetbaggers, this reconstruction captures the tragic imagination with its tale of lost causes and miscarried opportunities.

The other reconstruction, far more effective than the first, albeit less conspicuous, had little to do with freedmen, the South, or forty acres and a mule. It, too, leads from the Civil War with piquant tales of official corruption and ambitious men—not a few of them knaves and rogues—seeking power and wealth. But this reconstruction ultimately replaced an American economy of local trade, modest production, and prudent investment with a corporate system of global scope. Political reconstruction involved the long-term eclipse of southern-dominated early America; economic reconstruction raised New York City to the first order of national and international prominence. "Eminent before, this chief metropolis of the seaboard," wrote business journalist James Medbery in 1870, "now assumed an absolute financial supremacy," underwriting the staggering railroad expansion.[127]

The roots of New York's influence over the postwar economy lay in the resources that it had secured in the prewar economy. America's premier entrepôt and the center of commercial capital, it gave rise to the most influential banks, and they in turn served as a powerful magnet, drawing the nation's cash reserves to Gotham. Through the call loan market, this pool of surplus capital was made broadly available and invested in railroad corporations. But the men who took the initiative to lead this new economy were not necessarily drawn from the large class of successful merchants or their progeny. Many were "new men," like the willful Commodore Vanderbilt and his younger contemporaries Gould, Drew, Fisk, and Carnegie.

Few New Yorkers grasped the implications of abstracting value from a physical commodity and placing it in certificates apart from the thing itself; or the moral or legal implications of selling long and short, using puts and calls, trading on margin, scheming on corners, and all of the modern techniques for investment and speculation. This unrestrained capitalism included some novel and—at least by established standards—unscrupulous schemes for making money and manipulating the process. Yet the institutions of law and government were disinclined to rein in the market for fear of damaging Gotham's seductive culture of venturesome endeavor and unhinging the boom prosperity. They followed the traditional counsel to doctors facing a difficult and dangerous situation: Above all do no harm. In the parlance of the day, this emerged as the broad doctrine of laissez-faire, of keeping hands off the economy.[128]

For the economy had become a thing of wonder in these growth years. The war had tested the political imagination and found it wanting. There was a time in the era of the American Revolution when political tumult had led to a deep and extensive national conversation on politics, on the relative merits of different models of government. The debates on the nature of man and government were filled with urgency and passion as the most engaged, and arguably the most intelligent and practical, men of the day sought political solutions to the outstanding problems of the age. But in the years following the Civil War, Americans grew disillusioned with politics. Its many failures had brought war, a bungled Reconstruction, an assassination, and a terrifying uncertainty for those freed from slavery.

The war had, however, stoked economic ingenuity and resourcefulness. Prosperity, industrialism, and the rise of big business held out possibilities for radically improved standards of living, a less tenuous life, and, on another plane, international leadership. In these years, economic prosperity came to stand for more than just affluence and wealth. It replaced politics as the key to a just and secure society.

Politics, badly compromised by its failures, backed off from confronting a market so ripe with promise. It was to the economy not the political arena that Americans now looked to guarantee their "pursuit of happiness." The resulting politics of inactivity opened a wide field of play for those who were willing to move first to test the new limits. New York State's "hands off" policies had fostered corporate growth and set the example for railroad policy nationwide. Despite levels of fraud and insider manipulation that a state railway commission labeled "startling," nothing was done to lay a hand on the corporations or to rein in their freewheeling activities. In the 1860s, the merchant-led New York Chamber of Commerce, whose members stood to benefit from state-imposed limits on railroad rates, nonetheless expressed their solidarity with a business ideology of laissez-faire, demanding "what right has the state to . . . unjustly interfere with the chartered right of railroad companies, and diminish their profits . . . ?"[129]

In the same years, for a too brief moment, New Yorkers glimpsed the possibilities of a growth program that promised to match Gotham's extraordinary economic achievements with ambitions for metropolitan splendor and salience. The Tweed coalition wove together disparate constituencies in common purpose and in celebration of modern possibility. The rise of a strong metropolitan coalition raised the expectation that a countervailing authority would hold corporate powers and "the rottenness that is in New York" in check. At a time when even reflective capitalists like Andrew Carnegie fretted about losing their ethical bearings, and overseas investors, just recently lured back to Gotham's securities market, were badly shaken by the Erie wars and the gold corner escapades, it would have been propitious for a strong metropolitan government to assert the right to exercise oversight. Especially in this early phase of the economic transformation, such an initiative would have set a lasting precedent.

But it did not happen. The city government that had put together the power to make such oversight possible had from the beginning lacked the integrity to carry this out, and with the fall of the Tweed Ring, this moment when New York City might have asserted a limiting authority over big business prerogatives passed.

The disgraceful collapse of the growth government resulted in a loss of confidence that cut deep. True, many New Yorkers were aware that the city regime under Mayor Hall (or, as Thomas Nast preferred, "Mayor Haul") was corrupt. But few had any idea of the magnitude and pervasiveness of the corruption, of the extent to which the entire process of graft had been made regular, that there were set percentages for payoffs, kickbacks, contracts, appointments, franchises, and so forth. The realization that day-to-day politics was merely a cover for a *system* of graft, that the city had been converted into a private fiefdom, and that its governance was merely a pretense, was chilling. The Irish, the poor, the new rich, the advocates of an ambitious city, all caught bitter blame.[130]

Tammany's fall brought down the entire house of generous city expansion and swiftly transformed New York from a bold, job-rich, deficit-defying, swaggering city of giddy prosperity to a chastened municipality forced into a corrosive retrenchment. Assigned the task of sweeping out the Augean stables, the advocate of up-city development, Andrew Green, ushered in a period of municipal austerity, throwing overboard the hugely excessive baggage of civil service, slashing salaries, and abruptly halting most development projects. Ambitious plans for monumental grace notes and programs for broad social services were abruptly terminated, leaving the population unprotected against the ravages of a looming, if as yet unrecognized, economic crisis.[131]

Green's own dream of a consolidated greater city, embracing Manhattan, Brooklyn, Queens, and other counties, became one of the first casualties of the "small city" temper. Reform mayor William Havemeyer, son of America's sugar king, even threatened to halt funding for the Brooklyn Bridge, denouncing "large and centralized schemes of local government" as dangers to "municipal liberty." As for consolidation, he declared that it was with Manhattan, "so long the City and County of New York," with which all the traditions and history and "all the conditions for our future greatness" were exclusively associated. *More, bigger,* and *better* had failed and was now replaced by an urge to pull back the exposure, to limit the possibilities of fraud, to return to a modest municipal system with statutory caps on spending and taxation. (First, though, taxes had to be raised higher than ever before to pay for the deficits.)[132]

Having failed so sensationally in its experiment in expansive, progressive government, the metropolis recoiled from centrally directed urban advance and refinement. Large-ticket government was now denounced as "by nature wasteful, corrupt and dangerous."[133] Rejecting policies for improvement and enhancement, the distrusting temper focused on what government must be *prevented* from doing. There were too many hidden corners in politics. The backlash reinforced a broader northern reaction among liberals against the national blunders of Reconstruction and against any local initiatives. If something needed to be done, it was best to leave it to the private sector.[134]

The 1870s had begun with the hope that New York City's powerfully focused machine government with its dramatic agenda for urban growth and modernization might strike a pragmatic balance among big business, merchant commerce, and labor, all of whom City Hall worked mightily to bring into its governing coalition. But these hopes foundered when the government that held out so much promise for making New York a model for aggressive urban leadership was toppled in 1871 by revelations of corruption on a scale that doomed for a generation any thought of entrusting economic regulation to local officials and legislators.

The flush buoyancy of the postwar years gave way to a period of recrimination, investigation, and disillusion. The confidence that had undergirded growth crumbled. European bankers once again pulled back their investments. The Berlin stock exchange stopped trading in New York municipal bonds. The easy hopes of reformers that a determined city policy would regulate the stock exchanges and the corporations were dashed. The discrediting of urban activism ceded the field to the advocates of laissez-faire.

Soon New York was in depression.

# CHAPTER 4

# The Fall and Rise of the New York Economy

*In the good old days . . . Wall Street did business on principles very different from those which prevail there now. Then there was a holy terror in all hearts of speculation. Irresponsible men might indulge in it and so incur the censure of the more respectable, but established houses confined themselves to a legitimate and respectable business. . . . [But] the mania for wealth leads many clear, cool headed men into the feverish whirl of speculation, and keeps them there until they have realized their wildest hopes, or are ruined.*[1]
—JAMES D. McCABE JR., *Lights and Shadows of New York Life*, 1872

TWEED LEFT BEHIND monumental budget deficits and a lingering distrust of activist government. His breathtaking mendacity put an end for some time to the notion that Gotham could build itself into a modern city through municipal initiative. Good government forces were confined to a fussy preoccupation with cutting expenditures and thinking mostly about which programs to slash. Not even the most devastating depression in the nation's history in 1873 would shake the municipal government from its new torpor, from its commitment to doing little and doing it inexpensively.

In the flush years following the war, the city economy had seemed to be planted on a cloud. A surfeit of European investment stimulated the market in railroad and municipal securities. But with the panic of 1873, that ended, too. The dismaying collapse of so many railroads, coming on the heels of Tammany's season of scandal, ushered in seven lean years. Countless businesses were thrown into bankruptcy, while those that survived were forced into competition so intense that they sought protection from the free market.

But others flourished in these hard times. A chastened Andrew Carnegie gave up his promiscuous speculations to build a steel business. Borrowing the techniques invented by the railroads, he invested in innovative technologies, and instead of lamenting declining prices (though they did decline precipitously), he built the world's most advanced facilities, pressed production efficiencies upon his workforce, and forged Carnegie Steel into the envy of the industrial world.

The spirit of the times also influenced Jay Gould toward greater responsibility. By the late 1870s, the erstwhile speculator had assembled a business empire that even the most conservative New Yorker had to respect. His empire consisted of railroads, telegraph, newspaper interests, and New York's municipal railway. The most hated man in New York, the consummate outsider, became a pillar of its establishment.

The depression of 1873 represented a test for the American economy as a whole, but it especially challenged New York. Here was the center of the economy of easy investment and endless promise, and it had crashed. Farmers and inland marketers had already begun the rural threnody that attacked the city and the changes that its economy had wrought, holding the "eastern establishment" accountable for skewering hardworking yeomen and honest laborers. Wall Street, venerated during the seven fat years as the awesome geyser of new businesses and gushing prosperity, was now denounced as a place riddled with deception and duplicity. Businessmen themselves felt trapped in a destructive spiral of plunging prices and cutthroat competition. And the flow of foreign investment dollars came to a swift halt. Three years into an extended downturn with the massive pileup of ruined railroads, banks, and brokerages—the core of the investment economy—the United States held a presidential election, offering Americans a referendum on corporate capitalism.

They were certainly eager to be heard. This presidential election attracted the largest percentage of eligible voters (82 percent of the electorate) to the polls in U.S. history. A plurality cast their votes for Samuel J. Tilden, the wealthy New York attorney with a background in railroad and real estate investment, and the law partner of Andrew Green. Almost perverse in his lack of charisma, the humorless Tilden was a man for this season, when Americans tired of Ulysses Grant and the politics of personality. An outspoken opponent of the Tweed Ring, Tilden stood for probity in government and business, but this millionaire attorney with a long corporate client list was no opponent of investment capitalism.[2]

By a plurality of more than three hundred thousand, Americans voted for the New Yorker. Even in the midst of a depression, voters showed no inclination to change the economic system or the role played by the New York investment market. In one of the most questionable of American elections, Rutherford B. Hayes was ultimately installed in the White House, though it made little difference to the Gotham business community, for he too supported the new investment economy.[3]

The election marked an important change in Gotham's place in the nation. Except for Martin Van Buren, no New Yorker had ever been elected president, reflecting the early dominance of the South with its agrarian outlook. But following the Civil War, Manhattan-based politicians took center stage in virtually every presidential election for the rest of the century. Not only was the metropolitan influence greatly expanding across the land, but its influence and the influence of a Gotham-based capitalist establishment, as represented by the New York Chamber of Commerce, became commonplace.

---

In April of 1873, the papers reported that the "saturnine little man [who] is forever 'putting up jobs' on the gentlemen who . . . dabble in . . . commodities" paid a visit to Wall Street. Jay Gould spent some time talking to business associates, and then he repaired to

Delmonico's for lunch. A man who turned out to be an attorney strode over to the scrawny manipulator, cursed him for bilking a client, and, as the frail Gould tried to shake him off, beat the reviled speculator around the face.[4]

Times had turned tough for Gould. The gold scheme had failed. His important friend Tweed had run away to avoid prison. Gould's personal finances were in disarray. He lost control of the Albany and Susquehanna Railroad, and his sworn enemy Cornelius Vanderbilt had acquired the Lake Shore road, placing the New York Central through to Chicago, quashing Gould's dreams of a railroad monopoly to the Midwest. The painfully withdrawn Gould had set the public welfare at bold defiance, and now his every move attracted attention and rebuke. Finally, in the early months of 1872, Erie's stockholders ousted him. But not before Jim Fisk, his one good friend, was fatally shot by his mistress Josie Mansfield's new lover. Of the flamboyant deceased, journalist J. G. Dudley would write: "We should not judge too harsh of James Fisk. He was a creature of circumstance—a legitimate fruit of [the] public and private morality existing when he began his career. He found legislatures corrupt and he purchased them; he found judges venal and he bribed them; he found a large part of society fond of vulgar display, dash and barbaric magnificence and he gratified the taste of that portion of society. . . . Let the mantle of charity cover his sins. . . ."[5]

The passionately despised Gould was still too much alive to merit similar dispensation. Fined $200, his tormentor told friends that it was money well spent. He had laid hands on the most hated man on the Street, a man "whose name built upon ruins, carries with it a certain whisper of ruin . . . whose nature is best described by . . . the burden of hatred and dread that, loaded upon him for two and a half years, has not turned him one hair from any place that promised him gain and the most bitter ruin for his chance opponents. They that curse him do not do it blindly, but as cursing one who massacres after victory."[6]

In 1873, the New York air hung heavy with the sensation of massacres following victory. Journals of opinion were reporting with a sense of foreboding about a runaway economy that was moving forward more on momentum than on strong fundamentals. Speculators, undertaking ever more hazardous ventures, seemed to be daring the market to punish them, asking for some sign to stop committing so much to risky investments.

The year started with troubling omens. The day following New Year's, the papers related that the Jay Cooke banking house, perhaps the most respected financial institution in the country, was relying on high political connections and payoffs to win business and that it had become entangled in shaky railroad investments. The price of gold was fluctuating, threatening stability. And Americans' appetite for continental finery and the expensive products of foreign manufacturers had saddled the nation with vexing trade imbalances. "A season of ruin and disaster threatens," thundered a financial report, "in which the small fry, as usual, will most certainly be consumed and in which the heavier operators must make or break."[7]

Over the next few months, businesses failed at a disturbing rate. Pressure on the money market sent loan rates as high as 1 percent a day. As important brokerages and underwriters folded, tens of millions of dollars in investments were wiped out. Then, in the third week of September, the Jay Cooke firm faced a crisis. Cooke, the hero of Civil War finance, had invested in the Northern Pacific Railroad, hoping, in the ambition of the age, to become a railroad titan. It took a very special genius to buy up troubled roads at bargain rates and make them into solid stocks, and Cooke, it became distressingly clear, lacked the touch. The Northern Pacific road, its books a sea of red, was sucking up capital at an alarming rate. Cooke struggled to raise money. But some twenty-five railroads had recently failed to meet their bond payments, and the bulls were fleeing the market. Northern Pacific found no buyers. Cooke dipped into client deposits to pay bills, hoping to raise the money to repay. Finally, on September 18, Cooke company officials called together influential Wall Street financial houses and tried desperately to peddle millions in discounted Northern Pacific bonds, hoping to stave off ruin. There were no takers, and Cooke & Co., the leading investment bank in the nation, tumbled into bankruptcy.[8]

In confident times, New Yorkers boldly swept up bargains on price dips. Not now. Panic gripped the markets as stock prices fell and investors rushed to unload their securities. Brokerages were caught with high margins on collateral (stocks) that was sinking in value. Depositors descended upon banks to demand their savings, too large a portion of which were invested in the declining securities. Country banks snatched back their reserves, constricting the funds available for loans. Call loans were summoned back, forcing speculators to liquidate. Within a week Wall Street's banks, brokerages, and insurance companies were reeling. Merchants, used to boundless good times and easy credit, kept begging for loans to tide them over, but the loan market froze over. With shocking swiftness, the underpinnings of a seven-year boom collapsed.[9]

For the first time since its founding, the New York Stock Exchange shut down. It did not reopen for ten days. European markets, also unsteady, provided no comfort. A slump that began in Vienna spread to other capitals, sending European markets into a tailspin.[10]

The railroads were the most vulnerable. Reckless assumptions about future growth had saturated the market with railroad securities representing roads that too often were little more than a plot of land, a sheaf of certificates, and a dream. Of 364 rail securities listed in 1872, only 104 brought in enough earnings to distribute dividends. Many could not even cover operating costs. Risk-eager banks and insurance companies had advanced them loans, and fast-talking underwriters had sold their securities overseas to buyers who knew little about the difference between Ashtabula and Philadelphia. Now the combination of collapsed brokerages, European panic, and lingering misgivings about Tweeded municipal paper brought overseas investment to a halt. The British market would not take American bonds, a journalist wrote, "even if signed by an angel of Heaven." Countless railroads busted, and western expansion ceased.[11]

The banker J. P. Morgan called in his loans. "Affairs continue un-precedentedly bad," he cabled his father in London. Before the end of the year, more than five thousand commercial businesses expired. Fifty-seven brokerages failed. "Everything looks dark," August Belmont wailed. "I have met with greater losses . . . than I have ever known. . . ." His son wanted to leave Harvard to join Dad in the business, but Belmont resisted, writing back in despair: "You cannot imagine the utter prostration." Finally the entire house of cards went toppling, "ushering in," in the words of historian Eric Foner, "the first great crisis of industrial capitalism . . . shattering faith in the inevitability of progress and exacerbating class conflict. . . ."[12]

To a relative contemplating a move to Gotham, metal mogul Uriah Hendricks instructed, simply, stay away. The city was "no place for men without money." As many as three million Americans were out of work in 1874. In Gotham, with one million inhabitants, an estimated one hundred thousand were jobless. Thousands were evicted from their homes, and over the winter more than ninety thousand citizens were lodged at one time or another in the city's police stations. "It is not pleasant to reflect," the *Herald* reported cheerlessly, "that there are two New Yorks, the one plunged in the most abject misery, wanting all the necessaries of life, shivering from cold, borne down by disease, crowded into the unwholesome tenement houses of the poor quarters, which are now in truth, dwellings of sorrow and affliction. . . . Hundreds wander, homeless, in this great city through the winter storm . . . in the midst of plenty they starve," while the rich went about their privileged lives. The *Herald* called for soup kitchens to feed the poor.[13]

Vast sections of the new economy were wiped out. *Half* the railroads in the nation fell into receivership, sending many of the foundries, mines, and factories that fed and clad the iron horse into ruin. Life insurance companies, heavily invested in the railroads, suffered. Of thirty chartered after 1861, only eight were still selling insurance in 1877. European investors lost $600 million, mostly on American railroad securities. "Never . . . ," wrote the New York

Chamber of Commerce in its review of the iron industry, "has a darker cloud rested over its prospects. . . ." William Steinway, unable to sell a single piano, hastened to incorporate his business to limit his liability. As Manhattan properties sank to half their 1872 values, vacancies cratered the most desirable commercial streets.[14]

Western farmers attributed plunging agricultural prices to sinister "eastern interests," but city-manufactured goods, including lighting, metal goods, chemicals, building materials, and household furnishings, all declined more steeply than farm crops. Heavy products like manufactured steel rails came down from $120 in 1873 to $48 in 1879. And destructive railroad competition pushed carrying fares down even more.[15]

With prices tanking, railroads closing, and Wall Street littered with the hulks of failed financial houses, one of the most successful of New York's new men turned from trading businesses and rigging securities to building an industry from the bottom up. For more than a decade, Andrew Carnegie had been extraordinarily successful playing the speculative markets, but depression had put an end to that. He kept his Broad Street office, but Tom Scott's wunderkind manipulator, who had so thrilled at making money that did not "come from the sweat of my brow," left behind the securities market to establish one of America's foundation industries, building steel into the country's first billion-dollar corporation. He never did get to Oxford University to acquire the refinement that he coveted, and he did not retire at thirty-five as he had promised himself, but he signaled his about-face by turning down Jay Gould's invitation to join in raiding the Pennsylvania Railroad in 1872. With that he abandoned the company of speculators.[16]

Carnegie had been an excellent trader, adept at misleading, bluffing, and deceiving. He had played with the fortunes of friends and others, and not always with integrity, to make his riches. But times had changed and he no longer felt comfortable winding in and out of businesses, leaving over the detritus of gutted corporations. He described the new approach (reflecting the changed business environment) in his *Autobiography*: Put "all your good eggs in one basket and then watch that basket," adding, "As for myself . . . I would concentrate upon the manufacture of iron and steel and be master in that." He had passed through half a dozen businesses in a decade, but in the course of a depression that laid waste other fortunes, his genius for risk taking and putting to excellent advantage his New York contacts made a business pioneer of this most complicated of industrial America's founders.[17]

Among his many earlier acquisitions, Carnegie held a controlling interest in the Freedom Iron Company, a producer of rails and assorted iron products. The typical iron foundry was a congeries of separate shops that produced pig iron, iron rails, nails, and stoves. Each division of the company would take orders and turn out its own product line, with little direction or control from above. "The cost of each of the processes was unknown," Carnegie recalled. "It was a lump business and until stock was taken and the books balanced at the end of the year, the manufacturers were in total ignorance. . . ." Applying his experience from the Pennsylvania Railroad, Carnegie centralized Freedom's operations, taking control over its many functions. In short order he integrated Freedom's diverse production units and established firm accounting procedures to create a cost basis for business decisions.[18]

After molding Freedom into a modern industrial mill, he became interested in steel. It was no secret that steel, with its superior tensile strength and suppleness, represented the material of the future. Yet American steel production was minuscule, and American mills were turning out an inferior product that was much more expensive than British steel. By 1870, the discovery in Michigan's upper peninsula of an immense field of pure and readily accessible iron ore, and the elimination of technical barriers preventing the use of Bessemer technology ("No improvement in practical metallurgy since the time of Tubal-Cain," *Popular Science Monthly* remarked about the Bessemer process, "realized such magnificent results in increasing the quantity produced and diminishing the selling price of a metal"), eliminated the most formidable obstacles to the growth of an American steel industry.[19]

Here was the basket into which Carnegie wanted to put all his eggs. He traveled to England to study the world's leading steel foundries, absorbing everything he could about steel production. He returned with large plans for steel. Rejecting the notion of converting some of Freedom's iron-making equipment and building a steel industry by inches, he selected a site along the banks of the Monongahela and designed a modern plant with the latest technology, from the foundation up.

By the time he was ready to begin, the hour had become less auspicious. Businesses were falling around him, credit had evaporated, and a number of his partners backed out of their commitments. Half the nation's railroads had defaulted on their bonds. Track construction had stopped. Cancellations on rail orders closed 50 percent of the nation's iron furnaces. His own iron mills fell behind in their receipts. Steel prices were dropping. But Carnegie refused to give up his plan to make American steel the standard worldwide.[20]

He needed more than $1 million to build. But if New York had taught him the need to focus and innovate, it had also made him wary of its penchant for playing with the futures of large businesses. If there was one lesson that he took from his salad days in securities manipulation, it was that he did not want to establish his business on the shifting sands of the stock market. He did not want Wall Street's brokers and plungers pushing prices up and down, making a plaything of his company and its reputation. Nor did he want get-rich-quick stockholders pressing him to declare high dividends at the expense of long-range development. He wanted to build for the long term and it would take New York's money market some time to make that adjustment. Instead, he packed up his drawings and projections, boarded a transatlantic steamer, and set out for London. There he sought out Junius Morgan, father of John Pierpont, who directed the largest American-owned bank in England. Carnegie laid out his dreams for American steel and walked out with a

$400,000 commitment. He raised some more capital by selling his Pullman and Western Union stocks. Then he sought more funding in the United States.[21]

The depression had badly wounded his patron, friend, and business partner, Tom Scott. On the edge of ruin, Scott desperately begged Carnegie to sign notes to get him over his crisis. In a decision that saddened Carnegie for the rest of his life, he refused to help Scott. Carnegie's decision ended Scott's career and hurried his death, but Carnegie wanted to establish a credible independence apart from his speculating partners. "Up to this time I had the reputation in business of being a bold, fearless and perhaps somewhat reckless young man . . . to have been rather more brilliant than substantial," he wrote. And he wanted to change that image. When he reported to his creditors that he had spurned his good friend to protect the interests of the company, "our credit," he recalled with pride, "became unassailable." He raised the money for his foundry and proceeded to erect the largest, most modern steel plant in the nation.[22]

Then he sold all his other holdings to "concentrate my attention upon our manufacturing concerns. No sound judgement can remain with the man whose mind is disturbed by the mercurial changes of the Stock Exchange. . . . Speculation is a parasite feeding upon values, creating none."[23]

The times were as hard as ever before in the century, but it all depended upon how you looked at it. By building in the depression Carnegie was able to shave 25 percent off the costs of construction. Based in New York, the headquarters for large undertakings, he assembled the plans, the money, and the human capital to build American steel. He attracted to the new project some of the most experienced steel men in the nation, bringing the charismatic father of American Bessemer production, Alexander L. Holley, to New York, where the two of them planned a Pittsburgh empire around the creation of a state-of-the-art steelworks. Carnegie stocked the new company with managers of proven excellence. He took no bargains in his senior officials, declaring, "There is no labor so cheap as the dearest, in the mechanical field."[24]

The ruthless competitive instinct that he had honed in Gotham he brought to steel, hard driving the plants, the managers, and the workers. Carnegie installed the latest technology, making frequent upgrades even when it meant expensive overhauls. ("We have equipment that we have been using for twenty years and it is still serviceable," an English steelman once remarked to Carnegie. "And that," he replied, "is what is wrong with the British steel trade.") The blast furnaces ran at a blistering pace. Foreign manufacturers warned that such "reckless" use would ruin the costly furnace linings. Carnegie remained unfazed. If he could produce fast enough and build demand high enough, the profits would pay for new furnace linings many times over.[25]

The other producers did not think this way. They couldn't; they lacked the figures and the accounting techniques that would allow them to arrive at a reliable projection of costs and to systematically weigh alternatives. Forced to rely on impressions and rough guesswork, they had only the most imprecise notion of the cost benefit of expensive innovations. Only Carnegie's mills employed the precise accounting techniques developed by New York's most advanced corporations to assess the effectiveness of production policies.[26]

Carnegie stayed in New York, keeping his distance from the mills. He wrote to his manager in the third month of operations, after the company had already turned an $18,000 profit: "It is a grand concern and sure to make us all a fortune . . . [w]ith you at the helm and me pulling an oar on the outside. . . ." This outside role was by design. It allowed him to keep his ear to the ground at his centrally located Broad Street offices, doing what the new crop of industrial executives were learning to do well: select experts, give them direction and financing, and hector them through frequent communiqués designed to stir the managing staff and set company strategy. An important part of that strategy was producing at a high standard, and he become furious when his foundries shipped defective goods. "I would rather today pay out of my pocket 5000 dollars," he wrote one manager after a complaint about imperfect rails, "than have this disgraceful failure occur."[27]

Six months after opening his Edgar Thomson (ET) steel works, Carnegie was gloating, "Where is there such a business!" Rails accounted for 90 percent of his output in these years, and he traded tirelessly on his railroad connections. "There was not a railroad president or purchasing agent in the entire country with whom he was not personally acquainted," his biographer writes. They divulged to him what rivals were charging, and he undercut the price. Competitors were "very bitter against us," his manager reported, but Carnegie was undaunted. "For my part, I would run the works full next year even if we made but $2 a ton," as long as he sold an immense number of tons.[28]

Carnegie's competitors, backed by the analyses of academic economists and their own colleagues, were convinced that falling prices were a catastrophe to be avoided at all costs. Carnegie went along with industry-wide agreements to limit production and fix price minimums, but when the market weakened, or he had some advantage to exploit quickly, Carnegie ignored the agreements. It was not only that he had disdain for his competitors, he believed that protecting high prices was not the way to launch a fledgling industry. Protecting price was a prescription for keeping the industry small and limited.[29]

From his Manhattan offices he planned a bold strategy for rapid continuous production so that his mills could mass-produce steel. The scale of operations was matched by no other industry but the railroads. While the other producers concentrated on competing against each other for wedges of the steel market, he set out to vastly enlarge that market, aiming to make steel into the most popular high-grade construction material in the world. He not only fought for dominance over the other steel companies but aggressively competed to win market share away from iron, wood, and masonry by dramatically reducing the price of steel through the economies of mass production.

Mass-producing steel in a dry market, no matter how efficiently, was laden with risk. It could result in truly ruinous losses if inventory piled up. But Carnegie entertained no doubt about his ability to sell as much steel as his mills could turn out. He boosted public awareness and confidence in steel at every opportunity. At dinner parties in Gramercy Park and intermissions at the New York Metropolitan Opera he zealously promoted steel. A member of the Committee on Exhibition Buildings for the 1876 U.S. Centennial Exposition, he induced the committee to change its main exhibition hall from wood to iron and steel. He won the contract to supply steel for the Brooklyn Bridge, highlighting the desirability of the "metal of the future." And it was Carnegie metal that went into America's first steel-framed office buildings. In an environment where one businessman testified "you could not give a rolling mill away," he continued to run his furnaces at full throttle, undercutting the competition, shaving costs, and prowling the land for sales.[30]

Carnegie, a partner once said, did not pay so much attention to profits. "He always wanted to know . . . cost." Two months after his ET mill began producing steel rails, it cost $56.64 to produce one ton. By 1878 he had improved efficiency to the point that production costs were down to $36.52, and over the next twenty years Carnegie brought the cost down to $12 a ton. Carnegie's mass production efficiencies actually brought the price of steel rails down below those for less-desirable iron, driving iron rails from the market. Focusing on "small profits & large sales," he rang up millions.[31]

Three years after its opening no one in the industry could match Carnegie's mills for production volume or efficiency. Yet, Carnegie remained almost pathological about cutting costs. Despite record earnings and a mounting financial reserve, he kept pressing for more. To the manager who telegraphed that he had broken all production records the past week, Carnegie shot back, "Congratulations! What about next week?" Waste products were turned into marketable commodities. Wood buildings were converted to iron to save on fire insurance. Obsessively collecting data about the entire industry, he would press his executives to outpace the competition. Then he set them against one another. Different plants, furnace teams, and production lines were placed in competition, and companywide quotas were set at the level of the most productive of the units.[32]

Well placed in New York to mingle with investors from all over the United States and the European industrial nations, his access to banking, shipping, and investment information gave him an extraordinary feel for the market, allowing him to take orders and set prices six months into the future with an uncanny ability to project demand and financial conditions both here and abroad. No amount of time at the Pittsburgh mills could give him this tactile grasp of the global market. It also gave him the confidence to wave aside the industry's parochial concerns with protecting price in favor of building an empire in the depression.[33]

There was another more subtle effect of his being removed from his Pittsburgh mills, directing operations from Manhattan. His distance from the local scene fostered a perverse outlook toward his partners, his competitors, and his workers. Almost from the beginning he went about shrinking the number of his partners, developing heartless strategies to force them to sell out, one by one, as he tightened his own grip on the steel empire that they had helped him erect. It was the same with the steel makers. Many trusted one another and worked together as a kind of community of steel men. He remained a metropolitan outsider aloof from their rules, disdaining their approval.

He was particularly distant toward labor. No cost attracted so much of his attention as the expenditures on wages. In this he mirrored the common business thinking of his Gotham colleagues. There was "no reason," August Belmont declared, "why laborer's wages should not be reduced in times of depression," as he proceeded to cut wages on his Long Island property from $2 to $1.50 a day. In 1876, New York replaced its municipal workers with day laborers, paring salaries by as much as 65 percent, while average annual earnings declined steadily nationwide from the predepression figure of $486 in 1872 to $373 in 1879.[34]

As technology transformed the working process, reducing many to low-skilled ciphers in a mechanized manufacturing system, industrialists adopted the self-serving viewpoint that labor was to be dealt with like machines and raw materials, as simple costs of production. And like any other cost, it had to be brought down as low as could be gotten. There were other ways to look at this. Carnegie's general superintendent, Captain William Jones, once wrote back after being ordered to reduce wages that the company ought to "leave good enough alone." The workers were doing their best to meet quotas. They were working long hours faithfully. If wages were again cut, "we will lose heavily." Jones knew Carnegie's feelings on the matter, so he underscored his recommendation. "Now mark what I tell you. Our labor is the cheapest in the country. Our men have Esprit de Corps. . . . Low wages does not always imply cheap labor. Good wages and good workmen I know to be cheap labor." But though Carnegie listened to Jones this time, he rejected Jones's thinking, relying instead on what he called the "Darwinian principle of the survival of the fittest."[35]

Carnegie hectored his managers mercilessly. "I learn that the Crane Iron Company is now paying but sixty cents a day for labor and," he emphasized, "the result is better than when they gave two dollars." When local ministers protested the seven-day work week for violating the Sabbath, Carnegie's plant supervisor "notified our bigoted and sanctimonious cusses that in the event of their attempting to interfere with these works, I will retaliate by promptly discharging any workman who belongs to their Churches. . . . If they don't want to work when I want them, I shall take good care that they don't work when they want to."[36]

In New York business circles it was not enough to make money, or to build a company that enjoyed technological supremacy, possessed the best managers, and boasted a growing financial reserve. Here was a man of some intellectual pretension, who had looked deep into his own psyche and warned that business would block out his other interests, that the urge to make money would consume him well beyond reasonable need.

And it had.

Capitalized in 1876 at $1.25 million, the company returned stunning profits of $300,000, one-quarter of its value, in its first year. An exultant Carnegie boasted of the firm's success to Junius Morgan, "Even if the tariff were off entirely [something manufacturers publicly equated with the death of the Republic], you couldn't send steel rails to the west of us." Yet despite rocketing profits, Carnegie continued to push wages down, to press managers to drive up output, and to force his partners out of the firm. His fierce competitiveness is hard to overstate. His compulsion to control steel was complete. He compelled associates who joined the company to sign an "Iron Clad Agreement" that prevented them from either selling or transferring their interest to anyone outside the small circle of owners. And he kept making that circle smaller, concentrating power and profit in his own hands. He insisted that William Coleman, a friend who had helped him with other ventures and was his brother Tom's father-in-law, be squeezed out of ET, assigning the distasteful task to Tom Carnegie. He bought out half a dozen other partners by taking advantage of their need for cash.[37]

Within a generation steel became the metal of choice for heavy machinery, railroads, bridges, elevated railways, and the tall office buildings that changed the face of metropolitan America. In 1870, U.S. Bessemer production stood at thirty-eight thousand tons, less than one-seventh of British output. A decade later, production had soared to more than one million tons. In 1881, when Carnegie Bros. & Company was formally reorganized with a $5 million capitalization, profits reached $2 million. Within another ten years, the United States was the single largest supplier of world steel; and by 1900, Andrew Carnegie's foundries produced more steel than all of Britain.[38]

Applying lessons learned from the railroads, Carnegie invested in innovative technologies and gambled on expanding the market. While competitors took profits in the form of dividends, Carnegie plowed earnings back into capital improvements. And while others circled to protect prices, he slashed them repeatedly, making steel competitive with other building materials. A pathbreaker in so many things, he also would go on to create a revolution in philanthropy, contributing more than $350 million toward improving society. Yet for all of his progressive thinking, he could not break free of the convention that rigidly separated business from good works. In business he continued to be driven by a feral urge for profit, helping mold the Wall Street trinity of laissez-faire, social Darwinism, and the market theory of wages that did so much to make late-nineteenth-century business an extension of the jungle.

For this he borrowed extensively from the English philosopher Herbert Spencer. Andrew Carnegie's first encounter with Spencer left him overwhelmed: "Light came as in a flood and all was clear." Spencer was grandly received upon his visit to New York in the 1873 panic year, collecting the honors that observers have suggested fall to the personality who perfectly captures the zeitgeist. Businessmen, who had paid little attention to formal philosophy before, lionized the English social theorist, devouring his books, which popularized the notion of "survival of the fittest." What some have labeled his "magnificent exegesis" transformed Darwin's biological hypothesis into a social imperative, declaring that in social (and especially economic) life as in biology, survival was a competition in which the strong succeeded (opened corporations and grew rich), the weak failed (became workers or unemployed), and natural (social) processes eliminated the unfit (the hapless poor). In the same unmediated way that natural selection drove the evolution of the species, free competition balanced the economy, maximized its productivity, and propelled economic progress. It was as perilous and futile to tamper with the workings of the market as it was to try to turn back biological evolution. Endowing cupidity with high moral purpose, Spencer's "social Darwinism" provided Carnegie and much of Wall Street with a rationale for laissez-faire and unbounded profit lust.[39]

Moses Taylor, the trader who discovered that finance was more lucrative than shipping and helped New York make the leap from commercial center to financial capital. (N.Y. PUBLIC LIBRARY PICTURE COLLECTION)

Gotham's first dry goods king, Alexander T. Stewart, modernized retailing and made "shopping" a middle-class pleasure, while centralizing the importation and production of dry goods. (N.Y. PUBLIC LIBRARY PICTURE COLLECTION)

Cornelius Vanderbilt, the shipping mogul who late in life built a railroad empire around the New York Central. Before he was finished, he controlled one of the largest rail networks in the hemisphere. (N.Y. PUBLIC LIBRARY PICTURE COLLECTION)

Civic leader, New York City comptroller, real estate attorney, and urban planner who helped lay out much of upper Manhattan, Andrew H. Green won the sobriquet "Father of Greater New York" for leading the campaign for the city's 1898 consolidation. (SEYMOUR B. DURST OLD YORK LIBRARY)

Wall Street's Mephistopheles, stock manipulator extraordinaire Jay Gould is seen here *(left)* planning one of his deals with railroad speculator W. A. H. Loveland. Gould ultimately put together an immense transit-transport-communications-information empire. (N.Y. PUBLIC LIBRARY PICTURE COLLECTION)

Over the course of a career that took him from immigrant bobbin boy to America's "Man of Steel," Andrew Carnegie built an early fortune from corporate investment. While competitors focused on protecting prices, his energies went into high-tech modernization and ruthless cost cutting. (N.Y. PUBLIC LIBRARY PICTURE COLLECTION)

History's best-known urban boss, William M. Tweed, honeycombed New York's municipal service with thousands of Tammany loyalists and controlled all the major municipal offices. He modernized the city, but the costs, both staggering and staggeringly dishonest, led to his downfall. (SEYMOUR B. DURST OLD YORK LIBRARY)

Corporate attorney and governor, New York Democrat Samuel J. Tilden won the popular vote for the presidency in 1876, reflecting a strong vote of confidence in the new corporate system despite the depressed times. (SEYMOUR B. DURST OLD YORK LIBRARY)

Junius Spencer Morgan, a successful New England merchant, resettled in London and became the leading American banker to the Atlantic investment community. Morgan scrupulously molded the American banking career of his son, J. P. Morgan. (ARCHIVES OF THE PIERPONT MORGAN LIBRARY, NEW YORK)

Founder of the Standard Oil Trust, John D. Rockefeller built the monopoly into a Gotham-based multinational conglomerate, even as he acquired the world's richest iron holdings along the Mesabi Range. He was a fierce advocate of business consolidation. (SEYMOUR B. DURST OLD YORK LIBRARY)

The man who dominated Gilded Age finance, John Pierpont Morgan rationalized the railroad industry, served as the U.S. government's banker, and was Wall Street's chief underwriter. He determined the destiny of countless new corporations and carried out the first billion-dollar consolidation by putting together U.S. Steel. (This photo was retouched to cover the rhinophyma that deformed Morgan's nose.) (ARCHIVES OF THE PIERPONT MORGAN LIBRARY, NEW YORK)

Erected in 1872–1873, the six-story marble headquarters of the Drexel, Morgan bank occupied the power corner of Wall and Broad Streets at 23 Wall Street, directly across from the New York Stock Exchange. (J. P. MORGAN CHASE ARCHIVES, NEW YORK)

Upper Fifth Avenue featured a vista of mansions, castles, and palaces built by the new nobility of Wall Street. This view of Millionaires Mile includes two Vanderbilt mansions. In such churches as St. Thomas and Fifth Avenue Presbyterian, seen here, *Baedeker's* reported, the clergy "preached to $250 million each Sunday." (N.Y. PUBLIC LIBRARY PICTURE COLLECTION)

Henry George, the popular reformer and author of the influential tract *Poverty and Progress*, ran for mayor on a labor ticket in 1886. He attracted more than a third of the vote, placing elite New York on notice that labor intended to use the franchise to protect its interests. (N.Y. Public Library Picture Collection)

New York's most famous cigar maker, English-born Samuel Gompers organized craft workers into unions and brought these unions together to maximize their power through the New York–based American Federation of Labor. (N.Y. Public Library Picture Collection)

A product of New York's reform Republican fringe, Theodore Roosevelt masterminded a career that carried him from the New York State Assembly to the White House. He championed a progressive politics to keep big business in check. (Library of Congress)

Wall Street in 1850. This artist's lithograph offers a wider-than-real-life perspective, dominated by Trinity Church and stately three-story buildings, many of them banks and insurance firms, including the flag-topped Customs House, which in 1862 became the U.S. Sub-Treasury. On the south side *(left)* stand private dwellings. (N.Y. Public Library Picture Collection)

This rendering shows Wall Street's 1890s profile. The towering new structures give the street its modern canyonlike character.

(Seymour B. Durst Old York Library)

Two views of the New York Stock Exchange. In 1850 *(top)*, its several dozen members would come together for the twice-a-day calling of the stocks. In 1865, the NYSE moved into permanent quarters in a marble palazzo-style building on Broad Street *(bottom)*. By the end of the century, the exchange was trading 1.5 million shares on some days. By 1901, the NYSE had outgrown these quarters; they were demolished and replaced in 1903 with the present Renaissance-style structure that features a cavernous trading floor. (Seymour B. Durst Old York Library)

The East River Bridge, better known as the Brooklyn Bridge, in the year it was opened, 1883. It joined the cities of Brooklyn and New York, which became one municipality in the consolidation of Greater New York in 1898. (N.Y. Public Library Picture Collection)

The depression and the changed business environment also worked its effects on the diminutive Mephistopheles, Jay Gould. His career had traced an inconstant line in the black art activities of speculation, manipulation, and market fixing. But after draining Erie and unabashedly threatening America's monetary system, Gould, whom adversaries hated and feared in equal measure (John D. Rockefeller called him the "smartest man in America"), turned to building an empire.[40]

When he was still presiding over the Erie Railroad late in 1868, Gould had developed a broad program to improve the railroad and make it competitive with the Northeast's principal trunk lines. He was not able to carry through his own plan, but his instinct for guerrilla capitalism and his facility for using the power of the New York money market to change business priorities spurred his competitors to expand in ways they had been quite prepared to avoid. Business historian Alfred Chandler suggests that by forcing the Pennsylvania and the New York Central to think continentally and to unify the railroad system, Gould exerted the single greatest impact on "system building in American transportation."[41]

Fighting to turn Erie around before he was deposed, Gould resolved to build a ramifying transport system that led from New York to the Midwest, with Erie at its head. This system he would splice together from smaller "feeder" roads, many of which already had cooperative agreements with the Pennsylvania Railroad. Or, to put it another way, he would raid his competitor.

Despite its size and importance, the Pennsylvania had deliberately limited itself to a core system of roads. It had avoided expansion through merger, construction, or acquisition in the belief that a road stretched longer than five hundred miles became too expensive and complicated to operate. To extend its reach to the interior, it relied on informal alliances with subsidiary roads that had pledged to transfer goods and passengers exclusively to the Pennsylvania. Its president, Edgar Thomson, explained: "The policy of this Company

[is] . . . directed to the procuring of . . . connections . . . without involving this company in the direct management of distant enterprises." This method avoided expensive construction and upkeep, and it had the additional benefit of not stirring up the national "prejudice against large corporations."[42]

A "raider by profession," Gould set out to strip his competition of these feeders by buying up enough shares in the smaller lines to gain a voice in their policies and switch them to his Erie. In the days before anonymous trading in company stocks it would take weeks or months to carry out each of these deals, and it would be impossible to keep it all secret. The Wall Street exchange made it possible to orchestrate this plan swiftly and quietly. It took Thomson weeks to realize what Gould was up to, but then he took the wake-up call. "[I]t became evident to your Board," the Pennsylvania president wrote in a report, "that this Company must depart" from its past policies "and obtain direct control of its western connections." The Pennsylvania moved decisively "to reach all important points in the West"—actually all major commercial and extractive centers in the nation—by buying, building, or merging with local lines. Once the Pennsylvania, the largest private company in the world, decided to buy and build, Gould could not match its power.[43]

He turned instead to snipping away the New York Central's feeders, this time rousing Vanderbilt's fears. In one of their competitive clashes, Gould and Vanderbilt sent the price of shipping upstate cattle to New York City tumbling from $125 a carload to $100 to $75 to $50 to $25, and finally to $1 a carload or a penny per head. When the Commodore realized what his nemesis was up to, he followed Thomson's lead, reversed his earlier aversion to system building, and began directly annexing western links to ward off Gould's incursions.[44]

Gould changed the industry. His own plans for the Erie never took off, and they failed to save him from wrath of its stockholders, but they did force others to think large. In just a few years, the Pennsylvania, the New York Central, and John W. Garrett's Baltimore and Ohio utilized the New York securities market to assemble extensive rail networks that reached far inland. Between 1869 and 1873, the Pennsylvania, for example, obtained roads leading to Columbus, Cincinnati, Indianapolis, and Louisville, as well as lines running from the lake ports and lumber region of Michigan. Through long-term leases and outright purchase, it acquired routes from Philadel-phia and other rail centers to New York; it ran lines to Washington, Baltimore, Chicago, St. Louis, Detroit, Buffalo, Toledo, and other leading cities. From a road with less than five hundred miles of track, it expanded into a national system of close to six thousand miles, capitalized at $400 million, or 13 percent of the value of all Ameri-can railroads.[45]

Gould had thrown many balls in the air and, it seemed, missed catching all of them. Ironically, though, when Erie's stockholders dispatched Gould from the board in March 1872, his departure sent the road's stock price soaring, making him a rich man again from the sale of his Erie holdings. This fortune he committed to reviving the scandal-plagued Union Pacific Railroad, the long middle section of the transcontinental that connected America's eastern roads with California's Central Pacific, the same Union Pacific that Carnegie, Thomson, and Scott had held briefly before they were dumped.[46]

But this effort was different. It was no get-rich-quick plunge. Gould immersed himself in the badly tarnished road's business. On numerous trips out west he studied the ranches, mines, and indus-tries that formed the UP's natural constituency. He talked to local business and political leaders to develop a sense of regional needs and potentials. He improved the line's performance and cut ex-penses, working hard to wipe away the stain of scandal from the road, while fortifying its earnings and lobbying legislatures to ward off unfriendly legislation. In November 1873, UP stock stood at $15. A year later, with Gould pumping new funds into the road's op-eration, UP stock had climbed to $30, and before another seven months it reached $78. Other roads were closing or cutting their rates in desperation, but Gould's UP raised its fares by between 40 and 100 percent and declared its first dividend ever.[47]

The times had changed and, like Andrew Carnegie, Gould had changed with them. No longer was he the speculating outlaw, playing fast and loose with stocks and company treasuries. He guarded every dollar that the Union Pacific spent and placed the road on solid financial footing. He pushed his frail body to the edge of physical endurance, improving the road while also expanding its business vertically into coal and express services. He even considered outfitting UP with its own sleepers to avoid buying from the Pullman Company. The fearsome competitiveness had not abated, but the combination of personal setbacks and the depression forced Gould to change his ways and to embrace more constructive goals.

Gould's treatment of labor, however, was no different from that of Gotham's other industrialists. The investors' perspective led to a corrosive detachment. Men like Gould knew very little about the lives of the individuals who worked for them—increasingly immigrants who shared neither culture nor language nor background with their bosses. And they cared much less. When industrialists joined class-based trade organizations to fight the depression, they formed a united front to drive down wages. Gould brought in throngs of Chinese laborers, chopping monthly salaries from $52 to $32.50. Over the next four years, he continued to drive wages down. By 1877, the UP's Chinese hands were being paid $27 a month and Gould was pressing for another $2 reduction. When labor fought back, Gould retaliated by pitting foreign against native workers, calling upon federal troops to defend company properties, and ruthlessly making war on strikers. With the same remorselessness he promoted white settlement in the UP's service area. To the Indians whose lands were being overrun, he sent a chilling forecast from New York: They would be annihilated. And the market, which read brute policies as a form of business virtuosity, carried UP from debt to dividend payouts of nearly $12 million in less than four years.[48]

After suffering a second beating on August 2, 1876, when a man named A. A. Selover grabbed him by the lapels and hoisted him over a railing, cudgeling the dangling millionaire as he promised to teach him a lesson for lying and cheating, Gould stopped walking the streets unescorted, increasingly confining himself to his brownstone on Fifth Avenue and 47th Street. But well before his thrashing, his business strategy had changed. He no longer worked in the shadows. He invested more constructively now, as part of a larger business design that aimed to build businesses rather than entrap the unsuspecting. His politics changed as well. He had in the past been a political consumer, buying politicians and parties as he needed them for his purposes. Now the erstwhile Democrat and good friend of Boss Tweed became a loyal Republican, a supporter of the politics of business stability. He contributed generously to presidential candidates from Ulysses S. Grant to James Garfield and replaced his departed sidekick, the fun-loving Jim Fisk, with Russell Sage. Twenty years older than Gould, Sage was a merchant and banker with a past in politics and a lucrative sideline in lending money at high interest, a man as colorless in his personal style as Fisk had been flamboyant. And with Sage, Gould turned his attention to the telegraph industry.[49]

Other industrialized countries, recognizing the vital significance of inland telegraphy, had established state-run wire monopolies. Britain, for example, nationalized telegraph operations under its post office in 1869. In the United States the telegraph was left in the hands of private capital, with Cornelius Vanderbilt laying claim to the richest tangle of wires in the world with his Western Union Company. Like Andrew Carnegie years before, Gould used his rail connections as a wedge into the telegraph industry, stringing his extensive rail territories with cable and calling the new firm the Atlantic and Pacific Telegraph Company (Carnegie's start-up was the Pacific and Atlantic). For a very short time, he utilized the talents of the erratic, if ingenious, Thomas Edison to expand the capacity of the message-bearing cables. Then he undercut Western Union. Old Commodore Vanderbilt might have fended off such an attack, but he died in January 1877, and his son William had more than he could handle defending his railroad properties from another Gould offensive. Instead of jousting with Gould, Vanderbilt agreed to buy the A&P at a premium and eliminate Gould from the telegraph business.[50]

Gould walked away with a handsome gain, but he was far from satisfied. He coveted Western Union. Within two years he started another wire business, the American Union Company, and once again rattled William Vanderbilt with a flurry of harassing campaigns, ranging from rate wars to undermining Western Union's agreements with railroads, to stock manipulations that threw the wire giant off balance. By January 1881, when Vanderbilt invited him to a meeting, Gould was the single largest shareholder in Western Union, and he dictated the terms of the buyout. His tone no doubt rueful, Vanderbilt emerged from the tête-à-tête commenting that he had "seen the Great Mogul." He had also delivered tribute. "The country finds itself this morning," the *New York Herald* wrote in its report of the Gould victory, "at the feet of a telegraphic monopoly"—a monopoly with the power to control the flow of information, restrain competition, and fix prices from its central offices in Manhattan. Once Western Union completed ironclad agreements with his railroads, Gould held the reins to the most powerful telegraph-railroad combination in the nation.[51]

The third pillar of Gould's empire was the New York City municipal transit system. In many other cities, urban expansion took the form of concentric rings of settlement. However, New York's long and narrow shape dictated a northerly development. With the middle and upper classes seeking to leave congested lower Manhattan, uptown land investors clamored for swift and dependable transit. "Several hundred thousand persons . . . ," wrote the *New York Tribune*, "earn their living . . . in that narrow corner of this island which lies south of Grand Street. We cannot live here. . . . We want facilities for getting cheaply [and] comfortably" from home to work and back. Civic boosters, health reformers, labor representatives, real estate investors, and transit promoters all joined the call for efficient and speedy transit. "The growth of the city," exhorted the *New York World*, "the comfort of the people, and the value of property all depend on it."[52]

London and Paris had their own municipal transit systems. This made a world of difference not only in the level of financing, but in planning, quality, and service. In New York, "public money employed by public officials," writes urban historian David Hammack, "had dredged the Erie Canal, developed New York harbor, and established New York's commercial supremacy early in the nineteenth century," but those days were long gone. Ambitious civic planning had been put to rest by the Tweed scandals. Gotham limited its role in public transit to awarding street franchises and refereeing among competing companies. Private companies made the decisions that shaped New York's urban transit. They designed the routes, selected the technology, and arranged the financing.[53]

Proposals for municipal railways went back to the 1830s, but serious progress on rapid transit waited until the 1860s, when, inspired by the opening of the innovative London subway, Alfred Beach tried to open a "pneumatic underground railway," only to run into Boss Tweed's opposition, as we have seen. But even after Tweed's fall and a go-ahead from the Albany legislature, the project languished. Underground transit was much more complicated in New York than, say, London, where much of the "underground" actually ran through open-air cuts in the landscape. An even larger obstacle, in the end insurmountable, was the expense. The most optimistic estimate placed the cost of creating a subway system at $1.5 million per mile, or twenty times the cost of the then conventional horse railways. The depressed security market made that level of funding unattainable, and in any event, no one advocated entrusting so ambitious a project to the municipality.[54]

The only other option for rapid transit—that is, for transportation that did not have to negotiate Gotham's glutted streets—was to run the trains in the air on elevated stilts above the city streets. Traction companies could not dream of buying rights-of-way through prohibitively expensive Manhattan properties. Instead, the state leg-islature granted them air rights over public thoroughfares.[55]

Charles Harvey and his associates raised the world's first elevated line in 1867. A crude single-track railroad supported by thin stan-chions, it was drawn by cable from the Battery to 30th Street, along Ninth Avenue. Many feared that the flimsy "one legged Railway" would come toppling down at any moment, but the proximate stum-bling block for the road was Jay Gould's Black Friday. The collapse of the money market caught Harvey's company short of finances, forcing it to suspend operations. Subsequently sold at sheriff's auc-tion in 1871, the railway was reorganized as the New York Elevated Railroad Co., with improvements like double tracking and steam en-gines. But the depression and the opposition of downtown property owners stymied its growth.[56]

In 1872, Dr. Rufus Gilbert, a surgeon with an interest in promot-ing public health through the dispersal of Manhattan's dense popu-lations, founded a second overhead line (later the Metropolitan Elevated Railway Company), only to slam directly into the 1873 de-pression. The panic forced the underfinanced doctor to sell Gilbert Elevated. The city's own moves toward developing a municipal sys-tem were quickly slapped down by Albany. Instead, the state legisla-ture established a commission that reviewed some forty proposals in 1875 and awarded contracts to the Metropolitan Company (the re-configured Gilbert Co.) to chug on rails strung along Second and Sixth Avenues and the New York Elevated (Harvey's old line) along Third and Ninth Avenues.[57]

While the franchise agreement forbade the two elevateds from combining into a single monopoly, the commission did see the merit in having a coordinated transit system. It had the two companies lease their operations for 999 years to a holding corporation called the Manhattan Company, whose sole purpose was to provide central management for the city's elevated transit. The two old lines con-tributed $9 million each to cover initial operating expenses and to fund extensions. The Manhattan Company was to pay dividends and monthly charges to each of the companies. Thus, a single holding corporation, owned equally by the Metropolitan Company and the New York Elevated, controlled all of New York's traction lines.[58]

The arrangement worked better on paper than in practice. The two railroad companies quickly fell to feuding over every detail, leading important early investors like Samuel Tilden to sell their holdings. By April 1881 the Manhattan Company's declining stock prices caught Jay Gould's attention. The same depression that had ruined so many others had not only restored his fortune, it had made him one of the most powerful men in the country. His acquisition of Western Union was complete, and he had consolidated several southwestern railways. His varied purchases had also brought him the *New York World* newspaper—a "mere accident," he insisted. Now he was intrigued by the partially erected municipal railway that ran in his backyard. The els, writes his biographer, Maury Klein, "were properties of enormous potential with checkered pasts, and futures rendered uncertain by legal snarls and corporate infighting." This was familiar terrain for Gould.[59]

The Manhattan Company, which held the rights to the lines, was inexperienced and ineffective. The newspapers blasted its poor management, none more damagingly than Gould's recently acquired *New York World*. The talk of money problems and bad management was confirmed when New York State Attorney General Hamilton Ward brought suit on May 18, charging the Manhattan Company with inefficiency and even fraud and asked the courts to hand it over to a receiver. Attorneys general do not commonly single out companies for such attention unless there is some complaint. Yet there was no record of such complaint. In early July 1881, with the nation absorbed in President Garfield's shooting and his unsuccessful fight for life, the case was moved to Kingston, New York, before Judge Theodore R. Westbrook, who proceeded to appoint two distinguished receivers to bring the company back to health. The receivers, he determined, were not only distinguished, they were disinterested, lacking "relations of a professional, official, or business character with the elevated railways." They were, however, firmly in Jay Gould's employ. Judge Westbrook was so unconcerned with this that he even held a number of sessions related to the case in Gould's New York City headquarters in the Western Union Building. Meanwhile, the Manhattan Company had fallen more than thirty points, hitting a low on August 5 of $15.25.[60]

Then Judge Westbrook, in a move described by Gould biographer Maury Klein as "breathtaking in its . . . indiscretion," secretly contacted the counsel for the Manhattan Company, Wager Swayne (who was a friend of Gould's), and fed him information about the case, making clear that he would not allow the company to collapse. He went so far as to coach him on points that he should make before the court (that is, before himself) on behalf of the Manhattan Company. Then the severely misguided jurist went looking for an investor who could bail out the franchise. It occurred to him that in New York—brimming with investors and men of substance—there was one man who could provide the needed financing. Faced with "great practical questions . . . in which the arms length etiquette of courts is useless [!]," he wrote to Swayne that he was compelled "to go to the very edge of judicial discretion" and involve Gould in "saving the property."[61]

This much is clear. While others may have thought the Manhattan Company was finished—New York Elevated's president, Cyrus Field, declared that he wouldn't "give a dollar for as many [Manhattan receiver certificates] as a jackass could draw downhill!"—Jay Gould knew from the bench that the court was prepared to do what it could to support the Manhattan's stabilization. Curiously, while Judge Westbrook called upon him to "save the property," his *World*'s "Wall St. Gossip" column kept attacking the Manhattan Company, charging rotten deals and assorted swindles, predicting the stock's continued decline. Gould himself continued to badmouth the Manhattan's chances, hammering down its value, while he and his associates quietly bought almost a third of all its outstanding shares. Only after they had completed their purchases at distress sale rates on October 8 did the *World* offer its new analysis: The company had remarkably improved in health and was poised to climb in price.[62]

And the *World* was right. Judge Westbrook dismissed the dissolution proceedings. Gould brought together the disputing parties, closed out all outstanding suits, and announced an end to Manhattan's receivership even before the court made it official. By the second week in October, the price of the Manhattan Company—recently so close to the graveyard—stood at $45. Gould now controlled the holding company that ran the entire New York City rapid transit system. As with so many of Gould's operations, there were charges of impropriety, though not enough proof to convince a formal inquiry. Only Judge Westbrook's reputation (though perhaps not his pocketbook) suffered. And on November 19, 1881, the Manhattan Company was reorganized with Gould as president.[63]

The speculator who had some years before set the nation's monetary system at peril had lost none of his talent for dealing at the margins of business practice, but his focus had changed. He had assembled a portfolio that included the telegraph monopoly, the coveted center link of the transcontinental railroad, New York's rapid transit monopoly, and a number of important Western railroads, as well as a newspaper. In his hands he held a shockingly substantial part of America's new economy. There was no end to Gould's greed and power plays, but he held too large a stake to remain the insurgent speculator. He had become a very important part of New York's new industrial establishment.

---

D id Americans feel comfortable with an economic establishment in which Jay Gould played so prominent a role? In 1876, the new urban/corporate/investment–based economy faced an important test, the first presidential election following the financial collapse. Coming three years into an extended downturn, it offered

Americans an opportunity to register their reaction to the changes that had taken place.

New York and its postmercantile money market had been implicated in setting off the collapse. It was in Manhattan that the dominoes had begun their fall, as Jay Cooke's failed banking house set hundreds of other banks and businesses tumbling. Here a colossal mendacity had thrown business and politics into each other's embrace, resulting in nefarious rings, corners, and manipulators. Here was the home of Jay Gould, Jim Fisk, Cornelius Vanderbilt, and the entire brigade of speculators and traffickers in virtual business, not to mention Boss Tweed, who had greatly advanced the art of municipal corruption. One might expect that the misery brought on by the economic crisis would arouse opposition and anger at the new market that had rewarded seamy speculation so munificently; that the many across the nation who had suffered would assail New York City and its investment houses for the depression; that they would skewer its culture of accumulation and its banks, commercial emporiums, and lawyers, its accountants and brokers; that its businessmen would be maligned and reviled.

Most Americans still lived in rural areas, many worked on farms or as laborers. If they feared the new economy or opposed it, this was their chance to register their objections. In the midst of a later depression, in the 1890s, the Democrats would select an anticity, anti–Wall Street candidate to run for the presidency. Yet hard times incited no anticorporate paladin to lead a protest against the new scale of business and rally the citizenry around checking its advance in 1876. Instead, the Democratic Party nominated a man deeply involved in the metropolitan economy, the "first genuinely wealthy man to run for the presidency," New York governor Samuel Tilden, to be their standard-bearer, and he won a plurality of the votes cast, affirming a fundamental acceptance of the existing order.[64]

This election underscored how much that order had changed and how much American politics had changed along with it. The founding elite of the early Republic was composed largely of Virginia planters. Washington, Jefferson, Madison, and Monroe had fastened upon the nation the ethos of Richmond and Monticello. From the early days of the nation, New York's politics had often placed the city at odds with much of the rest of the nation, reflecting its distinctive role as a commercial port in an agricultural land. In the American Revolution, mercantile New York was the colony that was most loyal to the British. Decades later, in the agonizing months before the Civil War, New Yorkers, prompted in no small measure by a regard for the cotton trade, led the effort to avoid hostilities through compromise. Yet for all of its importance, New York could no more swing the nation around a moderate political course than stop the rancorous debate over slavery.

America's presidents after the Civil War were neither farmers nor southerners. The changes that transformed the national economy and placed Gotham at the forefront of modern business raised to prominence new men of urban background and broad mien. Intimately acquainted with the new corporate economy, New Yorkers proved pivotal in each presidential election after the Civil War. Samuel Tilden, Chester Arthur, Grover Cleveland, Theodore Roosevelt, New Yorkers all, extended the metropolitan aegis nationally.

And so, in the midst of the worst depression to that time, a plurality of voters cast their ballots for a city man, a New York native, a man of the new economy, one of Gotham's shrewdest and most successful corporate lawyers renowned for bringing order to the chaos of railroad economics, whose vast fortune was built from mergers, consolidations, and takeovers, from stock shares, and from investing the savings of others. Known as "the Great Forecloser" for taking lines thrown into bankruptcy and financial distress and reorganizing them, Samuel Tilden had accepted retainers from such Wall Street luminaries as Jay Gould (though exactly what Gould and Fisk bought for their $10,000 was disputed by the principals). His familiarity with the courts, the corporate headquarters, the balance books, and the director's offices was consummate.[65]

Samuel J. Tilden had risen to prominence in the Democratic

Party, organizing the New York State ticket behind Andrew Johnson, going on to chair the New York State Democratic Committee
for several years, and serving as New York governor Horatio Seymour's campaign coordinator in his run for the presidency in 1868. It
was in this contest that Tammany was charged with bringing as
many as twenty-five thousand recent immigrants before pliant
judges to expedite their naturalization and then paying the newcomers to vote Democratic. According to some calculations, the total
votes cast for Tammany exceeded by close to 10 percent the entire
voting population. Seymour's candidacy was beyond even such help,
but Tilden and Tammany did succeed in installing a governor, a
mayor, and assorted state and city officials, the foundation blocks of
Tweed's machine. After the election, the editor of the *New York Tribune*, Horace Greeley, addressed a stinging open letter to Tilden, defying him to make his party clean or leave it.[66]

Instead Tilden worked with Tweed on fund-raising, patronage,
and distributing funds to local candidates. Democrats did not hesitate to beseech him to approach Tweed for money on their behalf:
"Bring it up with you," an upstate candidate telegraphed Tilden, referring to a sum of between $20,000 and $30,000, "in Currency . . .
in $5 & $10—mostly $5."[67]

Tilden was perhaps the most sought-after corporate attorney in
New York, a leading figure among New York's Democrats, and an
adviser to presidents. He was close enough to both the business and
the political scene to have understood what was going on in Tweed's
New York quite early. Yet it is a telling reflection of the confusion
and paralysis faced by even the more upright of New York's citizens
that a man of his standing and integrity fell into a strange diffidence
when he confronted the sordidness of the times. It took the Erie
wars and the gold corner to move the "Sage of Gramercy Park" to
drop Gould and Fisk as clients in 1870, and longer still to attack
Tweed. "A hero of last moments," Tweed biographer Alexander Callow has called him, "a skillful general when the enemy was in retreat," though this is perhaps less a comment on Tilden than upon

the environment of corrosive prosperity that had so overtaken Gotham.[68]

The *Times* disclosures finally forced Tilden to confront the extent of the corruption. He had tolerated patronage in politics, but a politics whose *purpose* was patronage and graft he could not accept. He mobilized a reform crusade against the Tweed Ring, winning national attention as he pledged to make "New York . . . the envy of other governments . . . the pride of all lovers of liberty the world over." Promising to restore probity in government, he led a team of investigators—an accountant and an assistant actually camped in his house—in assembling the case against the ring, even picking up the tab when his finicky friend, Comptroller Andrew Green, turned back some of the legal fees. "Sir," the coldly forbidding Tilden (made even more forbidding as a result of having lost most of his teeth when he was twenty-two years old) once admonished a lawyer who was less than assiduous on the Tweed prosecutions, "a man who is not a monomaniac is not worth a damn." Bringing the ring to justice and restoring integrity became "his wife, his religion and his hope of heaven."[69]

As for a flesh-and-blood wife, the remote bachelor took none. When he was elected governor in 1874, after serving in the New York State Assembly, he was sixty years old, and he had made no place in his life for domestic pleasures. He was ill at ease among women and, according to friends and acquaintances, took little interest. In the genteel circumlocutions of his day, Tilden assured his biographer and good friend John Bigelow "that he had never had any acquaintance or relations with the female sex, of which he would have hesitated, from motives of delicacy, to speak with his mother or his sisters." Another biographer, Alexander Flick, speaks elliptically of "something fine grained in his makeup, a delicacy of feeling and a modesty of behavior . . . ," of being "inordinately shy of the gentler sex," and of his "sexual inhibitions . . . not a man's man." Civic issues absorbed this blue-eyed gentleman of medium height, slender frame, prematurely puckered mouth, and swift, jerky walk as no woman did. "Strangers," writes Flick, "spoke of him as queer." Since 1842, he had been close with another lifetime bachelor, his erstwhile law partner and now city comptroller, Andrew H. Green, who moved into his office and looked after his law practice when his friend went to Albany.[70]

Occupying the upper rungs of Manhattan's fluid, postmercantile class structure, this "largely friendless, admired but not liked," New York State governor, once described "as cold as a damn clam," improbably rode his vigorous display of municipal rectitude into national prominence. From Albany, Tilden was swiftly projected into presidential politics. He is "connected with the moneyed men of the country," one of his backers wrote, "and will be supported by the bankers. . . . This is exactly what we want." Some in the West mistrusted this "Wall Street man," but they could not rouse much of an opposition to his candidacy. Against the stormy background of Reconstruction and the ethically challenged Grant administration he trumpeted the cause of government integrity on a platform that called for an end to federal intervention in the South, support for free trade, gold currency, and low taxes—an end, in short, to the expansive program introduced by the Republicans during the Civil War.[71]

Tilden shared the thinking of a collection of metropolitan intellectuals and professionals who rejected the intrusive state, among them E. L. Godkin, Carl Schurz, and James Garfield. "The Government must," Godkin admonished, "get out of the 'protective' business and the 'subsidy' business and the 'improvement' and 'development' business. . . . It cannot touch them without breeding corruption." In an address before the American Social Science Association in 1876, Governor Tilden explained that "even those uncertain things that depend on human will" come together in "order, method [and] law," so long as government does not interfere. Too much tinkering, he remarked on another occasion, had brought the depression: "The fruits of a false and delusive system of government finances are everywhere around us. All business is in a dry rot. . . .

The truth is that our body politic has been overdrugged with stimulants." An advocate of the least government necessary, he announced to a Chamber of Commerce audience in 1877: "I am myself depressed this evening, and yet a little joyous, for I have just left at Albany 270 bills. . . . But when I think of the several hundred bills that were not passed, my melancholy turns into joy."[72]

How large a role did the issue of corporate business growth and monopoly play in this campaign? None! With much to complain of, there was no questioning of the "system," no rejection of entrepreneurial leadership. The opposition of antimonopolists, farmers, and workers faded before a more general and more widespread agreement on the desire for retrenchment and recovery. Neither Tilden nor the Republican, Rutherford B. Hayes of Ohio, opposed the recent changes in business or cast the issue as a complex problem requiring correction or reform. There was no debate over the radical implications of big business and the consolidating impact of New York's money market. On the contrary, both candidates affirmed the need to promote business growth and spur investment. Both Tilden and Hayes indicated that government's proper role was to help business, not regulate it. In the shadow of the depression, they talked about the South, tariffs, and gold money, and Tilden, returning to a favored theme, spoke out against combinations of workers and strikers who violated the natural laws of free enterprise. These matters overshadowed all other economic issues in the campaign, affirming a fundamental acceptance of the existing order.[73]

Early returns on election night showed Tilden, with a quarter million votes more than Hayes, headed toward victory. However, disputes loomed over the electoral vote in four crucial states. Tilden would have to fight for the presidency, but he lacked the burning ambition to fight for anything but his own reputation. Flick writes of him that he "was incapable of vigorous expression of personality." Not fighting for the presidency represented for him a moral act of self-abnegation, the discipline to stand aside from power and honor. He hovered maddeningly above the fray, offering no direction to emissaries who were involved in negotiating over the disputed votes. Rectitude alone offered him no clue about how to deal with the complexity of American politics.[74]

Tilden turned out to be a misfire for his New York backers. By the time the decision was ratified, many who had come to know too well the shimmering surface with little of iron or brilliance or passion beneath were quite unperturbed by the fact that he was cheated out of the White House. Physics teaches that gravity without weight creates no force. Even before the deals that gave the presidency to Rutherford B. Hayes were sealed, many in New York's business community threw their support behind the Ohioan. Hayes promised to end Reconstruction, symbol to many New Yorkers of the instability created by government's "overstepping." The words Hayes chose reflected precisely the prescription New York business wanted to hear. The benighted South, asserted Hayes, suffered from "too much politics and too little attention to business." This, he said, was "the bane of that part of the country."[75]

The words highlight the fact that in a nation that was still composed primarily of rural communities and very much in a depression, capitalist development was widely seen as a solution and not a problem. With more than 80 percent of those eligible voting, the election was split closely between a wealthy New York business lawyer and an Ohioan whose party was the best friend new business had.

Although Rutherford Hayes came from Ohio, his campaign, like Tilden's, was run from New York. And his running mate was a New York lawyer and banker. The nation's relationship with Wall Street was complex. Side by side with Main Street's frequent complaints about bankers and speculators and its genuine sense of grievance at being bullied by large, distant forces, was a respect for Gotham's role as the new economy's linchpin, the underwriter of western development, the indispensable link to international markets.[76]

The economic collapse of the 1930s led to the election of Franklin Roosevelt and the inauguration of a comprehensive New Deal. It radicalized a certain proportion of the working classes and set in motion broad reforms intended to help the most vulnerable "one-third" of society. But the 1873 depression was different.

First, for all of the pain and loss that it inflicted, the 1873 depression was not as thoroughgoing in its effect as the 1930s depression. The 1873 plunge devastated stocks, banks, and railroads and pushed down prices over a wide range, but it also accelerated the growth of domestic industry as new and developing businesses took advantage of declining imports to grow. Moreover, as early as 1875, manufacturing output started to climb back. Indeed, after the panic year of 1873, when more businesses failed than were opened, the total number of businesses continued to rise for the rest of the decade. And while it is true that the number of *unemployed* Americans grew, so too did the number of those who were *employed*, just as the decline in wages was matched by an even steeper drop in the consumer price index, which brought down the cost of living. Despite the general malaise, the gross national product grew. So did the gross domestic product. National income rose, as did the index of manufacturing. Indeed, by 1876 America achieved its first positive balance of payments since before the Civil War.[77]

Second, the 1873 depression was perceived as a producer's depression, one when declines in prices and skidding profits primarily hurt business. Not only businessmen, notorious for projecting economic trends from their own pockebooks, but also the leading economic thinkers of the day saw in the depression a threat to business. Influential economists like Jeremiah Jenks, David Wells, and the first commissioner of labor, Carrol D. Wright, thought, in Wells's words, that recent economic changes had given "the wage-earning class a greater command over the necessities and comforts of life," while signaling diminished opportunities for producers.[78]

Declining prices rattled producers, but the falling price index brought benefits to middle- and lower-class families. As declining prices sent real wages up, even in the depression years, the less privileged saw their standard of living improve. Consumer goods, foods, and household items that had been available only to the rich became more affordable, placing them within broader reach.[79]

In the light of such trends, it is not surprising that voters chose to endorse rather than reject the economic changes that Wall Street had done so much to bring about. Democrats and Republicans both feared big government more than big business. As for the depression, many concluded that it was a business problem, a problem of too many new businesses being opened with unsteady financing in the euphoria of good times, resulting in overproduction and destructive cutthroat competition.[80]

If the 1930s depression brought labor together and made workers more conscious of common class needs and vulnerabilities, the 1873 depression had a similar impact on business. Capital responded to the depression by banding together to moderate market competition, limit risks, and restore stability. Shipowners, rail managers, cigar producers, iron and steel manufacturers, stevedore contractors, piano builders, stove manufacturers, and merchants of all stripes banded together to form associations, pools, and trade organizations to restrict price competition, prevent unwelcome legislation, and combat labor unions. "All industries in our day stand or fall together," wrote E. L. Godkin. The business community came closer together, abandoning earlier protestations that America was a society without class divisions. "The temper of employers," sums up one scholar, "had changed." Organizations that in the past had fought for programs of civic uplift and urban improvement narrowed their focus to avoiding taxes and keeping government small. In the 1850s, when bad times hit, the city's commercial elite provided relief to help the poor. By 1873, in the wake of the Tweed scandals and the more pronounced division between the classes, the elite of the city rejected notions of responsibility to the needy and unemployed.[81]

The purging of the notorious Tweed Ring from government led to a regime of probity and retrenchment, a cold, dispassionate probity that rejected sensitivity and compassion for the less fortunate. Taking over after Tweed's fall, Comptroller Andrew Green instituted policies so tightfisted that workers and contractors were forced to endure long delays in payment. "We have kept our men at work without pay just as long as we can," a sanitation superintendent remonstrated. "Their grocers refuse to trust them any longer, and in some instances, their landlords have turned them into the street. . . . Dangerous results may follow."[82]

On a frozen January day in 1874, thousands of Gotham's poor gathered at Tompkins Square Park to demand work and bread. Mayor William Havemeyer, heir to a sugar fortune, refusing to acknowledge the demonstrators, dismissed the gathering as a "body of crazy men." The police were sent wading into the crowd, scattering the assembled, in the words of the *Herald*, "like wild birds." Samuel Gompers, the future labor leader, was forced to scamper into a cellar to avoid a bashed skull. He remembered the police action as an "orgy of brutality." Mayor Havemeyer applauded it. "Nothing better could have happened," he said. Genteel New Yorkers, made anxious by the depression, agreed. The *Herald* delivered a stiff lecture on the facts of laboring life: "He shares in the prosperity and when a season of difficulty arrives he must be prepared to bear patiently the suffering incidental to hard times."[83]

In 1871, a very good year, the city distributed close to $43,000 in public relief to 19,157 individuals. Four years later, in the depths of the troubles, the city stopped relief entirely. Private charities soon exhausted their funds, but the wealthy mayor adamantly declared that public works "belonged to other countries, not ours." The commissioner of charities and correction could not have been more plain. Better a few should "test the minimum rate at which existence can be preserved" than to allow poverty to lose its terror. Why, demanded Havemeyer, should Gotham tax those who "by thrift and industry had built up their houses," in order to succor those who "by strikes and the like contributed to the current state of things themselves"? New York stood at the proud center of a system that reached across oceans and continents, and this priceless arrangement, he insisted, must be protected from any "unjust and unnecessary exactions."[84]

The depression, the sense of increased isolation and foreboding from an immigrant workforce, the fear that labor and other interest groups were benefiting at their expense, the perception that government had not done enough to protect the prerogatives of capital, all helped promote a sense of community and shared outlook among Gotham's entrepreneurs. In other cities, businessmen were not numerous enough to form a world quite so separate, but in New York, with the nation's leading corporations, banks, and investment houses, this population formed a critical and self-contained mass.[85]

Corporate executives and investors worked with a fixed universe of banks, insurance companies, brokers, law firms, and accounting concerns. They belonged to many of the same churches, interacted socially, attended the same entertainments, served on the same civic boards, and worshiped together the corporate theology of the invisible hand. Men who in the past had not thought of themselves as part of a distinct class found themselves in the same organizations, listening to the same speakers, discussing the same issues. They heard economists tell them that the depression hurt capital more than labor. They heard from social thinkers that to distribute charity did no good but much harm. They heard from reformers that corrupt machine government was the natural result of allowing the poor and the foreign born a voice in government. They shared the comfortable assumption that the economy steered social progress and that property rights were privileged above other liberties. And, as New York ascended to the first level of national political importance, a significant number of them participated in a New York–Washington political community, enjoying easy access to cabinet members and even to the White House.

More than ever before, the wealthy peeled away from the quotidian concerns of common life to create an elite "society" of fancy balls, exclusive homes, and lavish dress. Boarding schools, museums, and gentleman's clubs adopted overt policies of exclusion and elite solidarity. Old and new wealth, notoriously dismissive of each other's social pretensions in the past, smoothed over their differences. The change was perhaps best represented by the gala "Bouncer's Ball" in December of 1874, where invited guests from fresh wealth blithely mingled with "old society's" elite bachelors who had invited them. "No other social group ever abdicated power," Mary Van Rensselaer exclaimed about the old merchant elite, "in more sumptuous surroundings." Wealth became a more powerful signifier than bearing or birth. In the Gilded Age, it finally became possible to buy class.[86]

The depression, Robert Davis observed in the 1874 *Journal of Social Science*, was separating "classes more than ever." There was more talk of *dangerous classes*, of antagonisms between *capital and labor*, of alien agitators, of "rabble," and of the natural imperative (by way of Herbert Spencer) for survival of the fittest, a kind of *natural* class. During the Tweed scandals, the *Times* had called out an agitated admonition: "We are in this city over the crust of a volcano," threatened by dangerous classes, ill prepared to nourish the delicate virtues of liberty, "who burrow under the roots of society and come forth . . . in times of disturbance to plunder and prey." The depression intensified talk about "explosive and terrible forces." This trope of a barely restrained underclass became a common rhetorical device invoked to interpret strikes, reject outspoken demands for public assistance, and read signs of menace and threats to order into expressions of labor solidarity. The effect was to create a deliberate estrangement between the classes by seeding the divide with sinister suspicions.[87]

Fears of mobs and class violence attenuated predepression ideals of civic uplift and classless harmony. Genteel critics rallied the softhearted to recognize the dangers in free soup: "It is no morbid imagination," lectured E. L. Godkin, "which finds not only official corruption, but possible communistic horrors also, in the dregs of the bowl of municipal free soup." Even the champions of the needy, such as the Association for the Improvement of the Conditions of the Poor, voiced distrust and misgivings. "There is a dangerous class in New York," the association announced gravely, warning that there is no "greater social and economic concern than that relating to the industrial classes, which numerically embrace more than two-thirds of the City population."[88]

The combination of Tweed scandals and depression fueled a genteel pessimism regarding democracy and active government and resulted in an elite campaign to limit the political effect of the working classes. Denouncing as fallacious the idea that humanity could be made better through legislation, many of New York's "best men" condemned active government as "by nature wasteful, corrupt and dangerous." The idea of municipal issues being determined at the ballot box, with so many of the voters drawn from among the foreign born, easily corrupted, poorly informed, often inebriated, and religiously misguided shook the upper class's trust in democracy. "Expressions of doubt about universal suffrage are heard constantly . . . among . . . the most intelligent, the most thoughtful and the most patriotic men," the *Atlantic Monthly* reported. Rejecting government based on "mere majorities," the city's privileged sought to insulate public policy from workers and immigrants by reserving more power to "the highly cultivated members of society."[89]

In 1877, the Committee to Devise a Plan for the Government of Cities in the State of New York (appointed by Governor Tilden) completed two years of study and published its solution to the problem of urban misrule. It proposed strict debt limits for city projects and called for vesting fiscal power in the hands of a select Board of Finance elected by property owners and large rent payers. This proposal appeared technical and innocuous, but it called for nothing less than instituting a two-tier system of voting—the proletariat limited to electing representatives to debate over street names while the wealthier citizens held power over the city purse. The commission hoped by this plan to eliminate the influence of the poor, the ignorant, and the foreign born. Led by the Chamber of Commerce, all major business groups, including the New York Stock Exchange, lent their enthusiastic support to the proposal. They were joined by the governor, the strongest newspapers in the city, and its wealthiest denizens.

The plan passed its first hurdle in 1877, but then it ran into Tammany. Although Tammany went along with budgetary retrenchment and draconian cutbacks in city spending, it drew the line at a restricted franchise that would deprive it of its power base. In the face of growing opposition, the supporters of elite government were forced to recognize that while they might have the money, they could not persuade the poor, who had the numbers, to give up their franchise.[90]

The effort to restrict lower-class voting did not succeed, but it did lead to a new activism on the part of New York's venerable Chamber of Commerce. The centerpiece of Gotham's business establishment, the Chamber of Commerce of the State of New York ("State" in the title referred to the source of its charter, not its geographic scope, which was the city) had in the past limited its work to behind-the-scenes business advocacy. But in the years following the ouster of the Tweed regime and the depression, the Chamber shed its customary diffidence to take a stronger hand in city government, extending the influence of the city's capital class over issues that it deemed too important to leave to an undependable electorate.

Founded by Manhattan's leading merchants and traders at Fraunces Tavern in 1768, in the days before the American Revolution, the Chamber of Commerce gathered business information and refereed commercial disputes among New York's merchants. Its role in supporting the boycott of British goods before the Revolution and backing the Union with loans and contributions during the Civil War burnished the Chamber's reputation for loyalty beyond its own short-term business interest. Still the Chamber remained a largely ceremonial organization, known primarily for its unequaled commercial library and its gracious dinners for visiting dignitaries. Following the Civil War, the Chamber, long dominated by import-export men like Moses Taylor and Abiel Abott Low, opened the organization to corporate leaders, bankers, and the owners of large retail emporia. Its prewar roll of some three hundred members expanded so rapidly that the Chamber was forced to cap membership at one thousand associates.[91]

From its early days, the Chamber of Commerce had always seen itself as a group of principled city leaders who happened to be merchants. They recognized no conflict between high-minded public interest and their exclusively commercial makeup. Chamber members conceived of business broadly as a benign civic institution dispensing the benefits of modern technology and a higher living standard. Exporters, investors, bankers, and insurance men promoted the public good, and the Chamber's mission was to protect this accomplishment by supporting a sturdy economy and a conservative city.[92]

Led by pragmatic traders, the Chamber usually avoided doctrinaire positions. It backed laissez-faire and free trade but lobbied for harbor improvements and other policies that promoted commerce, even if they came with some government involvement. It was unequivocal in its opposition to greenbacks (demanding solid gold, "honest money"), and labor organizations, its president declaring that the only true threat to "the prosperity of our port and the city" was the "combinations of men" who kept driving wages up to unreasonable levels. And though the Chamber was no more critical of Tweed than most New Yorkers at first, it took over the anticorruption crusade, once it got going, assailing corruption and attacking the growth agenda for saddling New York with "costly parks . . . unnecessary boulevards, [and] costly ornaments."[93]

With the bosses and the plungers discredited and its responsible, conservative voice more powerful and assured than ever before, the Chamber became a much more active presence in city politics, especially in its demands for retrenchment. The leading voice of business said no to poor relief, declaring "time offers the only solution of easing the difficulties." Actually, the Chamber had made highly visible contributions to ease the effect of fires and floods on communities in the United States and overseas. As recently as 1873, it contributed $20,000 to those suffering from yellow fever in Savannah, Georgia. It made President Garfield's family a gift of some $360,000 after his assassination, but it made no similar gesture toward New Yorkers thrown out of work by the depression.[94]

Business also made the Chamber liberal on some issues. The "commercial senate" piously denounced ethnic restrictions on the Chinese in these years, when open immigration for Asians meant cheap and easily manipulated workers. The effort to limit the number of Chinese, exclaimed the esteemed China trader and Chamber president Abiel A. Low, "is . . . opposed to the law of our National being; to all the traditions connected with our growth, and continued increase in wealth. . . . We are a nation of immigrants, and have no right to shut the door against the Chinese any more than . . . against the people of Ireland." Of course, there was a subtext: "The Chinese government," Low added, "would have the right to abrogate its treaty of amity, commerce and navigation," if discriminatory rules were passed.[95]

The Chamber, as one might expect of a house of merchants, devoted much of its attention to issues of transport and traffic. As early as the 1840s, it became entranced with the advances promised by the railroad's "annihilation of commercial distance [which] will render the trader practically omnipresent." The Chamber even came out in favor of state subsidies for the Erie Railroad. But in the years since then it had come to fear the unmatched size and power of these corporate leviathans. In an address in 1873, Chamber president Low expressed concern about the troubling sway that "gigantic corporations" exerted over the lives of citizens and businesses. Even more, Low and his colleagues feared that these roads threatened to erase the advantages that New York's superior harbor facilities and unequaled water connections had given its merchants. "Rail competition," writes historian Lee Benson, "became the leading problem confronting the New York mercantile community for it permitted rivals to take advantage of all the new opportunities presented by the Communications Revolution." The Chamber could not object to that, but it did strongly protest the collusion of the Erie and Central Railroads to raise New York rates above those charged shippers in other cities.[96]

Even before the depression the Chamber of Commerce had investigated regional inequities in rate schedules and asked the Albany legislature for redress, a charmingly quixotic exercise in the age of Tweed, when in the words of one historian, "legislatures were commonly regarded as another form of railroad property." By 1873, with Tweed facing a jail sentence, the picture had changed. Across the country railroads were collapsing, and surviving lines were joining pools to fix rates and allocate territories. Forty New York–area rail lines signed the Saratoga Compact in 1874 to eliminate competition in rail charges and to assign noncompetitive routes.[97]

By this, time the New York Chamber of Commerce was the leading commercial voice in the nation. Its word carried weight in Albany and Washington, and with businessmen throughout the land. It had moved to the forefront of civic leadership with its successful fight against the corrupt machine. Breaking with the laissez-faire orthodoxy that had come to dominate business circles, it leveled a strong attack on the railroads for their collusive practices and monopolistic pricing, demanding that Albany regulate the railroad price policies. The blunt attack on the carriers captured headlines and attracted the support of farmers and merchants across the nation. The dismayed carriers responded by flailing back, rebuking the Chamber's "destructive communistic characteristics . . . [and] socialistic principles." The ill-tempered reaction was a sign of how seriously the railroads took this breach in what had been a common wall of business ideology.[98]

It was also a sign that the Chamber had abondoned its traditional reserve. In 1873, the Chamber had resisted issuing a resolution supporting the retention of business favorite Andrew H. Green as city comptroller, on the grounds that it must avoid interference in city politics. Over the next few years, it remained in the background, wielding its influence by indirection, leading the movement to curb the influence of the "dangerous classes" on politics. But after its effort to restrict the franchise of the city's poorer citizens failed, the Chamber moved to the forefront of city government. Some members ascended to City Hall, and others joined investigative commissions and took appointive posts.[99]

Not only did the Chamber become more actively involved in government, it also made government more active, acknowledging that the nation's center of capitalism and premier metropolis required a more positive agenda than just cutting budgets and keeping government honest. Over the next decade, the "parliament of the region's business interests" turned its attention to rationalizing city transit.

Circulation about the streets, writes David Hammack, was "the most important and controversial issue of economic policy to emerge in Greater New York" in these years. The primitive array of street railways, carts, and horse-drawn wagons barely served the thriving metropolis. Free enterprise had given New York the less than optimal els, but there was a practical limit to the number of high-slung tracks that could be thrown across the city. Moreover, these crudely erected sky roads that set noisy behemoths chugging overhead exacted a high price. They blocked the sun, spewed fumes, and sprayed dirt and ash all over; and for their entire length they undermined adjoining property values. Powerful landowners like A. T. Stewart and the Astors kept the elevated structures off Broadway and Fifth Avenue. And laissez-faire had allowed the rapid transit system to fall under Jay Gould's unyielding thumb. None of this resembled anything close to an efficient, well-managed system; nor did it offer much reassurance about government serving the city's needs into the next century.[100]

Toward the end of the century, the Chamber (whose vice presidents at different times included Cornelius Vanderbilt, J. P. Morgan, Jacob Schiff, and John D. Rockefeller) moved deftly among the counterposed interests of the real estate lobby, employers, working families, and organized labor to mobilize a metropolitan consensus for a $50 million subway construction project. It assembled the professional specialists and the funding for a project that was unprecedented in scope and complexity, to build Gotham a transit system for the new century.[101]

---

Soon after the 1876 presidential election, William B. Evarts, the new secretary of state and a longtime member of the New York Chamber of Commerce, addressed its annual banquet. Evarts spoke warmly to this audience of his former colleagues, promising them the full cooperation of his department. He would conduct special studies for their businesses and have the consular service "act as earnest cooperators with the industry of manufacturers and the zeal of commerce" to expand business overseas. "And now," he went on to tell the appreciative audience, with the agony of Reconstruction "ended, and forever," the sad chapter of the Civil War was finally closed, heralding a new era of national comity and unified economic growth. The economy was finally turning up.[102]

The upbeat message was exhilarating. The words, encapsulating what many there so much wanted to hear, were received with loud applause. The audience's mood was especially buoyed by the unusual show of support and respect that accompanied the message. For attending the banquet with Evarts was the new president, Rutherford B. Hayes, who had also brought along the secretary of the interior, signifying Gotham's unquestioned dominion over national commerce, investment, and banking.[103]

---

Charles Francis Adams and Henry Adams published their lapidary accounts of corporate knavery in New York at the close of the 1860s. Their essays read like dispatches recounting a trip through distant jungles. Wall Street is "a haunt of gamblers . . . a den of thieves; the offices of our great corporations . . . the secret chambers in which trustees plotted the spoliation of their wards; the law . . . a ready engine for the furtherance of wrong; . . . the halls of legislation . . . a mart in which the price of votes was higgled over, and laws, made to order were bought and sold. . . ." Charles Francis's history of the Erie wars left no doubt about the cause: "It is but a very few years since the existence of a corporation controlling a few millions of dollars was regarded a subject of grave apprehension, and now this country already contains single organizations which wield a power represented by hundreds of millions. These bodies are . . . establishing despotisms which no spasmodic popular effort will be able to shake off."[104]

As commodities came to be represented by paper; gold and other money by notes; cotton, pork, sugar, tobacco, and wheat by warehouse certificates; and the ownership of companies by stock documents, these new forms of capital had become a basis for speculation and investment. As each transaction added efficiency of use or place or time to the commodity, it dilated the market and, not incidentally, expanded the opportunity for shady practice. By the early 1870s, the economy, much like the metropolis with which it was entwined, was becoming wealthier, larger, and ever more imposing. Tweed was giving the city what it wanted, and the economy was generating unparalleled prosperity, but the process had corroded the city's soul.

Gotham supporters glibly dismissed critics. "Were hundreds of millions to change hands every day in a church filled with saints," the *Times* commented mordantly, "we presume it would not be wonderful if an adventurous thief would now and then be caught in their midst." An unattractive hubris had taken hold as well. There was no other place for investors with serious money, boasted the *Herald*. "There is then one asylum left for capital and substantial money interests," the daily crowed in 1870. "Paris has gone into total eclipse and London trembles toward her sunset. The westward star of empire is in the zenith of New York." "Nowhere," declared a besotted

*Times*, "is commercial integrity more generally prevalent, more deeply cherished or more widely confided in."[105]

Social Darwinism gave the pursuit of unlimited business profits high moral sanction. Tweed landed in prison, Carnegie built steel, and Gould turned from speculation to erect a business empire. Tilden was cheated out of a White House victory. A long depression and the wholesale withdrawal of European investment subdued the excessive exuberance of the market and its boosters. Yet even in bad times a majority of Americans voted their confidence in the new economy. And for all the failures, bankruptcies, and cutbacks, the postwar economy was able to draw upon its internal resources not only to recover but to expand. Indeed, it is worth noting that unemployment in New York City was markedly lower than for the nation at large, suggesting that not only was it better for Andrew Carnegie to work from New York, but that workers too fared better here, even in hard times.[106]

The depression lingered on for much of the decade and many businesses formed pools to protect prices, but this solution proved delusive. Andrew Carnegie's response to the depression was more inspired. He paid scant attention to protecting prices. Indeed, he kept cutting them by introducing efficiencies in production. Instead of protecting market share through industrial agreements, he focused on expanding the market for steel. This was the approach favored by the New York investment community, which, in the teeth of a depression, continued to pour fresh money into industry. In each year of this seven-year depression the net value of plant and equipment, as measured in fixed dollars, kept rising. Clearly, a growing population and a vast demand for fresh construction in cities, factories, institutions, and residential neighborhoods offered far more important sources for economic renewal than did price fixing.[107]

Already the center of capital before the depression, Gotham continued to attract the nation's largest fortunes and most successful entrepreneurs. The meat-packing Armours from the Chicago stockyards; the California-based railroad tycoon Collis P. Huntington; John D. Rockefeller, who founded his multinational oil conglomerate in Cleveland; and James B. Duke, the North Carolina architect of the American Tobacco Company empire, all came to the Capital City to consolidate their businesses. And while Albany barely defeated genteel proposals to restrict the role of the lower orders in municipal governance, control over city growth passed from professional politicians to a class of businessmen with the time, money, and inclination to shape a modern metropolis in their own image.

## CHAPTER 5

# Shaping Modern Capitalism

*It is the numbers and the success of these [captains of industry] . . . ,
—their ability to work unfettered in a free economic field,—which de-
termines whether a nation shall be great or little, whether it shall advance or recede,—whether its cities shall house throbbing life, like
London or New York or only gloomy monuments of a buried past, like
Carthage, Tyre or Rome today.*[1]
    —CHARLES A. CONANT, *Wall Street and the Country*, 1904

*A corporation is only another name for the means which we have discov-
ered of allowing a poor man to invest his income in a great enterprise.*[2]
    —JAY GOULD, TESTIMONY BEFORE CONGRESS, 1883

IN THE EARLY 1880S, in the midst of an economic crisis, Cyrus
Field sent the London banker Junius Morgan a cable: "Many of our
businessmen seem to have lost their heads. What we want is some
cool headed strong man to lead." Over the next thirty years, Morgan's son, John Pierpont, came as close as anyone ever has to filling
that position.[3]

If any man exemplified Wall Street in its age of banker dominance, it was J. P. Morgan. Ron Chernow, the historian of modern
moguls, writes that it is the titanic Morgan who "define[s] our image
of the tycoon as . . . big bellied, top-hatted and frock-coated, a fierce,
swaggering buccaneer . . . a big time financier as P. T. Barnum might
have conceived him, with a thunderous voice and a dagger-like gaze,
a portly man of vivid appearance and kaleidoscopic moods. . . . Morgan epitomized the high testosterone tycoon, blessed with a lusty ap-

petite for big deals, big boats, and big . . . women." "[B]efore his sway," wrote the socialist daily the *New York Call*, "monarchs made obeisance. . . . He was the very typification of capitalism." The *very typification of capitalism*, "the embodiment," wrote the *New York Sun*, "of the heroic age in American industrial history." Or as a woman who knew Pierpont said simply, "He was the king. He was *it*."[4]

We do not know as much as we would like about this imperious man because he did not want us to. For more than thirty years, he corresponded regularly with his banker-father, often twice a week, writing detailed, revealing letters, sometimes as long as twelve pages, reporting financial and political news, proposing business deals, and making recommendations for investment. These arresting letters traced Pierpont's own development from a bold and sometimes heedless investor to a correct, conservative, and trusted international power broker. Pierpont collected the letters in handsome leather bindings. But the man who on the mantle of his private study had a message that read in French, "Think much, say little, write nothing," put this privileged view of the great age of private banking to flame two years before he died.[5]

What we do know is that Jupiter, as he was often called, at one time controlled one-fifth of all corporations trading on the New York Stock Exchange; that with the creation in 1901 of U.S. Steel—the first billion-dollar corporation—he controlled about 70 percent of the steel industry; that he dominated the three largest insurance companies in the country; that besides the Morgan bank, he controlled three or four other top banks. When, in passing, he commented that "America is good enough for me," William Jennings Bryan's newspaper the *Commoner* suggested that as soon as Mr. Morgan grew tired of it he could "give it back." Frank A. Vanderlip, president of National City Bank, wrote to a colleague shortly after Pierpont's death: "There will be no other king; . . . Mr. Morgan, typical of the time in which he lived can have no successor, for we are facing other days."[6]

Columnists liked to point out that Morgan was unusual in another way. Unlike A. T. Stewart, Jay Gould, Jim Fisk, Andrew Carnegie, and Cornelius Vanderbilt, he did not rise from penury. With no apparent irony, the *Review of Reviews* declared: "To be a rich man's son is a fearful handicap. Sympathize with the poor always; but the present-day talk about the dreadfulness of poverty is mostly sentimental twaddle. . . . Poverty is the diploma of ambition. . . . Success, in this country, at least, has had its hardiest growth in the soil of poverty." Morgan's was planted in business.[7]

Descended from a string of pious New Englanders with a background in banking and mercantile investment, John Pierpont was, in 1837, to enterprise born. His father, Junius Spencer Morgan, received from his own well-to-do father a share in a Connecticut dry goods business that he ultimately helped build into J. M. Beebe, Morgan and Company, the largest exporter in Boston. In 1853, George Peabody, himself a transplanted Yankee, invited Junius to join his thriving London bank as a partner. It took Peabody a year to persuade Junius to move to England, but once there Junius proved extraordinarily successful in selling American railroad securities to the investment-hungry British. When the austere and childless Peabody retired in 1864, he left Junius Morgan in charge of the most prominent American bank in England, with offices in London and New York and affiliates in leading capitals.[8]

If Pierpont lacked the tempering experience of great deprivation, he did have the benefit of an overbearing father whose expert, unsparing hand shaped him for the first fifty years of his life. Junius taught Morgan *fils* to dress, speak, behave, and think like a banker. Pierpont was sent to study in Switzerland and then Göttingen, Germany, where he excelled in math and roamed cathedral grounds collecting discarded shards of beautiful stained glass. In these years the young Pierpont absorbed the entwined cultures of cosmopolitan urbanity and international finance that influenced the rest of his life. Briefly, the young Morgan alarmed his family with the thought of becoming a China trader. But his father, described by an acquaintance as "all will," would not have it. In 1857, he placed twenty-one-year-old Pierpont with Duncan, Sherman and Co., one of New York's leading private financial houses, to have him schooled in American banking. The handsome and well proportioned banking scion with the piercing black eyes settled in fashionable Washington Square and learned to move with ease among New York's commercial and banking elite.[9]

"Slow and sure," Junius wrote in one of his letters to Pierpont, "must be the motto of every young man," as he sought to instill in his sometimes brash son the conservative convictions of the continental banking fraternity. Concentrate on the long term, "remember," he wrote Pierpoint, "that there is an Eye above that is ever upon you & that for every act, word & deed you will one day be called to give account." Called to war in 1863, Pierpont, instead of troubling himself about the "Eye above," displayed a prosaic concern for his own safety. He purchased a $300 exemption from military service. He also married Amelia Sturges, only to lose her tragically to illness less than four months after the wedding. He went on to complete his apprenticeship with Duncan, Sherman and join his cousin James Goodwin in opening a branch of the Morgan banking firm in the United States. His father continued to lecture him by post about building a fortune *together with* a reputation, but Pierpont found it impossible to ignore the quick profit opportunities that flourished in Gotham's war atmosphere, including one, a gold scheme that *The New York Times* described as a "shrewdly conceived . . . manoeuvre" that netted Morgan and Co. $132,000.[10]

Junius was appalled, exasperatedly telling Goodwin that he just could not understand how Pierpont could risk a "snug good business" on some short-term speculation. People who can "lose twice their capital by speculation are not safe people to be entrusted with the business of others—to say nothing of their ability to protect and look after such interest." He feared that in Pierpont's enthusiasm for fast and chancy money he detected a troubling flaw, an inability to withstand the allure of New York's financial daring and shoddy speculation. Fuming that "P so utterly disregarded my warnings," he informed the young partners that he was "transfer[ing] from you all our business on the 1st of April." He did not carry out his threat to break off business relations with his only son, but Morgan *père* did secure an experienced older partner for Pierpont, the estimable Charles Dabney, whom he expected to bridle Pierpont's recklessness and train him in the traditions of financial rectitude.[11]

Dabney, Morgan & Co. made a fine reputation, brokering securities and funding merchant trade as the Manhattan branch of Junius Morgan's bank. Credit specialists Dun & Co. described the New York firm as "a conservative, paying bus. & . . . safe for their engts." Pierpont Morgan they profiled as "excellent char., extra ability, shrewd, quick of perception"—adding, however, that "his peculiar brusqueness of manner has made him & his house unpopular with many." Blunt and quick-tempered Pierpont may have been, but his father and the deliberate Dabney taught him well. There were no more embarrassing ventures pursuing quick profits.[12]

Shortly after forming the new company, Morgan remarried, taking Frances Louisa Tracy, the daughter of a prominent Wall Street attorney, for his bride. Fannie did not do well with New York's noise and quick pace. It all grated on her delicate nerves, and she asked Pierpont to move to New Jersey's quieter suburbs. But he would not hear of leaving New York, the heart of the banking business and the money market, everything that was critical to his work. Here was concentrated the circle of wealthy investors to whom he and the other Wall Street bankers pitched securities and other investment opportunities. Moreover, he craved Manhattan with its kinetic stimulation, dense social attachments, and spirit of innovation. He refused to move, even if it meant more frequent separations from his young wife as she increasingly went for long stays in the country or for visits to friends and relatives. But the pace took its toll on Morgan as well, and in 1871, when the venerable Dabney announced his retirement, Pierpont, whose fits of fatigue and disabling headaches often set off bouts of despondency, wrote his partners that he too was preparing to withdraw from "active business, and liquidate."[13]

Of course, he was denied the last word. Junius would not allow this. He was not prepared to have his son relinquish his strategic outpost at the crossroads of exchange and communication and join the class of indolent rich. Anthony Drexel, one of America's most gifted young bankers, happened to be in London, and he sought the elder Morgan's advice about expanding his Gotham offices. Junius brought Drexel, whose family bank boasted a string of affiliates in Boston, Philadelphia, New York, Paris, and London, together with Pierpont, and the two struck up an easy relationship. They came to a quick agreement about a partnership that Pierpont scribbled on the back of an envelope. Laying aside his plans for early retirement, thirty-four-year-old Pierpont joined the new firm of Drexel, Morgan & Co.[14]

Morgan took the helm of the New York office and also became a full partner in the Philadelphia Drexel bank and in Drexel, Harjes of Paris. But first, directly after launching the new firm, Pierpont took a year off. He would say that he could do twelve months' work in nine, but not in twelve. What he failed to say was that he sometimes had great difficulty stringing two years of work together, nine months or twelve! "The only son," writes Vincent Carosso, "of a great London merchant banker," Pierpont did not forgo the perquisites of his birth. He remained very much his father's work in progress, going from extremes of intense focused banking activity to a full surcease of business, racing between the world of New York finance and a world of elsewhere with its baths (Carlsbad), its art (the continent), and its ancient artifacts (Egypt).[15]

Drexel, Morgan opened its doors on July 1, 1871. Within a year it moved to a new site at 23 Wall Street, at the corner of Broad and Wall, the corner where nearly a century before, George Washington had taken the oath of office. *Harper's Weekly* breathtakingly calculated that the purchase price of $1 million came to $21 million per acre, making 23 Wall the most expensive piece of real estate on the globe. Within months Pierpont had reason to question his decision to stay in banking, as the 1873 depression hit, taking down as many as four hundred banks, including some of America's most established financial houses. But advancing maturity and a caution stemming from the need to answer to his father had made a conservative banker of Morgan. With a sure feel for New York's investment environment, and a ripening appreciation for the reserve that his father had so often commanded, he was able to come out of the crash intact.[16]

Indeed, when the Cooke firm collapsed in September 1873, he wrote to his father with pride: "We had in Bank and Call-Loans enough money to pay in two hours every dollar we owed to everyone, assuming that every depositor we had should draw every cent of money out instantly without notice. How many firms do you suppose, doing such a business as we are, could make such a statement?" Despite this cushion, he refused to take risks. He called in every Drexel, Morgan loan. Tony Drexel thought that it was a mistake to cancel the high-interest loans, but Pierpont insisted that he would rather make no money than take the chance of being seen losing it. The step proved inspired. While other firms were closing, Morgan wrote London that by investing solely in bonds that "can be recommended without a shadow of a doubt," his bank finished the year with profits of close to $500,000. Representing "unassailable" companies exclusively, Drexel, Morgan won a reputation for gold-plated investment service, handled with Victorian caution, precision, and integrity.[17]

Prudent he may have been, but Morgan's enthusiasms were not modest. Other businessmen too spied rare opportunities in these depression years, refusing to settle for merely surviving the season of economic ruin. Carnegie built his steel works, Rockefeller conceived Standard Oil, Armour and Morris created their meat-packing empires, and Bell won funding for his telephone. Like these entrepreneurs, who devised new business forms and erected America's cornerstone industries, Morgan capitalized on the widespread dislocations to adapt investment banking to the financial needs of an industrializing America. With a small circle of Wall Street financial houses, he transformed a loose fraternity of former merchants who provided loans and services to businesses into an elite group of banking institutions that actively shaped America's ascent to international economic leadership.[18]

The most prestigious and most powerful of Europe's banks were the institutions run by the court bankers, grand European houses like Baring and Rothschild that were molded in the *haute banque* tradition of privileged access and government service. Friends and confidants to kings, princes, and governments, they influenced the course of history, stabilizing regimes, securing national economies, underwriting wars, and latterly funding the grand infrastructure projects of their homelands. Of course, government banking required the resources to advance the large sums that states might require upon short notice. With no private American bank in a position to offer such services before the war, the United States was forced to depend upon foreign houses for its loans.[19]

But by the early 1870s, some New York banks were big enough to compete for this business. Between 1871 and 1879, as the United States required $1.4 billion to refinance its Civil War debt, Washington found that it was no longer limited to negotiating with Europe's unsympathetic and demanding *haute banques*. Only a few years back, Drexel, Morgan, J&W Seligman, Levi Morton, and August Belmont had financed mostly trade cargoes. Now, their coffers filled with postwar boom profits, Wall Street banks succeeded in putting together five successive transatlantic syndicates to underwrite the largest funding contracts in history. Aside from peeling back another layer of foreign economic domination, the fact that these transactions were handled locally meant that the substantial commissions and management fees were funneled back into domestic industrial investment and business growth. And it was easier for Washington to deal with Americans, even if they were in New York, than to negotiate with foreigners whose loyalties were elsewhere. Perhaps most striking of all was the realization that New York had become like Paris, London, and Vienna, a seat of national financing. By

1876, European governments were coming to 23 Wall Street for loans.[20]

With Junius nominally at the head, the two Morgan branches, London and New York, formed a closely linked financial structure, bringing the European and American worlds of investment, commerce, and exchange together more intimately than ever before. Pierpont continued to defer to his father's notions of sound banking etiquette. Soundness, as in sound money, sound practices, and sound investments, became a Morgan byword. But the balance of power between London and New York was shifting, and Pierpont placed some distance between his firm and Junius's continental sensibilities. There was a sharper edge to the American bank, removed as Pierpont was from London's high reticence; a New York edge. "I have but one desire in relation to our business," he wrote to one of the Drexel partners, "to extend it in every way where it can be done profitably, and at the same time satisfactorily. . . ."[21]

The American practice of mixing banking with politics, for example, made Junius uncomfortable. Nonetheless, Drexel, Morgan and its syndicate partners each contributed $5,000 to Republican Rutherford B. Hayes's campaign in the controversy-racked 1876 presidential election. "Defeat," Drexel, Morgan cabled by way of explanation, "means inflation." "Such contributions," Pierpont protested to a less than enthusiastic London office, were "most *advantageous* for the future syndicate business and facilities." He even pressed his reluctant father into contributing an additional $5,000, though the elder Morgan insisted that his name not appear.[22]

So *advantageous* did these contributions prove that President Hayes installed the bankers' favorite politician, Ohio senator John Sherman, as secretary of the Treasury. Sherman did not let his benefactors down, consistently assigning the maximum allowable commission for their loans. So *advantageous* were these contributions in cementing a New York–Washington axis that Pierpont would drop in on the secretary of the Treasury and call upon the president for a quick hello whenever he was in Washington. Nor did Pierpont allow

London's skittishness to prevent him from joining other syndicators to reward a key Treasury official with cash "for his kind offices." Other civil servants were also offered a "suitable return" for their assistance to the bank.[23]

Father and son also disagreed over funding the work of Thomas Edison. Junius Morgan wanted to have nothing to do with the eccentric inventor and his bulb experiments; Pierpont was captivated by the possibilities opened by electrification and incandescent lighting.

Edison had made a reputation as a brilliant, if somewhat unsteady, inventor as he worked himself up from a job as a telegrapher to direct what amounted to an invention factory at Menlo Park, New Jersey. Here he developed and patented scores of important new gadgets and industrial processes and went on to become one of a few inventors at work on perfecting an inexpensive and dependable form of electric energy, as well as a host of related new products, including the incandescent lamp.

Junius wanted no part of Edison's various start-ups. In New York's much more venturesome environment, however, Pierpont was inclined to look beyond Edison's eccentricities. Cheap, safe, and accessible energy would become the largest industrial project in national history, bringing a higher standard to home life and transforming manufacturing. Pierpont was not interested in turning away this kind of business. He went personally to Menlo Park to investigate Edison's experiments on electrical power and came away impressed. He became an enthusiastic backer of the electrical work and made his home one of the first to boast Edison incandescent lighting. Then he bought as much of an interest in the unpredictable genius's electric business as Edison would sell him. In 1880, the Edison Company initiated construction on a Pearl Street power station in downtown Manhattan. Two years later, on September 4, 1882, the inventor, attired in a new Prince Albert frock, inaugurated the station's twenty-seven-ton generators before walking over to 23 Wall Street to throw the switch that bathed Drexel, Morgan's Manhattan offices in Edison lamp light.[24]

Father and son also differed over what Pierpont came to consider the empty conventions of continental banking etiquette. Junius, bedazzled by the Rothschild name and fortune, respected the venerable banking house as Europe's senior bankers. Just being listed as a co-underwriter with the Rothschilds meant a great deal to him, and he easily surrendered pride of place to them on joint syndications. He would not dream of excluding them from an underwriting venture. But Pierpont suffered no such compunctions. He bore a grudge against the Rothschilds' American representative, August Belmont, for snubs both real and imagined. Moreover, Belmont, an outspoken and highly partisan Democrat, proved to be a burden to other bankers in this Republican era. Pierpont closed Belmont out of the last of the Civil War refunding syndications, peevishly cabling his father that Morgan London needed to recognize that it owed more to its New York partners than to the house of Rothschild.[25]

By the late 1870s, having coordinated a string of successful syndications, Pierpont was emerging from beneath his father's domination. When 23 Wall Street closed a set of negotiations on the U.S. debt without consulting London, Junius Morgan sent his son a stinging complaint. Pierpont wrote back to the incensed Junius that the short deadline had allowed him no time to confer. But he offered no regrets. The momentum of the last twenty years had moved the center of financial innovation across the ocean to New York. Cautious and slow was fine for Europe, but Pierpont could no longer run all decisions—even multimillion-dollar ones—past Junius. Things not only moved faster in Gotham, a Drexel, Morgan partner wrote London, they also required "direct personal experience on the spot." If the Europeans were not willing to trust the Wall Street office, there were others in New York to take their place. Junius Morgan wrote back stiffly that he accepted Pierpont's explanations, "which modify our views."[26]

Pierpont's growing national stature also asserted itself in a matter unconnected to his work as banker to the government. In 1877, a year of intense labor unrest, Congress adjourned without having adopted a budget to pay the army. The men in uniform were furious, adding to the widespread sense of insecurity and discontent, but no one was prepared to do anything, and it would be months before Congress convened again. Morgan stepped in, announcing that he was interested in "protecting a class of men whose interest should in our judgement, command the greatest and most earnest solicitude of the Government and the Country." He provided the War Department with $550,000 a month to be disbursed in twelve centers around the country. Congress had not approved funding, but Pierpont committed a total of some $2.5 million to the army payroll, money that was later repaid.[27]

Fall 1877 marked one of those formal occasions that offer tribute at the same time that they mark a gracious, if unspoken, transition. New York was treated to a festive celebration of Junius Morgan's banking career. More than one hundred of Gotham's political and economic elite attended the dinner at Delmonico's. The *Times* described the guests, including four governors, leading business and banking executives, and a sprinkling of the most respected cultural and intellectual figures in the nation, as "the wealth and brains of the Union . . . probably never before . . . equaled at any gathering of the sort in the history of the Metropolis." The turnout offered homage to Junius's career while also honoring Pierpont's new stature. Pierpont had made Wall Street a leading power in government funding. Through the next decade, he would lead it in exerting unprecedented influence over the development of the new corporate order.[28]

In the mid-1870s, the railroad industry was growing at a faster pace than ever. The pursuit of growth had been programmed into the industry from its early days, when its pacesetters had barreled past fierce obstacles and blasted through mountains in order to lay track. Yet well past the pioneering stage, railroad leaders continued to think that success lay in expansion, that they must either continue to expand their roads or risk being overtaken by others who would create a more efficient and successful system. Laying more track, even as with every new mile they increased their debt, the railroads flirted with bankruptcy. In this volatile business environment, investors turned more guarded. In 1877, *Banker's Magazine* noted the "plethora of capital which is seeking employment." "Capital," declared one railroad industry scholar, had gone "on strike."[29]

With many clients among the railroads and among investors who held millions in road-based securities, Pierpont Morgan had no choice but to become involved in this crisis. Aside from his personal skills as a banker and respected voice of fiscal authority, he brought to this effort several important gifts. Pierpont had credibility. He had funded American government debt for a decade. He had paid the army. He had achieved eminent stature in the international banking community. And he controlled a blue-chip list of investors who looked to him for advice about where to invest their capital. With this immense leverage, his influence over an industry that was kept alive by the steady infusion of banker-negotiated capital grew large.

Morgan had already demonstrated that he was a different sort of railroad banker. Where other investment houses kept their distance, accepting the reports of the roads as definitive and then passing these on to their investors, Morgan pursued a more hands-on approach. When his client the Cairo and Vincennes Railroad came close to bankruptcy in 1873, he had his own staff conduct a thorough analysis. Then in blunt terms he threatened to cut the road off from its funding lifeline—and very few other banks were going to come in after J. P. Morgan had left—unless it adopted a long list of his demands for reform. He revamped the company management, installed a Morgan-dominated board, and for the next *eight years* kept the company on a tight leash. He did the same with the highly regarded Baltimore and Ohio road. Despite the fact that its president, the venerable John Work Garrett, was a friend of his father's, he pressed for direct oversight over the road's management, writing: "I should be derelict in my duty to . . . [investors] if I did not frankly state to you exactly what I deemed essential."[30]

Morgan's stature grew even more once the role he played in helping William H. Vanderbilt unload the New York Central became widely known.

When Cornelius Vanderbilt died in 1877 at the age of eighty-three, he left behind a New York Central system that stretched 4,500 miles into the American interior. It connected Chicago and a rich hinterland to New York City and the eastern ports. Intent on keeping this rail empire unified, he bequeathed close to 90 percent of its stock to one son, William Henry, who proved unequal to the challenge of keeping the gift intact.[31]

By this time, the old orthodoxy of laissez-faire had lost some of its power to ward off state regulation. Even businessmen who in the past had recoiled at state intervention now feared the railroad monopolies and their power over the market. In New York State, a politically potent coalition of farmers and merchants, threatened by railroads that charged them two and three times the rates quoted in Boston and other cities, pressed the legislature to regulate rail transport rates. This resulted in a pioneering state investigation of the railroads.[32]

Chaired by Republican Alonzo B. Hepburn, the probe released more than 4,000 pages of evidence and testimony detailing railroad frauds and abuses of corporate trust. In his testimony, William H. Vanderbilt revealed that his father had simply created more than $50 million in paper value out of thin air and added it to company books during the 1869 consolidation of the New York Central and the Hudson River roads. Railroad officials denied under oath that they offered special pricing agreements, rebates, or kickbacks, but the Hepburn committee uncovered more than 6,000 such arrangements for just the first six months of 1879![33]

The hearings made a powerful impression across the land, leading to an expanding movement for regulation. The hearings also shook William H. Vanderbilt, who lacked his father's swashbuckling nerve. The railroad heir feared that the legislature would use his New York Central, the last major railroad trunk still controlled by a single family, as its whipping boy, punishing it with restrictions and prohibitive taxes. He decided to sell off more than a third of his Central inheritance, a quarter million shares of railroad stock, to stop the attacks. To coordinate this great divestiture, which had to be carried out with care and discretion to avoid undermining the price of the stock, Vanderbilt sought out Drexel Morgan.[34]

Morgan demanded conditions before he would take on the assignment. Vanderbilt had to guarantee an 8 percent dividend on the stock for the next five years, *regardless of company profits.* And he had to place Morgan on the New York Central's board of directors to represent the interests of the investors. This was unprecedented. The idea of brokers dictating terms may have disturbed the Vanderbilt scion, but this was Pierpont Morgan who was doing the dictating, and Vanderbilt needed his services. He bowed to the conditions, granting Morgan a large say in the affairs of the New York Central. Morgan developed an elegant strategy, taking the sale to England and smoothly distributing the stock without rousing any suspicions. Not until all the securities had been sold did the papers report and praise Morgan's "grand financial operation."[35]

The same year, Morgan assembled a consortium to underwrite more than $40 million in mortgage bonds, the largest corporate bond transaction ever made in the United States, to fund 1,600 miles of new track for the Northern Pacific line. This was the line whose debt had sunk Cooke & Co. in 1873 to set off the depression. But Morgan had proved that he could accomplish wonders with roads of questionable background. Using the full resources of Drexel, Morgan's correspondents in New York, Boston, Baltimore, London, and Paris, he placed the Northern Pacific bonds, which were all sold on *the first day they came to market.* So quickly did these securities sell that in New York alone sales exceeded $10 million. Pierpont begged his overseas partners for more bonds for favored clients, but there were none to be had. The issue had been subscribed more than five times over! By the end of 1880, Pierpont was giddily reporting to London that "negotiations of great magnitude follow each other with great rapidity."[36]

Still, Junius had reservations. He did not like the idea of Pierpont taking so direct a hand in the companies he was financing. The senior Morgan thought that there should be a firewall separating bankers from their borrowing clients. Pierpont disagreed. Joining corporate boards, overseeing company policies, and even playing a strong part in management *were* banking duties, perhaps not in England, but in New York, with its tradition of Gould-ed railroads and such corporate eminences as Daniel Drew and Commodore Vanderbilt, it was important to make certain that shareholders were not held hostage to the easy virtue of courts and legislatures. Only his direct role in companies like the Northern Pacific allowed Pierpont access to continental pocketbooks for America's cash-hungry railroad carriers.[37]

Pierpont's outside activities may have displeased Junius, but he had even more ambitious plans for 23 Wall Street to use its banking clout to wrestle the railroad industry into more rational shape. This involved Morgan in developing a new business model for the railroad industry; it also made him an enemy of Andrew Carnegie's.

Andrew Carnegie's empire was producing staggering profits throughout the 1880s, but the steel king would not stop obsessing over costs. He hunted down every technical innovation, every practical twist, every opportunity to cut labor and other expenditures. One thing fell tantalizingly beyond his control, the carrying costs for his steel. On this issue, writes his biographer, he was "almost paranoiac." Extraordinary profits could not still his torment, especially when he learned that the Pennsylvania Railroad was giving other shippers better deals. In 1884, the steel mogul toyed with leading a citizens' march in Pittsburgh to protest the Pennsylvania monopoly. "We do not agree to be singled out & discriminated against," he cabled the railroad. "We [will] send a circular to every shareholder & failing here we [will] make our appeal to the general public whose opinion no corporation these days can successfully withstand. . . . Every manfr. in Pittsburgh & in the West will rise in indignation. It is infamous & I give you due notice you can't impose upon us." Only after his own officials suggested that it was not so smart to stir up working-class mobs who might have some unkind things to say about wages at his steel plants did he back down from leading a protest against the rail octopus.[38]

Meanwhile, the Pennsylvania had been carrying on a fierce competitive war with the New York Central. Each road made bold incursions on the other's turf. When Carnegie learned that William Vanderbilt aimed to punish the Pennsylvania's intrusion into the New York Central's Hudson territory with a "get even" road in southern Pennsylvania that would reach almost to the door of his steel works, he joined John D. Rockefeller and others to subscribe $5 million to the project. The plans were drawn, the rails ordered, the money raised, and work on cutting roadbed out of the most rugged terrain in the East was begun. Hundreds of lives were lost blasting tunnels through solid rock and setting the bridge piers in the Susquehanna as the industrialists made ready to tame the imperious Pennsylvania.[39]

This smaller episode of a much wider battle captured the attention of local producers, but all of Wall Street was mesmerized by the larger "struggle for preeminence" between the railroad titans. The war threatened disaster for the entire industry. It would result in huge losses and lead investors to flee the securities markets. Dismayed by the mad efforts at mutual destruction, Pierpont, who had been involved with both roads, summoned the executives to a meeting in July 1885 on board his yacht, the *Corsair.*[40]

He spoke bluntly to both sides, telling them that the senseless war reflected a deeply flawed reading of how to do business in this industry and threatened to undermine the climate of investment. For a full day he hammered at both parties. Nothing, not the volume of business, not the number of track miles, not even the level of earnings, was as important as stability. They must stop seeing each other as competitors for the same limited number of customers. Such a model was a prescription for disaster. Their most important concern must be not victory, but rather a sound business environment in which profits were secure and investor confidence was protected. Both sides must recognize each other's right to exist and to its own sphere of influence. Morgan got the two roads to sign what came to be called the "Corsair Compact." They would respect each other's natural market and abandon the competitive roads that each had undertaken in the other's primary territory.[41]

Andrew Carnegie was furious with Morgan for undermining his effort to sow competition, but railroad men were relieved. Wall Street, hoping that this agreement might signal a new spirit of comity in the industry, celebrated, recognizing with some unease that Morgan, in seeking to replace the competitive jungle with an approach borrowed from imperial diplomacy, had placed himself at its center.[42]

Morgan followed the Corsair Compact with regional railroad pools to eliminate cutthroat competition and shore up prices. But in the end, these voluntary agreements proved impossible to enforce. The typical industry official, said one railroad man, viewed rate agreements as "binding no longer than he thinks it for his interest to be bound by it." Short periods of calm rapidly faded into bouts of ruthless industrial battle, especially in the West, where a history of ill will, mistrust, and colossal vindictiveness yielded the longest and most bitter of these destructive wars. In 1886, the *Railroad Gazette* described the situation as "open warfare," with rates in a free fall, changing from hour to hour. Collis P. Huntington, head of the Southern and Central Pacific systems, reflected the industry's take-no-prisoners attitude when he declared starkly: "Nobody shall carry freight between New York and San Francisco any better or cheaper than we do." Millions were wasted on spite.[43]

Morgan did not allow the industry's disorder to discourage him from buying up choice railroad properties that had fallen on hard times, of which in this extensively overbuilt industry there was no shortage. From 1875 to 1897, seven hundred railroad companies representing one hundred thousand miles of track—more than half the nation's total—defaulted. Mobilizing billions in investor funds,

Drexel, Morgan sifted through the best of these roads, selecting more than twenty in all, and acquired precious equities by buying their debt. The ensuing reorganizations transferred crippled roads from local investors who had originally financed them to Drexel, Morgan at cut rates.[44]

From 1886 to 1890, Morgan reorganized three major roads, the Philadelphia and Reading, the Baltimore & Ohio, and the Chesapeake and Ohio, in each instance recasting debt, installing dependable management, and restoring profitability. Assisted by his partner, Charles Coster, whom Wall Street expert John Moody described as having "a mind in a generation for detail," Pierpont absorbed the endless details about each of the roads and then restructured them. The characteristic clause in a Morgan reorganization (aside from the million-dollar fees) placed control over management with Morgan people for a specified period of time. Through these "Morganizations," Drexel, Morgan took over company operations and molded the roads into modern enterprises. "Our absolute control," Junius Morgan wrote in one of his letters, "must be undoubted." At one point, Coster sat on fifty-nine separate corporate boards. By 1890, when Morgan *père* died, Pierpont stood as the virtual czar of railroad capital, his movements, wrote *The New York Times*, "watched more carefully than those of any other man in the financial world."[45]

In the past, financiers had been limited to putting up money and collecting interest. But Morgan changed this, converting "financiers," in Ron Chernow's words, "from servants to masters of their clients." The process resulted in a clutch of railroad companies that were national in scope and controlled by a small group of Wall Street banks. Vincent Carosso reports that by 1893, "thirty three railroad corporations with a capitalization of $100 million or more operated 69 percent of the railroad mileage in the U.S. . . . coordinat[ing] . . . the flows of smaller connecting systems."[46]

But the railroad market proved difficult to tame. The roads continued to build parallel lines and undercut price standards. Morgan railed at the blind pursuit of railroad growth (throughout the 1880s, more than $5 billion was poured into new railroad ventures, adding close to seventy-five thousand miles of new track), terming it "suicidal" for the $10 billion railroad industry. Finally, he summoned more than a dozen of the top railroad executives and leading underwriters to his home at 36th Street and Madison Avenue. The "financial buccaneering that had bankrupted many properties and undermined the reputation of railroad securities generally," he warned, must end. Investors would not stand for such mindless squandering of their resources. If it did not stop, the bankers would cut off their support. Over the next few months, Morgan fashioned a railroad cartel to enforce "reasonable, uniform, and stable rates" and deny financing to any road that violated the agreement. That eliminating competition seemed to violate a key principle of the free enterprise economy did not disturb him. Such matters concerned ideologues; Wall Street bankers focused on stability and profits.[47]

Reared in the customs of international finance, John Pierpont Morgan married the Victorian traditions of continental high banking that he had absorbed from his father to the more vigorous practices of the Wall Street financial community. A decade spent syndicating government bonds made him extraordinarily wealthy as he led American banking out from under the shadow of European domination, putting an end to the Baring and Rothschild monopoly over U.S. government financing. Ensconced at 23 Wall Street, with Junius in London, Anthony Drexel in Philadelphia, and another partner, John Harjes, in Paris, he came to recognize, through these successful syndications, what a well-organized cooperative industry could accomplish by avoiding destructive competition. He might mouth the conventional pieties of free enterprise ideology, but he had become disillusioned with the competitive market. Business's highest obligation to its investors was to minimize instability while protecting profits. The railroad corporations had proven themselves more adept at wondrous feats of construction and organization than at developing a coherent and effective business strategy. Through the Corsair Compact and the rail cartel Morgan imposed a level of active financial control over corporate enterprise that even the *haute banques* never wielded. He emerged as the leading banker of the age and the foremost example of active financier domination of corporate enterprise.[48]

By the close of the 1880s, Pierpont was the leading figure in American banking, and he had made this mean much more than it ever had before. In one generation, Morgan had managed to transform the role of banker from simple money broker to active business leader, wrapping his huge arms around the largest, richest, and most important industry in the world, an industry that, while deeply flawed, generated the profits for America's next quantum leap in industrialization. Buoyed by their past successes, Pierpont and his Wall Street colleagues prepared to lead this next stage in corporate growth and consolidation.

---

Twenty-three Wall Street and the funding syndicates ventured to replace the uncertainties of competitive business with stable and orderly profit streams. But the financiers lacked the practical means to enforce harmony and cooperation. It fell to 26 Broadway, an address as important to global industry as Morgan's was to banking, to develop the administrative and legal devices for industrial consolidation.

"Rockefeller, you know," the philosopher William James wrote in a letter to his novelist brother, Henry, in 1904, "is reputed the richest man in the world, and he certainly is the most powerfully suggestive personality I have ever seen. A man ten stories deep, and to me quite unfathomable . . . , flexible, cunning, quakerish, superficially suggestive of naught but goodness and conscientiousness, yet accused of being the greatest villain in business whom our country has produced."[49]

John D. Rockefeller originated Standard Oil in Cleveland and by a process of ruthless annexation managed to solve a problem that confounded Pierpont Morgan: how to make sure that a price, having been fixed, remained fixed; that corporations, having agreed to rationalize the market by controlling competition and manipulating distribution, were prevented from reverting to feral market practices. Through a centrally managed holding company, Rockefeller developed a strict rationalization in oil that did everything the bankers had hoped to accomplish with railroads, ridding his industry of redundancies and consolidating control over prices and markets.

By the time it was the largest corporation in the world, Standard Oil Trust was operating its global oil empire from New York, extending its petroleum-based operations both vertically and horizontally, from refining to production to distribution and marketing. Standard controlled four dozen American companies plus a wholly owned subsidiary in England. It participated in joint ventures in Germany, Holland, Italy, and Denmark and ran a huge export business to Latin America and the Far East. It owned more than four thousand miles of pipelines, a railroad tank car fleet that collected and delivered oil nationally, and a small navy of transoceanic tankers. Cascading profits, "arguably the most stupendous cash flow ever produced in American industry," allowed the trust to finance its own expansion (and buy up its competition) from its own reserves, leading Rockefeller to boast that he did not need J. P. Morgan to put his business together.[50]

John D. Rockefeller was born poor. "Because he was born in 1839," the *World Telegram* wrote insightfully, "and was—according to the standards of his own day—ruthless to the nth degree, he was on the stage, and ready to act his part when the curtain rose on the American era that began with the Civil War." War shortages accelerated the growth of the oil industry as many turned to kerosene (petroleum's most important product before 1900; only later was it gasoline) to replace embargoed southern turpentine.[51]

"He was smart," a *New York Post* columnist would write, "when he was twenty two, . . . he refused to join up for the Civil War and, taking seventy five more years to die, got rich. Was ever better evidence offered that Pacifism Pays?" Twenty-three years old in 1863, just a few years after oil had first been discovered in Pennsylvania, he entered the refining business. He realized that the best opportunities for profits lay in processing the gooey black ooze. The refining of oil added 100 percent to its value; it was also the sector of the petroleum business most open to technological innovation and the economies of scale.[52]

With the business still in its early stages, Cleveland-based John D. dispatched brother William to set up Rockefeller and Co. in New York to handle distribution and financing. It did not go easy. The banks were preoccupied with the railroad boom and, in any event, leery of a business where a single fire could destroy an entire company. John D. never forgot the humiliation that such dependency brought. "We had to go to the banks—almost on our knees—to get money and credit," he recalled later.[53]

Perhaps the experience strengthened Rockefeller's resolve to be independent and in control; certainly it provided the joyless and driven entrepreneur with a rationale for his extreme competitiveness. In 1870, when he incorporated Standard Oil with three partners, the refinery began pressuring strapped railroads to cut the rates they charged Standard. The crippled Erie, for example, was forced to rebate 75 percent of its regular charges. With carrying charges accounting for the petroleum industry's largest business expense, this edge allowed Standard to capture the regional market and to begin swallowing up its competitors.[54]

The tough, dour Rockefeller earned a reputation for pennypinching, and not only in business. When one of his investments in a sanitarium in Cleveland went bad, this by now impressively wealthy man moved his family into the large building. With all of the extra rooms, he and his wife (equally dour and equally frugal) hit upon the idea of entertaining people at the home and lodging them in the rooms that lined the upper floor. Before long, John and Laura were charging acquaintances for their stay at the establishment as "club guests." More than a few friends were taken aback upon returning home to find a bill from the Rockefellers waiting for them.[55]

Profit conscious and inordinately driven, Rockefeller proceeded to lash together the leading petroleum processors to form a confederation that fixed prices and pressed the railroads for discounts and kickbacks. The group also demanded drawbacks—that is, they demanded to be paid forty cents on each barrel shipped *by a competitor*, driving up their own receipts while taking a bite out of competitor profits. But, like many similar plans for industrial solidarity, the combination soon fell apart, and members of the group took to undercutting one another. Henceforth, Rockefeller dismissed all efforts at voluntary controls as useless "ropes of sand," no better than paste and bailing wire. He set out instead to systematically capture the industry.[56]

When the 1873 depression sent oil values into a tailspin, he pressed forward, annexing desperate competitors. Through methods benign, callous, and even criminal, he wove his refining empire. Rockefeller articulated the principle in the most kindly tones. "We wanted the old struggle to cease. . . . We wanted these men to pull together . . . to join us, . . . and thus work together" in a postcompetitive world. But his methods were relentless. Some competitors sold voluntarily, others joined Standard Oil as partners, and yet others were bludgeoned by threats into selling. Those who resisted his overtures Rockefeller with little apparent irony, denounced as "selfish people forever stirring up trouble or creating annoyances, blackmailers, sharpsters and crooks." By 1876, Standard Oil had eliminated these "troublemakers," annexing more than a score of firms and absorbing more through outright purchase. Five years later, with forty affiliates, the cartel controlled almost 90 percent of the nation's oil-refining capacity.[57]

The arrangement binding the processors was ingenious. They exchanged stock in one another's companies, creating an interlocking financial relationship, while each individual company retained its formal independence. A secret central administration dictated noncompetitive prices, allocated distribution, and negotiated concessions from suppliers and carriers. While the Standard Oil cartel stopped short of welding the companies into one integrated unit under a single management, it was the most powerful business combination ever developed.[58]

In 1879, the New York State Legislature's Hepburn investigation of monopolistic practices sought to uncover Standard Oil's secret world. It summoned Standard executives to testify. Rockefeller remained secluded in Ohio, beyond the committee's reach. Colleagues who could not avoid the committee provided truculent and uncooperative testimony. One of the Standard men was asked to explain his duties as a director. "I am," he replied flippantly, "a clamorer for dividends. That is the only function I have." Directed to return the next day to complete his testimony, the man bristled. "I have given today to the matter. It will be impossible for me to be with you again." Others simply refused to answer. Despite the evasions, the committee reconstructed a maze of hidden contracts and rebates. "There is no question about it," William Vanderbilt confided to the committee, "but these men are smarter than I am a great deal. . . . I never came in contact with any class of men as smart and alert as they are in their business." Standard's power, Vanderbilt declared, was unprecedented. "One man could hardly have been able to do it; *it is a combination of men.*" He was referring to Standard's accomplishment in achieving what had eluded the railroads: concentrating the power of the entire industry while avoiding the heavy hand of the bankers. The committee concluded that Standard was "a mysterious organization." Its chief counsel was less circumspect. He called it a "monstrous monopoly."[59]

The legislature created a commission to thwart the oil combination's power over the railways, but Standard was well ahead of them. Crude oil interests had begun introducing pipeline technology as a means for avoiding the railroads and their Standard-induced surcharges. Once the first pipeline was completed in July 1879, Rockefeller appropriated the idea, installing his own system of wholly owned pipelines. The new delivery system, requiring a new level of cooperation among the oil refiners, spurred Rockefeller to seek a thoroughgoing integration of the cartel. Unification under a single management would permit Standard to rationalize the industry, from planning new product lines to modernizing some plants while closing others. It would allow Rockefeller to build new technologically superior superrefineries and assign specialized tasks to the less efficient ones—in short, to make a single integrated business of the entire industry. However, under the loose cartel management then prevailing, no refining company executive could be expected to allow his plant to be closed down for the benefit of the larger alliance.[60]

Rockefeller wanted to make one large company of the individual units, but if he wanted to combine what historian Glenn Porter has aptly called a "patchwork of subterfuges" into a single corporation, he would have to overcome legal obstacles. State incorporation laws, for example, prohibited the merging of separate corporations, especially corporations that had been chartered in different states. Rockefeller once explained why he admired Napoleon: "There was none of the stagnant blood of nobility or royalty in his veins. . . . He could think quicker and along more individual and original lines than any of the [monarchs of Europe]." John D. knew what he wanted, and he assigned Standard Oil attorney Samuel C. T. Dodd to sweep away the legal obstacles.[61]

Dodd had been admitted to the Pennsylvania bar in 1859, the year oil was discovered in western Pennsylvania. Specializing in the new field of corporate law, he fought the Rockefeller interests on behalf of transportation companies, independent oil producers, and consumers. As a delegate to the 1881 Pennsylvania Constitutional Convention, he cast legislation to criminalize the sort of rebates that Rockefeller was extracting from the railroads. That same year, John D. Rockefeller lured him over to the side of Standard Oil and brought him to New York (where, in a step that no doubt endlessly nettled his heirs, Dodd refused to accept Rockefeller's gift of Standard Oil stock, on the grounds that this would unduly influence him!).[62]

The following year, Dodd conceived the trust, a "corporation of corporations." Forty separate Standard corporations turned over their stock to a newly formed board of trustees, receiving in exchange trust certificates of equal value. Rockefeller, who later testified that he had restructured the business so that he could bring poor people cheap energy, went to a great deal of trouble to cover this "charitable work" with a veil of secrecy, hoping to avoid the scrutiny of antimonopolists. Internal negotiations resembled wartime diplomacy, with secret bargaining among the units, an espionage network to guard against leaks, contracts drawn with the intricacy of international treaties, and a lobbying team that prompted the great muckraker Henry Demarest Lloyd to declare famously that Rockefeller did everything with the Pennsylvania State Legislature "except to refine it."[63]

All trust affiliates in each state were consolidated under a single business umbrella. These state corporations were then collectively joined under a central managing unit directed by nine trustees and an army of specialists from Manhattan. Here experts sifted information on finance, prices, trade, and transport, managing the dispersed branches through field executives (many of whom wielded more power than state governors) and coordinating their efforts. The executive committee, which established company policy and charted Standard's future, worked in secret in order to shield its members from internal pressure. Each of the branch companies was held to a profit standard determined through an advanced system of record keeping and accounting that crunched an astonishing array of numbers to wield informed control.[64]

John D., who held 44 percent of the titanic trust, routinely denied any understanding of how Standard Oil worked, but he was the force behind its policies. Like Carnegie, he refused to distribute the company's high profits in the form of dividends. Remembering too well what it had meant for his brother to go begging hat in hand to the New York bankers, he insisted on using Standard's earnings to grow the company and create a reserve so that the oil giant would never have to turn to a bank for funds.[65]

Not too many years before, such a business would have been inconceivable. The changes in American business that reduced the complexities of ownership to negotiable paper certificates easily convertible into yet other forms of negotiable paper made the trust possible. J. P. Morgan had used his mastery over the money market to consolidate the railroad industry, but his control over industry policy was imperfect at best. Rockefeller's trust offered the more effective model for tightly controlled authority over an entire industry. Moreover, it *kept control within the industry.* "This movement," Rockefeller would later exclaim, "was the origin of the whole system of modern economic administration. . . . The time was ripe for it. The day of the combination is here to stay. Individualism has gone, never to return."[66]

Like Morgan, Rockefeller hardly gave much thought to this departure from the prevailing business credo. Both men focused on goals, leaving others to work out the theoretical implications. Each man viewed capitalism as a general system that offered enough flexibility to build his businesses and not as a straitjacket that dictated a narrow set of market relations.[67]

Rockefeller had begun to spend more time in New York in the late 1870s, especially during the busy winter months. In the fall of 1882, he moved his legal residence there. Cleveland had been a perfect place for a reclusive mogul, especially when he sought shelter from public attention, but once the trust was planted in Manhattan, he needed to be close at hand. He moved to West 54th Street and filled the neighborhood around his home with Standard Oil men and their families. Not far away he built heated stables for his horses. While he religiously avoided New York's beau monde round of parties, balls, operas, and clubs, carriage racing was one of the few exceptions to his parsimonious lifestyle. Just the year before, when his equally abstemious wife commented that they needed a new coach, Rockefeller, one of America's richest men, replied that they first had to trade in the old one. He still enjoyed his simple breakfast of milk and bread (unless there was an executive committee meeting, which he often liked to hold in the early morning at his home), followed by a ride on the Sixth Avenue elevated to his office. Riders would see the gaunt millionaire jot reminders and memos on his shirt cuffs on the trip downtown to the trust's offices, recently moved from 140 Pearl Street to 44 Broadway.[68]

That same year, the trust purchased a $500,000 tract of land on lower Broadway and in May 1885 completed a nine-story neoclassical headquarters at 26 Broadway. The stern granite structure became the nerve center for the entire Standard Oil operation, where important men in stiff collars hammered out policy for the giant trust's multinational operations. Ruthlessly efficient, the trust reduced the total number of refineries from fifty-three to twenty-two (most of them in Brooklyn and Manhattan) and launched a number of super-refineries. It slashed refining costs by two-thirds and, with its centrally unified purchasing power, bypassed the petroleum exchanges (putting them out of business within the decade) to buy directly from crude oil producers.[69]

With control over refining and distribution uncontested, Standard next moved into production, by 1891 extracting 25 percent of all crude oil in the country. Once it controlled all aspects of petroleum production, from excavating to shipping, refining, and delivering the finished product, the trust next turned to directly marketing its oil, replacing exporters with wholly owned subsidiaries that sold to central and Western Europe. From the center of its web at 26 Broadway, in the span of less than a decade, the Standard Oil Trust consolidated every step in the petroleum oil business from the extraction of crude through its processing to its shipment and sale across the nation and around the world.[70]

In 1888, the New York State Senate again took up the issue of monopolies. This time John D. Rockefeller, described by the *Herald* as "this $15 a week clerk of fifteen years ago who handles a business of $20 million per annum, and . . . pushes all competitors into . . . failure and bankruptcy . . . [and] stands head and shoulders above all businessmen in the country," deigned to testify. Immaculate in his frock coat, his hair and mustache perfectly trimmed, and his eyes liquid with earnestness ("Ah, how he glowed," sneered a witness), he testified, in the words of one less than credulous account, to "the glorious missionary work which the trust had accomplished! Beginning with $70,000,000 capital, which by thrift and care, it has increased to $90,000,000, this charity has . . . reduced the price of kerosene." Another observer scoffed that Rockefeller had described Standard Oil as "the greatest philanthropy of the age, a sort of missionary society engaged in spreading the evangelical light of kerosene oil over the dark places in a naughty world."[71]

Rockefeller's sanctimonious depiction of the trust made great copy, but his pronouncements on industrial cooperation as the means for advancing American business interests in the world market were more noteworthy. The king of oil derided competition as wasteful, inefficient, and uncivilized. And who could dispute what monopoly had done for Standard Oil! Two score companies had turned over their business to a central synod that worked in the dark, bowed before no authority but John D. Rockefeller, and with invisible threads had woven a combination whose power was immense, unchecked, and mysterious. Its holdings, reported the senate committee, represented "the most active, and possibly the most formidable money power on the continent."[72]

Back in the first years of the business boom following the Civil War, industrial expansion had taken the form of an increase in the number of firms, without much change in their size. Prodded by the aggressively competitive market, businesses formed industrial associations to limit competition and production. These simple nonbinding arrangements fell apart under the pressures of economic depression. The next step was to create pools that replaced the associations and sought to manage prices and markets. The railroads and producers of salt, wallpaper, pig iron, rails, and nails all joined industrial syndicates, but these loose agreements proved no more effective than the associations in limiting the uncertainties of a competitive market. But Rockefeller's formula for consolidation through merger, annexation, and purchase quickly inspired imitators.[73]

With the help of prominent New York corporate attorney Elihu Root, Henry O. Havemeyer "Standardized" American sugar refining, bringing more than 75 percent of the industry under one trust umbrella. The grand southern staple, smoking tobacco, was brought to New York in 1884 by way of Durham, North Carolina's James B. Duke, who founded the American Tobacco Company to manufacture cigarettes (most tobacco users still took their pleasure in the form of pipes, snuff, cigars, and chewing tobacco). Duke built a mechanized production line capable of mass-producing a quarter million units of the nicotine-laced product. To bring the market up to this scale, he turned to New York's blossoming advertising industry (another of the major subspecialties spurred by the Wall Street market). In one of the first manufacturer-based ad campaigns, Duke succeeded in creating international demand for cigarettes. By the end of the 1880s, his Bonsack machines were turning out more than 800 million sticks of ground tobacco a day, and the American Tobacco Company had bundled its five leading competitors into the cigarette trust. In rapid succession, ten processing businesses in metals, foods, and consumer products formed trusts. Eight of these trusts were directed from New York. The American way of doing business, especially big business, was changing, and New York was leading the change.[74]

---

The rise of this New York–based corporate system roused adversaries as varied as western populists, urban merchants, and social reformers. "It must be remembered too," *The New York Times* added, "that the success of capitalists is often not so brilliant as it appears, and is gained by anything but moral means. . . . There is little in the history of most of our capitalists to cause the country to ardently desire more of them, or to wish the smaller property holders to be merged in the larger. A vast deal of money has been made by individuals in this country by very doubtful and selfish means." Of even greater concern than the way wealth was being made was the inordinate power and influence of the large new trusts and the Wall Street money market. Posing real threats to the rights and independence not only of small businesses, but of citizens, consumers, and workers, the concentration of economic control afforded the new companies broad sway over the market, profits, jobs, and politics. These hulking new aggregations bristled with authoritarian and even tyrannical possibilities.[75]

Yet the very fact that so much of this wealth and influence came to be concentrated in a city of kaleidoscopic diversity, with its reform and labor movements and traditions of adversarial politics, impeded the rise of a united, untrammeled business class. The unique Manhattan social environment promoted an array of checking forces that helped moderate big business's influence. Men like Morgan, Carnegie, and Rockefeller shaped the new capitalism with their investments and initiatives, but this capitalism was also molded by New York's emerging labor movement and the modifications that reformers and politicians inscribed upon the free market. The capitalism that formed in New York was shaped by many lines of development.

In 1892, greater New York contained 1,265 millionaires, 30 percent of the country's total. They and the city's other wealthy controlled newspapers, telegraphs, railroads, banks, topflight law firms, and investment houses—and more than a few aldermen and judges. In another setting, the swift rise of a powerful business class might have created an economic tyranny, but in New York, consistent, unified power eluded this group. Members of the proliferating upper class tended to compete with, rather than to reinforce one another. Carnegie, Rockefeller, and Morgan, for example, distrusted one another. Rather than work together to advance a big-business hegemony, they kept their exchanges to a minimum at a level that was barely civil. Suspicion and business individualism doomed every railroad pool that was tried. While corporate leaders might uniformly back the gold standard for currency, on so fundamental an issue as laissez-faire they disagreed, often quite diametrically (Andrew

Carnegie, disconsolate over being denied a cheap alternative to the Pennsylvania Railroad, demanded that the state legislature regulate the railroads to set equitable rates). Nor was there unanimity among New York's businesses on whether the state should own or control utilities or offer generous succor to the needy.[76]

New York's circle of businessmen was too large and too diverse for any one group or interest to dominate. The business "class" included, in addition to the new corporate enterprises, banking and securities houses; long-established trade and commercial firms; varied fields of manufacture; the information, real estate, and entertainment industries; and myriad retail businesses. "No society in the world," Julius H. Browne wrote in his 1869 study, *The Great Metropolis*, "has more divisions and subdivisions than ours—more ramifications and interramifications,—more circles within circles—more segments and parts of segments." They shaped a complex, variegated, and internally divided economic interest.[77]

The import-export traders (more than 40 percent of New York's millionaires) who had dominated the old city and its Chamber of Commerce formed a still potent mercantile elite, together with their lawyers and political allies. Many were Protestants from wealthy New England backgrounds. But many others had risen from poor homes, and yet others were foreign born, giving New York its surfeit of rags-to-riches success stories. Merchants included those who sold their goods overseas, others who supplied the American interior, some who sold manufactured products, and others who trafficked in raw materials. Even those in the same line of business, whose interests might appear similar, often competed fiercely against one another. Each wedge of the merchant class represented a different and not infrequently competing interest.[78]

New York's manufacturing businesses, which numbered 11,000 in 1880, more than doubled to 25,000 in 1890. In the past, merchants had controlled much of the city's manufacturing. They would buy raw goods and contract with middlemen to have them finished, often providing the financing and distribution as well. By the 1880s, the merchants no longer held in such control. Independent manufacturers came into their own. Employing an industrial army of more than 340,000 workers, they produced garments, printed materials, tobacco, meats, and liquor. New York's manufacturing interest alone accounted for $750 million in finished merchandise.[79]

Other elites in railroads, investment, communications, and real estate formed separate interest clusters among Gotham's businessmen, while the growth of specialties in business management, accounting, law, advertising, and a host of related fields created an influential service class with its own professional societies, codes, identities, and interests. Ethnic, religious, and social divisions fragmented the many economic categories, compounding the complexity. Even the most homogeneous of these groups, the English Protestant business elite, was divided, with devotees of the "sporting style" known for their conspicuous wealth and display, others who reveled in the distinction of ancestral peerage, and yet others, the "earnest and public-spirited class," who sought civic attainments and cultural renown. Among this last group were millenarians, who proselytized their traditional Christian faith, while others, equally active though less pious, placed their faith in social melioration through New York's plethora of voluntary organizations and reform societies.[80]

In the fullness of New York's economy, the metropolitan business elite were so divided in their needs and interests, in their outlooks, preferences, commitments, and beliefs, that they never managed to form a single power elite or to exert consistent political control. This lack of unity did not prevent them from recognizing a common fear. Jay Gould was not being disingenuous when he testified before the U.S. Senate in 1883 that capital feared the rapidly accumulating masses of "uneducated ignorant people" from abroad, who might turn against property. Periodic outbreaks of labor violence only deepened these fears. The rich did not need reformers and socialists to remind them that they were but a minority and that they ought not treat too cavalierly the smoldering bitterness of the poor.[81]

This helps explain the new philanthropic urge among the corporate class. Earlier millionaires had not made much of an impression with their giving. The superwealthy, a *New York Times* editorial declared in 1879, were "very cheap here," meaning that they abounded in the metropolis, though the *Times* would also accept the second meaning. "A man has the right to do as he likes with his own," the paper continued. "No one will gainsay this; and we all know what most of our millionaires like to do with their own. . . . But that so many of our exceedingly rich citizens should acquire their wealth here, and evince no appreciation of its source not to mention gratitude, is a curious, strikingly unpleasant, disclosure of human nature." William B. Astor died with his fortune intact. Cornelius Vanderbilt left his money only to those who carried his name (while the city got a frieze emblazoned with his likeness). A. T. Stewart had no children to leave it to, but he parted with precious little nonetheless. William Rhinelander, another of New York's rags-to-riches crowd, ignored the city where he had made his fortune. Elsewhere, the wealthy did good, but, the editorialist griped, not in New York.[82]

It was not long, however, before the "new wealthy" adopted a style of giving at great variance with the "modest" Stewarts, Vanderbilts, and Astors. Morgan, Carnegie, and Rockefeller ushered in a regime of philanthropy on a monumental scale. Endowed with more generous budgets than the United States Treasury, and possessing a freedom of action that no official body could match, the Carnegie and Rockefeller charities, for example, with perhaps $1 billion between them, went on to attack disease, build public libraries, reform medical education, erect low-cost housing, fund Negro colleges, and advance an agenda for social and cultural progress, while Morgan hauled more art to New York than the Medici gave Florence. Not the least of their projects involved furnishing New York in a single generation with a grand cultural infrastructure, outfitting the cold city of capital with the warming glow of centuries-old art and, willy-nilly, a fashionable high culture with a transatlantic worldview.

For all the physical and social separation that New York's expanding landscape placed between the rich and the poor, it did not blind the corporate elite to the dangers of segregated cultures. The class talk and class-based appeals that the elite heard from politicians, reformers, and radicals impressed upon them the dangers of an embittered and isolated working population. Concerned that the family and the church were losing their power to transmit conservative values and provide stability, especially in an increasingly foreign population, the business elite deemed it critical in this metropolis of capital to cultivate a common cultural tradition, a shared esteem for high civilization and its masters. Many agreed with the Metropolitan Museum's early founders that New York's rapid growth made it imperative to counter vice and villainy with beauty and culture to refine, uplift, and infuse the working classes with morality and dignity.[83]

By endowing museums, orchestras, and libraries, "responsible capital" aimed to assimilate these masses under the didactic cultural assumptions that supported the free market, private property, and a reassuring esteem for knowledge, piety, and taste. "No progress is possible," the Metropolitan's executive committee asserted at its founding, "which is not based on what has gone before. This knowledge must not only be possessed by artists, but also by the public." New York's worker citizens were too many and too independent to simply be pounded into a docile proletariat. The elite programs of cultural uplift made clear that concerned capital recognized that New York City was a shared space.[84]

Old Cornelius Vanderbilt may have uttered the oft quoted remark, "Law! What do I care about the law? Hain't I got the power?" but neither Morgan, Rockefeller, nor Carnegie felt so secure in his wealth to court mass disfavor or disregard. Perhaps Cornelius Vanderbilt and Jay Gould reveled in the pose of millionaire outlaws, but in an environment where organized labor, social and religious reform movements, tenement voting blocs, an active and inquiring press, and antimonopoly forces all played important roles, the new robber barons could not be so disdainful or oblivious.

Moreover, John D. Rockefeller, Andrew Carnegie, and J. P. Morgan all succumbed to a tempering regard for respectability, a longing, if not for a transcending legacy, then at least for justification in the eyes of their neighbors, friends, and fellow citizens. Instead of boasting about his business conquests, Rockefeller in his *Random Reminiscences* offers an apologia for his great wealth and the manner of its acquisition. Andrew Carnegie, who could have delighted in the pure joy of making money, agonized instead over the gospel of giving. Before his death, J. P. Morgan spoke earnestly of a desire to serve his country. The new philanthropy, which borrowed the unprecedented scale and system of the corporate business order, aimed, it is true, to weave the benefits of corporate largesse deep into the fabric of social and cultural life, to make it indispensable, but in the process capitalists too learned to yearn after transcendence. We understand very little about some of these men, even Morgan, Carnegie, and Rockefeller, if we ignore how much they were influenced to moderate their own inclinations.

We have seen that Andrew Carnegie had little sympathy for his workers. Yet in 1886, at the height of intense and bloody labor struggles, Carnegie wrote two articles preaching enlightened tolerance toward labor. Workers, he wrote in what represented important codewords for the union movement, were "independent contractors" with a "sacred right" to unionize. He exhorted management to "search . . . out the causes of disaffection among . . . employees," understand their needs, and meet the men more than halfway. Public sentiment, he informed his colleagues, supported worker demands for fair wages and hours. Employers must not replace strikers. As for those crossing picket lines, he tells scabs that there is an "an unwritten law among the best workmen: 'Thou shalt not take thy neighbor's job.'" Admittedly, Carnegie's words do not comport well with his behavior during the bloody Homestead strike in 1892, when hundreds of Pinkertons were imported to replace steel strikers, and the ensuing clashes resulted in fourteen deaths and hundreds of injuries. He was a poseur, driven by a hunger for the respect of intelligent men, but the issue is not the earnestness of his words as much as the fact that in the company of New York's thinkers, the milieu he so craved to be part of, he felt compelled to utter them.[85]

That is another way of saying that Gotham's capitalists, who ostensibly needed to answer to no one, were nonetheless profoundly influenced by their New York environment to moderate capitalism's more extreme possibilities. More than just a hub for business and business leaders, New York was a center for social reform, the labor movement, intellectual radicalism, elite philanthropy, and the social gospel. Its local politics empowered working-class voters, introducing them into the city's electoral pool almost as soon as they arrived.

The new corporate capitalism, with its investor-based financing and its vast scope and power, was very much a product of Gotham's complex social environment. Capitalism, after all, is not an abstract intellectual process. Capitalism is not a *thing*, a fixed object, it is an active *process*, a working definition that is continuously being refined and modified, and this was true especially during these turbulent years of pioneering industrialism. These powerful men were part of a dynamic environment where countervailing forces often forced them to compromise and to make necessary adjustments. Capitalism developed out of an evolving system of social, political, and cultural relations that shaped its nature. If the unique energy and reach of this corporate capitalism was New York made, it was also refined through a series of puissant metropolitan filters—civic values, countervailing business and economic interests, the impact of churches, the news media, intellectuals, reformers, and the labor movement—that gave it a self-interested flexibility, ultimately softened it, and bridled its more oppressive possibilities.

———————

One of the most important of these moderating influences was the labor movement. This is not to argue that unions and worker politics won great success in these years. On the contrary, labor unions were repressed by the government, starved by job hunger, and regularly denounced as subversive. Even temperate business opinion thought that workers should be grateful for their lot rather than demand more. Nor were they a privileged commodity. "If I wanted boiler iron," the Chicago, Burlington and Quincy railroad's general manager asserted before a Senate committee, "I would go out on the market and buy it where I could get it cheapest, and if I wanted to employ men I would do the same."[86]

The year 1877 was pivotal for American labor. After four years of hard times, railroads cut wages and extended workloads, setting off a long simmering bitterness. In July, the Baltimore and Ohio announced a 10 percent wage cut. Workers walked out. The strike—"a protest against robbery, a rebellion against starvation," in the words of one labor reformer—spread to the major eastern carriers, the Pennsylvania, the Erie, and the New York Central, before moving westward. The disruptions quickly escalated. Embittered workers tore up tracks, torched buildings, and disabled locomotives. Bloody clashes spread to a dozen cities, resulting in hundreds of casualties and considerable property loss. Fearing a "national insurrection," President Rutherford Hayes called out the federal troops. Samuel Gompers recalled the 1877 eruptions as "the tocsin that sounded a ringing message of hope to us all." Karl Marx wrote to Friedrich Engels that the strikes represented "the first outbreak against the associated capital oligarchy that has arisen since the Civil War."[87]

Preoccupied for so long with the Civil War and the politics of Reconstruction, Americans were forced to confront a new fault line, this time between capital and labor, and to commit the troops just recently called back from the South to protect railroad property from strikers and the enemies of the new corporations.[88]

In New York City proper, there was not much sympathy for the "insurrection." The *Tribune* characterized the uprisings as "Communistic and law defying" and called for meeting any violence with rifles. *The New York Times* used thirty-seven different adjectives to refer to the strikers, including agitator, brigand, rapscallion, and worthless fellows. Another journal called for "exterminating" the mob, if that proved necessary. Renowned Brooklyn preacher Henry Ward Beecher offered labor his sympathies, while instructing workers that Providence in laying plans for the world had "meant that great shall be great and that little shall be little . . . [and they must] reap the misfortunes of inferiority." Wage earners must live modestly. "The man who cannot live on bread and water," instructed the great divine, "is not fit to live."[89]

Local activists made plans to demonstrate their solidarity with the strikers, and New York officials prepared for war. The mayor canceled all police leaves. The National Guard was called out, and City Hall hastily completed a telegraph hookup to Manhattan's armories. Railroad property was fortified. Gatling guns were placed at the head of the financial district, and a force of volunteers surrounded the subtreasury. Gun-toting guards patrolled Central Park, while sailors and marines were posted at the Customs House and other federal property. On July 25, 1877, twenty thousand New Yorkers gathered at Tompkins Square to hear speeches and then went home after two hours. Except for some minor incidents, the protest did not amount to much, except that a jittery city hastened plans for future emergencies. When Andrew Green refused to release funds for a massive new Seventh Regiment fortification, Gotham's elite raised more than a $500,000 to erect the finest armory in the world with doors carved from half-foot-thick oak.[90]

Over the next few years, little changed for New York's workers except for the Central Labor Union's introduction of Labor Day. Borrowing from older artisanal traditions of worker festivals and parades, the CLU inaugurated a holiday celebrating labor and the dignity of work. New York's first Labor Day parade in 1882 drew more than ten thousand, featuring floats, marchers, and skits. By 1886 the parade, open to all who toiled with their hands (lawyers and politicians were excluded), attracted twenty thousand marchers in Manhattan alone and spread to neighboring Brooklyn, as well as to Chicago, Boston, and Washington.[91]

For all of the fanfare, labor lacked power, focus, and unity. Anarchists, nihilists, socialists, and communists were mixed together with union activists of all stripes, some of whom rejected all ideologies. The minority of laborers who had joined unions were ill prepared to challenge their bosses. When the Brotherhood of Telegraphers became embroiled in a labor dispute with Jay Gould in July of 1883 and rashly called a strike, they held no more than $140 in the local till and barely $1,000 in the national brotherhood treasury. So one-sided was the conflict that the strikers even won the sympathy of *Banker's Magazine*.[92]

The sympathy did Western Union's workers little good. They had assumed that the communications giant would compromise to avoid a shutdown, but they were wrong. Gould, like other business leaders, reckoned the cost of capitulation not in the wage increases that the workers were demanding, but in the potential cost of what an ascendant labor might ultimately extract. He was prepared to "close every office" rather than relinquish control over wages and work hours. Wages, he proclaimed, must be determined by supply and demand (that is, as low as he could get away with), *not* negotiation. By August 15, he had broken the strike.[93]

Labor expanded its membership and built some muscle over the next two years. The Knights of Labor, founded in 1869 in Philadelphia, had managed to survive both the depression and the violence of 1877. It led successful strikes that forced Western Union to rescind the 1883 cuts and in 1885 succeeded in squeezing wage improvements from the Gould-dominated Wabash Railroad. Knights of Labor president Terence Powderly also won a face-to-face meeting with Gould. These triumphs brought publicity and new members to the Knights, who promoted a mélange of goals, including the eight-hour workday, the union of all "producers" (that is, workers) in a cooperative commonwealth, and a new social order.[94]

In 1886, the year of "great upheaval," Knights membership jumped from about 100,000 to 725,000, raising expectations and encouraging militants to force concessions from capital. Close to

700,000 workers demanding higher wages and job security shut down thousands of plants and industries. The stoppages on the Gould roads attracted the most attention, beginning with a wildcat strike in February on the Texas & Pacific, a strike that the Knights leadership did not authorize. Instructing his son George to close the struck shops and if necessary to "suspend the whole payroll during the continuance of the strike," Gould was determined to break the union.[95]

When workers on other Gould lines went out in solidarity with the Texas & Pacific strikers, they confronted a "grim, unswerving fixedness of purpose." Management rolled back previously granted concessions and within days discharged all strikers. Replacements were brought in, leading to pitched battles between strikers and scabs. In half a dozen towns, strikers stormed the yards and closed them down. In East St. Louis, police deputies fired upon a mob, killing six bystanders. The Methodist bishop there prayed for "someone [to] take him [Gould] by the neck and kick him through New York, so long as he wasn't killed." Gould would not relent, and in the end the Knights of Labor leadership was saddled with responsibility for a strike they had not authorized and could not win. "In all the history of labor controversies," wrote the *New York Tribune*, "perhaps there was not another strike more unreasonable in its inception or unwise in its conduct." By May 4, it was crushed.[96]

Trade unions proceeded with unrelated plans for a nationwide one-day general strike in favor of the eight-hour day on May 1, 1886. Three hundred thousand walked off their jobs, with close to forty-five thousand joining the walkout in New York. In Chicago, tensions were heightened by a four-month-long McCormick Harvester strike that had been marred by violent incidents and fatalities. A demonstration on May 4 at Haymarket Square attracted a relatively small turnout amid a drenching rain. The meeting was about to break up when a troop of police appeared. A bomb was thrown into the crowd of officers, wounding dozens, of whom ultimately seven died. The police fired back blindly into the crowd, resulting in about seventy more casualties. The Knights, fearing a backlash, quickly denounced the anarchists, who despite the absence of hard evidence were accused of inciting the violence.[97]

The failed strikes and the Haymarket tragedy put an end to the Knights of Labor's spectacular growth. Drawn to politics, utopian schemes, social reform, and militant strike action, they had managed to attract much attention, but by the end of the year, employers were goading the locals into strikes that they then smashed, as the national union stood by helplessly. Over the next few years, the Knights of Labor declined into a regional organization confined largely to west of the Mississippi.[98]

New York cigar maker Samuel Gompers had meanwhile been building a different union, one that accepted the legitimacy of industrial capitalism and was determined to arrive at a policy of creative coexistence. One can debate Gompers's famous description of New York as the cradle of the modern labor movement, but it is impossible to ignore the impact of Gompers's own work on moderating the power of corporate capital.[99]

Thirteen-year-old Sam Gompers arrived in New York with his parents from England in 1863. They settled in the working district that Theodore Dreiser described as "that very different and most radically foreign plexus, known as the [Lower] East Side," where the teenager immediately began working, making cigars alongside his father in the family tenement. He earned enough over the next few years to marry at the age of seventeen. A year after the wedding, he moved his young wife and their newborn infant into their own modest apartment, which they furnished, he would later recall with pride, for "cash" and not by paying installments "on time."[100]

From New York's yeasty labor environment with its labor forums, adult schools, and socialists of every stripe and nuance; from his readings in the journals, newspapers, and polemical literature that flooded the Lower East Side; and from the refugee intellectuals and their "vast quadrille [of] political and economic groups, . . . constantly changing partners, occasionally all joining together for one brief turn only to separate again to form a new pattern," Gompers pulled together the elements of a labor perspective. He became an avid student of classes, books, and brilliant men. For more than a decade, Gompers grappled with the many ideas and theories to which New York exposed him. He tested a succession of approaches—"on labor matters my thought was wild"—and borrowed from many of them. From Marxism he adopted the stirring rhetoric and righteous indignation of labor discourse, though ultimately he dismissed the *Communist Manifesto* as a pithy analysis but an impossible solution. In time he tired of the succession of small ideological organizations with their dogmatic intellectuals and host of pretenders, given to falling out spectacularly over abstruse doctrinal disputes. He turned to extracting from his New York experience a sense of what might work in practice.[101]

He joined the cigar makers union and rose rapidly to become president of Local 144. In seeking an example to follow, Gompers looked not to Gotham's many charitable, political, or volunteer organizations, but to New York's large businesses. Successful businesses did not rely on volunteers or informal administration or pinchpenny budgets. Unions too needed to be well staffed by professionals, and they needed to charge real dues in order to support real budgets. Soft dreams for improving the world were no substitute for a strike fund. Impoverished unions, he knew, lacked credibility and often acted rashly to prove that they were serious. Like weak boxers, they invited a mauling.

He had another reason for high dues. He wanted members to recognize the union as something substantial in their lives and to demonstrate their commitment. The Knights of Labor had grown quickly but had fallen just as quickly. Labor needed soldiers who could be counted on not to abandon the cause. Giving pennies did not make soldiers. Moreover, unions needed to be financially independent to avoid the tawdry deals by which too many poor locals sold out their members to the bosses.

Gompers believed that labor had to be clear about its interest and limit its demands to what was achievable. He was convinced that American labor was different from its European analogue. American labor lacked the sense of implacable immobility that annealed many of the European movements. It also lacked the homogeneity. Too many Americans believed that their children would live better lives than they did to unite around a labor ideology. After all, this was the economy that had drawn them to leave their homelands and cross the ocean. Moreover, labor in America was no melting pot; workers remained too varied and separated by religion, nationality, race, and background to form a unified class. Gompers repudiated schemes for social change, leaving it to Europe's radical labor parties to agitate for revolution and to make war on new technology.

American labor, he was convinced, did not bear the responsibility for remaking society. Weak, defenseless labor was not obliged to carry the battle for assorted utopian causes and get itself bloodied fighting for subversive experiments in glorious sharing. He espoused a narrow labor interest, avoiding universal crusades and demands, rejecting any idea larger than the material improvement of his members. At the same time, he insisted that the burdens and benefits of industrial progress must be more widely shared. Workers who had invested a lifetime in their craft and contributed to America's extraordinary material advance could not simply be discarded every time a new machine came along, not if they were expected to support the system with their votes and to reject the allure of radical ideologies. This "New York" model of "unionism pure and simple" honed a narrow practical focus, pursuing recognition, collective bargaining, and improved conditions.[102]

In 1883, when the Senate Education Committee launched its investigation into the relations between capital and labor, Gompers was called to testify about strikes. Before addressing that topic, he painted a picture of the evils of homework. More than two thousand New York families had been forced to convert their living quarters into miserable, foul-smelling cigar-finishing shops, where the disease of the tenements, tuberculosis, spread. Later, New York passed a law outlawing "homework." But then the courts overturned the legislation. The lesson for Gompers was clear. For all of the attractiveness of solving difficult issues in one swift legislative act, the political process was tangled. The courts had the last word, and the legal system, anchored in precedent, was inclined to keep things as they were rather than define new rights and novel protections for labor. And business could afford the best lawyers. Moreover, the case was impossible to make by pure logic. Start with the assumptions of business, and it is the investor and business proprietor who created the conditions for capitalist development. His rights in property entitle him to the fruits of his risk taking and enterprise. Substitute labor theories, and it is the sweat and skill of the worker that creates the commodity value. Substitute other assumptions, and they lead to yet other conclusions.[103]

American tradition assigned to property a privileged place in law and society, defining property rights as a facet of personal liberty and placing these rights largely beyond the reach of the state. Few had thought through the consequences of chartering corporations, which recently had accumulated such large stores of wealth that their rights in property now threatened to encroach on the general rights and freedoms of vast numbers of citizens; much less had they thought through the implications of the new corporate monopolies concentrating property in fewer and fewer hands. Once government and the courts extended "equal protection" rights to this fabricated entity, the corporation, it became quite possible to frame a legal argument against passing factory or safety or tenement legislation, because such laws treated corporations differently from other citizens and therefore infringed on their "equal rights."

Gompers understood that this route led down a blind alley. Better to rely on hard-fought but contractually negotiated benefits won in direct encounters with business. Labor had to choose its fights carefully and keep its issues clear, discrete, and within reasonable locus of its own influence. Asked by a Senate committee to describe the unions' ultimate goals, Gompers's colleague Adolph Strasser replied,

"We have no ultimate ends. We are going on from day to day . . . fighting only for immediate objects." They did not fight capitalism or even monopoly, focusing instead on getting labor a good wage and winning a place at the table with management. Strikes were to be used sparingly, not to destroy business, but to persuade it to work cooperatively, and only if they could be won.[104]

Business had already begun to organize regionally, and Gompers and his crowd of "gentleman proletarians" (at meetings "practically every man wore a silk hat and a Prince Albert coat") concluded that labor must match that scope by consolidating locals into a national alliance of craft unions. They formed the American Federation of Labor (AFL) in 1886, appointing the thirty-seven-year-old Gompers as president. Unlike the Knights of Labor, the AFL accepted only skilled workers. Its members prided themselves on their craft traditions and their bargaining power. The union was an interest group, not a benevolent association. It chose not to carry the burden of vulnerable and easily replaced unskilled workers, who often operated the new machines that were supplanting the craftsmen whose interest was closest to Gompers's heart.[105]

Between the end of the Civil War and the close of the century, New York labor forged a union movement of national scope. The AFL developed its own considered approach to the problem of subordination and the equitable distribution of industrial profits. Union membership fluctuated, but by the end of the 1890s, the federation represented close to half a million workers. The numbers only begin to indicate the attention workers attracted as their stories, their photographs, and their lives moved closer to the center of American consciousness. State legislatures investigated their treatment, and the United States Senate gathered copious testimony advancing the new discourse about relations between capital and labor. Years before, in a column devoted to the "labor question," the *Herald* had advised its readers that the chief cause of labor unrest was not low pay, but that "from one-third to one-half of the money paid out to the lower classes of labor finds its way into the tills of the liquor dealers."

Serious newspapers no longer dismissed aggrieved laborers as whiskey-swilling malcontents and anarchists bent on mindless violence and the overthrow of capitalism. As labor took on a new prominence in American life, the New York–based AFL advanced the practical strategies that carried labor over the threshold of the twentieth century to wider sway and a countervailing influence on big business.[106]

In 1886, New York's mayoral election contest demonstrated the broad interplay of the city's varied interests. More strikingly, it offered evidence of a level of labor power that few had suspected. This election ultimately recast the Democratic coalition that ran City Hall. Three candidates ran for office, each representing a different political approach to the relationship between labor and capital. The candidates included a forceful, maverick Republican whose campaign helped move him along a political path that eventually led to the first progressive presidency. Yet Theodore Roosevelt was not the most intriguing of the mayoral candidates. That honor went to red-bearded Henry George, the best-known radical in America.

Following the rout of the Tweed Ring, from 1872 to 1884 each mayor elected to office was a wealthy merchant drawn from the city's commercial and social elite. Workers could vote, and did, but they had little influence at City Hall. Even Tammany had backed away from the eight-hour day. Workers found it particularly galling as another of the city's periodic scandals made the headlines, that the very same traction companies that had tenaciously fought to cut pennies from their wages had disbursed hundreds of thousands of dollars to purchase state senators, aldermen, and ultimately a transit franchise. *The New York Times* census of city government officials offered scant reassurance: fifteen aldermen out on bail; three in flight from the country; one at large; one protected by his status as an informer; and two dead. The scandal highlighted the difference between the way the courts had harshly punished strikers and picketers while they showed an exaggerated deference to the transit interests. Declaring, "Honest men can be elected to administer the affairs of government," the Central Labor Union, with some fifty thousand affiliated members, determined to shake up the two parties and run its own candidate for mayor.[107]

Driven, funny, filled with restless energy and a passion for social reform, Henry George had come from humble origins and persevered through difficult early years as a wage earner and printer to eke out a living. He had visited New York as a reporter for a San Francisco paper in 1869 and found the contrast with pre–Civil War Gotham jarring. The pleasant, attractive, decent-scaled town that he remembered had lost its sense of balance. It had become too large, too rich, and too poor. "There and then I made a vow," he later recalled, to solve the mystery of poverty amid plenty. Following the year of bloody labor uprisings in 1877, George wrote his classic reform tract, *Progress and Poverty: An Inquiry into the Cause of Industrial Depressions and of Increase of Want with Increase of Wealth.*[108]

Capitalism perplexed him: "Where the conditions [for] . . . material progress . . . are most fully realized, we find the deepest poverty. . . . Amid the greatest accumulations of wealth, men die of starvation, and puny infants suckle dry breasts." Yes, the American economy offered both competition and liberty, but these were not sufficient to assure a just economic system. Competition among unequals was a deceit and a pretense, placing upon the poor the responsibility for their own failure. He traced the problem almost exclusively to the system of private landholding and rent, which he denounced in an oft quoted passage as "a toll levied upon labor constantly and continuously." The landlord, adding nothing to his land, claims the full benefit when a productive economy pushes up property values, creating an undeserved bonus that "debases, and embrutes, and embitters . . . it sends greed and all evil passions through society as a hard winter drives the wolves to the abodes of men." George's solution was for government to reclaim this benefit through a 100 percent tax on the "unearned increment." Income from this tax alone would eliminate the need for all other excises and usher in "a great co-operative society." *Progress and Poverty* became the most popular book in print. A sensation on both sides of the ocean, it ultimately sold millions.[109]

While George favored government ownership of railroads and municipal utilities, he did not favor a government-run economy. He recognized the right to private property, distinguishing between property in land and property in goods. He had no quarrel with the essential structure of American capitalism and preached no implacable struggle between labor and capital. To Karl Marx (whom George termed "the prince of muddleheads"), *Progress and Poverty* was an attempt to "save the capitalist regime," an example of "bourgeois political economy" by a "panacea monger. . . ." American labor embraced the bourgeois radical for just this reason, because he gave voice to disaffiliation *within* the framework of capitalism.[110]

Informed that George was considering a labor candidacy, a Tammany Democrat sought him out. Tammany's man assured him that he could not win. The machine had its ways. Regardless of the vote, he would not be "counted in." When the politico offered him a deal, George wanted to know why they were going to all of this trouble if he could not win. "You cannot be elected," came the reply, "but your running will raise hell." George was charmed. "I do want to raise hell."[111]

He also wanted to run a respectable campaign. He demanded thirty thousand signatures as a sign that the newly formed United Labor Party had some real voting strength. He got that and more. Union members fed the campaign with their dimes and quarters. Samuel Gompers, laying aside his principle of nonpolitical unionism, coordinated George's campaign, bringing the candidate to Manhattan's street corners, churches, and shop floors. George captivated the working population with attacks on Jay Gould, business greed, and Tammany, "the gamblers, saloon-keepers, pugilists, or worse who have made a trade of controlling votes, and of buying and selling offices and official acts. . . . [T]hrough these men . . . rich corporations and powerful pecuniary interests can pack the Senate and the Bench with their creatures." To the poor who had been taught Christian resignation, George preached that poverty was the outgrowth of an inequitable system. His message, a supporter would write, "came to the weary and heavy laden as the talisman of a lost hope."[112]

New York had never seen such a campaign. The coalition of reformers, laborites, social gospelers, liberal Catholics, and many in the immigrant population rattled New York's business class. Of course, it was not hard to find fault with George's single-tax scheme. How serious could the reformer be about turning over millions in tax money to the local politicians and have them run the telegraphs, railroads, and other utilities? "Every man who reads the papers knows what sort of men we have as Aldermen," exclaimed *The New York Times.* But who could miss the larger point? Labor was attracting serious attention throughout the city in an election that offered voters the choice of a lifetime.[113]

Opposing George was sixty-three-year-old former congressman Abram Hewitt, a man of vast wealth, moderate opinions, and impeccable refinement. Described by *Nation* magazine as "just the kind of man New York should always have for Mayor," Hewitt had won Tammany's support. The Republicans ran twenty-eight-year-old, Harvard-educated Theodore Roosevelt, a scion of one of New York's most prominent families. With a family fortune from banking, investment, and real estate, Roosevelt had turned his back on business to make a difference in politics. He had written three books and had returned from cowboy excursions in the Badlands to found the City Reform Club and advance a politics of civic virtue. His aggressive integrity excited good government Republicans, and in 1882, with J. P. Morgan's support, he had run a successful campaign for the New York State Assembly.[114]

He had arrived in Albany green as grass, a twenty-three-year-old "dude," hair parted in the center, sporting a cutaway coat, gold-tipped cane, silk hat, a monocle attached to a gold fob, and a mouth full of teeth that "seemed to be all over his face." His aristocratic accent hardly disciplined his piping screech of a voice as his boyish laugh reverberated through the legislative chamber. He also brought with him, in the words of a none too keen observer, "a wealth of mouth." His contempt for Democrats was profound: "The average [C]atholic Irishman . . . as represented in this Assembly," he confided to his diary, "is a low, venal, corrupt and unintelligent brute." His assembly committee he described as split between those who were "positively corrupt and the others . . . , singularly incompetent." In an early form of the "big-stick" policy, he showed up one day to a committee hearing that he was chairing with a rough slab of lumber at his side, telling all that he would tolerate no scheming from his tainted colleagues.[115]

Fellow reformers quickly gathered round and made him their leader. Indiscreet, impulsive, and driven to vanquish the old politics in one cyclonic round, he defied the legislature's neighborly customs. "What on earth will New York send us next?" the *Tribune* wondered when the Republicans made the self-righteous dervish minority leader.[116]

Bristling with an insurgent spirit, he proclaimed Jay Gould a member of "that most dangerous of all dangerous classes, the wealthy criminal class." But Roosevelt was no radical. He affirmed the rights of property, and although he voted to cut the fare on Gould's elevated transit line, he soon regretted it: "[W]hen I voted for this bill . . . I weakly yielded, partly in vindictive spirit toward the infernal thieves and . . . swindlers . . . and partly to the popular voice in New York." But government had no right to dictate even to bad businesses. Moved by the plight of the worker, he was nonetheless not yet willing to set wages or limit hours, denouncing reformers who backed such moves as "professional agitators . . . always promising to procure by legislation the advantages which can only come to workingmen . . . by their individual or united energy, intelligence and forethought." Frustrated by Roosevelt's careful gradualism, the

*New York Sun* seethed, "The popular voice in New York will probably leave this weakling at home hereafter."[117]

Homework changed his mind. When the legislature first took up a measure to outlaw work in the tenements, he initially opposed it. Government, he was certain, had no right to prevent a family from working in their home for wages that they agreed to. But when Samuel Gompers insisted that the young legislator come with him for a tour of the tenements to see this homework firsthand, Roosevelt agreed. What he saw—children and parents working amid dangerous conditions for sixteen hours a day and piddling wages—swept away his reservations. Back in Albany, he grabbed two colleagues and took them on the same tour. "Whatever the theories might be," common sense and humanity dictated intervention. He voted to outlaw homework (a bill that he agreed was "in a certain sense a socialistic one") and helped convince a hesitant Governor Grover Cleveland to sign it. But then the courts threw out the law. This decision, Roosevelt would write, "first waked me to a dim and partial understanding . . . that the courts were not necessarily the best judges of what" an evolving industrial society required. Law, he came to sadly conclude, sometimes stood "against justice." It was an insight that would develop over the years into a fully formed progressive vision.[118]

On February 12, 1884, his wife, Alice, gave birth to a daughter. Roosevelt received the good news by wire and, after reporting fourteen bills out of committee, headed downstate for home. The trip was filled with trepidation, for the telegram had reported that Alice was doing "only fairly well" and his own mother, who was living with them, was dying of typhoid fever. Two days later, she succumbed to the disease, and in a desolating tragedy, Alice died the very same day, two days after her baby's birth. "The light," he wrote in his diary, "has gone out of my life."[119]

Overcome with grief, he poured his energies into political reform, pushing to conclusion a broad investigation into the government of New York City that gave him a rare insight into the structure and abuse of municipal politics. He drove through the legislature six separate bills designed to cleanse city government by removing power from the aldermen and placing it in the hands of a strong and accountable mayor.[120]

Then he retired from the assembly to seek refuge in the uncomplicated frontier that so refreshed his energies. He also returned to writing history. By 1886, when he wrote the secretary of war, volunteering to "raise some companies of horse riflemen" to straighten out a border incident with Mexico, the old itch for larger challenges had returned. He accepted the backing of Gotham's Republicans for the mayoralty. He won support from the *Times*, *Tribune*, and the *Commercial Advertiser* and some businessmen who opposed Tammany, but other moderates, fearful of splitting the anti-George vote, backed the Democrat. Hurt by the defection of men who were his natural constituency, he dismissed these "emasculated professional humanitarians" as the "timid good" and despite the disappointments went on to run a vigorous, articulate campaign.[121]

The Democrats had selected shrewdly. Abram Hewitt was a self-made man, an iron manufacturer and the son-in-law of New York's best example of a business radical, the philanthropist Peter Cooper. Supported by the Catholic hierarchy, Tammany, and many in the business community, Hewitt was not averse to making populist appeals. He reminded workers that he had supported them in Congress and had kept his mills running during the depression, despite his losses, in order to protect jobs. He also criticized the wealthy class—despite his own considerable estate—for disregarding its fair share of civic obligations. He campaigned as the balanced voice of decent, respectable New York, the best alternative to George's radicalism.[122]

The contest, one of the most high-minded in city history, was unusual for the quality of the candidates and the new ideas about the rights of labor and the imperatives of capital. It attracted a huge turnout, and as expected, Hewitt won with 90,552 votes. But in a year marked by union defeats and the Haymarket tragedy, Labor

Party's George, with no political experience and running on a new party ticket, in a campaign fed by nickels and dimes, polled about one-third of the votes, 68,110, more votes than Roosevelt's 60,435 total.[123]

A delighted George declared that his campaign had lit a fire that "would never go out." Even *The New York Times*, which had earlier published an editorial entitled "How to Insure George's Defeat," was forced to concede that "this vote is . . . the most noteworthy and significant feature of this election." This was not the vote of a violent fringe. "That view which denies to" the impressive George turnout "any reasonable cause for existence, which lumps these 68,000 voters indiscriminately together as Anarchists, vagabonds, cranks and tramps, and which conceives no way of dealing with the new force save to fight it and put it down, implies an understanding of our Republican Government," declared the editorial, "quite as densely stupid and violently wrong as that of the Anarchists themselves."[124]

Tammany's partnership with Hewitt's forces of genteel rectitude soon collapsed. Hewitt took up the long inactive municipal improvement agenda, paving streets and promoting harbor rehabilitation and rapid transit. But he bridled at Boss Richard Croker's demands for patronage and influence. An unapologetic product of the age of Protestant merchant preeminence, he also refused to bow to New York's new populations. Caught up in the spirit of Protestant triumphalism that was sweeping through the city, he came out in support of cutting immigration and extending to twenty-one years the residency requirements for naturalization. "America," he declared, "should be governed by Americans." For the first time in twenty-seven years, the mayor of New York refused to participate in the St. Patrick's Day parade, observing that "the Irish furnish more than double the number of [prison] inmates" than their proportion in the population.[125]

In the time it took for New York's newest voters to demonstrate their distaste for intolerant Protestant cultural reform by turning Abram Hewitt out of office, Tammany absorbed the deeper message of George's surprising showing. The Democratic machine abandoned the genteel element to court the newly active tenement populations. Within two years, Boss Croker embedded a newly invigorated Tammany machine in the tenement community more thoroughly than anything Tweed had accomplished before. Striking deals with labor unions and ethnic organizations in return for the bloc votes that these groups contrived to deliver, Tammany acknowledged labor's new importance with patronage and party favors. It also backed pro-labor legislation and had the police ease up on union pickets and strikers. Croker also brought big business into the Tammany coalition, reviving a relationship that had been dormant in the fifteen years since Tweed. With both labor and big business under its tent, a resurgent Tammany mediated between capital and labor, providing an important check on corporate power.[126]

The chief metropolis of the American urban system, and the center of the national money market, New York led the corporate transformation that greatly expanded the scope of American business. With its expansive financial base, broad expertise, and, latterly, its strategies to consolidate entire industries into trusts that effaced market influences, Wall Street spearheaded the postwar economic ascent that thrust the United States to the forefront of the international economy. Over a score of years, the innovative business form of the corporation was tested and refined by the railroad and telegraph industries. It managed to attract global investment in historic proportions, established innovative management systems, and stimulated unprecedented technological innovation. Its proven economic success drew a virtually inexhaustible labor supply from the depleted lands of Europe.[127]

This corporate transformation was molded in Gotham's extraordinarily diverse environment amid an array of counterposed business, social, and economic interests. Its highly competitive press (numbering more than twenty dailies under some of the most distinguished editors in the nation, and of late energized by the pungent sensationalism of Joseph Pulitzer and his imitators) practiced an exuberant journalism of exposure and criticism that no business could safely ignore. Interest groups, political factions, and reform leaders, often no more than tiny splinter groups elsewhere, exerted a significant influence in the metropolis, frequently accounting for shifts in the balance of Gotham's political coalitions. New York's thinkers and activists, participants in the transatlantic discourse on government, business, and the rights of citizen workers, sparked important movements to moderate economic inequality. This center of corporate America represented an apt example of the balancing factionalism that James Madison lauded in his famous *Federalist No. 10* as the most salient practical check on the abuse of power.[128]

In these years, criticism of the emerging corporate capitalist economy came to a decisive point. The farm-based populist movement formed a party of opposition. Raised on epic myths of taming the wilderness and conquering the frontier, America's western farmers confronted decline: frontiers closing; dwindling water supplies; the rise of Wall Street. They responded with a politics of complaint and indignation, declaring war on the transforming forces of their times, attacking the city, and launching an incoherent assault on the corporate economy, agitating to peel back progress. Their impact on the essential nature of corporate capitalism remained limited.[129]

Labor ideologues proved no more successful in articulating a broad alternative movement. In 1877, thousands of railroad men joined what became a nationwide protest against long hours and low wages. Between 1881 and 1890, the federal Bureau of Statistics estimated that workers took part in close to 10,000 strikes and lockouts. In 1886 alone, the year of "great upheaval," 1,432 strikes and 140 lockouts involved close to 700,000 workers in stoppages and labor actions. Violence and death marred too many of the clashes. In the end, however, workers rejected violent confrontation and radical ideology in favor of the bread-and-butter movement led by Samuel

Gompers. The New York–based AFL embraced the capitalist perspective. Working within the established political and economic order, Gompers and his trade unionists built a national federation that made practical progress toward a place for workers at the bargaining table and a growing share of capital's prosperity.

Henry George's popular single-tax treatise, *Progress and Poverty*, stirred one of the most far-reaching radical crusades of the century, but this movement and the mild forms of socialism advanced by others did little to halt the legitimation and acceptance of corporate capitalism. What George's mayoral candidacy, as well as the movement for regulation of monopolies and early efforts at factory legislation, did accomplish was to subdue some of capitalism's more extreme possibilities.

It was the other losing candidate in New York's historic 1886 mayoral campaign, however, who would go on to forge historic changes in corporate capitalism, giving it a progressive resilience that ultimately made it more stable and durable. "I feel it incumbent on me to try to amount to something, either in politics or literature," Theodore Roosevelt wrote in his diary in 1889, "because I have deliberately given up the hope of going into a money making business." One of the most important effects of the 1886 election was the continued molding of Theodore Roosevelt's progressive consciousness. His extensive investigations of municipal affairs, which made him one of the best-informed students of city government, taught him firsthand about the social effects of industrialization and big business. This led him to think in new ways about the need to curb business's excessive power. The campaign familiarized him with the city's many communities and neighborhoods and taught him to interact with citizens of all types, not just those of his class, but also bricklayers and day laborers, immigrants and African Americans. He became an unabashed champion of diversity, telling a black audience in his exuberant screech: "I like to speak to an audience of colored people." With this campaign he initiated what was to become an ongoing conversation with reformers and good government groups about finding a middle course between free enterprise and economic justice.[130]

Colleagues might dismiss Roosevelt as, in the words of New York assemblyman Newton M. Curtis, "a brilliant madman born a century too soon," but he was one of the most open, curious, and promising politicians on the horizon. His defeat for the mayoralty at the age of twenty-eight was no blemish on a career just beginning to win broad attention. Concluded the *New York Sun:* "To be in his youth the candidate for the first office in the first city of the U.S., and to poll a good vote for that office, is something more than empty honor. . . . He cannot be Mayor this year, but who knows what may happen in some other year? Congressman, Governor, Senator, President?" He told close friend Henry Cabot Lodge that he had run in order to gain "a better party standing." He would go on to become police commissioner and then governor and one of the most important progressive political leaders in the nation's history. And he would draw upon his metropolitan background to confront more directly than any president before him the need to think in new ways about the power of capital and monopolies.[131]

As the examples of Roosevelt, George, and Gompers suggest, most critics of the new corporate system wrought by the Morgans, Rockefellers, and Carnegies objected to details and not the system. They did not intend to halt the progress of corporate growth or even to uproot monopoly. Reformers might denounce the great concentrations of wealth, and the unions might chafe at capital's control over the conditions of labor and its reward, but despite these and other real objections, the new economic order attracted millions of immigrants from around the world (and many tens of thousands from America's disaffected farm regions) who chose to participate in just this system. Imperfect, corporate capitalism had nonetheless proven effective in promoting growth, encouraging technology, making comfortable peace with change, and mobilizing America's latent resources. It offered a capacious, flexible vision for the modern industrial economy.

Mechanization and the manufacturing process gave businesses additional sway over the lives of workers, introducing regimes of the clock and of industrial discipline, but this process brought benefits as well. The more arduous and often most dangerous tasks were increasingly carried out by machine. And more New Yorkers than ever before could boast that they "wore no man's livery," as the number of maids, butlers, servants, and valets, occupations that had been staples of lower-class existence, declined, while the number of jobs as well as wage levels and the standard of living all rose.[132]

The new economy did concentrate power, and big business sought to keep all of the options in its own hands, making pools, fixing prices, and building monopolies. But New York's diverse checking influences made capital more pliant. The debate over slavery in the 1850s became an ideological clash between irreconcilable forces. Both sides wrapped themselves in their exclusive certainties and marched off to war. But corporate capitalism did not develop in its own section of the nation insulated from challenge. It developed in the dynamic environment of New York, where it was forced to wrestle with the substantial influences of a growing labor movement, a competitive and increasingly outspoken press, a coalition style of municipal government, and a tradition of active urban reform. This subdued some of its more extreme possibilities. It also contributed to capital's ideological and tactical flexibility, giving it a resilience and wide acceptance that ultimately made it more stable and durable. It is worth noting, as historian Marshal Sklar points out, that the corporate movement's rise represents the most peaceful change of such vast scope in American history. With all the opposition, the adversaries of the corporation and the industrial system did not mount a sustained or meaningful resistance.[133]

E. L. Godkin, one of New York's "best men," an editor and social critic, missed the old days when hard work and inspiration brought slow, steady success; when those who succeeded shone with integrity and practiced a modest frugality. How different was the modern system, where wealth arrived in a rapid rush through "lucky strokes" and "bold and ingenious combinations." He longed for solidity and honor while all around him he saw instead shrewdness and daring. He excoriated "the worship of wealth, in its coarsest and most un-draped form," the materialist mood that had overtaken New York and the nation. But for many others, release from the iron grip of birth, family, tradition, and poverty was enough of an attraction. They pursued material success as the first step to a decent life. And they credited the vigorous new economy with making this possi-ble.[134]

Little wonder that the colorful New York communist Gustav Schwab, with no little irony, described New York's business elite as America's true revolutionaries. These revolutionaries uprooted the values of small-scale proprietary capitalism and supplanted a busi-ness culture that emphasized measured growth and local scale with audacious investment and global scope. For all their differences, the New York business elite, from Gould to Carnegie to Rockefeller, preached as one of the principal virtues of the free market that poor men of modest backgrounds could aspire to great wealth. And who could tell this story better than they.[135]

# CHAPTER 6

# The Age of Morgan

*J. P. Morgan was the mightiest figure in international finance. Up to the time of his death he was the leader of the financial interests in this city and country and of international bankers. In this country he stood supreme in the world of money . . . and through the occupation of the leadership of the chain of banks actually controlled the economic destinies of the nation. It was generally conceded that he was the motive power behind the political government of the country, and it is well known that before his sway monarchs made obeisance.*[1]
—*New York Call,* APRIL 1, 1913

*The molder of the railroad history of the nation, the man who gave character to broad financial operations, the man who financed the nation itself and who first opened the doors for American participation in world financial undertakings. . . .*[2]
—*Chicago Record-Herald,* APRIL 1, 1913

AS MIDNIGHT GAVE WAY to the first of January, 1900, the new century descended with muted deference upon John Pierpont Morgan. The man some referred to as the most powerful figure in the United States sat alone in the library of his Madison Avenue brownstone on this night of celebration, arranging solitaire cards at his desk. He was surrounded by the rare manuscripts and Old Master paintings for which he had searched the ends of the earth. Pierpont had become a collector, pursuing cachet art with a passion, acquiring cherished canvases by the crateload, along with priceless miniatures and ornate objects of surpassing beauty and value. Indulging his lust for possess-ing objects of splendor and rarity, he had acquired a Gutenberg Bible, an original of Keats's *Endymion*, ancient Babylonian tablets, and myriad sacred relics.[3]

Morgan derived immense pleasure from these precious objects of magnificence and grace, not so much from their substance—he did not have the time or inclination to read the ancient documents or study the distinctive details of the exquisite drawings—as from the contentment he took from images and words bathed in the glow of history, validated as it were by their resilience, gorgeousness, and durability. His art was old, his furniture heavy, his rooms crammed with priceless possessions. Age, heft, and mass reassured Morgan and brought him great comfort.[4]

Nearing his sixty-third birthday, the thickly built man of six feet and well over two hundred pounds savored the isolation of his over-flowing library. His home on the northeast corner of 36th Street might not compare with the outré splendor of the Vanderbilt broth-ers' matched set of Fifth Avenue show palaces, but no one said of him, as Edith Wharton did of the old Commodore's descendants, that he was "entrenched in a *thermopylae* of bad taste." He could be kind, courteous, and even gentle, though the clerks and subordinates who worked for him considered it a supreme act of tenderness when he kept his sulfurous temper in check. He remained a man brimming with energy and ambition. And a huge diseased nose. Even the best intentioned could not ignore its deforming eruptions. "No nose in any caricature," declared the art dealer James H. Duveen, "ever as-sumed such gigantic proportions or presented such appalling excres-cences." The piercing hazel eyes continued to shine with a terrifying intensity. He had begun to rely on a cane to get around, but he still possessed the implacable dynamism that Wall Street broker Henry Clews compared to "the driving powers of a locomotive." Contem-poraries referred to him as Jupiter.[5]

As he relaxed with his playing cards, Pierpont's crackling assertive-ness and powers of imagination were barely held at bay. No longer young, he remained fresh, filled with plans to build and create. He wanted to expand Morgan & Co.'s investments beyond railroads and state loans, to extend the glory of his church, to clothe the city in grandeur, and to build a showcase for his inestimable art collections. Even discounting the aura that wealth imparts, and art and power and sheer physical heft, and a titanic will, there was still something that made Morgan one of the most magnetic, masterful, and imposing men of his time. Newspapers spilled gallons of ink over his words, his charities, even the quotidian events of his daily life, discussing the mystery of his lost coat at a church convention.[6]

Several times in his earlier years, he had threatened to leave the banking business. Now he was the colossus of the economy even when he traveled the world, sometimes for months at a time, in search of venerated art and the serenity with which escape provided him.[7]

The shadow of his father had begun to fade by the late 1880s. The senior Morgan died in April 1890, soon after suffering an injury in Monte Carlo, a week short of his seventy-seventh birthday. "Probably no other foreign banker," the *Tribune* eulogized, "was so well and widely known and liked, or exerted so great an influence in the United States as he did." Pierpont was the principal beneficiary of his father's estate and assumed his father's position as senior partner at the London firm.[8]

The decade following his father's death was as difficult and trying as any period Pierpont had ever experienced, testing him and the new corporate system that his bank had come to symbolize. The depression of 1893 had confronted the new economy with the most severe financial collapse in the nation's experience. It was even more devastating coming as the third economic crisis in three successive decades. In these troubled years, it was far from clear that Morgan and his fellow capitalists would escape responsibility for the economic disaster. Then, even before the nation recovered from the depression, a gold emergency hit, threatening to undermine the American monetary system and its money markets. This crisis was hardly over when the

1896 presidential election turned into a referendum on corporate capitalism, as the Democrats joined western populists on an agrarian economic platform that deeply unnerved Wall Street. This was followed by an imperial war in Cuba and the Philippines, which Morgan opposed (not solely because it claimed his yacht, the *Corsair*, for the U.S. Navy), and finally by the most aggressive merger movement in American history. As this turbulent decade unfolded, few could sanguinely predict that Morgan and the system he piloted would lead the national economy to the dawn of the American Century.[9]

As he sat alone with his cards, Morgan refused to dwell on the past. With his largest projects still before him, the future excited him more. He had large plans for consolidating railroads and the steel, telephone, and farm machine industries into Northern Securities, U.S. Steel, Bell Telephone, and International Harvester. He would craft each of these industries into giant monopolies to make production more efficient and prices less competitive. These dreams made others tremble, for they would transfer power from the market to the hands of a small coterie of bankers and industrialists. But he did not give these concerns much thought.

For a smart, powerful man, he was quite unreflective. Though he himself had done so much to construct this new system, he preferred to see it as the outcome of larger forces that must not be tampered with. He viewed the amalgamation of power and property as the legitimate effects of natural processes. His view was distorted, of course. It ignored the efforts of his own bank and the other financial barons to transform American industry from modest privately held firms into publicly owned corporate monopolies, efforts that had more to do with the plans of forceful capitalists who shared a Wall Street perspective than with the invisible workings of disembodied market forces. In time, an effective progressive movement would challenge Morgan's comfortable self-delusion. But for now, while revelers made merry in the streets, his concentration on the cards was unclouded by doubt. He greeted the American Century with an unprecedented momentum for business growth behind him.

N ew technology and advances in management and manufacturing had sent production output soaring throughout the 1880s, bringing more business, more jobs, higher living standards, and greater prosperity, but also a lingering fear that a runaway economy was increasing its debt load at too rapid a pace, riding a giant magic carpet that must at some point succumb to the laws of physics. By 1890, this fear took on an unsettling reality.

Pumped up by easy credit from Europe's respected Baring house, Argentina had undergone a parallel expansion in commerce and industry, only to fall before a killer combination of rapid inflation, unsupported debt, and epidemic corruption. "Rarely," wrote *Banker's Magazine*, "has there been a failure of such magnitude." The collapse toppled the government and imperiled Baring. It sent shock waves throughout the Western financial community. Compelled to bail out the Baring bank, London financial houses pulled back from other commitments and called in their loans, forcing British investors to dump American securities.[10]

The wholesale withdrawal of foreign investments worsened an unfolding American gold crisis. Between 1890 and 1893, American gold outflow went from $4.3 million to $87.5 million. Over the same period, the volume of consumer perishables, whose spectacular climb had so greatly enhanced living standards, began a disheartening decline, while the production of durables tanked even more rapidly. For a generation, America's railroad industry had pumped up the economy. But as too many iron horses competed with one another, rates on competitive routes tumbled. This led to wage cuts and resulted in bitter strikes that roiled the industry. By February of 1893, the respected Philadelphia and Reading Railroad had run its debt up to $18.5 million. With no more than about $100,000 in its treasury, it went bust. Other railroads folded. Orders for rails and rolling stock were canceled. Early in May, the giant National Cordage Trust ran short of working capital. Under normal circumstances the rope cartel should have been able to arrange a loan, but a panicked credit market had turned impossibly tight. National Cordage collapsed. A healthy economy could absorb these shocks, but too many industries were overextended and the economy was far from healthy.[11]

Exports, housing construction, and railway investment all declined. The volume of new stock releases went from $165 million in 1890 to $94 million in 1893. By June, *Banker's Magazine* was reporting a "storm" moving "from Wall Street to the West, where banks, trust companies and corporations have fallen before the cyclone like cob houses, and left its path strewn with wrecks."[12]

June 29, 1893, was one of those days that leave their imprint for a generation. For much of the month, merchants had not been able to borrow for less than 15 percent. On this day, short-term interest rates hit an incredible 50 and then 75 percent, as the loan market closed down and a terrible anxiety gripped the financial community. Only the New York Clearing House committee's rescue efforts, putting together an emergency loan fund of $6 million, brought the rate back down closer to normal. But the markets failed to recover. The confidence that had kept the economy gliding along the surface of good times evaporated into a gloom filled with endless frictions.[13]

New York merchants initially dismissed the troubles as limited to the speculating community. But as the crisis spread, it revealed a deeper precariousness, not of any single class, but of the new economy itself. The money markets had worked up speculative fever well beyond any practical basis. The crash of unsound investments had pulled down the credit markets, leading to frenzied efforts to liquidate. The ensuing panic crushed some sixteen thousand firms nationwide. One-third of all railroad companies went careening over the edge of solvency. In New York alone, seventy-five thousand inhabitants were without jobs, twenty thousand without homes. Daily newspapers reported New Yorkers found starved to death and others frozen. They also carried the response of President Grover Cleveland to demands for assistance to the poor. It was, he lectured, the duty of the people to support the country and not the other way around.[14]

Stocks fell. Businesses closed. Banks suspended. Colleges, even Ivy League schools, reported large drops in enrollment. Scores of students who paid their tuition by tutoring "their more opulent and pleasure loving classmates" lost their patrons. Harvard and the University of Chicago laid off faculty. Salaries declined across the land. Foreign capital fled. "As fast as Europeans can dislodge their holdings in America," moaned the *Commercial and Financial Chronicle*, "they take their money away." Immigrants stopped coming. In 1892, 480,000 people had come to the United States, most of them in search of economic security. Three years later, immigration was down by four-fifths. By the end of 1893, new stock issues, already sluggish, declined another 60 percent, to under $37 million.[15]

The Morgan bank, like its sister institutions, was forced to redraw its forecasts and take note of the disasters playing out around the nation. It could not escape the fear that enveloped so many in the business community that the crisis signaled something serious, not in its large number of unemployed, for that was not what made a depression, but in the rapid decline in prices. The 1893 depression seemed to augur a future filled with depressed prices and cutthroat competition that would drive prices down to a hair above profitability. This analysis, with its promise of recurring panics followed by wholesale crises, greatly unnerved the business community.

As he worked first to understand the meaning of the crisis and then to pull the nation's financial leadership together, Pierpont Morgan's banking partner Tony Drexel suddenly dropped dead at the age of sixty-six, in June 1893. *Banker's Magazine* eulogized Drexel as "a king. . . . [F]rom the realm of finance a sovereign has departed." Such a loss would have been hard at any time, the journal continued, but in the face of "the gravest problem that has taxed financial genius since the funding experiences of Alexander Hamilton," it was a tragic loss. Drexel's son replaced his father for a while, but he displayed no interest in allowing fiduciary responsibilities to distract him from society life and after a few months retired to less demanding pursuits. Pierpont moved to concentrate international power at 23 Wall Street. The Philadelphia and New York branches were fully merged. Pierpont became the senior partner in the Paris bank, now to be known as Morgan, Harjes & Co., and while the London firm remained nominally independent, he headed that house as well. Renamed J. P. Morgan & Co., the four houses were now united under a single commanding figure, who at the age of fifty-eight directed the most powerful banking conglomerate in the country.[16]

His first step was to respond to the rapid depletion of the U.S. Treasury's gold. The nation's gold reserves served as a rough barometer of financial stability, and they had been plummeting since early in the 1890s, leading, said *Banker's Magazine*, to "doubt, fear and semi-panic." By the time of Grover Cleveland's second inauguration in March 1893, the reserve dipped below $100 million, the level that Americans had come to view, in the new president's words, with "a sort of sentimental solicitude" as the required level for safety. The rapid decrease of this primary metal threatened to undermine the basis of American exchange on international markets, with consequences that Morgan considered nothing short of disastrous.[17]

Even before taking office, Cleveland began talks with the major international banks about the feasibility of a large bond sale to replenish the gold reserve. The Rothschilds were hesitant, but Morgan assured the president-elect that his bank could syndicate a large issue. Cleveland backed away at the last minute, fearful of offending the antibank forces in Congress. Over the succeeding months, the full weight of the depression fell upon the president's shoulders, but he was preoccupied. On June 30, under a cloak of secrecy to avoid further agitating the economy, the president slipped out of Washington and traveled to New York. There, aboard a friend's yacht in the East River, he had a malignancy removed from his mouth. He recovered and returned to office determined to address the gold crisis, to "put beyond all doubt . . . the intention . . . of the government to fulfill its pecuniary obligations in money universally recognized by all civilized countries."[18]

As the gold reserve continued to decline, Cleveland pleaded with Congress for a new bond issue to bring in gold to avoid "a national calamity and our country's disgrace," but inflationary interests led by the farm caucus defeated the bill. Desperate to fend off default, the president released notes under his emergency powers, but the effort was poorly executed. Only the New York banking community's co-ordinated purchases saved the Treasury from what Cleveland acknowledged would have been "a disastrous failure." The fitful release of bonds on the open market failed to stanch the drain. By February 1895, with the reserve depleting at the rate of $2 million a day, the gold supply was down to $41 million. Still, Congress refused to grant Cleveland authority to stabilize the gold supply. Those who owed debts saw their burdens eased as inflation made money less valuable, and they were well represented in Congress, where the majority had no desire to pass a bill that might make bankers happy at the expense of debtors.[19]

Cleveland finally turned to New York for help. Say what you might, Wall Street knew how to plan a bond sale by bringing together leading underwriters, preparing the market, and retailing the debt to a gilt-edged overseas clientele. Pierpont Morgan wired his London partners, "We are disposed to do everything our power to avert calamity & assist U.S. Govt."[20]

With the assistant secretary of the Treasury shuttling back and forth between Washington and Morgan's library to hammer out the details, Pierpont assembled a consortium to underwrite up to $100 million in bonds on terms that were better than what could be gotten from the European banks. At the last minute, a strong anti–Wall Street campaign forced Cleveland to cancel the deal. The White House informed Morgan that the United States would sell the bonds directly to the public without any bank help. Stunned by the turn in events, Pierpont ordered the White House to delay any public announcement, instructing August Belmont Jr. (the Rothschild interests had joined the Morgan-led syndicate) to meet him, and cabled London: "Going Washington. . . . We consider situation critical, politicians appear to have absolute control," adding: "If fail . . . it is impossible [to] overestimate result U.S. Must admit am not hopeful." He boarded the private car that was attached to the Pennsylvania Railroad's *Congressional Limited* and hastened to the nation's capital.[21]

Arriving in Washington late in the afternoon, Morgan was greeted by the secretary of war, Daniel Lamont, who informed him that it was useless to see the president. The decision was firm. Fixing Lamont with his icy gaze, Pierpont said tartly: "I have come down to see the President and I am going to stay here until I see him." Around midnight, Morgan buttonholed Attorney General Richard Olney to tell him that an unmediated sale in the depressed environment would do little more than recycle gold that was already in the United States. American investors would simply redeem their legal tender notes for gold and buy the bonds with gold withdrawn from the Treasury, producing little net gain. He needed to see the president. At a few minutes past two in the morning, Morgan wired London that he had an appointment for 9:30 A.M. at the White House. He would do his best.[22]

The meeting involving the president and his cabinet officials dragged on into the afternoon. Morgan reported afterward that Cleveland seemed intent on ignoring him as he sought a solution that would avoid a fight with Congress. But as reports drifted in from the New York Subtreasury with the latest figures on the declining gold balance, the air became more urgent. Yet the officials could not come up with anything practical. Finally, Cleveland turned to Morgan and asked his opinion.[23]

Pierpont replied that fresh gold was needed quickly to avoid a default that would wound American markets. His syndicate was prepared to underwrite a bond issue for up to $100 million, drawing mostly on European rather than American gold. Cleveland wanted to know how Morgan could be sure that European investors would not simply cash in *their* securities for American gold to buy the new bonds. He demanded a "guarantee that this will not happen." The remarkable request would require an extraordinary level of intervention in international gold markets. Backed by a banking empire that spanned two continents, Morgan answered simply, "Yes, sir." They agreed on a $60 million contract.[24]

Morgan wrote London that he was "more than satisfied" with the agreement. "Could not have better document." When the bonds were released, the entire issue sold in less than twenty minutes, with the underwriters turning away business. "You cannot appreciate the relief to everybody's mind," Morgan wrote with a sense of backing away from the precipice of national default. "The dangers were so great, scarcely anyone dared whisper them."[25]

Morgan's pledge to protect the Treasury reserve for the duration of the contract did not prove easy. The bonds, which were issued to investors at $112.25, climbed within two weeks to $124. If European bondholders, who held about $30 million of the new notes, began selling them to the American market to take quick profits, they would drain off millions in gold dollars. Morgan pressed his European syndicate partners to block such sales. He also used his good offices to discourage American importers from shipping out gold, even when this meant paying a premium for overseas goods. When gold levels began faltering, the syndicate bought gold on the open market or used its own holdings to replenish withdrawals. Morgan's farrago of clever juggling and financial intimidation fortified the reserve. Soon *The New York Times* was reporting that the syndicate had won "a prominent place in financial history" by restoring "buoyancy" to the markets."[26]

Never before in peacetime had the United States borrowed on such a scale. Washington's own attempts had proven feeble and ineffective. Only Wall Street could attract overseas gold in the midst of the depression. Hailed for safeguarding the nation's credit and preserving its international credibility, the bankers had also braced their own institutions. Morgan himself had cabled his London partners: "We all have large interests dependent upon maintenance sound currency US." He fully expected the deal to "pay good profit." But in the end, many agreed with the *Times* that if for "a mere $5,000,000," Morgan et al. had shored up the American financial system, the money was well spent. One could not buy that kind of security anywhere else.[27]

What in fact did the syndicate earn in profits? Even congressional investigators could not get the bankers to divulge the information. Estimates have ranged from $8.4 million to more than $18 million. In fairness, at the time that the deal was made, the signatories had no assurance beyond their own projections that it would prove as successful as it did. The closest student of this deal, Vincent P. Carosso, calculates that total syndicate earnings for the American consortium came to about $2.1 million. J. P. Morgan & Co. (New York) claimed roughly $300,000 (about $5.4 million in year 2000 dollars), an amount that Carosso concludes was well within range for transactions of such "magnitude, risk and duration," though it was far from cut-rate.[28]

Much later, Grover Cleveland asked Morgan what had made him think that Europe's banking houses would buy bonds on his terms. "I simply told them," Jupiter replied, "that this was necessary." This was the kind of thing he had become used to doing. Cleveland, more accustomed to dealing with a tangle of contending interests that each needed to be accommodated, discovered that banking was different. A quiet word from Jupiter "and," recalled Morgan, "they did it."[29]

Earlier in the century, few Americans had been prepared to sanction a financial link to international banking. President Andrew Jackson used the specter of a vast money power, dominated by foreign and elite interests, to portray the Second Bank of the United States as an enemy of the people and ultimately to destroy it. But now Wall Street's elite banking houses, working closely with their overseas partners, had bailed out the Treasury and President Cleveland had nothing but praise for Morgan's "large business comprehension and . . . remarkable knowledge and prescience," calling him a "great patriotic banker." Nevertheless, the old misgivings surfaced anew. Joseph Pulitzer's *World* condemned the banker's syndicate as a cabal of bloodsucking Jews and aliens.[30]

"We face an immense amount of criticism," Morgan's New York office reported to London. His every move attracted attention. "Am watched & followed; attacked in papers," he wrote. It was not Pulitzer, however, that Morgan and Wall Street feared most. It was the rising populist campaign that had brought together a collection of grievance movements and was making great headway in the West. Conceiving the economy as a zero sum game, the populists seethed over banker's profits that they were convinced came at their expense. "There are but two sides in the conflict that is being waged in this country today," declared a populist manifesto. "On the one side are the allied hosts of monopolies, the money power, great trusts and railroad corporations, who seek the enactment of laws to benefit them and impoverish the people. On the other are the farmers, laborers, merchants, and all the other people who produce wealth and bear the burdens of taxation. . . . There is no middle ground." They blamed Wall Street, foreign capital, and big business for their hard times.[31]

There was, of course, real pain and suffering behind their disaffection. The decent livelihood they believed was their due for hardworking the land, for living in isolated circumstances, for keeping faith with the Jeffersonian vision of America, was proving ever more elusive. Farmers' exports were especially hard hit in the depression, and the forces that had brought prices down in consumer goods—greater efficiency, mechanization, and intensified competition—had reduced the price of staple cereal grains to as low as a sixth of their previous figures. Meanwhile, expenses for borrowed money, transport, and warehousing cut deeply into what was left of profits. Perhaps most wounding of all, the cities—which the farmers saw as inimical to their values—were growing, replacing the stolid vision of a yeoman America with an exciting and prosperous urbanity. It did not lessen the pain that many of their own sons and daughters were abandoning the land for the city's bright lights and seductive opportunities.[32]

Populist politics proposed a retreat from the new economy. They aimed to take back economic power from the corporations and banks. Unable to accomplish this themselves, they called for federally imposed redress. Fiercely independent in the past, farmers now turned to the government to protect their lands, adopt debtor-friendly financial policies, and closely regulate those who stored, processed, shipped, and distributed their produce. They called for nationalizing the telegraph and railroads. As one of the cavalcade of unlettered speakers who toured the western regions wrote: " . . . dont the government Successfully Run the post offic [?] and implys in the pestal Servis Receve living Wagges Without any Striks[.] the railRoads can be Run on the Same plan[.] government can essue Stampt tickets from one mile up to one thousen[.] a purson Can Buy a ticket for eny number of miles he Wish for instints if he is going to Chicago. . . . Culd be cuntrold in the Same Way as the postal servis."³³

Bewildered by the transformations that had so profoundly shifted their own status, they blamed Wall Street for their torment. "The fruits of the toil of millions," declared the 1892 Populist Party platform, "are boldly stolen to build up colossal fortunes for a few. . . . [F]rom the same prolific womb of government injustice we breed the two great classes—tramps and millionaires." The populists characterized the new economy and its center, New York City, as an alien space populated by Jews, bankers, and those who mercilessly conspired to bilk the upright, homespun-attired plain folk of the farm.³⁴

A split over gold defined the two sides. Commercial interests defended the gold standard, denouncing inflationary programs as dishonest "repudiation." In contrast, the agricultural West and South held gold responsible for strapping them to a confining monetary system, a "cross of gold" that enriched foreign and domestic bond investors while depriving debtors of the benefits of "soft money." This debate dominated the contest for the Democratic Party presidential nomination in 1896. Split between eastern and western wings, the Democrats abandoned Cleveland conservatism in favor of Nebraska's William Jennings Bryan, the eloquent voice of the western cause. The "silver-tongued orator" ran a searing campaign of grievance, promising to push back the changes that were transforming his America. Bryan's electrifying acceptance address rejected any Cleveland-like deals with bankers, condemning the gold standard as a Procrustean tool of eastern capital and America's cities as ungrateful parasites living off the prairie while scheming to cheat its farmers of a decent living.[35]

With the gold reserve plunging once more, Wall Street arrayed to fight Bryan and his simple nostrums. On July 23, the day after Bryan won a second line on the presidential ballot as the Populist Party candidate, New York's international bankers convened at 23 Wall Street to form a $50 million "guarantee syndicate," placing Pierpont Morgan at their head. For the next four months, until after the election, forty-nine of New York's leading financial institutions functioned as a central bank, exchanging foreign currencies and debt receipts among the members in order to satisfy most foreign gold charges internally to avoid having to ship gold out of the country. "The New York people have come up well," Assistant Treasury Secretary William Curtis wrote in a letter, "& we see the curious spectacle of the U.S. finances being controlled by a committee, of which J. P. Morgan is the chairman & the majority of whom are Hebrews, while the Secretary of Treasury sits, practically powerless in his office."[36]

While less than enthusiastic about the Republican candidate, former Ohio governor William McKinley, Morgan and his colleagues loathed Bryan. Andrew Carnegie paid for printing five million pamphlets against "that light headed, blathering demagogue," while Morgan finally came around with $250,000 (about $4.5 million in year 2000 dollars) for the campaign. John D. Rockefeller matched this contribution, and the rest of the business community fell in line for a total that has been estimated at as much as $7 million, though $3.5 million is probably closer to the truth. Bryan, limited to the quarters and dollars of his homespun crowd, raised no more than a tenth of that amount.[37]

McKinley may have had a backbone of jelly, as Morgan once lamented, but he was no fool. He refused to be drawn into a debate with the rhetorically gifted Bryan ("I may just as well put up a trapeze on my front lawn," the reticent Ohioan declared, adding, "I have to think when I speak"). He fastened himself to his front porch and sent a swarm of surrogates to make the Republican case. Offered a remarkably clear choice between two rival economic visions, voters handed McKinley and his "business principles" platform a decisive victory, 51 to 47 percent, over Bryan's anticorporate crusade.[38]

In the midst of a depression that had lingered for more than fifty months, voters dismissed the narrow premises of prairie populism in favor of broad-gauged urban capitalism. Even in the farm regions there was opposition to Bryan's promise of a return to modest-scale agricultural economics. For many of these farmers, banks, including the very New York banks that Bryan excoriated, were profoundly liberating, advancing capital to those with only limited resources, allowing them to buy land or invest in a business by borrowing against potential earnings.

These banks occupied the central place in American finance. Morgan and his New York colleagues had raised $262 million in gold to tide over the economy, and now McKinley's victory and a brightening trade environment brought recovery. With the recurrent gold crises that dominated the first half of the decade ended and a new Republican ascendancy, the banks turned their attention from underwriting government bonds to sparking an era of business consolidation that remains unmatched in American history.[39]

Many had warned that the 1893 depression would profoundly reshape the free enterprise system. Some even thought that it might lead to a revolution, but few predicted that it would lead to the most fully developed effort to curb competitive capitalism in American history. This effort was not spearheaded by radicals or populists or labor unions or even Washington; in its vanguard stood Pierpont Morgan and Wall Street.

Used to thinking in terms of the 1929 depression, we look for changes issuing from the 1893 economic crisis such as unemployment insurance or welfare relief or any of the scores of programs designed to place the state between the citizen and extreme want that came out of the New Deal. Of course there was none of this, nothing of the social safety net, no National Recovery Administration, no WPA, nor any state initiative to mitigate the depression's impact or tackle its causes. Nineteenth-century depressions were not read as a call to help the displaced and needy. The most significant message taken from the 1893 collapse by the business community was a warning to business about cutthroat competition and the need to protect industry against the uncertainties of the market—that, to put a fine point on it, if anyone needed protection from depressions, it was *business*.

The depression had caught the railroads perilously overextended. For years the recurring complaint of the giant industry had been that the roads were building beyond any rational need. Charles Francis Adams, who had become president of the Union Pacific, in 1884 warned four years later that, "The railroad system of this country . . . must inevitably lead to disaster. . . . There is among the lines . . . an utter disregard of those fundamental ideas of truth, fair play and fair dealing, which lie at the foundation of . . . civilization itself. . . . Great corporations, one after another, have contracted the madness, and have built hundreds of miles of road, almost paralleling each other." The result—destructive, competitive battles "unprecedented in the whole bad record of the past"—confronted many of these multimillion-dollar companies with ruin. In the seismic shakeout that followed the 1893 depression, one-fourth of the national rail system—192 roads, capitalized at $2.5 billion and operating forty thousand miles of track—fell into the hands of receivers, mostly Wall Street investment banks, who pruned more than thirty years of wild railroad growth into a neater arrangement of centrally coordinated systems.[40]

Carrying out the most thorough and most important of these reorganizations was the same bank that had ridden the gold crisis to dominance, J. P. Morgan & Co. The transfer of power was swift, surgical, and unforgiving. Though Morgan had serviced some of the very roads that went under with the depression, few blamed him for the industry's troubles. He had been admonishing the industry for close to a decade about wastefulness and senseless redundancies. He had tried pools, alliances, and formal agreements but had not succeeded in restraining the roads' illusions of individual dominance. Nothing he did brought about a cooperative approach.[41]

Now, with scores of railway lines bankrupt, carriers from every region flocked to him, and Morgan selected the most attractive roads for salvage. Taking charge of the discredited boards of directors, he cleared out ineffective management, slashed costs, and forced upon the roads an unaccustomed discipline. With what the *Commercial and Financial Chronicle* called "exceeding frankness," Pierpont reorganized the fallen businesses. He made the Southern Railway system's security holders deposit their certificates with his bank so that they could not speculate on the road during rescue efforts. With other roads he made stockholders dig into their own pockets to contribute to operating costs; yet other investors he pressed into accepting a reduction in the number of their shares. When officials objected to his rough handling of *their* roads, he bellowed, "*Your* roads! Your roads belong to my clients," the clients who were putting up money for the refinancing. He eliminated entire lines that he judged redundant or inefficient, and those with wasteful habits he "Morganized." These roads, among the most powerful corporations in the world, meekly surrendered their independence.[42]

When a Morgan-led syndicate was appointed receiver of the oft maligned two thousand-mile-long Erie, it had passed through three receiverships only to skirt disaster once again in 1893. Pierpont assigned Morgan Bank partner Charles Coster, described as his "right arm . . . with great energy, organizational genius, very cautious, and with fine negotiating skills," to the task. It took two years to complete a meticulous study of the entire Erie system before Coster charted a comprehensive reorganization. Then Pierpont rammed through a "Morganization," unifying the Erie's subsidiaries under one management, rehabilitating its finances, and placing the "Scarlet Woman of Wall Street" on the path to long-term stability.[43]

Morgan & Co. did not work cheap. At the same time the bank pressed reductions upon the securities holders, it charged $500,000 for the Erie restoration, with Morgan accepting payment in stock shares to demonstrate confidence in a reconstituted Erie. By the time the syndicate closed its Erie accounts several months later, the shares had tripled in value. Erie's recovery offered one more indication of Wall Street's power. Investors were willing to forgive even the scarlet woman's irregular past once she was safely in Morgan's arms.[44]

In addition to the Southern and the Erie, the Morgan bank reorganized the New York Central, the Philadelphia and Reading (this restructuring brought $2.75 million in commissions and another $650,000 in fees), and other major roads. "No other private banker in the United States," writes Vincent Carosso, "was so heavily engaged in so many large operations of such far-reaching consequence." The New York Central alone involved the sale of nine major securities issues worth $125 million, an almost impossible task in the risk-averse depressed economy. Yet Morgan managed to pull it off.[45]

For years Morgan had warned railroad executives that it was suicide to keep building and competing, but as long as they were able to stay above water, they refused to relinquish their dreams of dominance. The 1893 avalanche of railroad defaults put an end to that. Humbled and, more important, bankrupted, these roads fell into his hands. What he had not been able to accomplish through persuasion and exhortation he accomplished through an unyielding consolidation, imposing stability upon the nation's notoriously chaotic transportation system and converting railroad equities from highly speculative properties into prudent investment vehicles. Morgan emerged from the 1890s with more than one-sixth of the nation's railroad industry under his control. Together with Kuhn, Loeb's Jacob Schiff (the only other financier who matched Jupiter's influence), he wove these disparate lines into interlocking super roads. By 1900, the nation's vast railroad network had been consolidated into six huge systems run largely from New York City.[46]

Though the "colossus of American finance" apparently found a way to do all the work and relax with his art and his excursions, those who worked for him were not so lucky. Charles Coster left the office each evening with stacks of papers that he analyzed into the night, only to return the next morning to face a new round of troubled businesses. He would hurry from meeting to meeting, mastering the details of each railroad placed under his direction, studying the books, reviewing the management, and creating an overall plan, which Morgan would then force through.[47]

The job was a killer, but with his grasp of detail and brilliant organizing mind, Coster became the national expert on railroad rehabilitation. It was to him as much as any person, the authoritative *Commercial and Financial Chronicle* wrote, that the Morgan house's success in reorganization was to be attributed. Coster and his equally brilliant associate Samuel Spencer (who, it was said, held in his head the cost of every item from that of a "car brake to the estimate for a terminal") directed the reorganizations with guidance from Morgan's outstanding legal staff.[48]

Shortly after J. Hood Wright, another of the favored Morgan partners, dropped dead at the age of fifty-eight, the bank wooed Harvard alumnus (1880) Robert Bacon to New York. All remembered Bacon, a star sportsman (and according to classmate Theodore Roosevelt "the handsomest man in the Class and . . . as pleasant as he is handsome"), as one of Cambridge's most gifted. Undecided at first, Bacon ultimately could not resist. When he informed colleagues at Boston's Lee, Higginson and Co., the president wished him well but cautioned: "Don't overwork like Coster just because you can and like to do it. He is wonderful, and unwise to do so." Three months into his new job, Bacon was hooked. "I am really working for the first time in my life," he wrote his wife, apologizing for backing out of a holiday in France. "I shudder to think of the responsibility which I feel. My life is simply engrossed in this maelstrom."[49]

In 1897, Walter Burns, Pierpont's brother-in-law and head of the London Morgan bank, collapsed and died. Three years later Charles Coster expired at the age of forty-seven, *The New York Times* attributing his early death to "demands upon his time and strength and the responsibilities he had assumed, far heavier than any one man ought to bear, or could bear with safety." The business journalist John Moody mused on the number of Morgan men claimed by "the gigantic, nerve-wracking business and pressure of the Morgan methods and the strain involved in the care of the railroad capital of America."[50]

The following year, a London partner visiting the Morgan empire on Wall Street found there a "prodigious amount of nervous excitement and energy," adding: "Old Pierpont Morgan and the house occupy a position [in America] immensely more predominant than the Rothschilds in Europe." The two banks, which he thought controlled roughly similar sums of capital, differed, however, in their approach. Morgan's was far more "expansive and active," with "few of them liv[ing] through it to advanced years except . . . giants like Morgan, who has something Titanic about him. . . ." Only Pierpont came "through the soul-crushing mill of business, retaining his health energy, vigor and energy," remarked Moody.[51]

This killing work advanced the most extensive industrial rearrangement in American history.[52] Indeed, within only a few years after the passage of America's pioneering Sherman Act in 1890, a law designed to outlaw trusts that restrained trade, Morgan created the shared community of railroad interest that he had long sought and helped set off the most intense wave of industrial consolidation and monopoly building in history.

---

In the early 1890s, the stocks listed on the New York Stock Exchange consisted primarily of railroad shares. Fewer than ten *manufacturing* securities were listed, and of those most were in some way connected to the railroad; *The Wall Street Journal* carried no entry for "Industrials." Manufacturing was still predominantly entrepreneurial and capitalized by private owners who managed these often family-run businesses. The largest manufacturing company in the world, the Carnegie Steel Company, was privately owned and managed.[53]

Only a handful of businesses like H. B. Claflin's dry goods, Procter & Gamble, P. Lorillard, and Westinghouse had converted partnerships into industrial corporations or formed combinations like the cottonseed, lead-smelting, sugar-refining, and whiskey trusts.[54]

One of the earliest of these combinations involved the sugar-refining industry. In the 1880s, bitter competition brought prices down to their lowest point in thirty years, leading the largest companies to join forces in a cartel. "We were all practical men . . . ," recalled one of the participants. "We all knew that the only way to make sugar refining pay was to stop overproduction." With their businesses at stake and Henry Havemeyer, scion of a wealthy New York sugar family, leading them, the refiners combined to impose industrial order and stability. Over the next few years, profits rose by 18 percent. In 1890, New York State brought suit against one of the participating firms, charging that the combination was illegal. The refiners responded by disbanding their cartel.[55]

Shortly before, the New Jersey State Legislature, eager, in the words of corporate lobbyist James Dill, "to pass promptly any law which tended to improve the general scheme of incorporation," and working closely with corporate executives, passed new legislation making it easy to consolidate business corporations in New Jersey. Until then, state-chartered enterprises were prevented from absorbing or merging with out-of-state corporations. Manufacturers, for example, could not assemble corporate affiliates across the nation to control price, quality, quantity, and profits. The new law changed that, expressly permitting corporations to purchase stock in other corporations and to acquire property outside the state—in other words, to set up interstate corporations. The law also provided other inducements, including tax advantages, fee abatements, and an over-all climate of business permissiveness.[56]

Fine-tuned in the next few years, New Jersey's incorporation statutes eliminated what had been a practical limit on the size and spread of corporations. Now, for a small fee, businesses could com-bine into one integrated, centrally managed holding company. Within two years, close to 1,200 firms, 6 of them trusts, incorpo-rated in New Jersey. "A strange revolution is going on in the indus-trial world," exclaimed *Banker's Magazine*. Competition had led to enormous losses, "but instead of resorting to the old-fashioned rem-edy of killing out the weaker," businesses discovered a new method "uniting all conflicting interests in what is popularly known as a trust, or . . . converting them into . . . ordinary corporations."[57]

In January 1891, John Dos Passos (father of the famous novelist), a brilliant New York criminal lawyer who had switched to the lucra-tive new specialty of corporate law, provided the disbanded sugar re-finers' cartel with a new legal shell for its efforts to fix prices and limit competition. He incorporated the American Sugar Refining Co. as a trust—in New Jersey, naturally. Other companies remained hesitant, fearful that they might be made the target of the recently passed Sherman Anti-Trust Act, which outlawed combinations in restraint of trade. And indeed, the antimonopolists did assail the sugar trust. "Never," cried *The New York Times*, "has competition been more completely suppressed by a combination in a prominent industry." From Congress came demands that "the people of the country [be] protect[ed] from the exactions of such great monopolies as the sugar trust." In May 1892, a suit was initiated against the E. C. Knight Co., charging its parent company, the American Sugar Re-fining Co., with conspiring to monopolize "the manufacture of re-fined sugar and . . . interstate commerce. . . ."[58]

After four years making its way through the courts, the U.S.

Supreme Court decided the case in January 1895. The High Court declared that while the law prohibited monopoly in *commerce*, it laid no similar ban on *manufacturing*. Federal authorities were therefore powerless to punish or restrict combinations of producers and manufacturers like the sugar refiners. (Later, in the *Addyston Pipe and Steel* decision, the Court made its rule even more clear and more limited: The Sherman law forbade informal, cartel-type combinations but did not outlaw incorporated mergers that carried state sanction, no matter how large or powerful the resulting company.) The path had been made safe for others to follow. And they did.[59]

As business activity picked up, confidence that had been shattered in the 1893 meltdown was restored, setting off a new expansion boom. Businessmen learned from their experience that size mattered a great deal. Cartels, corporations, and trusts survived the depression far better than more modest enterprises. Even before the crash, unincorporated businesses had sold for three times earnings while desirable joint stock corporations commanded seven to ten times earnings. Part of this had to do with the liquidity that the stock form of ownership provided. Much more had to do with the fact that the stock exchange made a company's hopes and dreams fungible, so that a mere promise of future earnings inflated market values, making it easier to capitalize such companies. And soaring capitalization was the key to modern industrial success. Capital paid for new research, the application of new technologies, and the expansion for mass production.[60]

Unable to take advantage of mass-production efficiencies, the smaller businesses had made ineffective efforts to hold prices. But the most successful businesses recognized that such limited steps were futile. Prices had been falling in every major category of production for decades (New York City's wholesale price index in 1866 was 174 but less than half that in 1890). Industrial consolidation promised more effective results through the economies of mass production and managed markets.[61]

Pioneering trusts in the oil, sugar, and tobacco industries had achieved these efficiencies through mergers and monopoly, and with the path cleared by the *Knight* decision, manufacturers adopted their example. In the quarter century after the Civil War, investment capital had gone into creating the American railroad system. Now it went into consolidating American manufacturing. In a remarkably short span of time, hundreds of smaller firms merged into large, integrated industrial combinations. The rise of the industrial corporation created a new form for business. It altered social and class relations and substantially reordered the everyday world of American life. Abraham Lincoln, no stranger to threats to the Republic, may have exaggerated the effect but not the scale of importance when he warned at the dawn of the new era: "Corporations have been enthroned . . . and the Republic is destroyed."[62]

Behind the throne stood Wall Street.

At first the manufacturers handled the mergers themselves, but buying out competitors was expensive. Before long, much like the early antebellum industries that were forced to turn to Moses Taylor and other New York bankers for funding, the industrial capitalists too were "tempted," writes William Roy, "by the prospect of Morgan's millions" into "their Faustian bargain." They relinquished managerial control in return for access to foreign and domestic capital. Led by Morgan and Jacob Schiff of Kuhn, Loeb, Wall Street's "rich and able men," in the words of *The New York Times*, used the power of the purse to seize the reins of the corporate revolution. They approved the mergers, paved the legal path, underwrote the securities, appointed the managers, and framed the policies. "Big deals are not possible," the *United States Investor* declared in 1899, reflecting on the past few years, "if banking assistance is withheld."[63]

Better known and more trusted than the companies they took on as clients, the bank underwriters became the instruments of incorporation, the initial purchasers and therefore the guarantors of corporate securities. Unregulated, working behind closed doors, often in collusion with other bankers, they set the initial stock values for new issues that they then marketed to a gilt-edged international clientele. Companies that failed to get their approval did not make it to market.[64]

These underwriters followed an unspoken etiquette based on a shared regard for conservative economic principles and patrician discretion—and, of course, the bottom line. Only three or four banks had the necessary standing and resources to serve as principal underwriter. One or two of these would assemble the rest of the syndicate, drawing upon a second tier of investment banks and insurance companies. The managing partner, usually the initiating bank, wielded autocratic power. "Nobody," Jacob Schiff was wont to say, "participates in a syndicate by any right; whoever participates, participates by the good will of Kuhn, Loeb & Co." Schiff would notify those selected what proportion they had been allotted and the extent of their involvement.[65]

Syndicate members worked together in noiseless calm and hierarchical diffidence. "There is an air of omniscience as if nothing unexpected could ever happen," reported an observer. "Doors do not slam, men walk softly upon rugs, voices are never lifted in feverish excitement over profit and loss; no one is permitted even to call off the prices from the tape. There is first a feeling of space. . . . Ceilings in a banking house are higher than ceilings anywhere else." Syndicate members recoiled at asking for an accounting of expenses and stifled any word of criticism, apprehensive of offending. Once invited to join, bankers beneath the top rung did not think of declining, even if they had doubts, for fear of never being invited again. While the financial houses made a show of not competing for this business, it brought them cascading profits (a 1902 estimate: 20 percent of the value of the securities being issued) as they took liberal advantage of clients whose dependence upon them was total.[66]

As mentioned, the most influential syndicator other than Morgan & Co. was Kuhn, Loeb & Co., the leading representative of New York's elite Jewish investment houses. By the 1890s, Kuhn, Loeb, headed by the imperious and brilliant Jacob Schiff, serviced an A list of the world's principal investors and leading railroad firms. Descended from a long line of rabbis, scholars, and businessmen, Schiff had been born and raised in Germany. He left school at the age of fourteen to apprentice in a mercantile firm and then took a job in his brother-in-law's bank. Headstrong—"he already feels that Frankfurt is too small for his ambition," his father wrote—he left for the United States in 1865, when he was eighteen. Before boarding the transatlantic liner that took him across the ocean, Schiff wrote to a family friend in St. Louis, seeking help in finding a suitable position "in one of [America's] large cities. I am," he explained, "at an age when I must make my decision for the future."[67]

Within a year of landing in Manhattan, young Schiff rose from a clerk to opening his own brokerage, Budge, Schiff & Co.; but the pressures of being without family, alone and on the make, were not inconsiderable. Thirty-five years later, he would recall the challenges that confronted him as a young "stranger in this great city . . . [with] greater aspirations than to satisfy alone bodily wants and desires." He returned home. But when a visiting Abraham Kuhn offered him a banking post in Gotham, he accepted. He was made for America, his mother assured him.[68]

Abraham Kuhn himself had made a similar transit across the ocean some thirty years before. With his partner, Solomon Loeb (whose sister he later married), he peddled merchandise out west. The two men combined their earnings and became merchants and then war suppliers, finally moving to New York and opening a bank in 1867 on Manhattan's Nassau Street. Brokering government bonds and servicing the German Jewish mercantile community, Kuhn, Loeb & Co. formed part of the closed circle of New York's German Jewish banking houses that included August Belmont, Philip Speyer, J. S. Bache, the Seligman brothers, Henry Lehman, and Marcus Goldman, many of whom had also arrived in the 1830s and 1840s and had capped spectacular success stories with investment banks on Wall Street. Bound together by kinship, nationality, and religion, their "our crowd" circle of select families worked and worshiped together and frequently intermarried.[69]

In its early years, Kuhn, Loeb followed a policy of doing "business with people who come to us." But the determined young Schiff shook off this reserve, selling railroad securities to Jewish investors in Paris, London, and Hamburg, giving the firm a bold international profile. Solomon Loeb in particular was uncomfortable with the techniques of aggressive securities banking, but he deferred to the punctilious Schiff, to whom in May of 1875, he gave his daughter, Therese, in marriage. By the age of thirty-eight, in 1885, Schiff was head of Kuhn, Loeb.[70]

Schiff's banking style was similar to Morgan's. Both were tough and unremitting, but morally exact. With his aristocratic bearing, piercing blue eyes, and thick German accent, Schiff made probity a company byword. "If [trust] is gone," he once told an associate, "our business is gone, however attractive our shop window might be."[71]

He managed his business affairs like his personal life, with an inflexible Junker precision that venerated routines and rules. "I have made it a rule to spend Friday evening exclusively with my family," he told a business associate who wanted to meet with him, "and I can under no circumstances vary from this." He chose his words so carefully that his sentences seemed crafted on a lathe. If an appointment was more than fifteen minutes late, he could not be persuaded to wait. He responded to mail on the same day he received it. His brother-in-law and partner, Paul Warburg, described Schiff as very generous, distributing 10 percent of his personal wealth to charity, in addition to his hundreds of philanthropic projects, but he "had a perfect horror of waste." He saved string from packages and bundled old newspapers to donate to prisons and hospitals. "He could get very indignant when he found that money was spent wastefully, and when Mr. Schiff became indignant," Warburg recalled, "he had a way of expressing himself clearly and forcefully. People who became the object of his criticism would not easily forget it."[72]

Son Mortimer remembered Jacob Schiff as a strict and demanding father. After inheriting his parents' Fifth Avenue mansion, Mortimer quipped that it was "wonderful to be the master of a house in which I have been spanked so often." Uncomfortable with the sort of display that typified some of the other moguls, Schiff shunned the glare of publicity. His most conspicuous outlays were for civic undertakings. Genuinely modest, the literate and stiffly elegant financier cultivated a circle of high-level friendships with half a dozen leading bankers in England, France, Scotland, and Germany, the warmest and most enduring of which was with Ernest Cassel of London, whom he met in 1879. For forty years thereafter, the two collaborated on business and exchanged ideas about markets, about mutual acquaintances, about national affairs, and about their families. Only about his secret conversion to Catholicism from his inherited Jewish faith did Cassel not breathe a word to his older friend.[73]

Like Morgan, Kuhn, Loeb, specialized in railroad financing during the last quarter of the century. From 1881 on, it was the principal banker for the Pennsylvania Railroad, releasing more than $1 billion in securities for the line. Schiff also managed Jay Gould's railroad investments in his post-Erie period and Edward Harriman's adventurous campaigns for transcontinental railroad mastery. By the end of the century, Kuhn, Loeb included among its clients ten of the largest railroad systems in the United States.[74]

Schiff and Morgan were sometimes thrown into competition, but they dealt with each other as rival heads of friendly states and treated each other with elaborate deference. When he was approached about reorganizing the Union Pacific, Schiff at first demurred, declaring, "That is J. P. Morgan's affair. I don't want to interfere with anything he is trying to do." Only after Morgan assured him that he was not interested did Kuhn, Loeb take on the account.[75]

When once the two bank giants found themselves pursuing the same company for their respective clients—something they generally avoided—Schiff received a note from Pierpont explaining that he had been left no choice in the matter. He insisted, therefore, that Kuhn, Loeb share substantially in the profits of the transaction and he would not relent until Schiff accepted. On another occasion, "caring much as I do for your respect and good opinion," Schiff personally wrote Morgan a 1,700-word letter to explain a complicated series of events that had set off a bidding war between their respective interests, taking pains to reassure his colleague that there was no intent to "do aught means to be antagonistic to you or your firm, and that, as far as my partners and I are concerned, we have at all times wished, as we continue to do, to be permitted to aid in maintaining your personal prestige, so well deserved."[76]

That personal prestige for both men was greatly extended as they moved their respective houses beyond railroad work to reorganize the new industrial economy along monopolistic lines. Using their favored access to investors in the world's principal cities, they changed the face of American industry in the closing years of the century. Between 1897 and 1904, in what remains the most intense period of merger activity in American history, 4,277 firms were amalgamated into 257, as Wall Street created trusts in every field.[77]

One of Pierpont Morgan's earliest forays outside the railroad business (after completing with Schiff the merger of New York's municipal railway) was the organization of the General Electric Trust in April 1892.[78] Three years before, Morgan had joined Kuhn, Loeb and the Deutsche Bank to underwrite the creation of a diversified electrical energy and equipment company, Edison General Electric Co., by merging Edison's original light company with six other concerns. Two other electrical energy powerhouses, Westinghouse and Thomson-Houston, competed with Edison General Electric for the growing electrical energy market, which caused periodic price wars. In preliminary discussions aimed at forming some sort of alliance to restore price stability and eliminate the duplication of very expensive production equipment, Westinghouse made clear that it was not interested in cooperating. For its part, Thomson-Houston was more interested in absorbing Edison General Electric than in discussing short-term expedients.[79]

Thomas Edison opposed a merger, but Morgan, who handled Edison's finances, had long understood that the irascible inventor was not much of a business executive. The other companies were better managed and had done better in marketing their products. Morgan had Charles Coster draw up detailed merger plans that he then proceeded to press upon Edison, who reluctantly signed the agreement to form the new $50 million General Electric Corp. Furious at the erasure of his name from the firm and at terms that placed his former rival at the head of the new corporation, Edison attended one board meeting before turning his mercurial interest to other things. Nevertheless, the General Electric Trust went on to become one of the world's leading electrical monopolies.[80]

Morgan had been seeking to moderate competition and rationalize industry for years. "The old idea that we were raised under, that competition is the life of trade, is exploded," Morgan would later say. "Competition is no longer the life of trade. It is cooperation"—a very limited form of cooperation, however, cooperation among businesses to replace market competition with the dictate of New York's bankers. Labor, consumers, small businesses, and environmental reformers might harbor grave doubts about this new approach, but what William Roy calls "an ideology of monopoly," a conviction that industrial consolidation was necessary in order to assure large profits, captivated America's industrialists. For them and for the bankers who financed and steered them, bigness represented progress. Monopoly made it possible to afford the latest machinery. It streamlined the workforce, eliminated duplication of plants, machinery, and inventory, and made it feasible to mass-produce on a scale heretofore unimaginable. Size translated into power to buy in larger quantities, dictate better terms, and exert firmer control on wages, expenses, and prices.[81]

Morgan may not have been as light of foot as he turned sixty, but he had become used to thinking in ever larger terms—in terms that, combined with the resources he controlled, made him the most formidable economic force in the land; formidable and audacious, for he recognized no limits to the possibilities open before American industry. In 1901, in a historic sequence of mergers, Jupiter marked the high point in Wall Street's era of business consolidation by mobilizing New York's leading capitalists to form United States Steel, the world's first billion-dollar corporation.

Early in the 1890s, the prince of steel, Andrew Carnegie, surveyed John D. Rockefeller's $24 million portfolio of non–Standard Oil holdings—sixteen railroad companies, nine real estate firms, half a dozen shipping lines, nine banks and investment houses, and plants that produced steel, lumber, paper, and nails, as well as two orange groves in Florida—and announced that "Reckafellow" was "one of the poorest investors in the world." One of the oil baron's investments, however, was in a pine-forested property stretching approximately 120 miles across north-central Minnesota. ("It is," Frederick Gates had said to Rockefeller in convincing him to make the investment, "the opportunity of a lifetime, one of those opportunities, the seizing or failing to seize, which marks the difference between success and failure in life.") It was the great Mesabi Range, the richest iron ore lands ever discovered in North America.[82]

Carnegie himself had passed on these properties, writing his partner: "If there is any department of business that offers no inducement, it is ore. It never has been very profitable and the Messaba [*sic*] is not the last great deposit. . . ." Rockefeller continued to scoop up land in the mineral-rich territories surrounding the American Great Lakes, and by 1895 his Lake Superior Consolidated Iron Mines was bringing $10 million a year in profits. Carnegie no longer ridiculed "Reckafellow's" ore investments, especially as some were saying that Rockefeller had plans to enter the steel business. In fact, as Rockefeller approached sixty, his pinched visage corrugated by wrinkles, his interest was turning away from business. In December 1896, he signed a long-term agreement with Carnegie Steel to ship (exclusively on Rockefeller-owned carriers) 1.2 million tons of iron ore at a fixed price for a period of fifty years. *Iron Age* called it "Carnegie's greatest achievement." In one deal, the steel man locked away long-term rights to the richest deposits in the land and also eliminated the most important threat to his steel empire. "All hail 1897," exulted Carnegie.[83]

It turned out to be a very good year for steel. Despite a long-term trend that dramatically reduced steel prices—rails, for example, went from $67.50 per ton in 1880 to $17.50 in 1898—the steel industry was generating huge profits. And it was not hard to see why Carnegie was leading the pack. While each dollar invested by the average steel firm bought 112 pounds of steel production, Carnegie was squeezing 153 pounds of steel out of the same dollar. Between 1880 and 1900, Carnegie Steel's investment budget multiplied tenfold. And now the orders were pouring in to build the new generation of heavy machinery and the new factories, bridges, and tall buildings. Already the most successful manufacturers in the world, American steel producers ordered twenty-two new furnaces in 1897 to keep up with demand. And the war on Spain that broke out in the following year brought urgent new orders for munitions, heavy armaments, and forgings.[84]

Carnegie opposed war. Indeed, his rancorous denunciation of the president in connection with the war led cabinet officials to fear that he had lost his mind. But Carnegie had a higher principle, and when the War Department ordered steel plate for ships, the pacifist grasped the import with a laserlike clarity: "There may be millions for us in armor." Willing to trade his principles, but not inexpensively, Carnegie formed a pool with Bethlehem and other steel corporations to fix the prices that he charged his country, pegging profits at 250 percent of production costs. When the government accused the industry of irregularities, he whined sanctimoniously. But secretly he boasted to a friend, "Ashamed to tell you the profits these days. Prodigious." Profits in 1897 of $10 million more than doubled to $21 million and doubled again the following year. "Where is there such a business," Carnegie exclaimed.[85]

Illinois Steel was the largest iron and steel producer west of Carnegie. When it broached the idea of a plan to protect prices on industrial steel, the Scotsman flatly refused. "Our policy," he declared "is to stand by ourselves alone. . . ." Coexistence did not interest him. "The enemy [Illinois Steel]," he wrote his colleagues, "is at our mercy . . . let us not be foolish enough to throw away the fruits of victory." To protect its own business, Illinois Steel set out to create a steel combine of a scale to compete with Carnegie, sending chief counsel Elbert H. Gary to 23 Wall Street early in 1898 to secure the funding for a series of purchases of mines, furnaces, foundries, shipping lines, and rail links. He also asked Morgan to orchestrate the buyouts, mergers, and takeovers.[86]

Charles Coster and Robert Bacon took three months to design the consololidation plan and begin folding rich ore fields, modern steel foundries, a host of fabricating mills, and high-capacity carriers into a coordinated steel monopoly. Capitalized at $200 million, the combination brought Illinois Steel and American Steel and Wire (itself recently formed out of five other companies) under the umbrella of Federal Steel. To run the Federal Steel monopoly, Morgan did not choose an industrial expert. In this age of mergers and monopolies, it was more important to understand finances and the law. He installed the brilliant counsel Gary as president, and Gary proceeded to bring close to forty new companies under Federal Steel's billowing cape. Within the year, Coster, Bacon, and Morgan engineered another steel amalgamation, bringing fourteen manufacturers together as the $80 million National Tube Company.[87]

Though he dismissed the mergers as mere stock schemes, the rival monopolies posed a genuine threat to Carnegie, who predicted that the scheme "will fail sadly." Carnegie already dominated the industry's "stage one" ore-mining operations as a result of his exclusive rights to Mesabi ore. With four steel plants, two iron mills, and highly advanced operations, Carnegie Steel also led in "stage two"— that is, the production of primary steel products. Now Carnegie instructed Charles Schwab, the president of his steelworks, that "our policy should be to make finished articles," competing with Federal Steel and National Tube for "stage three," manufactured goods. He wanted to manufacture wire and nails and all the steel items stocked by general stores, but also boilers and, he wrote to Schwab, "finished railroad cars as well, as soon as you can do it." He was prepared to slash prices. Struggle, he wrote, was "inevitable . . . it is a question of the survival of the fittest."[88]

With the nation's largest industry one step away from chaos and his panicked steel clients mewling that Carnegie was going to "wreck us," Morgan conceived another consolidation, only this time on a scale only Jupiter could imagine.[89]

They were not fast friends, but Andrew Carnegie and Pierpont Morgan had occupied the same business universe for close to three decades. They had worked together on protecting the gold reserve and had clashed over the Pennsylvania Railroad. Carnegie disapproved of Morgan's uninhibited womanizing and resented his efforts to build up Carnegie Steel's competitors. For his part, the banker saw Carnegie as a maverick whose war to win uncontested control over all phases of the steel industry had "demoralized steel" by undermining coordination, order, and, ultimately, stability.[90]

Carnegie Steel's thirty-eight-year-old president, Schwab, impressed him, however. In December 1900, the two men attended a University Club dinner, one of the typical New York affairs that brought together the Wall Street business circle to honor one of their own (also in attendance were Jacob Schiff; E. H. Harriman, president of the Union Pacific; H. H. Rogers, Standard Oil's chief executive; and others of their ilk—it would have been difficult indeed to imagine so high-powered a dinner in any other city). That evening Schwab delivered an address on the possibilities open before the American steel business. He suggested that self-interest dictated cooperation and went on to draw the possibilities of a fully integrated steel combination. Intrigued, Morgan invited him to come to his home to carry these discussions further. They met in January and talked through the night.[91]

This was, of course, more than piquant coincidence. Wall Street was in the midst of a merger craze. Carnegie, while trumpeting a battle for markets, was molding a new life project in philanthropy (leading banker James Stillman to remark: "His vision of what might be done with wealth had beauty and breadth, and thus serenely overlooked the means by which the wealth had been acquired"). Morgan, as king of American finance, had been leading efforts to tame the undisciplined market. He had been thinking about steel for more than a year. Both thought that an American steel colossus would dominate the world market, but Morgan was unwilling to work with the notoriously independent-minded Carnegie. He asked Schwab to pry from the steel mogul a sales figure for his steel holdings. He would handle the rest.[92]

Schwab brought back to Morgan an asking price of $480 million, twelve times annual earnings. It was an astounding figure (equivalent to $5.5 billion in year 2000 dollars). That year the federal budget stood at approximately $350 million. Morgan peered at the scrap of paper with the numbers and immediately accepted. With that he had the centerpiece of the new United States Steel Corporation. Equally important, writes Morgan son-in-law and biographer Herbert L. Satterlee, it replaced "disturbing personalities" (read "Carnegie") with the "right men to run the great corporation . . . more or less" cooperatively. Morgan's lieutenants systematically brought the other steel interests into the combine, but John D. Rockefeller, who had a lock on the world's largest ore properties, remained critical to the project.[93]

Jupiter and the emperor of oil had their differences, too. Morgan did not appreciate John D.'s disdain for Wall Street. Ron Chernow recounts a London banker's testimony that Morgan "inveighed bitterly against the growing power of the Jews and of the Rockefeller crowd." Fond of luxury, Pierpont inhabited a world for the superrich that he had helped create, a world of yachts, extensive travel, kept women, priceless art, and sybaritic indulgence. He viewed the rail-thin Baptist, who struggled to avoid sin, as a prune, "devoid," in Chernow's words, "of manly charms and vices," while Rockefeller once said of the arrogant Morgan: "I have never been able to see why any man should have such a high and mighty feeling about himself." Rockefeller would often complain that while Kuhn, Loeb treated him fairly, Morgan froze him out of the best syndications, assigning him the more chancy issues that offen as not lost him money. Still, both men detested competition, and Rockefeller, like Carnegie, was turning his attention to philanthropy.[94]

Morgan went to Rockefeller's West 54th Street home to make an offer. John D. was cordial but sweetly told the banker that he would have to discuss business with his son, who was now in charge. By the time John junior met with Morgan, this time at 23 Wall Street, much of the consolidation had already been completed. Junior recounted to his father that when he called on Morgan, the banker was preoccupied, as if completing the final sweep of "the room, and we seemed to be the crumbs around the edge which of course must be swept up and expect to be swept up and which it was most annoying to find at this late date still on the floor." How much did the Rockefellers want for their properties? Morgan asked. "I think there must be some mistake," Junior shot back. "I did not come here to sell. I understood you wished to buy." The riposte gave the elder Rockefeller great pleasure, though it paled before the enormous profit he made from the deal. It brought his personal fortune to some $200 million (or about $3.5 billion in year 2000 dollars) and made him the second richest man in the universe.[95]

Coordinating more than three hundred underwriters, including bank presidents, insurance executives, and some of the toughest businessmen in the nation, Morgan made them all fall in line like obedient schoolboys. He assembled eight giant conglomerates with seven more companies that were added before the end of the year to form U.S. Steel, the world's first "billion-dollar corporation." Capitalized at $1.4 billion, hugely in excess of the company's material value (the U.S. Bureau of Corporations later concluded that the amount of securities issued exceeded proven worth by roughly 50 percent), U.S. Steel was incorporated in New Jersey. In capitalizing the new corporation at one-sixth of the total value of all American manufacturing, Morgan followed the time-honored Wall Street practice of factoring potential worth into the initial offering price, based on his own self-serving projections. Others called it watering the stock. For a management fee—aside from all other profits—the J. P. Morgan bank took $12.5 million.[96]

Carnegie alone received $240 million for his shares. When Morgan encountered him shortly thereafter, he saluted him as the "richest man in the world." Carnegie was less gracious, sourly predicting that the combination would soon fail, because Pierpont "knows nothing about the business of making and selling steel." He added: "I will then foreclose and get my properties back, and Pierpont and his friends will lose all their paper profits. Pierpont feels that he can do anything because he always got the best of the Jews in Wall Street. It takes a Yankee to beat a Jew and it takes a Scot to beat a Yankee!"[97]

Carnegie was wrong. He never got his steel company back, and nobody beat Morgan.

Morgan appointed Schwab president of the new corporation, placed Gary at the head of the executive committee, and made Morgan partner Robert Bacon chair of the finance committee. Morgan himself and three other partners took seats on the board, leaving no question about who was in charge. Rockefeller was also included on the board, but he soon resigned over differences with Jupiter. "Pierpont Morgan is apparently trying to swallow the sun," exclaimed Henry Adams. Finley Peter Dunne's fictional saloon keeper, Mr. Dooley, animadverted a bit more lengthily on the Morgan majesty: "Pierpont Morgan calls in wan iv his office boys, th' prisident iv a national bank, an' says he, 'James,' he says, 'take some change out iv th' damper an' r-run out an' buy Europe f'r me,' he says. 'I intind to reorganize it an' put it on a paying basis,' he says. 'Call up the Czar an' th' Pope an' the Sultan an' th' Impror Willum, an' tell thim we won't need their sarvices afther nex' week,' he says."[98]

*The Wall Street Journal* called the merger "the high tide of industrial capitalism." In less than a decade, Wall Street had converted an economic landscape filled with an abundance of independent manufacturers into a system dominated by horizontally integrated monopolies. In 1893, manufacturers had still served a local clientele and few products were recognized beyond their immediate region. Publicly traded manufacturing firms were capitalized at no more than $33 million. Only one decade later, mergers like the U.S. Steel consolidation had woven together hundreds of businesses to form 318 trusts that were national in scope, the bulk of them incorporated under New Jersey's statutes. These companies boasted an aggregate capitalization of more than $7 billion. With their many functions and international buyer base, the conglomerates became the nation's most influential businesses, surpassing the railroads in size, earnings, and importance.[99]

Bringing competitors together under one umbrella, the mergers consolidated control in the hands of monopoly managers who set prices, created purchasing cartels, dictated wages, and rationalized production across entire industries. Woodrow Wilson would write in his history, *The Making of the Nation*, that Americans had now reached a stage beyond competition of the survival of the fittest type. The new economy offered them the "triumphs of cooperation, the self possession and calm choices of maturity."[100]

These calm choices were made by J. P. Morgan, Jacob Schiff, and the restricted coterie of Wall Street investment bankers who came to exert wide and unchecked influence. Through their banks, the financiers organized the mergers and underwrote the new trusts that concentrated the economy in a small number of corporations. Transforming the scale and compass of American manufacturing, they formed trusts across a broad spectrum: in food production, from sugar and whiskey to bananas and meat; in equipment, from heavy machinery like harvesters and electric generators to small devices like typewriters, cash registers, and sewing machines; from industrial goods like iron rails and structural beams to consumer goods like cigarettes and automobiles; in rubber, steel, copper, nickel, glass, tin cans, farm equipment, and photographic film.[101]

The New York Stock Exchange was the ultimate test for Wall Street's trust makers (underwriters who could not sell the securities they endorsed were left holding very expensive paper). Here the new businesses were retailed to the broader population in the form of securities. Not long before, the stock market had been viewed as a raffish arena for contests between the unwary and their slick cozeners. But the exchange won back the confidence of investors. On banner days in January of 1899, trading volume exceeded 1.5 million shares, indicating to *The New York Times* "many gauges of coming and lasting prosperity, supplemented by confidence in the future of securities." Ownership in $150 million of *businesses* routinely changed hands daily. By 1901, daily trading on the NYSE, which now listed more than one thousand industrial corporations, surpassed three million shares. More than 4.4 million Americans, close to 6 percent of the national population, were investors.[102]

To these investors and to the rest of the nation, Morgan's steel consolidation called attention to the new face of American manufacturing. In the past, manufacturing had been scattered across the country in family-owned local units that were passed on from father to son. These plants, mills, and factories carried out single, uncoordinated lines of economic endeavor. In one swift burst of merger activity, Wall Street mobilized the nation's long-term capital (and a not inconsiderable portion of overseas capital as well) and replaced this economic scheme with large, integrated, investor-owned conglomerates, taking American industry from almost entirely privately held to public ownership. This change profoundly reoriented American manufacturing, framing large-scale enterprise in the structures of corporate capitalism. "The investment bankers in effect tore up the social roots of the capitalist order," writes Daniel Bell. "By installing professional managers—with no proprietary stake themselves in the enterprise, unable therefore to pass along their power automatically to their sons, and accountable to outside controllers—the bankers effected a radical separation of property and family."[103]

And like the giant railroad corporations before them, these immense conglomerates were drawn to New York. In 1895, 298 major American businesses, each worth more than $1 million, were headquartered in Manhattan, a number greater than the next four metropolitan centers combined. The largest of these businesses were the awesome trusts that cast a hulking shadow over the new century's business profile. In 1900, 70 of the nation's 128 largest conglomerates were run from lower Manhattan, more trusts than in all of Chicago, Pittsburgh, Philadelphia, San Francisco, Boston, Baltimore, St. Louis, and New Orleans taken together. Chicago, the closest competitor, held 18. "It is a revolution so radical in its sweep, so wide in the area affected," John B. Walker, the publisher of the *Cosmopolitan* magazine, wrote about the U.S. Steel merger, "that in comparison the most important movements of history become insignificant. . . . Governmental decisions will cease to exist except as means to carry out mandates decided upon in the executive offices of the world's commercial metropolis."[104]

O UR TRADE AMAZES LONDON, roared a *Times* headline. And with good reason. Great Britain, with its dominion over commercial water routes and its pioneering production in iron, coal, and finished textiles, had been the acknowledged leader of the older industrial order. As a result, the Sceptered Isle was able to provide its citizens the richest array of consumer goods and the highest standard of living in the world. But after the first Industrial Revolution, it reached a point of stasis in an economy dominated by "small, single function, single product, personally managed enterprises." The introduction of the railroad, which proved so critical in the United States, had a limited impact on the British economy. The iron horse stirred no economic revolution, serving merely to reinforce existing patterns of business and enterprise. Even England's schools of higher learning venerated the past more than the future. For English gentlemen, the notion of introducing vocational training at the university level, even in such fields as engineering, was scorned. In contrast, American and German schools adopted new programs in engineering and applied technology. Having achieved primacy, England did not feel pressed to innovate. As late as 1879, Great Britain remained the world's leading industrial power, accounting for 32 percent of total industrial production. The U.S. share was 23 percent, and Bismarck's Germany held 13 percent.[105]

The United States with its rich farms and immense frontier remained largely agricultural longer than its European counterparts. Moreover, the vastness of the land, with its many small, disconnected agricultural communities, delayed the development of a nationally integrated economy. In America, the railroad proved revolutionary, linking this proliferation of localities into a burgeoning domestic hinterland anchored by the New York entrepôt. At the same time, the railroads became America's largest employers, most inventive businesses, and its first large private corporations. Where England was careful and slow, American investors proved no less than audacious. The scale of railroad construction and its thirst for capital pushed the roads into the eager and venturesome embrace of Manhattan's investment markets.

The far-flung railways pioneered new techniques in management, organization, and marketing and in the second half of the century triggered a spectacular expansion that resulted in bruising struggles for market primacy. This led eventually to a wave of banker-designed amalgamations that served as the model for a historic round of fin de siècle industrial consolidations. The resulting conglomerates magnified America's production capacities in such widely divergent areas as processed foods, metals, oil, light machinery, and electrical equipment, as they ushered in a new era of managerial capitalism.

These developments wove together an expansive modernizing American economy, greatly amplifying the economic power inhering in the nation's immense geographic domain and bold business culture. Remarking on the spectacular rise of the American economy, a prominent London banker revealed more than he realized when he said: "The United States is rather too enterprising for the peace of mind of Europe." The new corporate giants—integrating across the length and breadth of industry to maximize production efficiency—exploited the new technologies and adopted continuous mass production, daring to produce well in advance of demand for the opportunity to cut costs and build profits through volume. Having ripped out the outworn and confining system of demand-driven production, they replaced it with techniques for manipulating and stimulating demand through advertising, branding, and marketing.[106]

By century's end, agricultural America had reinvented itself as a modern industrial power, rapidly outstripping the slower-paced, more modestly drawn entrepreneurial capitalism of the old world. Farm produce had been reduced to 18 percent of national product, while manufacturing and industrial production—the primary symbols of modernization and economic advance—mushroomed to 44 percent of the total, propelling the American economy to the forefront of global industrialization. With 30 percent of the world's industrial output, the United States displaced Britain, which by 1900 was reduced to 20 percent, while Germany filled 17 percent of world orders.[107]

What in Europe, with its much larger governments, was done by the state—providing the funding and training for modern large-scale regulation and administration of technologically advanced industry—was done in America by private hands, mostly from New York. No other city could match Gotham's deep reserves of expertise in law, advertising, accounting, and management, the access to information and communication, or the cachet of a prestige Manhattan address. Already the nation's commercial, mercantile, and financial hub, with the largest concentration of industrial workers and manufactured output value, New York's investment community made Gotham into its corporate headquarters as well.[108]

Innovative technology had electrified American industry, catalyzing great advances, but what so radically reconfigured the modern economy was not new science. More than anything else, it was the New York capital market—recognized as the crossroads of international financing—that drove this process. Through its underwriters, exchanges, and investment banks, Gotham mobilized economic reserves from all over the world and placed these resources at the disposal of America's new companies. "It was the investment in the new and improved processes of production," writes Alfred Chandler, "not the innovation—that initially lowered costs and increased productivity. . . . [I]investment . . . created . . . the modern industrial enterprise—and . . . built . . . the new or reshaped industries in which further, cumulative innovations in product and process would come." It was investment, concludes Chandler, that drove the second industrial revolution, casting the "modern legal, financial, and educational environment in which the modern industrial enterprise operated in the U.S. throughout the twentieth century."[109]

---

At the dawn of the twentieth century, more than five decades of commercial and financial development had concentrated the nation's investment resources in lower Manhattan's narrow canyons in the hands of Gotham's elite syndicators. Pierpont Morgan, Jacob Schiff, and a very small group of others controlled billions of dollars of other people's money, and the businesses that this money bought, and the economy that these businesses dominated. Following the U.S. Steel consolidation, President William McKinley held that Pierpont Morgan was "not only a financier but a statesman." How important Morgan and the system he represented had become for American stability was made clear when an anarchist shot McKinley just six months into his second term. Reporters camped outside Morgan's bank to await a reassuring statement. There was no doubt that such word must come from 23 Wall Street, and it did. Jupiter reassured the stricken nation, urging Americans not to worry, that "the financial situation is absolutely good" and that "the banks will take care" to assure that nothing would "derange it."[110]

Critics agreed that the banks were taking care of the economy; it was the nature of that care that concerned them. Congressional investigators would in time condemn the tight group of major investment bankers as a sinister money trust. Concern about the concentration of power was already widespread. Even detractors conceded that the modern industrial economy, with its giant conglomerates and global supremacy, had vastly improved profits, job opportunities, living standards, and industrial wages. What they feared, however, was that these same conglomerates exerted a disturbing influence over the rights and freedoms of workers, smaller competitors, and plain citizens. "Do not worry" came easily from Morgan's lips. After all, this was the system he had wrought. But others were very troubled by oligopoly's vexing disparities. They were concerned about how to rein in the new superbusinesses in order to protect rights and opportunities without disabling the great engine of economic prosperity that Gotham had built.[111]

Control of the expanding corporate community had become a critical concern to one New Yorker in particular, who had given some thought to the implications raised by the new economy. It is perhaps no more than ironic symmetry that at the same time that J. P. Morgan assumed such mastery over the economy, another of Gotham's forceful men of destiny ascended to the top political office in the land and helped keep this power in check. Described by the great Emporia, Kansas, newspaper editor William Allen White as "the coming American of the twentieth century," Theodore Roosevelt had become a reform fixture on the New York political scene since his days in the New York State Assembly. His daring exploits in the Spanish American War had made him a national hero, and in 1900 he went on to become New York's "boy Governor."[112]

Himself the wealthy scion of an aristocratic New York family, Roosevelt displayed a skeptical disregard for the men of his class. "I do not see very much of the big moneyed men in New York," he wrote in July of 1900, "simply because very few of them possess the traits which would make them companionable to me or would make me feel that it was worth while dealing with them. To spend the day with them at Newport, or on one of their yachts, or even to dine with them save under exceptional circumstances, fills me with frank horror." Similarly, he made no secret of his disdain for "corrupt wealth . . . the Pierpont Morgan type[s] . . . with their equally tainted political counterparts."[113]

As New York governor, he had urged a more "rigorous control" of utility conglomerates whose means "are utterly inconsistent with the highest laws of morality." He had backed a law permitting the state to investigate thoroughly the inner workings of corporations and to embarrass the corporations into becoming better citizens by publishing the findings. He tried to calm Republican Party stalwarts, assuring them that he was not given to impractical forays into "altruism," but he remained firm in his support for a controversial tax on corporate property. "I had heard from a good many sources," New York senator and Republican kingpin Thomas Collier Platt wrote, chiding the governor, "that you were a little loose on the relations of capital and labor, on trusts and combination, and, indeed, on those numerous questions which have recently arisen in politics." How far, he now wondered, had "the notions of Populism" infiltrated the governor's mansion?[114]

Pratt's rebuke elicited from Roosevelt the clearest expression of his thinking on these issues. He wrote back to the man known as "Boss Platt" that he rejected "Bryanism" as deeply harmful to progress. But the "representatives of enormous corporate wealth" were as unwholesome as the populists. The proper course for a modern party, he declared, was to secure "a just balance," opposing populists and socialists, but also "improper corporate influence." "[T]he dangerous element as far as I am concerned," Roosevelt confided to his friend, *New York Post* editor Joseph B. Bishop, "comes from the corporations.[115]

Little wonder that party leaders sought a safe place to hide the

Rough Rider. They finally decided, Roosevelt wrote to a friend in April of 1900, to "kick me upstairs," to have him run for the office left vacant by the death of Vice President Garrett Augustus Hobart. With few illusions about what this meant—"I really do not think there is anything for me to do and no reputation to make" as vice president—the forty-three-year-old New York governor agreed nevertheless to "take the veil" (no doubt hoping to position himself for the presidency) and join incumbent William McKinley on the Republican ticket.[116]

TR may have been a progressive, but he was also one of the shrewdest of American politicians, and with his complex makeup, he was often of at least two minds on many important issues. He knew that a little bit of iconoclasm went a very long way and that his political future depended upon working with or around, but not against, the political establishment. Shortly after the 1900 election that took him to Washington, he wrote to Elihu Root, one of the impeccably traditionalist men upon whom he relied to tame his rebellious tendencies, "I am hard at work trying to assume the Vice Presidential poise." He was tendering a formal dinner in John Pierpont Morgan's honor. "You see," he teased, "it represents an effort on my part to become a conservative man, in touch with the influential classes."[117]

His efforts did little to calm their nerves. When President McKinley was assassinated in September 1901 and the forty-three-year-old Roosevelt became the youngest man to assume the presidency, Republican stalwart Mark Hanna blurted that anything could happen now that the "the damned cowboy" was taking the helm. "I am afraid of Mr. Roosevelt," J. P. Morgan told a journalist, "because I don't know what he'll do." TR was amused, chirping that Morgan feared him because he knew only too well "what I'll do."[118]

In his first message to Congress in December 1901, Roosevelt issued notice that he was prepared to address the new economic realities: The free economy had given rise to colossal combinations whose size and power was disturbing. These giant corporations had brought much prosperity, but some of these companies were responsible for "real and grave evils." The corporations were a "natural" part of modern America, and they could not be eliminated, but the old laws and customs were no longer sufficient to contain them. Government had a duty to learn as much as it could about these new monopolies and to regulate them.[119]

Just two months after this address, Roosevelt had his attorney general file suit against the Morgan-engineered Northern Securities combine, a new $400 million railroad trust chartered in New Jersey in November 1901 that merged the country's major carrier empires and threatened to eliminate rail competition over a vast expanse of America's Northwest. Morgan, Schiff, and William Rockefeller were all prominently involved as underwriters, stockholders, and gray eminences in this giant holding company that represented the latest example of New York's financial and industrial concentration. Roosevelt's bold application of the antitrust statutes hit the moguls like a "thunderbolt from a clear sky."[120]

The thunderbolt clearly piqued Morgan, who declined an invitation to a White House dinner following the announcement. Henry Adams was gleeful. "Our stormy petrel of a president" had "without warning . . . hit Pierpont Morgan, the whole railway interest, and the whole Wall Street connection, a tremendous what square on the nose. The wicked don't want to quarrel with him, but they don't like being hit that way." Picking up two senators along the way, Morgan rushed to Washington to instruct the new president on the proper handling of Very Important Capitalists, suggesting to Roosevelt that he send "your man [the attorney general] to my man [Morgan counsel Francis L. Stetson] and they can fix it up." A generation earlier, Jay Gould had paid good money to buy access to Ulysses S. Grant. Now an indignant Morgan directly confronted the president for overstepping his proper boundaries and rudely intruding into business affairs.[121]

He did not understand why the government would not work with him cooperatively, instead of making attacks upon the well-run companies he had put together. His mergers had eliminated much wasteful fighting and competition, had created a secure market for equities, and had won the confidence of investors both domestic and foreign. Why disturb it? From Morgan's point of view, the government was not a superior authority, but rather an equal one, whose proper domain was distinct and apart from his own. Or to put it bluntly, its budget was much smaller than the ones he worked with, and it should mind its own business and not his. Roosevelt was unmoved. The courts backed the president, ordering Northern Securities dissolved. "Even Morgan no longer rules the earth, and other men," declared a journal, "may still do business without asking his permission."[122]

Some in the business community feared that Roosevelt would go on to attack all trusts and dismantle the new order. But his intent was far more circumscribed. TR's trustbusting may have been a cold slap to J. P. Morgan, but it posed no essential threat. Roosevelt represented a new spirit for the American Century, a president of metropolitan background who had given serious thought to the issues raised by the new corporate economy, but he was no radical. A product of New York's elite reform movement, Roosevelt meant no harm to capitalism, even corporate capitalism.

He accepted, endorsed, and helped secure the new capitalist order, including the role of New York's money trust with its megamillionaire syndicators and the monopolies they erected. For better or worse, he saw these as a natural and unassailable outgrowth of large-scale industrial capitalism. The giant corporations had brought much prosperity. They had thrust the United States to the forefront of international commerce. Roosevelt himself had reflected to his English friend Sir Cecil Arthur Spring Rice that despite the "very unhealthy sides of the concentration of power, in the hands of the great capitalists; . . . in our country . . . I am convinced there is no real oppression of the mass of the people by these capitalists. The condition of the workingman and the man of small means has been improved."[123]

What he rejected was the idea that Washington had no role but to stamp Wall Street's initiatives. Some of these companies had become harmful and dangerous. His quarrel was with illegal behavior, with those who exploited their extraordinary advantages to abuse others. He insisted on government's obligation to regulate the large new business aggregations not so much to address the inequalities of wealth as to police its potentially distorting influence. TR's war on the trusts was an effort to reinforce the new system, not weaken or attack it. Even Morgan, who had done much to establish a business climate of probity, had not avoided questionable behavior (including approving political payoffs). Jupiter did not take kindly to being brought down a notch, but nonetheless TR—more given than Morgan to thinking about the capitalist system—helped brace the new corporate order by reforming it. His brand of progressivism, earnest but vague and very mild, represented no attack on corporate capitalism or upon the New York spirit of speculation and profit that promoted it.[124]

What Roosevelt did do was raise some important questions about economic balance and fairness. The answers to these questions were of necessity partial and imperfect. Roosevelt's solution was far from a resolution of the difficulties, but it offered more of a response than Washington had ever made before. Consistent with Roosevelt's New York experience, his politics aimed to restrain the more extreme aspects of corporate capitalism in order to sustain its viability.

———

This era viewed largeness itself as progress, as a solution to problems that were seen as primarily the result of outdated isolation and fragmentation. Consolidating separate entities, whether businesses, or farms, or communities, promoted comprehensive approaches, global thinking, a broader view. To take an example very much on the mind of contemporaries, a small business could not hope to win a national market, dictate to labor, invade overseas economies. Only a consolidated business monopoly could do that. It was even more likely to accomplish this if it diversified its lines of production. Similarly, the coming together of populations from the isolated separate existence of small farm life into more centrally organized, more complex town and urban communities led to advances on many levels.

It is therefore not surprising that the same society that was merging and expanding its simple, single units of capitalism into complex, integrated corporations underwent similar demographic changes, as individual families left the farms for complexly arranged cities, and that these cities, with New York in the forefront, were themselves annexing their neighbors in order to increase efficiency and power, and also to attain metropolitan grandeur.

In 1860, 16 percent of America's population lived in cities. Thirty years later, the urban share was fully one-quarter of a vastly larger population. New York's own population totals over the same period soared from 814,000 to 1.44 million. Its shift from a port city to world-class metropolis was marked by audacious signatures of urban accomplishment: awesome new skyscrapers; stunning steel ligatures connecting distant metropolitan districts by rail, bridge, and elevated railway; and imposing cultural temples crammed with the proudest artifacts of Western tradition. And it culminated in the most significant urban annexation in American history, the formation of Greater New York in 1898.[125]

As early as 1827, there had been talk of uniting Brooklyn and Manhattan. In 1856, Henry C. Murphy, a former mayor of Brooklyn, declared: "It requires no spirit of prophecy to foretell the union of New York and Brooklyn at no distant day. The river which divides them will soon cease to be a line of separation, and, bestrode by the colossus of commerce will prove a link which will bind them together." In 1874, the New York State Legislature considered a unification plan to upgrade the harbor and knit the region's cities into a single system. But the spirit of post-Tweed retrenchment and mistrust of large urban undertakings killed the bill. Talk of unification revived with the completion of the Brooklyn Bridge and the dispersal of many of Manhattan's workers and middle-class proprietors to Brooklyn. "What the bridge has joined," wrote *Truth* magazine, "let not the politicians keep asunder."[126]

The city had long before outgrown its earlier boundaries. In 1890, more than forty million people crossed the bridge. If Gotham was to hold on to its status as the nation's leading metropolis and its economic center, it needed more than a bridge and splendid new Fifth Avenue mansions. Columbia University president and former Brooklyn mayor Seth Low observed with some alarm that New York was losing its middle class to Brooklyn, resulting in a "weakened . . . tone of public sentiment." Others added that New York's magnificent but ill-divided harbor must be brought under one unified and efficient management if it was to continue to serve as America's gateway. Yet others demanded a modern rapid transit system to link the commercial and industrial city with its surrounding bedroom suburbs. In sum, if Manhattan were to fully realize its regional advantages, it must transcend its outdated Lilliputian scale and annex the nation's fourth largest city, Brooklyn.[127]

By the late 1880s, the New York Chamber of Commerce, the most powerful coalition of New York's business community then or ever, was sufficiently moved by the city's physical decline to shed its earlier diffidence. Dismayed by the terrible toll that small and parsimonious government had taken on New York's development, it issued a frank assessment of the city. The grand harbor had deteriorated dangerously. Lower Manhattan's streets were clotted, rotted, and running with filth. The central city's primitive infrastructure had not kept pace with population growth. Levels of overcrowding in Manhattan's tenement neighborhoods approached 250,000 per square mile. Sewers, water, transit, all demanded urgent attention. The commercial leaders also sounded a note of alarm about the rise of other ports. New Orleans, Baltimore, Boston, and Philadelphia were all growing and modernizing, and the soaring capitalist powerhouse of Chicago with a population of more than 1.1 million was expanding more rapidly than Manhattan.[128]

Mayor Abram Hewitt, a prominent Chamber of Commerce member, shared these concerns. He proceeded to revive the growth program that had been sidetracked by Tweed's fall, calling for a host of new projects for the harbor, streets, rapid transit, and public health, capped by a string of "salubrious and attractive parks." Hewitt concluded grandly that with these improvements, New York's "imperial destiny as the greatest city in the world is assured. . . ." The Chamber added its own enthusiastic endorsement. In the past, it had recoiled from such breathtaking itineraries, but with receipts from the booming economy now filling city coffers and men from its own ranks in important municipal commissions, the Chamber backed the aggressive new public works agenda, assuring Gothamites that "nothing yet reached in municipal grandeur is beyond the aspiration of New York." The astute magazine editor Albert Shaw commented before the end of the century, "We are governed in this city today, and governed splendidly, by the New York Chamber of Commerce."[129]

The Chamber also advanced a plan that had been advocated by Andrew H. Green, New York's consummate nineteenth-century planner. For years Green had urged consolidating the municipalities that surrounded the New York port. In the nineteen years since he had first made this proposal to the state legislature, the population had surged, the economy had advanced spectacularly, and the Brooklyn Bridge had linked the two cities closer together. But nothing had been done to consolidate regional resources, which remained divided among the various cities, each working separately. Much like Rockefeller absorbing his many competitors to prevent "wasteful duplication," the Chamber called for unifying the fractured political jurisdictions into a single, streamlined metropolis under one government, one budget, and one plan.[130]

Annexations had become fashionable in this age when progress and size were thought to be synonymous. "There is destiny in this consolidation," proclaimed a resident from Brooklyn. "The consolidation will be in keeping with the tendency of the times. This is an age of unions and combinations." Philadelphia had absorbed a ring of independent suburbs, expanding from two to thirty miles. By 1889, a resurgent Chicago, making spectacular progress after its fire, had swallowed much of its present South Side, adding 133 square miles to its area. Almost every major city expanded its borders.[131]

Green, backed by the Chamber of Commerce, pressed the state legislature to create a Greater New York Commission. After the initial proposal failed in 1889, the following year Green got the bill passed and the commission elected him its president. Boosters, real estate interests, and merchants united behind the commission, forming a consolidation coalition, advocating New York's "manifest destiny" to annex its neighbors and challenge recently consolidated London for the title of world's metropolis. "New York would undoubtedly lose a great deal in prestige the world over," warned the *Real Estate Record*, if it lost its status as America's largest.[132]

It was more than simply honor. The secretary of Green's consolidation commission, Albert Henshel, explained that Gotham had been tangibly hurt because Chicago "by municipal consolidation and a unity of effort . . . succeeded in wresting from us the [1893] World's Fair," which Congress had awarded to the burgeoning midwestern metropolis. Consolidationists cautioned that if New York failed to keep pace, its great banks would relocate to Chicago, costing the city at least $50 million a year. And the dominoes would keep falling: European financial houses would resettle their correspondents. Then the corporations would depart, followed by the publishers and the entire service industry. Next would go the exchange markets and then industry. All for want of the prestige of first place. That, admonished Henschel, was what had happened to Philadelphia after 1850, when New York took over.[133]

Fourteen American cities already exceeded New York in size. How much longer could Manhattan remain dominant if it held to its narrow boundaries? In this age of empire, a single imperative guided the great urban centers, whether Philadelphia or Chicago or New York: Grow or step aside. Only the regional metropolis could support the level of economic development, transport, waterfront, and transit that greatness demanded. Only the large metropolis could mobilize the resources for modern services, amenities, and protections. Only the greater city could exploit the economies of scale and its enlarged tax base to span and clear and dig and build to secure the commercial basis of urban prosperity.[134]

Chauncey M. Depew, New York State's senior senator, placed the issue in global perspective. Great cities, world cities, did not bow before geography. London's Thames was spanned by bridges modern and old. Despite its great poverty, Rome spent millions to knit old and new settlements together across the Tiber. Florence and Vienna annexed their surrounding regions in the cause of metropolitan progress. "The essence of the marvelous development of the nineteenth century is combination," declared the former chief officer of the New York Central Railroad. "It is the strength, the force, the motive power of our age. It . . . created modern Germany. It made Rome the capital of Italy. It is inspiring the Slav and the Scandinavian for government and liberty on broader lines. It has made London, Paris, Berlin, Vienna and Rome, Europe. It has drawn all the surrounding towns to Chicago, Philadelphia and St. Louis. The lesson," Depew went on to say, was "for union, and in union strength. . . ."

"Prosperity of incalculable value, which is accorded to the unquestioned metropolis of a country"—was within Gotham's grasp, but only if she grew. Join Manhattan with Brooklyn and the other cities, promised Depew, and New York would be entrenched as the metropolis of the hemisphere "forever." Not only would it remain the economic powerhouse of the continent, but its science and "educators . . . will make the city the university of the country. The intellectual life of the country will concentrate here. . . . [A]rtists will seek a reputation in New York. The grandeur of the city, the rapidity of its growth, the majesty of its power, the splendor of its civilization, the prosperity of its people, and the intelligence of its citizens will compel honest government and pure administration. In twenty years the office next to the President of the United States will be that of Mayor of Greater New York."[135]

, If Depew provided the soaring rhetoric, Andrew Green offered the clearest rationale. His lengthy "Communication" to the state legislature, blending history with an understanding of urban policy around the world, laid out a sweeping brief for growth. Green had studied the world's great cities firsthand and had worked with Olmsted and Vaux, as well as with corporate and real estate moguls. He had strong ties to the legal, financial, and merchant communities and had spent many years pinching the city's budget as comptroller. A veteran of city politics, he had planned bridges, museums, grid-defying thoroughfares, and much of upper Manhattan. This broad urban knowledge and rich experience he infused into his design for the city and its future.

Tough, confident, and biting, Green laid out the arguments for largeness in an age that measured progress in square miles. Yes, the waters and mountains did form natural barriers between the cities, but great cities proved themselves by taming nature, not by ratifying its limits. Those citizens of Brooklyn, Queens, and Richmond who fought to protect their private little flags and their precious local identities Green attacked as "the retreating forces of the tribal system," who insisted on their familiar paths even if they led to insignificance. With words that might have come from Morgan or Rockefeller, he recommended instead the "coming forces of the co-operative system." New York must reject small futures. "Cities are the crowns, the signs, the factors of empire," he wrote, and New York must seize her destiny as the imperial city of the nation. "The name of a great city," Green exhorted, "is a tower of strength. Magnitude is not a thing of vapory dimensions, but a solid, substantial and determining factor, of which it would be folly to deny ourselves the advantage. . . . All the great cities of the world," he pronounced with finality, "have attained their rank and eminence by the proceeds of annexation and consolidation."[136]

Green proposed a progressive, powerful greater city, whose

grandeur, scale, and magnitude would balance the massing private interest. The greater city would take on a wider identity and institutional importance, stimulating broader domains of fulfillment. Elevated railroads, Central Park, skyscrapers, the bridge, sanitary reform, worker housing, museums, the opera, the waterworks, and the zoos already formed a metropolis not only of wealth, but of that which wealth makes possible. These were not mere accoutrements of city life, they lifted civic life to a new level of social importance. Expand it, expand the metropolis by uniting the cities into a broad-gauged municipal government, and they will do more, mean more, attract greater loyalty, and in the end prove capable of imposing a civic imperium upon the economic interest.[137]

It took a while for the idea to catch on. Doubters in Brooklyn thought that the future might hold better things than submerging their identity under the boss-run immigrant-beset city across the river. Nor was all of Manhattan convinced by Green's arguments that it was worth taking on the responsibility for financially strapped Brooklyn. But the collection of reformers, real estate interests, commercial groups, and major newspapers would not relent. Consolidation would break up lower Manhattan's awful slums, rid the government of bossism, free the city from the overweening hand of the state legislature, "attract the wealth and culture of the continent, and would make [New York] in time the greatest city in the world."[138]

In a nonbinding referendum in November of 1894, city voters approved consolidation. In Brooklyn, the very close contest was decided by fewer than three hundred votes. But in the end, each of the five cities affirmed its desire to combine into a greater metropolis. It took another four years for this vote to be translated into reality, but with the unyielding leadership of Republican boss Thomas Platt, who used his good offices to ram the consolidation bill through the legislature and then press Governor Levi P. Morton to sign the bill, Andrew H. Green's thirty-year dream was fulfilled on January 1, 1898. In this age, when growth was progress and progress divine, the consolidation of Manhattan, Brooklyn, Richmond (Staten Island), Queens, and the Bronx into Greater New York resulted in a city that covered 359 square miles and held twice the population of Chicago and more inhabitants than all but six U.S. states. In the entire world, only London was more populous.[139]

"More than any other community we have had greatness thrust upon us," declared the "Father of Greater New York." "There is scarcely room for doubt, that when the infant of this day shall reach maturity and come to cast his first vote," Green exulted, "he will be a citizen of a municipality which, in population, in wealth, and influence shall stand at the head of the line of great cities whose influences guide the destiny of the world and whose records embellish the pages of history."[140]

T he corporation emerged in the years after the Civil War to become the dominant institution of American economic life, much as the manor had been the chief organizing institution for Europeans in the Middle Ages. The corporation provided the institutional framework for modern capitalism. It determined how businesses operated, how money was made, work was ordered, products manufactured. It determined the state of the national economy. Stripped of such human frailties as conscience and feeling, the corporation was a sleek machine for profit. Courts argued about how far its rights as an individual and a citizen extended, but all agreed that this bloodless legal construct lived forever. Only one thing could kill it: the failure to make money. Even its activities that yielded no profit, whether disbursing charity or developing sympathetic personnel policies, were in the end justified—could only be justified— by the bottom line. So pervasive was the American corporation that "small business" (the euphemism for noncorporate enterprise) was seen as an endangered species. More recently, the federal government provided it special assistance as a kind of good deed, a grace note from an overwhelmingly "corporate" economy. The corporation remained the most powerful economic form for maximizing investment, attenuating personal responsibility, and driving profit.

Figure the number of Americans owning securities in one form or another and it becomes clear how extensive today is the association between Americans and their corporations—that is, as owners. Then add the numbers who work for corporations, and the total covers a much larger population. The ubiquity of the corporation as the primary American business form makes it seem natural, a kind of pure, simple, and spontaneous form of doing business among free people. Yet the corporation is very much the product of history and human contrivance, the result of decisions and contingencies, a construct of brilliant strategy and unintended consequences and economic "climates," rather than the impersonal "natural free market."

The corporate form itself had been used for centuries to charter cities, universities, guilds, monasteries, and even minority populations like the Jews in medieval Europe. It had been used to create distinct legal identities under government with unique rights, entitlements, and obligations. In the United States after the Revolution, its use was still limited primarily to state-sponsored undertakings of public purpose like roads, bridges, and canals. But state legislatures, responding to calls for greater democracy and reacting to a wave of corruption and corporate failures, put an end to the selective awarding of these charters, passing general incorporation laws that made the benefits of the corporate form much more broadly available.

Corporate-type business became an ideal vehicle for raising large sums, segmenting investment opportunity into venture-size chunks while offering protections that no other format allowed. Corporations begat trusts and trusts begat monopolies, resulting in a fundamental reordering of the American economy. And to a very large extent, the New York economy begat them all.

In its successive reinventions, New York did not so much transfigure its previous identities as add new ones. It did not relinquish its economic authority over any area, deepening the business it already had while pioneering entirely new fields of economic activity. As chief trading port and national banking center, it was well placed to fund and mold the new investment economy, an economy that transformed national business from the exchange in real goods to a trade in virtual property, signified by paper security certificates. This change greatly increased the volume of trade, the flow of profits, and the capacity to undertake projects of immense scope and importance.

The railroad leaders of the post–Civil War era, many of them now ensconced in corporate headquarters in Manhattan's rising office towers, raised business to new levels of investment, organization, management, and profit. The industry produced unprecedented new wealth, which while adding to the pool of capital for new expansion also triggered other investment. The direct impact of the railroad not only as a carrier but as a consumer sparked much new industrial growth as well. Moreover, the railroads also demonstrated the enhanced business efficiencies made possible by integrated management and industrial planning on a broad territorial scale.

Andrew Carnegie applied many of the managerial lessons from the railroads to the nascent steel industry, and John D. Rockefeller brought the nation's oil refiners together in a tightly organized, centrally coordinated monopoly, the Standard Oil Trust. Despite their anomalous financing (both of these world-class businesses did their best to avoid a dependency on Wall Street's famed investment banks), these businesses were run from New York, which offered the concentration of legal, administrative, and management expertise by now required by such international businesses. This location was also indispensable for communications and transport.

Meanwhile, a new generation of Wall Street investment banks, many of them opened after the war, were attracting overseas investors and taking over a large share of the government bond business that had previously been monopolized by Europe's *haute banques.* Wall Street's elite banks also assumed responsibility for protecting the nation's currency from a series of destabilizing gold crises. In the 1890s, their syndicates coordinated the national effort to protect the gold reserve and worked with the White House to syndicate large gold bond issues.

The banks also provided the expansion-addicted railroad industry with its capital lifeline. The radical separation between ownership and management that corporate business brought in its wake had left a huge gap. In the past, the owner-manager of a business, driven by the most simple of desires, the motivation to make a success of the venture and a good name for himself, exerted responsibility and oversight. But corporations were largely separated from their investors, the legal owners. And in this void there was immense room for schemers to wreak great havoc and much spoliation. Investors who had been burned often realized that they could not know all about the businesses whose securities they were buying. In seeking reliable advice about where to deposit their millions, they came to rely on New York's sterling investment banks. These banks became the deal makers.

In these years, New York achieved an influence unmatched by any other city. Money accumulated more rapidly here than anywhere else on the globe. New York banks set rates for borrowing across the country. Its stock market fixed the price of securities. Its investors dominated the large new corporations, and Wall Street became a synonym for money power, attracting the enmity of anticity, antigold standard, anti-industry forces, whose golden-voiced spokesman, William Jennings Bryan, rode the cresting anticorporate sentiment to the Democratic presidential nomination in 1896. Much about that election is remarkable, but most interesting is how the New York–based economy, made into the principal issue of the campaign, emerged unscathed. Indeed, the election was followed by the most intense period of Wall Street brokered–business concentration in American history.

As the economy recovered from its depression with restored confidence and investment interest, American business went through a swift and pervasive paroxysm of consolidation. Wall Street, entrenched as the dominant economic force in the land, converted American industry from single-unit family-owned enterprises into integrated corporations. Its elite banks, already the masters of their rail clients, formed a tight money trust, indispensable for the funding that assembled the cornerstone corporate industries of the American Century. Their power was not limited to providing crucial funding. By this time, they were actively managing businesses and setting industry policy, nowhere better demonstrated than by J. P. Morgan's work in creating U.S. Steel.

What proved especially important was New York's resilient ability to ride atop the changes that transformed the American economy. Other cities saw their importance pass as the national economy changed. But New York not only absorbed the changes, it retained its dominance in each successive economic iteration. Putting to great advantage the momentum of its mighty metropolitan economy, it seized the reins for national economic development. Still the world's most active port, the nation's banking, information, and trading center, and leading metropolitan manufacturer, New York became the world's corporate center. As the economy continued to change, Gotham continued to add new facets onto its old advantages. In each incarnation, from commercial hinge, to investment center, to railroad headquarters, to national money market, communication hub, banking axis, and corporate trailblazer, New York introduced the most innovative techniques, developed the most talented experts, bred the most intrepid risk takers.

The effect was cumulative and daunting. It gave to this audacious economy of many parts a unique level of importance so that the difference between New York and its rivals was not one of magnitude. It was a difference of orders of significance. If Chicago was the second city of the nation, serving as the great metropolis to the Midwest, New York was the central metropolis for the entire system of cities in the United States. It was the center around which other regional metropolises orbited, the great organizer of American commerce. From here the other cities received their goods, sent their

own products overseas, drew their working classes, took funding for
their capital projects, managed their surpluses, did their banking,
traded their securities, and ran their corporations.[141]

In the span of less than forty years, New York mobilized the financial, entrepreneurial, and managerial resources to lay out a powerful
new basis for American business, in the process filling a vast fron-
tiered nation with settlers and industry and capitalizing the land's
unequaled resources. When John Pierpont Morgan first came to
Wall Street, not a single industrial concern was listed on the New
York Stock Exchange. By the time he completed the U.S. Steel consolidation, more than one thousand such companies were listed, including the foundation businesses of the American economy. In the
process, the Wall Street banking syndicates converted an economic
system theoretically committed to laissez-faire to a market dominated by corporate conglomerates. These monopolies absorbed
competitors and swallowed up suppliers of raw materials, as well as
producers and distributors, eliminating competition. Corporate
managers, more than the market, determined production, prices,
and policies, greatly enhancing what Henry Adams called the "vigorous and unscrupulous energy" of these businesses.[142]

It certainly wasn't Marxism, but neither was this new approach of
bringing competitors together into one monopoly sympathetic to
free market competition. (Little wonder that *Banker's Magazine*, in
reviewing a new translation of *Das Kapital*, concluded that while one
might disagree with Marx, one "must admire the acuteness of his
reasonings, and his vast collection of facts . . . disposed as to throw a
brilliant light on a subject greatly in need of illumination.")[143]

It is, of course, one of the premises of this book that despite the
tendency to think about the Industrial Revolution, the rise of big
business, and metropolitan growth as a braided set of ineluctable
forces, the new corporate economy was built in New York by individuals. Out of New York's milieu of vast wealth and vaulting ambition, these individuals formed a new business culture that supplanted
an emphasis on measured growth and local scale with audacious in-

vestment and global scope. "All New York was demanding new men," Henry Adams recalled in his *Education*,

> and all the new forces condensed into corporations, were demanding a new type of man,—a man with ten times the endurance, energy, will and mind of the old type,—for whom they were ready to pay millions at sight . . . for the old one had plainly reached the end of his strength and his failure had become catastrophic. The Trusts and Corporations . . . were revolutionary, troubling all the old conventions and values. The new man could be only a child born of contact between the new and old energies.[144]

These fascinating "new men" were very much products and reflections of their times, though clearly in ways that were exaggerated and personalized. Their influence was seminal. No later American generation had open before it the range of economic options, the broad canvas, the untrammeled power and influence, and the political and economic license available to this group. Adams's new men carved the new tracks into the ground, fixing the course for the future as they built the fresh American metropolis of capital.

Indeed, the obituaries that marked their passing made clear that they were the remarkable products of a unique age that would forever bear their stamp:

Of J. P. Morgan, the editor and Whitman scholar Horace Traubel wrote: "He was a brute. His code was barbarous. He put us all under tribute. He walked over rather than round the humanities . . . [but] I am not satisfied when he is discredited. . . . He was a certain civilization. What the power of wealth stood for: he was that. He was stocks, bonds, banks, railroads, trusts, financiering, chicanery, profit. He was success. The victory was over innocence. . . . You can't consider him as an individual. As mister so and so. . . . *He was the shadow of his time. . . . We put his age away in the hole in the ground with him. . . .*"[145]

Added another eulogist: "[He] was the last of his line. . . . Never again will conditions of government make it possible for any financier to bestride the country like a Colossus."[146]

On John D. Rockefeller: "[B]ecause he was born in 1839 . . . he was on the stage and ready to act his part when the curtain rose on the American era that began with the civil war. It was an era of individualism uncurbed, of complete adherence to the Adam Smith philosophy." Or: "Like Napoleon . . . like J. P. Morgan . . . like Henry Ford he was a product of his time. He could have done what he did in no other setting. John D. Rockefeller was a great expression of a great age."[147]

With little premeditation, these men and their equally outsized counterparts constructed American corporate capitalism out of the unique mix of New York's business experience. Lacking guidelines, characterized by improvisational vigor and a chaotic potency, they drove the process by their private strategies. The corporation, Chief Justice Marshall has said famously, is but "an artificial being, invisible, intangible, existing only in contemplation of law." And law and practice change. The corporation was refined, modified, extended, and adapted out of the push and pull of nineteenth-century American experience. Corporate capitalism was a process that emerged from the market, the law, and the broader reaction to its effect. Much of that experience was cast in New York. And that meant that at the same time that the bankers and the industrialists were consolidating corporate capital, the labor movement, progressive reform, and the very diversity of the metropolitan business class worked their checks *into* the new system, helping save it from some of its own excesses.[148]

That same atmosphere gave rise to reform movements and Theodore Roosevelt's pragmatic progressivism. Corporate capitalists who brought rational order to huge businesses and organized intricate systems of labor and investment were taught to think in complex ways about success. Corporate planning at least suggested to them the merits of taking the long view, of pursuing profits *and* stability, of sinking deep foundations beneath class interests by thinking in broad social terms rather than narrowly about annual returns. One may dispute the ultimate result, but clearly the fact that corporate capitalism emerged from New York's rich diversity gave it a resilience and a complexity that helped account for its wide acceptance.

For it was widely accepted. In 1900, the majority of Americans still lived on farms and in rural communities (the distribution between farm and city did not tip to the urban until the decade between 1910 and 1920). Many of them did not understand the changes that the new economy was undergoing, and they had reservations about the large cities that shaped this transformation. They were especially suspicious about Wall Street, its bankers and brokers with their amoral business environment and the incomprehensible economic abstractions that they spouted. But while most Americans may not have fully understood the workings of the new economy, they did appreciate its benefits. Workers were impressed with the greater stability in employment, better wages, and cornucopia of consumer goods that prosperity wrought. That, and the possibility of economic advancement, if not for the laborers themselves, then for their children. In election after election, they ratified the great changes, and in the first election of the new century they elected a bully New Yorker to the White House, a man who understood the new economy and appreciated its benefits.

That same year, Henry Adams returned to New York after a long absence. New York was now consolidated Greater New York. Coming up the bay, he encountered a scene he took pains to describe in his *Education:* "[M]ore striking than ever—wonderful—unlike anything man had ever seen. Power seemed to have outgrown its servitude and to have asserted its freedom. . . . The city had the air and movement of hysteria. . . . Prosperity never before imagined, power never yet wielded by man, speed never reached by anything but a meteor. . . ."[149]

Herald of twentieth-century modernity, fin de siècle New York had formed itself into the center of world capitalism. Its political figures contended for high national office and set the terms of political discourse. Its disparate immigrant population cast the mold for national diversity and its bankers and industrialists guided America's economic reorganization. Even today our economy remains largely the invention of Gotham's Gilded Age.

# NOTES

## INTRODUCTION

[1]Robert Shackleton, *The Book of New York* (Philadelphia: The Penn Publishing Company, 1917), 3.

[2]Henry Adams, *The Education of Henry Adams* (New York: Modern Library, 1931), 462–63.

[3]Sigmund Diamond, *The Reputation of the American Businessman* (Cambridge, Mass.: Harvard University Press, 1955), 88, 118.

[4]Bayrd Still, *Mirror for Gotham: New York as Seen by Contemporaries from Dutch Days to the Present* (New York: University Press, 1956), 298.

[5]Andrew H. Green, "Communication on the Subject of Consolidation of Areas About the City of New York under One Government," March 4, 1890, *New York State Assembly Doc. No. 71, 1890*, 11–13; *New York Times*, October 11, 1895.

[6]Adams, *The Education*, 462.

## CHAPTER 1: FOUNDATIONS

[1]*Thirty Four Sermons by the Reverend Jonathan Mayhew Wainwright* (New York: 1856), in Sigmund Diamond, *The Reputation of the American Businessman* (Cambridge, Mass.: Harvard University Press, 1955), 52.

[2]Bayrd Still, *Mirror for Gotham: New York as Seen by Contemporaries from Dutch Days to the Present* (New York: University Press, 1956), 202.

[3]Ibid., 63–68, 73; Eric E. Lampard, "The New York Metropolis in Transformation: History and Prospect," in Hans-Jurgen Ewers, J. B. Goddard, and Horst Matzerath, eds., *The Future of the Metropolis: Berlin, London, Paris, New York* (Berlin; New York: W. de Gruyter, 1986), 35, 40.

[4]Still, *Mirror for Gotham*, 54.

[5]Robert Greenhalgh Albion, *The Rise of New York Port, 1815–1860* (New York: Charles Scribner's Sons, 1939), 16–37.

[6]Still, *Mirror for Gotham*, 55.

[7]Albion, *Rise of New York Port*, 38.

[8]Lampard, "New York Metropolis," 44–45; Edwin Burrows and Michael Wallace,

*Gotham: A History of New York City to 1898* (New York: Oxford University Press, 1999), 335.

9Albion, *Rise of New York Port*, 95–99, 119–120; Burrows and Wallace, *Gotham*, 335–36.

10James Ciment, "In Light of Failure: Bankruptcy, Insolvency and Financial Failure in New York City, 1790–1860" (Ph.D. dissertation, City University of New York Graduate Center, 1992), 21–50.

11Curtis P. Nettels, *Emergence of a National Economy, 1775–1815* (New York: Holt, Rinehart and Winston, 1962), 222, 235, 396; Burrows and Wallace, *Gotham*, 333–34; Elizabeth Blackmar, *Manhattan for Rent, 1785–1850* (Ithaca, N.Y.: Cornell University Press, 1989), 38, 75.

12Quote: Still, *Mirror for Gotham*, 74; Kenneth T. Jackson, *The Encyclopedia of New York City* (New Haven, Conn.: Yale University Press, 1995), 923; Burrows and Wallace, *Gotham*, 300–303, 333–38; Lampard, "New York Metropolis," 42–43; Nettels, *Emergence of a National Economy*, 222, 235, 396.

13Still, *Mirror for Gotham*, 68–69.

14Ira Cohen, "The Auction System and the Port of New York, 1817–1837" (Ph.D. dissertation, New York University, 1969), 5–24, 279–80.

15Frederic Cople Jaher, *The Urban Establishment: Upper Strata in Boston, New York, Charleston, Chicago, and Los Angeles* (Urbana, Ill.: University of Illinois Press, 1982), 177; Lampard, "New York Metropolis," 44–45; Albion, *Rise of New York Port*, 278–80; Ciment, "In Light of Failure," 54–55; Cohen, "The Auction System," 24–48.

16Albion, *Rise of New York Port*, 38–40, 237–38; Allan Richard Pred, *Urban Growth and City Systems in the United States, 1840–1860* (Cambridge Mass.: Harvard University Press, 1980), 143–45.

17Kenneth T. Jackson, "The Capital of Capitalism: The New York Metropolitan Region, 1890–1940," in Anthony Sutcliffe, ed., *Metropolis, 1890–1940* (Chicago: University of Chicago Press, 1984), 320; Lankevich, *American Metropolis*, 69; Albion, *Rise of New York Port*, 75, 85, 89, 90–91; Lampard, "New York Metropolis," 47.

18Quote: Charles Lockwood, *Manhattan Moves Uptown: An Illustrated History* (Boston: Houghton Mifflin, 1976), 24; ibid., 18, 28; Albion, *Rise of New York Port*, 261–62, 280; Burrows and Wallace, *Gotham*, 338.

19Albion, *Rise of New York Port*, 285–86.

20Ibid., 196–97; Allen Johnson, ed., *Dictionary of American Biography*, Volume 1 (New York: Charles Scribner's Sons, 1928–1958, 22 vols.), 397–99; Burrows and Wallace, *Gotham*, 337–38.

21Quote: Burrows and Wallace, *Gotham*, 411; Albion, *Rise of New York Port*, 197.

22Albion, *Rise of New York Port*, 197; Philip Hone, *The Diary of Philip Hone, 1828–1851*, Allan Nevins, ed. (New York: Dodd, Mead and Company, 1927), 847–48. Edward Pessen, *Riches, Class and Power Before the Civil War* (Lexington, Mass.: D. C. Heath, 1973), 25. For a more skeptical view, see ibid., 77–165, and Edward K. Spann, *The New Metropolis: New York City, 1840–1857* (New York: Columbia University Press, 1981), 233–34.

[23]Quote: Albion, *Rise of New York Port*, 241–42; ibid., 236, 241.

[24]Quote: Daniel Hodas, *The Business Career of Moses Taylor: Merchant, Finance Capitalist, and Industrialist* (New York: New York University Press, 1976), 5; ibid., 2–4; Albion, *Rise of New York Port*, 262.

[25]Ciment, "In Light of Failure," 60; Albion, *Rise of New York Port*, 182; Joseph Bucklin Bishop, *A Chronicle of One Hundred & Fifty Years: The Chamber of Commerce of the State of New York, 1768–1918* (New York: Charles Scribner's Sons, 1918); Hodas, *Moses Taylor*, 5–6.

[26]*New York Herald*, July 24, 1870; Albion, *Rise of New York Port*, 279; Harry Resseguie, "A. T. Stewart's Marble Palace—The Cradle of the Department Store," *New-York Historical Society Quarterly* 48 (April 1964): 131–33; Harry Resseguie, "A. T. Stewart and the Development of the Department Store, 1823–1876," *Business History Review* 39 (Autumn 1965): 306; Harry E. Resseguie, "The Decline and Fall of the Commercial Style of A. T. Stewart," *Business History Review* 36 (Autumn 1962): 255–86; Edward Crapsey, "A Monument of Trade," *Galaxy* 9 (January 1870): 94–110.

[27]Lockwood, *Manhattan Moves Uptown*, 85.

[28]Quote: Resseguie, "A. T. Stewart and the Development of the Department Store," 308; ibid., 302–3, 306–8, 311–13; Resseguie, "Marble Palace," 131–62; Pessen, *Riches, Class and Power*, 12; Thomas Kessner, *The Golden Door: Italian and Jewish Immigrant Mobility in New York City, 1880–1915* (New York: Oxford University Press, 1977), 11; Jackson, *Encyclopedia of New York City*, 1123.

[29]Quotes: Sarah Bradford Landau and Carl Condit, *The Rise of the New York Skyscraper, 1865–1913* (New Haven: Yale University Press, 1996), 43–44; Resseguie, "A. T. Stewart's Marble Palace," 131–44; Spann, *New Metropolis*, 97–98; Burrows and Wallace, *Gotham*, 668.

[30]Quotes: "ladies of this city," *New York Herald*, September 18, 1846, in Resseguie, "A. T. Stewart's Marble Palace," 142; "grand magazine," in ibid., 159; ibid., 139–40, 150; Resseguie, "A. T. Stewart and the Development of the Department Store," 316–17; Lockwood, *Manhattan Moves Uptown*, 85; Kessner, *Golden Door*, 11; Jackson, *The Encyclopedia of New York City*, 1123; Landau and Condit, *The Rise of the New York Skyscraper*, 43–44; William Leach, *Land of Desire: Merchants, Power, and the Rise of a New American Culture* (New York: Pantheon Books, 1993), 21.

[31]Quotes: "urban artifact," Alan Trachtenberg, *The Incorporation of America: Culture and Society in the Gilded Age* (New York: Hill and Wang, 1982), 131; "idle carping," Leach, *Land of Desire*, 22. "The only great store in existence" before 1876, John Wanamaker, who came to be known in his time as the greatest merchant in America, wrote to a friend in 1908, "was the A. T. Stewart store." Ibid.

[32]Resseguie, "A. T. Stewart and the Development of the Department Store," 319; Burrows and Wallace, *Gotham*, 668. His influence could be seen in Chicago's Potter Palmer and Marshall Field's, and in London's Selfridge's. John Wanamaker recalled that his own dreams of retailing were patterned after A. T. Stewart. Resseguie, "A. T. Stewart's Marble Palace," 134–35; Leach, *Land of Desire*, 32.

[33]Quote: Junius Henry Browne, *The Great Metropolis: A Mirror of New York* (New York: Arno Press, 1975 reprint of 1869 ed.), 293; ibid., 316, 319; Leach, *Land of Desire*, 147; Resseguie, "A. T. Stewart and the Development of the Department Store," 316–19; Resseguie, "The Decline and Fall of the Commercial Style," 257; Resseguie, "A. T. Stewart's Marble Palace," 150.

[34]Trachtenberg, *The Incorporation of America*, 131.

[35]Albion, *Rise of New York Port*, 15, 94–121, 260, 389.

[36]Quotes: "grand prize," ibid., 98–99; "The South . . .," ibid., 120; "All other," Jaher, *The Urban Establishment*, 178; "not a tree," Ciment, "In Light of Failure," 85; Albion, *Rise of New York Port*, 114–15, 284; Burrows and Wallace, *Gotham*, 119–20, 335–36.

[37]Albion, *Rise of New York Port*, 235–59, 265; Albion, "Commercial Fortunes in New York: A Study in the History of the Port of New York About 1850," *New York History* 16 (April 1935): 159; *Riches, Class and Power*, 47–48, 251–99; Sean Willentz, *Chants Democratic: New York City and the Rise of the American Working Class, 1788–1850* (New York: Oxford University Press, 1984), 25–26.

[38]Ciment, "In Light of Failure," 8–9, 69–70, 137–39; Herman Kroos, "Financial Institutions," in David Gilchrist, ed., *The Growth of the Seaport Cities, 1790–1825* (Charlottesville, Va.: Published for the Eleutherian Mills-Hagley Foundation by the University Press of Virginia, 1967), 104–35.

[39]Ciment, "In Light of Failure," 62–63, 65, 297.

[40]Hodas, *Business Career of Moses Taylor*, 22–23.

[41]Ciment, "In Light of Failure," 4–5; Hodas, *Business Career of Moses Taylor*, 6, 19; James Sloan Gibbons, *The Banks of New York: Their Dealers, the Clearing House and the Panic of 1857* (New York: Appleton and Co., 1858), 21, in Pessen, *Riches, Class and Power*, 44.

[42]Hodas, *Business Career of Moses Taylor*, 6, 21, 80, 90; Albion, *Rise of New York Port*, 263.

[43]Ciment, "In Light of Failure," 1, 291; Vincent P. Carosso, "A Financial Elite, New York's German-Jewish Investment Bankers," *American Jewish Historical Quarterly* 66 (1987): 67; Margaret Good Myers, *The New York Money Market, Volume I: Development and Origins* (New York: Columbia University Press, 1931), 94, 103, 125–26, 200; Jackson, *New York Encyclopedia*, 262; William Cronon, *Nature's Metropolis: Chicago and the Great West* (New York: W. W. Norton, 1991), 302; Burrows and Wallace, *Gotham*, 444–45.

[44]Ciment, "In Light of Failure," 85; Myers, *The New York Money Market*, 125–26, 132–34, 266–68.

[45]Ibid.; Albion, *Rise of New York Port*, 285.

[46]Myers, *The New York Money Market*, 94.

[47]Ibid., 90, 95, 97–99, 101, 140.

[48]Hodas, *Business Career of Moses Taylor*, 7, 26, 52–53.

[49]Stuart Bruchey, "Corporation," in *Encyclopedia Britannica*, Volume 6 (Chicago: 1969, 24 vols.), 525–34; William Roy, *Socializing Capital: The Rise of the Large Industrial Corporation in America* (Princeton, N.J.: Princeton University Press, 1997), 50.

[50]Arthur Hadley, *Railroad Transportion, Its History and Its Laws* (New York: Putnam's, 1886), 7, in John Steele Gordon, *The Scarlet Woman of Wall Street: Jay Gould, Jim Fisk, Cornelius Vanderbilt, the Erie Railway Wars, and the Birth of Wall Street* (New York: Weidenfeld and Nicolson, 1988), 40; Alfred D. Chandler, *The Visible Hand: The Managerial Revolution in American Business* (Cambridge: Belknap Press, 1977), 3.

[51]Quote: Alfred D. Chandler, "Patterns of American Railroad Finance, 1830–1850," *Business History Review*, September 28, 1954, 256 (emphasis added), 254–55, 259.

[52]Chandler, *Visible Hand*, 90; Hodas, *Business Career of Moses Taylor*, 89.

[53]Chandler, "Patterns," 263.

[54]Ibid., 262–63.

[55]Ibid., 261; Chandler, *Visible Hand*, 91–94; Chandler, *Henry Varnum Poor, Business Editor, Analyst, and Reformer* (Cambridge, Mass.: Harvard University Press, 1956), 89, 127–33, 147, 171–75; Vincent P. Carosso, *Investment Banking in America: A History* (Cambridge, Mass.: Harvard University Press, 1970), 12.

[56]Quote: Hodas, *Business Career of Moses Taylor*, 111; ibid., 7, 26, 52–53.

[57]Ibid., 94–95, 117–22.

[58]Ibid., 119; Chandler, *Visible Hand*, 132–37.

[59]Hodas, *Business Career of Moses Taylor*, 67–78, 96.

[60]Ibid., 126–27.

[61]Quotes: "bustling," Still, *Mirror for Gotham*, 81; "on the decline," Lockwood, *Manhattan Moves Uptown*, 23.

[62]Quotes: "worships," Gordon, *Scarlet Woman*, 34; "privations," James D. McCabe Jr., *Lights and Shadows of New York Life, or the Sights and Sensations of the Great City* (New York: Farrar, Straus and Giroux, 1970 reprint of 1872 ed.), 135; Jaher, *Urban Establishment*, 21, 178; Albion, *Rise of New York Port*, 235, 390–91. New York's merchants came, writes Robert Albion, from "decidedly varied backgrounds." Ibid.

[63]Quotes: "entirely safe," Jaher, *Urban Establishment*, 46; "great uneasiness," ibid., 23; ibid., 21, 181; Albion, *Rise of New York Port*, 235.

[64]Quote: Jaher, *Urban Establishment*, 75; ibid., 181; Albion, *Rise of New York Port*, 68, 253.

[65]Jaher, *Urban Establishment*, 35–37, 228–32; Chandler, *Henry Varnum Poor*, 10.

[66]Quotes: "R. W. Emerson," Albion, *Rise of New York Port*, 252; "thinking center," Jaher, *Urban Establishment*, 67; "licking up," Gordon, *Scarlet Woman*, 30; "provincials," Martin B. Duberman, *James Russell Lowell* (Boston: Houghton Mifflin, 1966), 445, fn 19.

[67]Willentz, *Chants Democratic*, 107.

[68]Sven Beckert, "The Making of New York City's Bourgeoisie, 1850–1886" (Ph.D. dissertation, Columbia University, 1995), 122. The dissertation has been revised and published as *The Monied Metropolis: New York City and the Consolidation of the American Bourgeoisie, 1850-1896* (Cambridge, Eng.,: Cambridge University Press, 2001). Albion, *Rise of New York Port*, 400; Paul R. Migliore,

"The Business of Union: The New York Business Community and the Civil War" (Ph.D. dissertation, Columbia University, 1975), 16–18.

[69]Quote: Lampard, "New York Metropolis," 47; Beckert, "Making of New York City's Bourgeoisie," 120–32, 135–37; Migliore, "The Business of Union," 119; Thomas C. Cochran and William Miller, *The Age of Enterprise: A Social History of Industrial America* (New York: Harper & Row, 1942), 98–99, 106; Emerson David Fite, *Social and Industrial Conditions in the North During the Civil War* (New York: The Macmillan Company, 1910), 108–9.

[70]Beckert, "Making of New York City's Bourgeoisie," 133.

[71]Quote: Cochran and Miller, *Age of Enterprise*, 112; *New York Herald*, October 24, 1860; Migliore, "The Business of Union," 120, 122–24; Fite, *Social and Industrial Conditions*, 106–9.

[72]Beckert, "Making of New York City's Bourgeoisie," 145–46.

[73]Quote: Edward Chase Kirkland, *Industry Comes of Age: Business, Labor, and Public Policy, 1860–1897* (New York: Holt, Rinehart and Winston, 1961), 15; Migliore, "The Business of Union," 142–43; Hodas, *Business Career of Moses Taylor*, 177–79; Carosso, *Investment Banking*, 14; Philip Paludan, *A People's Contest: The Union and the Civil War, 1861–1865* (Lawrence: University Press of Kansas, 1996), 108–9.

[74]Richard Franklin Bensel, *Yankee Leviathan: The Origins of Central State Authority in America, 1859–1877* (New York: Cambridge University Press, 1990), 248–49, 253; Carosso, *Investment Banking*, 15–16; Fite, *Social and Industrial Conditions*, 134; Ellis Paxton Oberholtzer, *Jay Cooke, Financier of the Civil War*, Volume 1 (Philadelphia: G. W. Jacobs and Co., 1907, 2 vols.), 143–59.

[75]Quote: Irwin Unger, *The Greenback Era: A Social and Political History of American Finance, 1865–1879* (Princeton: Princeton University Press, 1964), 17–19; Alonzo Barton Hepburn, *A History of Currency in the United States* (New York: The Macmillan Co., 1915); Fite, *Social and Industrial Conditions*, 114; Myers, *New York Money Market*, Volume 1, 20–32, 215–33, 264; Bensel, *Yankee Leviathan*, 364; Cochran and Miller, *Age of Enterprise*, 110.

[76]Quote: "vast pecuniary," Harold Woodman, ed., *The Legacy of the American Civil War* (New York: Wiley, 1973), 61; ibid., 94; Philip Sheldon Foner, *Business & Slavery: The New York Merchants & the Irrepressible Conflict* (Chapel Hill, N.C.: The University of North Carolina Press, 1941), 311; Bensel, *Yankee Leviathan*, 253.

[77]Victor Clark, "Manufacturing Development During the Civil War," in Ralph L. Andreano, ed., *The Economic Impact of the American Civil War* (Cambridge: Schenkman Pub. Co., 1962), 41–62.

[78]Quote: Cochran and Miller, *Age of Enterprise*, 109; ibid., 95.

[79]Quote: Fite, *Social and Industrial Conditions*, 46; ibid., 17–18, 47; Paul Wallace Gates, *The Farmers' Age: Agriculture 1815–1860* (New York: Holt, Rinehart and Winston, 1960).

[80]*Social and Industrial Conditions*, 18–19.

[81]Ibid., 3–21, 29, 30, 40, 41, 46, 79–81, 88–89; Cochran and Miller, *Age of Enterprise*, 113; Paludan, *A People's Contest*, 147; Burrows and Wallace, *Gotham*, 873–76.

[82]Resseguie, "A. T. Stewart and the Department Store," 319, 322; Resseguie, "A. T. Stewart's Marble Palace," 131; Fite, *Social and Industrial Conditions*, 167; *Land of Desire*, 21; Landau and Condit, *The Rise of the New York Skyscraper*, 51–52; Lockwood, *Manhattan Moves Uptown*, 89.

[83]Quotes: "single house," Ralph Hower, *History of Macy's of New York, 1858–1919* (Cambridge, Mass.: Harvard University Press, 1943), 47; "Next to the president," Still, *Mirror for Gotham*, 190; "was of the humblest," *New York Herald*, July 24, 1870; Resseguie, "The Decline and Fall of the Commercial Style," 256; Resseguie, "A. T. Stewart's Marble Palace," 131–62; Resseguie, "A. T. Stewart and the Department Store," 315. In the same year, 1870, R. H. Macy's staff numbered 270 at the peak of its sales season. Hower, *Macy's*, 192; Jay Cantor, "A Monument of Trade: A. T. Stewart and the Millionaire's Mansion in New York," *Winterthur* 10: 168.

[84]Bensel, *Yankee Leviathan*, 253; Kirkland, *Industry Comes of Age*, 2; Burrows and Wallace, *Gotham*, 444–45; Fite, *Social and Industrial Conditions*, 123–30.

[85]Quote: Ibid., 166–67; ibid., 45.

[86]*New York Sun*, March 24, 1865, in Fite, *Social and Industrial Conditions*, 151–52.

[87]Fite, *Social and Industrial Conditions*, 85.

[88]Cochran and Miller, *Age of Enterprise*, 110–11.

[89]Quotes: "high glee," *London Times*, November 3, 1863, in Fite, *Social and Industrial Conditions*, 259; "sybarites," *New York Herald*, February 1, 1863, in ibid., 268; "button their waistcoats," Norton, *A People & a Nation*, 414; "age of shoddy," Ibid.; Fite, *Social and Industrial Conditions*, 263–65.

[90]Paludan, *A People's Contest*, 113–14; Migliore, "The Business of Union," 43, 141, 171–72; Beckert, "Making of New York City's Bourgeoisie," 151, 180.

[91]Ibid., 160, 213 Jaher, *Urban Establishment*, 184.

[92]Quotes: "no hurry for peace," Paludan, *A People's Contest*, 145; "great state of prosperity," William E. Dodge to William B. Kinney, March 9, 1863, in Beckert, "Making of New York City's Bourgeoisie," 90; Fite, *Social and Industrial Conditions*, 84.

[93]Quote: Cochran and Miller, *Age of Enterprise*, 116; Fite, *Social and Industrial Conditions*, 158–69.

[94]Quote: *Commercial and Financial Chronicle*, January 12, 1866, in Fite, *Social and Industrial Conditions*, 165; ibid., 158–66; Cochran and Miller, *Age of Enterprise*, 116.

[95]Albion, *Rise of New York Port*, 267.

[96]Hodas, *Business Career of Moses Taylor*, 7, 26, 52–53.

## CHAPTER 2: NEW YORK'S NAPOLEON

[1]Walt Whitman, *Democratic Vistas* (New York: Liberal Arts Press, 1949 reprint of 1871 original), 11–12

[2]Samuel Sloan, "The Growth of New York," *The Architectural Review and American Builder's Journal*, 2 (1869), 8.

[3]Quotes (both): Bayrd Still, *Mirror for Gotham: New York as Seen by Contemporaries from Dutch Days to the Present* (New York: University Press, 1956), 172; Paul Renard Migliore, "The Business of Union: The New York Business Community and the Civil War" (Ph.D. dissertation, Columbia University, 1975), 405.

[4]Quotes: "magnanimity," Robert P. Sharkey, *Money, Class, and Party: An Economic Study of the Civil War and Reconstruction* (Baltimore: Johns Hopkins Press, 1967), 289; "enterprise of the North," Migliore, "The Business of Union," 356; Migliore, "The Business of Union," 403–4, 392–94; Stanley Coben, "Northeastern Business and Radical Reconstruction: A Reexamination," in Ralph Andreano, ed., *The Economic Impact of the American Civil War* (Cambridge: Schenkman Pub. Co., 1962), 138–39.

[5]James Livingston, *Pragmatism and the Political Economy of Cultural Revolution, 1850–1940* (Chapel Hill, N.C.: University of North Carolina Press, 1994), 35; Daniel Hodas, *The Business Career of Moses Taylor: Merchant, Finance Capitalist, and Industrialist* (New York: New York University Press, 1976), 193; Sharkey, *Money, Class, and Party,* 272–75, 288–90; see also George Milton, *The Age of Hate: Andrew Johnson and the Radicals* (New York: Coward-McCann, Inc., 1930), 289–90; Migliore, "The Business of Union," 388–89.

[6]Quote: Edwin Burrows and Mike Wallace, *Gotham: A History of New York City to 1898* (New York: Oxford University Press, 1999), 906; Migliore, "The Business of Union," 405–6.

[7]Ibid.; Stanley Coben, "Northeastern Business," 125–45; Hodas, *Moses Taylor,* 193, 238–40, 245–46, 252.

[8]Quotes: "loyal states," Eric Foner, *Reconstruction: America's Unfinished Revolution, 1863–1877* (New York: Harper & Row, 1988), 188–89; "absorb it all," David Moisseif Scobey, "Empire City: Politics, Culture, and Urbanism in Gilded Age New York" (Ph.D. dissertation, Yale University, 1989), 16; ibid., 76; Richard Bensel, *Yankee Leviathan: The Origins of Central State Authority in America, 1859–1877* (New York: Cambridge University Press, 1970), 251; Peter Passell and Susan Lee, *A New Economic View of American History* (New York: Norton, 1979), 226–30.

[9]Sven Beckert, "The Making of New York City's Bourgeoisie, 1850–1886" (Ph.D. dissertation, Columbia University, 1995), 206–7; Scobey, "Empire City," 70, 74, 73–74; Hodas, *Moses Taylor,* 194, 909; Richard B. DuBoff, "Business Demand and the Development of the Telegraph in the United States, 1844–1860," *Business History* 54 (Winter 1980): 459–799. By 1869, when the New York Stock Exchange merged with two competing exchanges, New York claimed more than 90 percent of the nation's trade in stock securities.

[10]Beckert, "The Making of New York City's Bourgeoisie," 207–9; Frederic Cople Jaher, *The Urban Establishment: Upper Strata in Boston, New York, Charleston, Chicago, and Los Angeles* (Urbana, Ill.: University of Illinois Press, 1982), 184; Scobey, "Empire City," 26.

[11]Sean Willentz, *Chants Democratic: New York City and the Rise of the American Work-*

*ing Class, 1788–1850* (New York: Oxford University Press, 1984), 11; Eric E. Lampard, "The New York Metropolis in Transition," *The Future of the Metropolis: Berlin, London, Paris, New York: Economic Aspects,* Hans-Jurgen Ewers, J. B. Goddard, and Horst Matzerath, eds. (New York: W. de Gruyter, 1986), 61–62; Beckert, "The Making of New York City's Bourgeoisie," 210–14.

[12]Margaret G. Myers, *The New York Money Market* (New York: Columbia University Press, 1931–1932), 242.

[13]Quote: Scobey, "Empire City," 78; ibid.; Burrows and Wallace, *Gotham,* 124; Paul B. Trescott, *Financing American Enterprise: The Story of Commercial Banking* (New York: Harper and Row, 1963); Myers, *The New York Money Market,* 213; Lawrence Friedman, *A History of American Law* (New York: Simon & Schuster, 1985, 2nd ed.), 190–96; Ronald E. Seavoy, *The Origins of the American Business Corporation 1784–1855: Broadening the Concept of Public Service During Industrialization* (Westport, Conn.: Greenwood Press, 1982); Bensel, *Yankee Leviathan,* 251.

[14]Quotes: "seven years," Beckert, "The Making of New York City's Bourgeoisie," 206; "Overturn," Allan Nevins, ed., *The Diary of Philip Hone, 1828–1851* (New York: Arno Press and The New York Times, 1970 reprint of 1927 ed.), 730; Kenneth T. Jackson, "The Capital of Capitalism: The New York Metropolitan Region, 1890–1940," in Anthony Sutcliffe, ed., *Metropolis, 1890–1940* (Chicago: University of Chicago Press, 1984), 990; *Real Estate Record* 1, no. 1 (March 21, 1868): 1, cited in Scobey, "Empire City," 26–27.

[15]This was the second Trinity, the historic old church having been torn down in 1839 and replaced by a grander version in 1846. Edward K. Spann, *The New Metropolis: New York City, 1840–1857* (New York: Columbia University Press, 1981), 3.

[16]Quotes: "turned myself out," Nevins, *Diary of Philip Hone,* 202. He originally paid $25,000 for the home at 235 Broadway in 1821, ibid., 201; "old . . . Christian church," in Spann, *The New Metropolis,* 3.

[17]Elizabeth Blackmar, *Manhattan for Rent, 1785–1850* (Ithaca: Cornell University Press, 1989), 30–33.

[18]Ibid., 100; Morgan Dix, *History of the Trinity Parish, Part V* (New York: Columbia University Press, 1950), 4, 266–72, 322–26, 359–61, 392–93; Spann, *New Metropolis,* 229–31, and the discussion in footnotes 51–54 on page 477.

[19]Quotes: "large and growingly important," in Eugene P. Moehring, *Public Works and the Patterns of Urban Real Estate Growth in Manhattan, 1835–1894* (New York: Arno Press, 1981), 60–61; "all kinds of roguery," Charles Lockwood, *Manhattan Moves Uptown: An Illustrated History* (Boston: Houghton Mifflin, 1976), 59–62, 171; *New York Herald,* July 24, 1870.

[20]Dix, *History of Trinity Parish, V,* 65–70.

[21]*New York Herald,* July 24, 1870.

[22]Ibid., October 3, 1869; Robert G. Albion, *The Rise of New York Port: 1815–1860* (New York: C. Scribner's Sons, 1939), 151–54, 268; Matthew Josephson, *The Robber Barons: The Great American Capitalists: 1861–1901* (New York: Har-

court, Brace and Company, 1934), 12; John Steele Gordon, *The Scarlet Woman of Wall Street* (New York: Weidenfeld and Nicolson, 1988), 51–59.

[23]Albion, *Rise of New York Port*, 240; *New York Herald*, October 3, 1869; Josephson, *The Robber Barons*, 14; Gordon, *The Scarlet Woman of Wall Street*, 65; *The Dictionary of American Biography*, Volume 19 (New York: C. Scribner's Sons, 1928–1958, 22 vols.), 171.

[24]Quote: Gordon, *The Scarlet Woman of Wall Street*, 63; ibid., 68; Josephson, *The Robber Barons*, 15; *New York Herald*, October 3, 1869.

[25]Chamber of Commerce of the State of New York, *Annual Report* (1865–1866), and *Real Estate Record* 9:203, quoted in Scobey, "Empire City," 146–47.

[26]Scobey, "Empire City," 56, 46–53, 100–101; Sarah Bradford Landau and Carl Condit, *The Rise of the New York Skyscraper, 1865–1913* (New Haven: Yale University Press, 1996), 9; Albion, *The Rise of New York Port*, 266.

[27]Scobey, "Empire City," 57–58; Burrows and Wallace, *Gotham*, 944–45.

[28]Clifton Hood, *722 Miles: The Building of the Subways and How They Transformed New York* (New York: Simon & Schuster, 1993), 49; ibid., 41; Landau and Condit, *New York Skyscraper*, 2–3; Scobey, "Empire City," 150; *New York Herald*, July 7, 1869.

[29]E. J. Hobsbawm, *Age of Capital, 1848–1875* (London: Weidenfeld and Nicolson, 1975), 21–75.

[30]Scobey, "Empire City," 68–69, 110–11; Donald J. Olson, *The City As a Work of Art: London, Paris, Vienna* (New Haven: Yale University Press, 1986); David Pinkney, *Napoleon III and the Rebuilding of Paris* (Princeton: Princeton University Press, 1958); David Harvey, "Paris 1850–1870," *Consciousness and the Urban Experience: Studies in the History and Theory of Capitalist Urbanization* (Baltimore: Johns Hopkins University Press, 1985); Carl E. Schorske, *Fin-de-Siècle Vienna: Politics and Culture* (New York: Alfred A. Knopf, 1980); David Owen, *The Government of Victorian London, 1855–1889: The Metropolitan Board of Works, the Vestries and the City Corporation* (Cambridge, Mass.: Harvard University Press, 1982); Harold M. Mayer and Richard Wade, *Chicago: Growth of a Metropolis* (Chicago: University of Chicago Press, 1969); William Cronon, *Nature's Metropolis: Chicago and the Great West* (New York: W.W. Norton, 1991); Anthony Sutcliffe, ed., *Paris: An Architectural History* (New Haven: Yale University Press, 1993).

[31]Quote: "Attila," Victor Fournel, *Paris Nouveau et Paris Future* (Paris: 1865), 220; Wolfgang Schivelbusch, *The Railway Journey: Trains and Travel in the 19th Century* (New York: Urizen Books, 1979), 178; Pinkney, *Napoleon III*, 214; Norma Evenson, "Paris: 1890–1940," in Sutcliffe, ed., *Metropolis*, 178, 190, 264–65.

[32]*New York Herald*, July 7, 1869.

[33]Quote: Pinkney, *Napoleon III*, 189; 174–186, 190–206.

[34]Quote: Charles Moore, *Daniel H. Burnham, Architect, Planner of Cities* (Boston, New York: Houghton Mifflin Company, 1921), 147, in Pinkney, *Napoleon III*; ibid., 218–20.

[35]Quotes: "blessing in disguise," Donald L. Miller, *City of the Century: The Epic of Chicago and the Making of America* (New York: Simon & Schuster, 1996), 178; "highest buildings," ibid., 16; Cronon, *Nature's Metropolis*, 346–47.

[36]Andrew Green, *Communication to the Commissioners of the Central Park Relative to the Improvement of the Sixth and Seventh Avenues, from the Central Park to the Harlem River; the Laying out of the Island above 155ᵗʰ Street; the Drive from 59ᵗʰ Street to 155ᵗʰ Street and other Subjects* (New York: W.C. Bryant and Co., 1866), 38–39.

[37]John Foord, *The Life and Public Services of Andrew Haswell Green* (Garden City, New York: Doubleday, Page & Company, 1913), 7–10.

[38]Quotes: "apply myself," ibid., 9; "I feel," ibid., 24; ibid., 9–12.

[39]Quote: ibid., 13; ibid., 19–21.

[40]Barry Kaplan, "Andrew H. Green and the Creation of a Planning Rationale: The Formation of Greater New York City, 1865–1890," *Urbanism, Past and Present* 8:32; George Mazeraki, "The Public Career of Andrew Haswell Green" (Ph.D. diss., New York University, 1966), 19–20; Foord, *Andrew Haswell Green*, 53; David Hammack, "Comprehensive Planning Before the Comprehensive Plan: A New Look at the Nineteenth-Century American City," in Daniel Schaffer, ed., *Two Centuries of American Planning* (London: 1988), 145.

[41]George Mazeraki, "The Public Career of Andrew Haswell Green," 2; Barry J. Kaplan, "Andrew H. Green and the Creation of a Planning Rationale: The Formation of Greater New York City, 1865–1890," *Urbanism Past and Present*, 8:32.

[42]Quote: *New York Times*, October 10, 1873; Mazeraki, "The Public Career of Andrew Haswell Green," 109.

[43]Quote: Foord, *Andrew Haswell Green*, 70; ibid., 7, 34–35, 359–60; Mazeraki, "The Public Career of Andrew Haswell Green," 146; Roy Rosenzweig and Elizabeth Blackmar, *The Park and the People: A History of Central Park* (Ithaca and London: Cornell University Press, 1992), 121–210; Scobey, "Empire City," 354, 371; *New York Herald*, August 17, 1869.

[44]Quotes: "No one but Green knows," Rosenzweig and Blackmar, *The Park and the People*, 186; "blood & sweat," ibid., 191; Hammack, "Comprehensive Planning," 146; Foord, *Andrew Haswell Green*, 71.

[45]Ibid., 66.

[46]Mazeraki, "Andrew Haswell Green, 113; Foord, *Andrew Haswell Green*, 72.

[47]Quotes: "first city," Bryant, "Can a City be Planned?" *New York Evening Post* March 16, 1868, in Scobey, "Empire City," 241; "daily experience," *New York Times*, October 16, 1868, in ibid., 308; "we want," *Real Estate Record* 3 (June 19, 1869), in ibid., 309.

[48]*New York Times*, November 22, 1868.

[49]Quotes: "how to plan," Rosenzweig and Blackmar, *The Park and the People*, 196; "fragment," Scobey, "Empire City," 381; "no compeer," *New York World* in 1868, quoted in Foord, *The Life of Andrew Green*, 86; Mazeraki, "Public Career of Andrew Green," 64; Green, "Communication to the Commissioners of the Central Park," 37; Scobey, "Empire City," 314.

[50] Quote: Andrew Green, "Communication to the Commissioners of the Central Park," 39; ibid., 40–41; Roy Rosenzweig and Elizabeth Blackmar, *The Park and the People*, 203–12; *New York Herald*, July 24, 1870.

[51] Quote: Andrew Green, "Communication to the Commissioners of the Central Park," 65; ibid., 8–9, 71–72.

[52] Quote: Spann, *The New Metropolis*, 104; ibid., 103.

[53] Landau and Condit, *The New York Skyscraper*, 2.

[54] Quote: "private-use planning," Andrew Green, "Communication to the Commissioners of the Central Park," 69; ibid., 25–33; Scobey, "Empire City," 336–38, 388–90.

[55] Ibid., 391.

[56] Rosenzweig and Blackmar, *The Park and the People*, 342; ibid., 350–53; Scobey, "Empire City," 373–75, 387–88.

[57] Calvin Tomkins, *Merchants and Masterpieces: The Story of the Metropolitan Museum of Art* (New York: E.P. Dutton, 1970), 15–18, 120; Rosenzweig and Blackmar, *The Park and the People*, 357–58.

[58] Tomkins, *Merchants and Masterpieces*, 22–24.

[59] Rosenzweig and Blackmar, *The Park and the People*, 341–49.

[60] Quotes: "erect, establish," Tomkins, *Merchants and Masterpieces*, 39; "upper," the preferred term for Gotham's wealthy, common in newspapers, also Burrows and Wallace, *Gotham*, 714 ff.; "the masses," Rosenzweig and Blackmar, *The Park and the People*, 352; "mysteries," "Disastrous Fire," *New York Times*, July 14, 1865, in Scobey, "Empire City," 43–44; Rosenzweig and Blackmar, *The Park and the People*, 351; David C. Hammack, *Power and Society: Greater New York at the Turn of the Century* (New York: Columbia University Press, 1987), 191.

[61] Quote: "get up a show," *New York Herald*, July 12, 1866, in Rosenzweig and Blackmar, *The Park and the People*, 353; ibid., 352; Kenneth Jackson, ed., *The Encyclopedia of New York City*, 78.

[62] Rosenzweig and Blackmar, *The Park and the People*, 353–54.

[63] Ibid., 267–68; Thomas Bender, *New York Intellect: A History of Intellectual Life in New York City, from 1750 to the Beginnings of Our Own Time* (Baltimore, Md.: Johns Hopkins University Press, 1987), 170.

[64] Quotes: "humanize," Rosenzweig and Blackmar, *The Park and the People*, 357; "most dextrous," Tomkins, *Merchants and Masterpieces*, 29–30; Daniel M. Fox, *Engines of Culture: Philanthropy and Art Museums* (Madison, Wis.: University of Wisconsin, 1963), 41.

[65] Quotes: "the Museum," Tomkins, *Merchants and Masterpieces*, 46; "furnishing," ibid., 120; Edwin Burrows and Mike Wallace, *Gotham*, 964.

[66] Quotes: "Mr. Green," *New York World*, in Foord, *The Life of Andrew Green*, 86; "It has," Andrew Green, "Communication to the Commissioners of the Central Park," 37; ibid., 12–13, 64.

[67] Quotes: "sustenance," George Mazeraki, "The Public Career of Andrew Haswell Green," 111; "Imperial City," Landau and Condit, *The New York Skyscraper*, 1–2; "too narrow," Scobey, "Empire City," 389; ibid., 92–93.

68Quotes: "many rooms," Olmsted in Scobey, "Empire City," 243; "a business man," Frederick Law Olmstead and Calvert Vaux, "Report of the Landscape Architects to the . . . Board of Commissioners on Prospect Park" (1868), in Scobey, "Empire City," 241; *New York Herald,* February 5, 1873.

69Foord, *Life of Andrew Green,* 116, 176.

70Quote: Scobey, "Empire City," 186; Foord, *The Life of Andrew Green,* 110–12; Mazeraki, "The Public Career of Andrew Green," 111.

71Jacob August Riis, *How the Other Half Lives: Studies Among the Tenements of New York* (New York: Dover, 1971 reprint of 1901 issue of 1890 publication), 212.

72Scobey, "Empire City," 3, 17, 26–28; Rosenzweig and Blackmar, *The Park and the People,* 268; Still, *Mirror for Gotham,* 171; Moehring, *Public Works and Urban Real Estate Growth,* 87, 306, 308; *New York Herald,* October 17, 1870.

73Quote: "everything," *Harper's Weekly,* August 14, 1869, 525, in Scobey, "Empire City," 29; ibid., 89–90.

74Landau and Condit, *The New York Skyscraper,* 3; Scobey, "Empire City," 24.

75Quote: Scobey, "Empire City," 25; ibid., 4, 45, 59, 175, 244.

76Quote: Still, *Mirror for Gotham,* 206; Landau and Condit, *The New York Skyscraper,* 19–62; Olmsted called the elevators "vertical railways," in Scobey, "Empire City," 59–62.

77Ibid., 219–20.

78Quote: Landau and Condit, *The New York Skyscraper,* 89; ibid., 50–51, 88–90.

79New York held some 85 percent of the national insurance market, a market worth hundreds of millions; Burrows and Wallace, *Gotham,* 940; Landau and Condit, *The New York Skyscraper,* 64.

80Ibid., 63–71.

81Ibid., 62–66, 82–83; Scobey, "Empire City," 62, 218–19, especially footnote 17.

82Quote: Still, *Mirror for Gotham,* 171; Scobey, "Empire City," 65.

83Quote: Scobey, "Empire City," 206; ibid., 429.

84Quotes: "narrow streets," New York City Department of Buildings, *Reports of the Superintendant of Buildings, 1862–1872,* 54, cited in Scobey, "Empire City," 206; "colossal wealth," Still, *Mirror for Gotham,* 178; "*Baedeker's,*" ibid., 228; "tributary," ibid., 158; ibid., 183.

85Quotes: "soon convert," ibid., 178; "sleeping-place," ibid., 175; "tranquil habitation," Olmstead and Vaux, "Report of the Landscape Architects," 155, in Scobey, "Empire City," 242.

86*New York Daily Graphic,* June 3, 1873, in ibid., 220.

87Montgomery Schuyler, "The Evolution of the Skyscraper," *Scribner's Monthly* 46 (September 1909), 259, in ibid., 253–54.

88Quote: "Changes in New York," *Leslie's Illustrated Weekly* 40 (May 22, 1875): 167, in Scobey, "Empire City," 214; ibid., 271.

89Lockwood, *Manhattan Moves Uptown,* 177, 258; Landau and Condit, *The New York Skyscraper,* 3; Scobey, "Empire City," 264; Edith Wharton, *The House of Mirth* (New York: Oxford University Press, 1994).

90Scobey, "Empire City," 207.

91Quote: Junius Henry Browne, *The Great Metropolis: A Mirror of New York* (New

York: America Pub. Co., 1975), 289; ibid., 293; Montgomery Schuyler, "A Modern Classic," *Architectural Record* 15, no. 5 (May 1904): 431–44; Jay Cantor, "A Monument of Trade: A. T. Stewart and the Millionaire's Mansion in New York," *Winterthur* 10: 177–82.

[92]Quotes: "Furniture and hangings," Jay Cantor, "A Monument of Trade," 189; "Mr. Stewart's New Residence," *Harper's Weekly* (August 14, 1869), 526; "far surpassed," Lockwood, *Manhattan Moves Uptown*, 301; Cantor, "A Monument of Trade," 192; Gordon, *Scarlet Woman of Wall Street*, 183–84, 188, 191; *New York Times*, April 11, 12, 1876; "Big Bonanza Buildings," *Real Estate Record* 17 (April 8, 1876): 255.

[93]Quotes: "ostentatious," Jay Cantor, "A Monument of Trade," 191; "profusion," ibid., 189–90. In 1904 Montgomery Schuyler, praising the new McKim, Mead and White structure that had replaced Stewart's mansion, delivered its epitaph, calling it a "monument of the architectural uncultivation of the most conspicuous New York millionaire of A.D. 1870." Ibid., 192; *New York Sun*, quoted in Andy Logan, "That Was New York, Double Darkness and Worst of All," *New Yorker* 34 (February 22, 1958): 82–84; "one edifice," "Mr. Stewart's New Residence"; *Harper's Weekly* 13 (August 14, 1869): 525–26, in Jay Cantor, "A Monument of Trade," 189.

[94]Quote: Scobey, "Empire City," 274; 230–35.

[95]Still, *Mirror for Gotham*, 178.

[96]Scobey, "Empire City," 17–23; Burrows and Wallace, 691–711.

[97]Walt Whitman, *Democratic Vistas* (New York: Liberal Arts Press, 1949 reprint of 1871 original), 11–12.

[98]Bertolt Brecht, "A Worker Reads History," *Selected Poems*, H. R. Hays, trans. (New York: 1947), 109.

[99]Quote: *New York Herald*, July 7, 1869; ibid., October 1, 1869.

## CHAPTER 3: THE ROTTENNESS IN NEW YORK WILL ULTIMATELY DESTROY IT

[1]"The Vanderbilt Memorial," *The Nation* 9 (1869):431–32, in Sigmund Diamond, *The Reputation of the American Businessman* (Cambridge, Mass.: Harvard University Press, 1955), 55–56.

[2]*New York World Telegram*, May 24, 1937, in ibid., 122–23.

[3]Seymour J. Mandelbaum, *Boss Tweed's New York* (New York: Wiley, 1965), 1–6; see also Max Page, "The Creative Destruction of New York City: Landscape, Memory, and the Politics of Place, 1900–1930" (Ph.D. dissertation, University of Pennsylvania, 1995), 5–18.

[4]Cochran and Miller, *Age of Enterprise*, 68.

[5]Quotes: Weber in Alan Trachtenberg, *The Incorporation of America* (New York: Hill and Wang, 1982), 58–59, italics added; "new spaces," in ibid.; Wolfgang

Schivelbusch, *The Railway Journey: Trains and Travel in the Nineteenth Century* (New York: Urizen Books, 1979), 89–90; Alfred Chandler, *The Visible Hand: The Managerial Revolution in American Business* (Cambridge: Belknap Press, 1977), 83, 88; Roderick D. McKenzie, *The Metropolitan Community* (New York: McGraw-Hill Book Company, 1933), 3–6.

[6]Quotes: "Land navigation" is Daniel Webster's term; Schivelbush, *Railway Journey*, 112; "American imagery," William G. Roy, *Socializing Capital: The Rise of the Large Industrial Corporation in America* (Princeton: Princeton University Press, 1997), 78; Trachtenberg, *Incorporation of America*, 59–60; William Cronon, *Nature's Metropolis: Chicago and the Great West* (New York: W.W. Norton, 1991), 79; Gordon, *The Scarlet Woman of Wall Street*, 67.

[7]Roy, *Socializing Capital*, 78.

[8]The description of changes in the wheat business is based on Cronon, *Nature's Metropolis*, 97–147.

[9]Ibid., 123–25.

[10]Gordon Wright, *France in Modern Times: From the Enlightenment to the Present* (New York: W.W. Norton, 1995, 5th ed.), 145.

[11]Quote: James Willard Hurst, *Law and the Conditions of Freedom in Nineteenth Century United States* (Madison, Wis.: University of Wisconsin Press, 1964, 2nd ed.), 86; Roy, *Socializing Capital*, 72–75, 78–79. In 1850, the New York State Constitutional Convention called for an end to Erie Canal–type undertakings, unanimously approving a prohibition on state-sponsored internal improvements. Lee Benson, *Merchants, Farmers and Railroads: Railroad Regulation and New York Politics, 1850–1887* (Cambridge: Harvard University Press, 1955), 3–5.

[12]Quote: Edward Chase Kirkland, *Industry Comes of Age: Business, Labor, and Public Policy, 1860–1897* (New York: Holt, Rinehart and Winston, 1961), 51; Chandler, *The Visible Hand*, 82, 122; Philip Paludan, *A People's Contest* (Lawrence, Kans.: University Press of Kansas, 1996), 139, 141–43; Thomas C. Cochran and William Miller, *The Age of Enterprise: A Social History of Industrial America* (New York: The Macmillan Company, 1942), 132; Eric Foner, *Reconstruction: America's Unfinished Revolution, 1863–1877* (New York: Harper and Row, 1988), 466; Wallace Farnham, "The Weakened Spring of Government: A Study in Nineteenth Century American History," *American Historical Review* 68 (April 1963): 662–80; Hurst, *Law and the Conditions of Freedom*; Morton J. Horowitz, *The Transformation of American Law, 1780–1860* (Cambridge, Mass.: Harvard University Press, 1977).

[13]Emerson David Fite, *Social and Industrial Conditions in the North During the Civil War* (New York: The Macmillan Company, 1910), 182; Glenn Porter, *The Rise of Big Business: 1860–1910* (Arlington Heights, Ill.: H. Davidson, 1973), 33.

[14]Roy, *Socializing Capital*, 139; Margaret G. Myers, *The New York Money Market* (New York: Columbia University Press, 1931–1932, 4 vols.), Volume 1, 290–99, Volume 3, 213; Fite, *Social and Industrial Conditions in the North*, 182;

David Moisseif Scobey, "Empire City: Politics, Culture, and Urbanism in Gilded Age New York" (Ph.D. dissertation, Yale University, 1989), 77–79.

[15] Quote: Foner, *Reconstruction*, 468; ibid., 123, 146; Scobey, "Empire City," 71; *New York Times*, June 10, 1868; Sven Beckert, "The Making of New York City's Bourgeoisie" (Ph.D. dissertation, Columbia University, 1995), 212.

[16] Chandler, *The Visible Hand*, 81–82, 96, 97.

[17] Ibid., 109–15; James Don Edwards, *History of Public Accounting in the United States* (East Lansing, Mich.: Michigan State University, 1960), 47–53.

[18] Chandler, *The Visible Hand*, 105; Foner, *Reconstruction*, 465–66.

[19] Thomas C. Cochran, *Railroad Leaders, 1845–1890: The Business Mind in Action* (Cambridge, Mass.: Harvard University Press, 1953), 26.

[20] Gordon, *The Scarlet Woman of Wall Street*, 57, 69–80.

[21] Quote: "stock jobbing," in Frederic Cople Jaher, *The Urban Establishment: Upper Strata in Boston, New York, Charleston, Chicago, and Los Angeles* (Urbana, Ill.: University of Illinois Press, 1982), 192; Gordon, *The Scarlet Woman of Wall Street*, 80, 69.

[22] Ibid., 82.

[23] Quote: Ibid., 84; ibid., 81–93; Cochran, *Railroad Leaders*, 22–24.

[24] *New York Herald*, October 3, 1869.

[25] Cochran, *Railroad Leaders*, 24–26; Gordon, *The Scarlet Woman of Wall Street*, 123.

[26] Quote: Maury Klein, *The Life and Legend of Jay Gould* (Baltimore: Johns Hopkins University Press, 1986), 79; Edward H. Mott, *Between the Ocean and the Lakes: The Story of the Erie* (New York: J.S. Collins, 1901), iii; Charles Francis Adams Jr., "A Chapter of Erie," *North American Review* 109 (July 1869): 30–106, reprinted in Frederick Hicks, ed., *High Finance in the Sixties: Chapters from the Early History of the Erie Railway* (New Haven, Conn.: Yale University Press, 1929), 29. Henry Clews wrote of the oleaginous Drew that he possessed the ability to "insinuat[e], with affected but well dissembled humility, which was highly calculated to disarm": Gordon, *The Scarlet Woman of Wall Street*, 4, 17–21, 25; Cochran and Miller, *The Age of Enterprise*, 70, 75–76; Matthew Josephson, *The Robber Barons: The Great American Capitalists, 1861–1901* (New York: Harcourt, Brace and Company, 1934), 18.

[27] Hicks, *High Finance in the Sixties*, 31.

[28] Quotes: Pulitzer in Gordon, *The Scarlet Woman of Wall Street*, 154; Adams in Klein, *Life and Legend of Jay Gould*, 76; ibid., 19; Gordon, *The Scarlet Woman of Wall Street*, 131; John A Garraty, ed., *Labor and Capital in the Gilded Age: Testimony Taken by the Senate Committee upon the Relations Between Labor and Capital, 1883* (Boston: Little Brown, 1968), 13; Josephson, *The Robber Barons*, 38, 192–95.

[29] Quote: Klein, *Life and Legend of Jay Gould*, 54; ibid., 25, 38–39, 45.

[30] William W. Fowler, *Ten Years in Wall Street* (New York: J. D. Denison, 1870), in Gordon, *The Scarlet Woman of Wall Street*, 22.

[31] Quote: W. A. Swanberg, *Jim Fisk: The Career of an Improbable Rascal* (New York: Scribner, 1959), in Klein, *Life and Legend of Jay Gould*, 80–82; ibid., 72–73;

Kenneth D. Ackerman, *The Gold Ring: Jim Fisk, Jay Gould, and Black Friday, 1869* (New York: Dodd, Mead, 1988), 6–7; Gordon, *The Scarlet Woman of Wall Street*, 132–34.

[32]Klein, *Life and Legend of Jay Gould*, 81; Gordon, *The Scarlet Woman of Wall Street*, 159, 178.

[33]Quote: Gordon, *The Scarlet Woman of Wall Street*, 165. "There is a man here on the bench . . . ," E. L. Godkin wrote to a friend regarding the Commodore's favorite judge, George Barnard. "Some years ago . . . he kept a gambling saloon in San Francisco, and was a notorious blackleg and *vaurien*. He came then to N.Y., plunged into the lowest depths of city politics and . . . married a rich woman. His reputation is now the very worst. He is unscrupulous, audacious, barefaced, and corrupt to the last degree. He not only takes bribes, but he does not wait for them to be offered him. He sends for suitors, or rather for the counsel, and asks for the money as the price of his judgements. A more unprincipled scoundrel does not breathe. There is no way in which he does not prostitute his office, and in saying this I am giving you the unanimous opinion of the bar and the public." E. L. Godkin to Charles Eliot Norton, April 23, 1867, in William M. Armstrong, *The Gilded Age Letters of E. L. Godkin* (Albany: State University of New York Press, 1974), 103. "One magistrate had forbidden them to move, and another . . . had ordered them not to stand still," in the words of Charles F. Adams, who described the fray in a display of epic overwriting: Charles Francis Adams Jr., "A Chapter of Erie," *North American Review* 109 (July 1869): 30–106, reprinted in Hicks, *High Finance in the Sixties*, 48; Klein, *Life and Legend of Jay Gould*, 82; Gordon, *The Scarlet Woman of Wall Street*, 180; Kenneth D. Ackerman, *The Gold Ring*, 18–20, 7.

[34]Klein, *Life and Legend of Jay Gould*, 83, 88.

[35]Quotes: Gordon, *New York Herald*, in *The Scarlet Woman of Wall Street*, 95; "thoroughly venal," Gordon, *The Scarlet Woman of Wall Street*, 180; Ackerman, *The Gold Ring*, 14; Klein, *Life and Legend of Jay Gould*, 80–82, 85.

[36]Quote: Ibid., 97; ibid., 85–86; Gordon, *The Scarlet Woman of Wall Street*, 189–94.

[37]Klein, *Life and Legend of Jay Gould*, 92; Gordon, *The Scarlet Woman of Wall Street*, 233–34.

[38]Edward Hungerford, *Men of Erie: A Story of Human Effort* (New York: Random House, 1946), 157–62; Klein, *Life and Legend of Jay Gould*, 77, 89–92, 152–57; Gordon, *The Scarlet Woman of Wall Street*, 233–24; Ackerman, *The Gold Ring*, 22.

[39]Quotes: Hicks, ed., Charles F. Adams, "Chapter of Erie," 32; *New York Herald* in Gordon, *The Scarlet Woman of Wall Street*, 206; "Scarlet," ibid., 90–92; "death," Ackerman, *The Gold Ring*, 27–28; ibid., 23–25; Cochran and Miller, *The Age of Enterprise*, 195–206.

[40]Ackerman, *The Gold Ring*, 39; Gordon, *The Scarlet Woman of Wall Street*, 179, 196; Samuel J. Tilden to Jay Gould, February 14, 1870, and Jay Gould to Samuel J. Tilden, February 21, 1870, John Bigelow, ed., *Letters and Literary Memorials of Samuel J. Tilden*, Volume 1 (New York: Harper, 1908, 2 vols.), 258–62;

297–301; Alexander C. Flick, *Samuel Jones Tilden* (New York: Dodd, Mead and Company, 1939), 193, 199; Cochran, *Railroad Leaders*, 63–66.

[41]Quote: Gordon, *The Scarlet Woman of Wall Street*, 208.

[42]Quotes: "cornering gold," Henry Adams, "The New York Gold Conspiracy," *Westminster Review* 94 (October 1870): 411–36, reprinted in Hicks, *High Finance in the Sixties*, 132; "nothing but . . . ," Gordon, *The Scarlet Woman of Wall Street*, 260.

[43]Vincent Carosso, *The Morgans: Private International Bankers, 1854–1913* (Cambridge, Mass.: Harvard University Press, 1987), 102; Ackerman, *The Gold Ring*, 46, 112; Gordon, *The Scarlet Woman of Wall Street*, 258.

[44]Kenneth D. Ackerman, *The Gold Ring*, 44–47.

[45]Ibid., 48; Gordon, *The Scarlet Woman of Wall Street*, 258–60.

[46]Klein, *Life and Legend of Jay Gould*, 102.

[47]William F. McFeely, *Grant: A Biography* (New York: W.W. Norton, 1981), 234–36, 253, 265. Contributors included the New York Stock Exchange and a host of business lions, including A. T. Stewart, William Astor, Daniel Drew, Samuel Tilden, and Moses Taylor. Daniel Butterfield to Moses Taylor, February 19, 1866; Daniel Butterfield to Ulysses S. Grant, February 15, 1866; Grant to Daniel Butterfield, February 17, 1866: Moses Taylor Collection, Box 209, New York Public Library; also Ackerman, *The Gold Ring*, 65.

[48]*New York Herald*, October 8, 1869; Kenneth D. Ackerman, *The Gold Ring*, 53–57; *New York Times*, March 1, 1870.

[49]*New York Times*, March 1, 1870; Gordon, *The Scarlet Woman of Wall Street*, 260–62.

[50]*New York Times*, March 1, 1870; Kenneth D. Ackerman, *The Gold Ring*, 77, 88, 75–77.

[51]*New York Times*, October 18, 1869, March 1, 1870, January 24, 1870; Gordon, *The Scarlet Woman of Wall Street*, 263.

[52]*New York Times*, October 18, 1869. The Garfield Congressional Commission report is summarized in *New York Times*, March 1–2, 1870; McFeely, *Grant*, 324, 330; Kenneth D. Ackerman, *The Gold Ring*, 88.

[53]*New York Times*, October 18, 1869, January 24, 1870, March 1–2, 1870; Kenneth D. Ackerman, *The Gold Ring*, 80, 84; Gordon, *The Scarlet Woman of Wall Street*, 264; Klein, *Life and Legend of Jay Gould*, 106; McFeeley, *Grant*, 324.

[54]Quotes: "undesirable," *New York Times*, October 18, 1869; "West would suffer," *New York Herald*, September 8, 1869; Kenneth D. Ackerman, *The Gold Ring*, 165; *New York Times*, March 1, 1870.

[55]*New York Times*, January 19, 1870, March 2, 1870; Klein, *Life and Legend of Jay Gould*, 102–3; Hicks, *High Finance in the Sixties*, 130.

[56]Kenneth D. Ackerman, *The Gold Ring*, 149; *New York Times*, September 24, 1869.

[57]Ibid.; Susan P. Lee and Peter Passell, *A New Economic View of American History* (New York: W.W. Norton, 1979), 4.

[58]*New York Times*, March 1, 1870; Kenneth D. Ackerman, *The Gold Ring*, 156.

[59]*New York Times*, March 1, 1870; ibid., September 30, 1869.

[60]Gordon, *The Scarlet Woman of Wall Street*, 266–71; Kenneth D. Ackerman, *The Gold Ring*, 100, 171–78; Klein, *Life and Legend of Jay Gould*, 105.

[61]Quotes: "history of," *New York Times*, September 25, 1869; "Gold, Gold, Gold," Gordon, *The Scarlet Woman of Wall Street*, 272.

[62]Quotes: "any part," *New York Times*, January 24, 1870; "nonsense talk," Kenneth D. Ackerman, *The Gold Ring*, 208–9. "One of those Roman Saxonians that belong to the 'chosen people,'" said Fisk in his description before the congressional committee: McFeely, *Grant*, 328; Klein, *Life and Legend of Jay Gould*, 112; Edmund C. Stedman, "Israel Freyer's Bid for Gold," *New York Tribune*, September 28, 1869; *New York Times*, September 25, 1869; ibid., October 3, 1869.

[63]Quotes: "prone," *New York Times*, September 27, 1869; "corpse," 41st Cong. 2nd Sess. House Report, *Gold Panic Investigation* (September 29, 1869), 1436–37; ibid., 171, 176.

[64]*New York Times*, October 3, 1869; "There is nothing left of him," said Fisk of his drained partner, "but a heap of clothes and a pair of eyes." Gordon, *The Scarlet Woman of Wall Street*, 276; Klein, *Life and Legend of Jay Gould*, 113; David McCullough, *The Great Bridge* (New York: Simon & Schuster, 1972), 141.

[65]*New York Times*, January 19, 1870, March 2, 1870, October 14, 1869; Kenneth D. Ackerman, *The Gold Ring*, 259–67.

[66]Quotes: *Herald*, in Kenneth D. Ackerman, *The Gold Ring*, 269; "no power," reprinted from *London Spectator* in *New York Herald*, October 29, 1869; "$20,000," Klein, *Life and Legend of Jay Gould*, 117; "foundations," *New York Times*, March 2, 1870; *New York Times*, September 29, 1869.

[67]Daniel Hodas, *The Business Career of Moses Taylor: Merchant, Finance Capitalist, and Industrialist* (New York, New York University Press, 1976), 177, 203–5, 263–64, 282.

[68]Albion, *Rise of New York Port*, 265; one Reverend Orville Dewey, D.D., authored a series of discourses entitled "The Morals of Trade," see Gordon, *The Scarlet Woman of Wall Street*, 12–14; Lawrence Friedman, *A History of American Law* (New York: Simon & Schuster, 1973; 2nd ed., 1985), 21, 391–405.

[69]Hicks, *High Finance in the Sixties*, 46; Lawrence Friedman, *A History of American Law*, 391–410.

[70]*New York Times*, December 10, 1868, October 2, 1869.

[71]Quotes: "great aim," ibid., December 10, 1868; "hasty profit," Hodas, *The Business Career of Moses Taylor*, 281; ibid., 197, 189, 279–80.

[72]Klein, *Life and Legend of Jay Gould*, 55–56, 128–29.

[73]Quote: "fatuity," Hicks, ed., Charles F. Adams, "Chapter of Erie," 82; *Law Review* in Gordon, *The Scarlet Woman of Wall Street*, 170.

[74]Quotes: *Cincinnati Gazette* in *New York Times*, December 3, 1868; *Harper's Weekly* in Gordon, *The Scarlet Woman of Wall Street*, 164.

[75]Klein, *Life and Legend of Jay Gould*, 115; *New York Times*, October 2, 1869; Alfred Eichner, *The Emergence of Oligopoly: Sugar Refining as a Case Study* (Baltimore: Johns Hopkins Press, 1969), 2.

[76]Joseph Frazier Wall, *Andrew Carnegie* (New York: Oxford University Press, 1970), 181, 232–33.

77Ibid., 222, 227, 419; David C. Hammack, *Power and Society: Greater New York at the Turn of the Century* (New York: Columbia University Press, 1987), 46.

78Jonathan Hughes, *The Vital Few: American Economic Progress and Its Protagonists* (Boston: Houghton Mifflin, 1965), 224–27; Harold C. Livesay, *Andrew Carnegie and the Rise of Big Business* (Boston: Little, Brown, 1975), 8, 12, 17, 22–23; Wall, *Andrew Carnegie*, 113–17.

79Quotes: "Eureka," Livesay, *Andrew Carnegie*, 40–41; "I'm rich," Wall, *Andrew Carnegie*, 189; ibid., 142–43, 171, 178, 187–89; Livesay, *Andrew Carnegie*, 41–51, 54–55; Hughes, *The Vital Few*, 227; Jean Strouse, *Morgan: American Financier* (New York: Random House, 1999), 131.

80Livesay, *Andrew Carnegie*, 24.

81Wall, *Andrew Carnegie*, 190. A judge wrote to his son: "It is only greenhorns who enlist. You can learn nothing in the army. . . . Those who are able to pay for substitutes, do so, and no discredit attaches. [A] man may be a patriot without risking his own life or sacrificing his health. There are plenty of other lives less valuable. . . ." Josephson, *Robber Barons*, 50; Livesay, *Andrew Carnegie*, 42.

82Livesay, *Andrew Carnegie*, 68–71; Wall, *Andrew Carnegie*, 222–23.

83Quote: Wall, *Andrew Carnegie*, 211; 200–11; Livesay, *Andrew Carnegie*, 65–66.

84Quote: Cronon, *Nature's Metropolis*, 122; Klein, *Jay Gould*, 196–202; Livesay, *Andrew Carnegie*, 61–62, 212.

85Livesay, *Andrew Carnegie*, 62–64; Wall, *Andrew Carnegie*, 214–20.

86Wall, 228–29; 267–73; Strouse, *Morgan*, 138–39. He actually earned a bit more. Reminiscent of the town wit who liked to go around saying that if he had the king's fortune, he would be richer than the king—he would put it in the bank and collect interest—Carnegie squeezed a low-interest $200,000 loan from the bridge trustees, which he then invested at a higher rate of interest for his own pocket. Livesay, *Andrew Carnegie*, 68.

87Livesay, *Andrew Carnegie*, 69; Wall, *Andrew Carnegie*, 268–69, 279–80, 282.

88Quotes: "You see," Wall, *Andrew Carnegie*, 290; "control," ibid., 287; 286–87.

89Wall, *Andrew Carnegie*, 288–92; Livesay, *Andrew Carnegie*, 70.

90Quotes: "$50,000," Wall, *Andrew Carnegie*, 224; "degrade me," ibid., 224–25.

91Quote: Ibid., 302; ibid., 224–25, 298–301.

92Quote: Bayrd Still, *Mirror for Gotham: New York as Seen by Contemporaries from Dutch Days to the Present* (New York: University Press, 1956), 204.

93*Commercial and Financial Chronicle* in Scobey, "Empire City," 146; "repulsive," Still, *Mirror for Gotham*, 187; "streets," ibid., 173; Scobey, "Empire City," 144–54; Mandelbaum, *Boss Tweed's New York*, 8–14.

94Quote: *New York Times*, November 22, 1868; Callow, *Boss Tweed*, 76, 82.

95Quote: Paul R. Migliore, "The Business of Union: The New York Business Community and the Civil War" (Ph. D. dissertation, Columbia University, 1975), 418; *New York Times*, November 22, 1868; Edwin Burrows and Mike Wallace, *Gotham: A History of New York City to 1898* (New York: Oxford University Press, 1999), 918–22; Mandelbaum, *Boss Tweed's New York*, 71; Callow, *Boss Tweed*, 78–83.

[96]*New York Herald,* July 2, 1870.

[97]Quote: Callow, *Boss Tweed,* 10; ibid., 152–56; McCullough, *The Great Bridge,* 127.

[98]McCullough, *The Great Bridge,* 127; Callow, *Boss Tweed,* 26–28.

[99]Quotes: Mandelbaum, *Boss Tweed's New York,* 69, 67; Callow, *Boss Tweed,* 34–39.

[100]Quote: "[T]his structure," McCullough, *Great Bridge,* 27; Callow, *Boss Tweed,* 32, 153–56, 181, 198–206; Leo Hershkowitz, *Tweed's New York, Another Look* (Garden City, N.Y.: Anchor Press, 1977), 138–40; Scobey, "Empire City," 443; Eugene P. Moehring, *Public Works and the Patterns of Urban Real Estate Growth in Manhattan, 1835–1894* (New York: Arno Press, 1981), 312–21; Mandelbaum, *Boss Tweed's New York,* 58, 71, 75.

[101]Quote: *New York Herald,* April 5, 1870; ibid., April 4, 6, 1870, July 2, 12, 1870; Foner, *Reconstruction,* 491; Beckert, "The Making of New York City's Bourgeoisie," 234, 279–80; Bernstein, *New York City Draft Riots,* 207–8; Mandelbaum, *Boss Tweed's New York,* 72; Iver Bernstein, *The New York City Draft Riots: Their Significance for American Society and Politics in the Age of the Civil War* (New York: Oxford University Press, 1990), 207–8.

[102]Mandelbaum, *Boss Tweed's New York,* 71–72; Callow, *Boss Tweed,* 226; *New York Herald,* April 4, 1870.

[103]Quote: Burrows and Wallace, *Gotham,* 931; *New York Herald,* July 2, 1870.

[104]Callow, *Boss Tweed,* 8, 105–6; Bernstein, *New York City Draft Riots,* 214–15, 224.

[105]Ibid., 195–99; Callow, *Boss Tweed,* 35, 42; McCullough, *Great Bridge,* 148.

[106]Quotes: "rich old men," *New York Times,* April 29, 1869; "improvements," Mandelbaum, *Boss Tweed's New York,* 70; *New York Herald,* April 11, 1870; David Schuyler, Jane Turner Censer, et al., eds., *The Papers of Frederick Law Olmsted: The Years of Olmsted Vaux and Company 1865–1874,* Volume 6 (Baltimore: Johns Hopkins University Press, 1992, 6 vols.), 38–40.

[107]Callow, *Boss Tweed,* 168.

[108]Bernstein, *New York City Draft Riots,* 200–202; Jonathan Teaford, *The Unheralded Triumph: City Government in America: 1870–1900* (Baltimore: Johns Hopkins University Press, 1983), 285; Chandler, *The Visible Hand,* 92–94; Edward Durand, *The Finances of New York City* (New York: The Macmillan Company, 1898), 375.

[109]Mandelbaum, *Boss Tweed's New York,* 77; Beckert, "The Making of New York City's Bourgeoisie," 234; Kenneth Jackson, ed., *The Encyclopedia of New York City* (New Haven, Conn.: Yale University Press, 1995), 166; Burrows and Wallace, *Gotham,* 931.

[110]*New York Times,* October 1, 7, 1870; Callow, *Boss Tweed,* 241.

[111]Quote: Callow, *Boss Tweed,* 242–43; Gustavus Myers, *History of Tammany Hall* (New York: Gustavus Myers, [self-published], 1901), 276–77; Dennis Lynch, *Boss Tweed: The Story of a Grim Generation* (New York: Boni and Liveright, 1927), 347.

[112]Quotes: "manifestation," *New York Times,* November 18, 1870; "Honest Democrats," Hodas, *The Business Career of Moses Taylor,* 195; *New York Times,* November 22, 30, 1870; Beckert, "The Making of New York City's Bourgeoisie," 236.

[113]Flick, *Samuel J. Tilden*, 195; Callow, *Boss Tweed*, 238–39, 254, 271, 279, 296–97; Mark D. Hirsch, "Samuel J. Tilden: The Story of a Lost Opportunity," *American Historical Review* 56 (July, 1951): 791–92; *New York Tribune*, October 20, 1869. Tilden worked with Tweed to redeem promises to Democratic operatives and to channel money for candidates. Isaiah Blood to S. J. Tilden, October 1869, Samuel J. Tilden Papers, Box 7, New York Public Library.

[114]Bernstein, *New York City Draft Riots*, 207.

[115]Quote: McCullough, *Great Bridge*, 102; Callow, *Boss Tweed*, 187; *New York Times*, December 20, 29, 1868.

[116]McCullough, *Great Bridge*, 126–33.

[117]Quote: Scobey, "Empire City," 442–43; ibid., 451.

[118]Ibid., 167–74; see also the relevant footnotes; *New York Herald*, April 6, 1870.

[119]Scobey, "Empire City," 350, 348, 351; Moehring, *Public Works*, 318.

[120]Callow, *Boss Tweed*, 180; Moehring, *Public Works*, 318–21; Callow, *Boss Tweed*, 8, 51–52; McCullough, *The Great Bridge*, 125.

[121]Teaford, *The Unheralded Triumph*, 288; Callow, *Boss Tweed*, 46, 175, 199–203.

[122]Callow, *Boss Tweed*, 23.

[123]Ibid., 175–78; Mandelbaum, *Boss Tweed's New York*, 70.

[124]Quote: Klein, *Jay Gould*, 88; Callow, *Boss Tweed*, 31; Alexander Flick, *Samuel J. Tilden*, 198.

[125]Mandelbaum, *Boss Tweed's New York*, 73; *New York Times*, October 2, 18, 1869, March 1, 1870; *New York Tribune*, December 13, 15, 19, 20, 30, 1871.

[126]Callow, *Boss Tweed*, 164–65, 256, 260–61.

[127]Scobey, "Empire City," 81.

[128]Chandler, *The Visible Hand*, 92; Hurst, *Law and the Conditions of Freedom*, 86.

[129]Quote: Benson, *Merchants, Farmers and Railroads*, 16; ibid., 6–8.

[130]"Mayor Haul," Callow, *Boss Tweed*, 38.

[131]Ibid., 271–72; Burrows and Wallace, *Gotham*, 1011; Scobey, "Empire City," 453; Beckert, "The Making of New York City's Bourgeoisie," 308. Data is based on Clarence E. Bonnett, *Employers' Associations in the United States: A Study of Typical Associations* (New York: Macmillan, 1922), 114, 119, 120, 140.

[132]Callow, *Boss Tweed*, 271–72; Burrows and Wallace, *Gotham*, 1011; Mandelbaum, *Boss Tweed's New York*, 110; Teaford, *The Unheralded Triumph*, 288, 294–95.

[133]Foner, *Reconstruction*, 492.

[134]Scobey, "Empire City," 454.

## CHAPTER 4: THE FALL AND RISE OF THE NEW YORK ECONOMY

[1]James D. McCabe Jr., *Lights and Shadows of New York Life: Or the Sights and Sensations of the Great City* (New York: Farrar, Straus, and Giroux, 1970 reprint of 1872 edition), 279–85.

[2]U.S. Department of Commerce, Bureau of the Census, *Historical Statistics of the United States, Colonial Times to 1970*, Volume 2 (Washington, D.C.: U.S. Govt. Print. Off., 1975, 2 vols.), 1072.

[3]The election figures are from Alan Brinkley et al., *American History: A Survey* (New York: McGraw-Hill, 1991, 8th ed.), appendices, xxv.

[4]*New York Herald*, April 30, 1873.

[5]Quote: John Steele Gordon, *The Scarlet Woman of Wall Street: Jay Gould, Jim Fisk, Cornelius Vanderbilt, the Erie Railway Wars, and the Birth of Wall Street* (New York: Weidenfeld and Nicolson, 1988), 336; ibid., 280–88, 319–31; Edward Hungerford, *Men of Erie: A Story of Human Effort* (New York: Random House, 1946), 166–70; Maury Klein, *The Life and Legend of Jay Gould* (Baltimore: Johns Hopkins University Press, 1986), 115, 116–29.

[6]Quote: *New York World*, September 1, 1873, in Klein, *The Life and Legend of Jay Gould*, 134, quoting *New York World; New York Herald*, April 1, 1873.

[7]Quote: Ibid.; Margaret Myers, *The New York Money Market*, Volume 1 (New York: Columbia University Press, 1931–1932, 4 vols.), 290; Eric Foner, *Reconstruction: America's Unfinished Revolution, 1863–1877* (New York: Harper and Row, 1988), 467; *New York Herald*, January 2, April 1, 17–18, 1873.

[8]*New York Herald*, April 17, 1873; Edwin Burrows and Mike Wallace, *Gotham: A History of New York City to 1898* (New York: Oxford University Press, 1999), 1020–22; Foner, *Reconstruction*, 512; Sven Beckert, "The Making of New York City's Bourgeoisie" (Ph.D. dissertation, Columbia University, 1995), 95; Thomas C. Cochran and William Miller, *The Age of Enterprise: A Social History of Industrial America* (New York: 1942), 148–49; Henrietta M. Larson, *Jay Cooke: Private Banker* (Cambridge Mass.: Harvard University Press, 1936), 428–32; Rendigs Fels, *American Business Cycles, 1865–1897* (Chapel Hill N.C.: University North Carolina Press, 1959), 100.

[9]Margaret G. Myers, *A Financial History of the United States* (New York: Columbia University Press, 1970), 188; Louis M. Hacker, *The Triumph of American Capitalism: The Development of Forces in American History to the Beginning of the Twentieth Century* (New York: Columbia University Press, 1947), 404; Fels, *American Business Cycles*, 85.

[10]Larson, *Jay Cooke*, 409–10, 419; Eric Hobsbawm, *Age of Capital: 1848–1875* (New York: Scribner, 1975), 70.

[11]Quote: Ron Chernow, *The House of Morgan: An American Banking Dynasty and the Rise of Modern Finance* (New York: Simon & Schuster, 1990), 36; Beckert, "The Making of New York City's Bourgeoisie," 95, 300–301; Myers, *Financial History of the United States*, 188–89; Hacker, *Triumph of American Capitalism*, 404; United States Commissioner of Labor, *First Annual Report: Industrial Depressions* (March 1886), 60–61.

[12]Quotes: "unprecedentedly bad," Ron Chernow, *House of Morgan*, 36; "dark," David Black, *The King of Fifth Avenue: The Fortunes of August Belmont* (New York: Dial Press, 1981), 419; "prostration," ibid., 422; Foner, *Reconstruction*, 512; Chernow, *House of Morgan*, 36; Fels, *American Business Cycles*, 100; A.

Ross Eckler, "A Measure of the Severity of Depressions: 1873–1932," *Review of Economic Statistics*, May 15, 1933; Beckert, "The Making of New York's Bourgeoisie," 302.

[13]Quotes: "no place," Foner, *Reconstruction*, 512; "two New Yorks," *New York Herald*, February 9, 1874; ibid., February 5, 1874; Hacker, *The Triumph of American Capitalism*, 403–4; Burrows and Wallace, *Gotham*, 1022; these figures are disputed by Fels, *American Business Cycles*, 108; Association for the Improvement of the Conditions of the Poor, *32nd Annual Report*, 1875, 33; Leah Feder, *Unemployment Relief in Periods of Depression* (New York: Russell Sage Foundation, 1936), 39; Edward O'Donnell, "Henry George and the 'New Political Forces': Ethnic Nationalism, Labor Radicalism and Politics in Gilded Age New York City" (Ph.D. dissertation, Columbia University, 1995), 171.

[14]Quote: Sven Beckert, "The Making of New York's Bourgeoisie," 95; ibid., 300–303; Foner, *Reconstruction*; Hacker, *The Triumph of American Capitalism*, 512; Burrows and Wallace, *Gotham*, 1022; Shepard Clough, *A Century of American Life Insurance* (New York: Columbia University Press, 1946), 136–39; *Historical Statistics*, Volume 2, 1057–59; Vincent Carosso, *Investment Banking in America: A History* (Cambridge, Mass.: Harvard University Press, 1970), 28; Vincent Carosso, *The Morgans: Private International Bankers, 1854–1913* (Cambridge, Mass.: Harvard University Press, 1987), 246.

[15]Fels, *American Business Cycles*, 109; *Historical Statistics*, Volume 1, 201–8.

[16]Joseph Frazier Wall, *Andrew Carnegie* (New York: Oxford University Press, 1970), 298–301; Harold C. Livesay, *Andrew Carnegie and the Rise of Big Business* (Boston: Little, Brown, 1975), 72–74.

[17]Andrew Carnegie, *The Autobiography of Andrew Carnegie* (Boston: Northeastern University Press, 1986 reprint of 1920 ed.), 170; Livesay, *Andrew Carnegie*, 93–95; Wall, *Andrew Carnegie*, 295.

[18]Quote: Harold Livesay, *American Made: Men Who Shaped the American Economy* (Boston: Little, Brown, 1979), 116; Livesay, *Andrew Carnegie*, 80–85.

[19]Quote: W. F. Durfee, "The Manufacture of Steel," *Political Science Monthly* 34 (1891): 743–44, in John A. Garraty, *The New Commonwealth, 1877–1890* (New York: Harper and Row, 1968), 90–91; Livesay, *Andrew Carnegie*, 80; Wall, *Andrew Carnegie*, 261.

[20]Carnegie, *Autobiography*, 182–83; Harold Livesay, *Andrew Carnegie*, 95; Foner, *Reconstruction*, 512; Wall, *Andrew Carnegie*, 264–66.

[21]Ibid., 315–22; Livesay, *Andrew Carnegie*, 95.

[22]Quote: Andrew Carnegie, *Autobiography*, 186; Livesay, *Andrew Carnegie*, 97; Wall, *Andrew Carnegie*, 298–303, 314–19.

[23]Carnegie, *Autobiography*, 148.

[24]Quote: Livesay, *Andrew Carnegie*, 99; Wall, *Andrew Carnegie*, 312, 318.

[25]Quote: Livesay, *Men Who Shaped the American Economy*, 118; Livesay, *Andrew Carnegie*, 88–89; Wall, *Andrew Carnegie*, 346–47.

[26]Peter Temin, *Iron and Steel in Nineteenth Century America* (Cambridge, Mass.: M.I.T. Press, 1964), 157; Livesay, *Andrew Carnegie*, 88–89.

[27]Quotes: "grand concern," Wall, *Andrew Carnegie*, 326; "rather pay," Ibid., 351.

[28]Quotes: "where," Wall, *Andrew Carnegie*, 353; "bitter," and "railroad president," ibid., 348; "my part," ibid., 349; Livesay, *Andrew Carnegie*, 103.

[29]Wall, *Andrew Carnegie*, 330–34; Jeremiah Jenks, "The Economic Outlook," *The Dial* 10 (1890): 252–54, in Livingston, "The Social Analysis of Economic History and Theory," *American Historical Review* 92 (February 1987): 69–91, 76.

[30]Wall, Andrew Carnegie, 291; David McCullough; *The Great Bridge: The Epic Story of the Building of the Brooklyn Bridge* (New York: Simon & Schuster, 1972), 30; Wall, *Andrew Carnegie*, 291.

[31]Quotes: "cost," David Brody, *Steelworkers in America: The Nonunion Era* (Cambridge, Mass.: Harvard University Press, 1960), 2; "small profits," Wall, *Andrew Carnegie*, 351–52; ibid., 326; Temin, *Iron and Steel*, 125–26, 131, 222, 270, 283.

[32]Quote: Wall, *Andrew Carnegie*, 346; ibid., 322–23, 328, 336–37, 340–42.

[33]Ibid., 352.

[34]Quote: Beckert, "The Making of New York's Bourgeoisie," 95; ibid., 304, 320; *Historical Statistics*, Volume 1, 165.

[35]Quotes: "leave," "lose," and "cheapest," Wall, *Andrew Carnegie*, 345; "Darwinian," ibid., 336.

[36]Quotes: "I learn," ibid., 343–44; "bigoted," ibid., 345–48; ibid., 343–55.

[37]Quote: Ibid., 329; ibid., 353–55; Livesay, *Men Who Shaped the American Economy*, 114; Carnegie, *Autobiography*, 144.

[38]Wall, *Andrew Carnegie*, 360; Thomas Hughes, *The Vital Few: American Economic Progress and Its Protagonists* (Boston: Houghton Mifflin, 1966), 234–35; Garraty, *The New Commonwealth*, 91; Livesay, *Men Who Shaped the American Economy*, 122.

[39]Quote: Thomas C. Cochran and William Miller, *The Age of Enterprise: A Social History of Industrial America* (New York: The Macmillan Company, 1942), 124; ibid., 124–49.

[40]Quote: David Freeman Hawke, *John D.: The Founding Father of the Rockefellers* (New York: Harper and Row, 1980), 189.

[41]Quote: Alfred Chandler, *The Visible Hand: The Managerial Revolution in American Business* (Cambridge: Belknap Press, 1977), 148; Hungerford, *Men of Erie*, 161–65; Gordon, *Scarlet Woman of Wall Street*, 340–41; Chandler, *The Visible Hand*, 136.

[42]Quotes: "The policy," Julius Grodinsky, *Jay Gould: His Business Career, 1867–1892* (Philadelphia: University of Pennsylvania Press, 1957), 174; "Prejudice," Chandler, *Visible Hand*, 136; Grodinsky, *Jay Gould*, 149, 151.

[43]Quotes: "raider," ibid., 25; "evident," 174; Jean Strousse, *Morgan: American Financier* (New York: Random House, 1999), 131.

[44]Klein, *Life and Legend of Jay Gould*, 97.

[45]Grodinsky, *Jay Gould*, 148–50, 151, 155.

[46]Hungerford, *Men of Erie*, 166–70.

⁴⁷Klein, *Jay Gould*, 145–50.

⁴⁸Ibid., 149–55, 157.

⁴⁹*New York Times*, August 3, 1877, in ibid., 205–6; ibid., 134, 174–75, 196.

⁵⁰Eric Hobsbawm, *Age of Capital, 1848–1875* (New York: Scribner, 1975), 61; Klein, *Jay Gould*, 196–205.

⁵¹Quote: Ibid., 280–81; ibid., 277–82.

⁵²Quotes: *New York Tribune*, February 2, 1866, in Charles Cheape, *Moving the Masses: Urban Public Transit in New York, Boston, Philadelphia, 1880–1912* (Cambridge, Mass.: Harvard University Press, 1980), 27; *World*, in ibid., 28; David C. Hammack, *Power and Society: Greater New York at the Turn of the Century* (New York: Columbia University Press, 1987), 231.

⁵³Ibid., *Power and Society*, 230–31; Cheape, *Moving the Masses*, 31.

⁵⁴Quote: Seymour J. Mandelbaum, *Boss Tweed's New York* (New York: Wiley, 1965), 43–46; Cheape, *Moving the Masses*, 29; Strouse, *Morgan*, 47–49.

⁵⁵Mandelbaum, *Boss Tweed's New York*, 126.

⁵⁶Clifton Hood, *722 Miles: The Building of the Subways and How They Transformed New York* (New York: Johns Hopkins University Press, 1995), 49–50; Cheape, *Moving the Masses*, 29–30.

⁵⁷Hood, *722 Miles*, 33, 50–51; Cheape, *Moving the Masses*, 32–33; Klein, *Jay Gould*, 282–283.

⁵⁸*New York Herald Tribune*, October 16, 1879; Cheape, *Moving the Masses*, 34.

⁵⁹Quote: Maury Klein, *Jay Gould*, 282; ibid., 283–84; *New York Times*, December 27–30, 1881; *New York Herald Tribune*, May 7, 1882; *New York World*, "Wall Street Gossip," May–October 1881; Maury Klein, *Jay Gould*, 545, note 31.

⁶⁰Quote: Ibid., 288; ibid., 184–88.

⁶¹Ibid., 288–89.

⁶²Quote: Ibid., 289; ibid., 283–89; *New York Times*, December 27, 1881; *New York World*, May 19–October 8, 1881.

⁶³*New York Times*, December 27, 1881; Klein, *Jay Gould*, 290.

⁶⁴Keith Ian Polakoff, *The Politics of Inertia: The Election of 1876 and the End of Reconstruction* (Baton Rouge: Louisiana State University Press, 1973), 288.

⁶⁵Robert Kelley, *The Transatlantic Persuasion: The Liberal-Democratic Mind in the Age of Gladstone* (New York: Alfred A. Knopf, 1968), 241; John Bigelow *The Life of Samuel J. Tilden*, Volume 1 (New York: Harper and Brothers, 1895, 2 vols.), 231; Alexander Clarence Flick, *Samuel Jones Tilden: A Study in Political Sagacity* (New York: Dodd, Mead and Company, 1939), 165, 203; Eric Foner, *Reconstruction*, 568; John Bigelow, ed., *The Letters and Literary Memorials of Samuel J. Tilden*, Volume 1 (Freeport, N.Y.: Harper, 1908, 2 vols.), 258–59, 297–301.

⁶⁶Polakoff, *The Politics of Inertia*, 72–73; Bigelow, *Letters of Samuel J. Tilden*, Volume 1, 219; Flick, *Samuel Jones Tilden*, 188–203. Greeley's letter of October 29, 1869, is in Flick, *Samuel Jones Tilden*, 18.

⁶⁷Flick, *Samuel Jones Tilden*, 190, 195; Bernstein, *New York Draft Riots*; Isaiah Blood to Samuel Jones Tilden, October 18, 1869, Tilden Papers, Box 7, New York Public Library; Flick, *Samuel Jones Tilden*, 197.

[68]Paul Sarnoff, *Russell Sage the Money King* (New York: J. Obolensky, 1965), 214–16; Callow, *The Tweed Ring* (New York: Oxford University Press, 1966), 254; Bigelow, *Letters and Literary Memorials of Samuel J. Tilden*, 258–59; 297–301; Flick, *Samuel Jones Tilden*, 193, 199.

[69]Quotes: "the envy," ibid., 224; "monomaniac," and "wife," ibid., 233; ibid., 33–36, 221, 226, 274; Callow, *The Tweed Ring*, 254.

[70]Quotes: "never had," Bigelow, *Letters and Literary Memorials of Samuel J. Tilden*, 373; "queer," Flick, *Samuel Jones Tilden*, 108–10; ibid., 59–80, 107–9. Tilden did offer a number of favored female friends financial advice and even suggestions about their clothing. He proposed once or twice but was turned down and failed to make the same offer in a situation where he was more certain of success; but he made peace with his isolation, and though the wives of friends would ever be aiming to set him up, he remained a bachelor: Tilden Papers, Correspondence, New York Public Library.

[71]Quotes: "admired," Robert Kelley, "The Thought and Character of Samuel J. Tilden: The Democrat as Inheritor," *Historian* 26 (February 1964): 177; "cold," Flick, *Samuel Jones Tilden*, 351; "connected," ibid., 278; ibid., 200; Foner, *Reconstruction*, 568.

[72]Quotes: "Government must," Foner, *Reconstruction*, 489; "uncertain things," Robert Kelley, "The Democracy of Tilden and Cleveland," in Peter B. Kovler, ed., *Democrats and the American Idea* (Washington, D.C.: Center for National Policy Press, 1976), 155; "fruits of," Robert Kelley, *The Transatlantic Persuasion* (New York: Alfred A. Knopf, 1968), 286–87; "depressed," *Nineteenth Annual Report of the Chamber of Commerce of the State of New York*, 14, in Edward Chase Kirkland, *Dream and Thought in the Business Community 1860–1900* (Ithaca, N.Y.: Cornell University Press, 1956), 126; Kelley, *The Transatlantic Persuasion*, 275–76; Flick, *Samuel Jones Tilden*, 280–96.

[73]Foner, *Reconstruction*, 514–18; Cochran and Miller, *The Age of Enterprise*, 137; Bigelow, *Life of Samuel J. Tilden*, 295.

[74]Quote: Flick, *Samuel Jones Tilden*, 9; ibid., 1–5, 110.

[75]Quote: Polakoff, *The Politics of Inertia*, 257; Foner, *Reconstruction*, 570–75; Flick, *Samuel Jones Tilden*, 312.

[76]Foner, *Reconstruction*, 567; Michael E. McGerr, *Decline of Popular Politics: The American North* (New York: Oxford University Press, 1986), 72–85.

[77]James Livingston, Eric Foner, and others see the 1873 depression as ushering in a twenty-three-year period of curtailed economic growth, with failures and losses arresting the upward trajectory of American economic development: James Livingston, "The Social Analysis of Economic History: Conjectures on Late Nineteenth-Century American Development," *American Historical Review* 92 (February 1987): 72; Foner, *Reconstruction*, 513. *Historical Statistics*, Volume 1, 130, 138–39, 165, 201, 211, 212, 214, 230–33, 240, 588; *Historical Statistics*, Volume 2, 667, 865, 867–68, 884, 897, 912–13, 1020, 1027, 1030; Fels, *American Business Cycles*, 111; Jenks, "The Economic Outlook," *The Dial* 10 (1890): 252–54; Beckert, "The Making of New York's Bourgeoisie," 95, 300.

[78]Quote: David Wells, *Recent Economic Changes* (New York: D. Appleton, 1889), 84–86, 406–22; James Livingston, "The Social Analysis of Economic History and Theory," 69–91, 75; Fels, *American Business Cycles*, 107–8.

[79]John A Garraty, *The New Commonwealth*, 128.

[80]Cochran and Miller, *The Age of Enterprise*, 137; David Moisseif Scobey, "Empire City: Politics, Culture, and Urbanism in Gilded Age New York" (Ph.D. dissertation, Yale University, 1989), 76, 211–12; Margaret Myers, *New York Money Market*, 1, 309.

[81]Quotes: Godkin in Foner, *Reconstruction*, 518; "The temper," Clarence Bonnet, *History of Employers Associations in the United States* (New York: Vantage Press, 1957), 119, in Beckert, "The Making of New York's Bourgeoisie," 307–8.

[82]*New York Tribune*, May 25, 1872, in Mandelbaum, *Boss Tweed's New York*, 90.

[83]Quotes: "body," "wild," "orgy," "Nothing better," all in Herbert G. Gutman, "The Tompkins Square Riot," *Labor History* 6 (Winter 1965): 54–56; "He shares," *New York Herald*, January 9, 1874.

[84]Quotes: "belonged," Gutman, "The Tompkins Square Riot," 55; "by thrift," *New York Times*, November 22, 1873; "test the," Beckert, "The Making of New York's Bourgeoisie," 319; "exactions," *New York Tribune*, October 19, 1872, in Mandelbaum, *Boss Tweed's New York*, 95; Barry J. Kaplan; "Reformers and Charity: The Abolition of Public Outdoor Relief in New York City, 1870–1898," *Social Service Review* (June, 1978), 202–3, in Beckert, "The Making of New York's Bourgeoisie," 319.

[85]Hammack, *Power and Society*, 47–50.

[86]Quote: "No other," John King Van Rensselaer, *The Social Ladder* (New York: Arno Press, 1975 reprint of 1924 ed.), 58; Beckert, "The Making of New York's Bourgeoisie," 309, 311; Nicola Beisel, *Upper Class Formation and the Politics of Censorship in Boston, New York, and Philadelphia, 1872–1892* (Ph.D. dissertation, University of Michigan, 1990), 5.

[87]Quotes: Robert Davis, "Pauperism in the City of New York," *Journal of Social Science* 6 (1874): 74; "rabble," James G. Sproat, *The Best Men, Liberal Reformers in the Gilded Age*, 205; *New York Times*, August 14, 1871, in Scobey, "Empire City," 428; Iver Bernstein, *The New York City Draft Riots: Their Significance for American Society and Politics in the Age of the Civil War* (New York: Oxford University Press, 1990), 229–36.

[88]Quotes: "morbid," *Nation*, May 9, 1876, 155, in Scobey, "Empire City," 456; "dangerous class," Beckert, "The Making of New York's Bourgeoisie," 321–22; Robert Davis, "Pauperism in the City of New York," *Journal of Social Science* 6 (1874): 74–87; Gutman, "The Tompkins Square Riot," 44–70.

[89]Quotes: "by nature," Foner, *Reconstruction*, 492; *Atlantic Monthly* in Sven Beckert, "The Making of New York's Bourgeoisie," 323–24; "mere majorities," Bernstein, *New York City Draft Riots*, 219–20; Migliore, *The Business of Union*, 436–37; William M. Armstrong, ed., *The Gilded Age Letters of E. L. Godkin* (Albany, N.Y.: State University of New York Press, 1974), 220; Burrows and Wallace, *Gotham*, 1032–33. John I. Davenport, a member of the Union

League, put together a full volume entitled *The Election and Naturalization Frauds in New York City, 1860–1870* (New York: 1894).

[90]Morton Keller, *Affairs of State: Public Life in Late Nineteenth Century America* (Cambridge, Mass.: Belknap Press of Harvard University Press, 1977), 110–14; Jerome Mushkat, *The Reconstruction of New York Democracy: 1861–1874* (Rutherford, N.J.: Fairleigh Dickinson University Press, 1982), 215; Burrows and Wallace, *Gotham*, 1032–33; Polakoff, *The Politics of Inertia*, 288.

[91]Joseph Bucklin Bishop, *A Chronicle of One Hundred & Fifty Years; The Chamber of Commerce of the State of New York, 1776–1918* (New York: C. Scribner's Sons, 1918), v, 65,76–91; Hammack, *Power and Society*, 52; Burrows and Wallace, *Gotham*, 277; *New York Encyclopedia*, 825.

[92]Bishop, *The Chamber of Commerce of the State of New York*, 66; Burrows and Wallace, *Gotham*, 498, 986, 1157, 1163; David Hammack, *Power and Society*, 52–54, 102, 138.

[93]Quotes: "combinations of men," Chamber of Commerce of the State of New York, *Report of Select Committee on Return to Specie Payment* (November 1867), New York Public Library; "costly parks," Chamber of Commerce of the State of New York, *Proceedings Annual Banquet 1874* (New York: 1875), 6; Chamber of Commerce of the State of New York, *Nineteenth Annual Report, 1876–1877*, 13, and Chamber of Commerce of the State of New York, *Eighteenth Annual Report, 1875–1876*, 18, in Beckert, "The Making of New York's Bourgeoisie," 317; Bishop, *The Chamber of Commerce of the State of New York*, 114–17.

[94]Quote: Chamber of Commerce of the State of New York, *Proceedings Annual Banquet 1873* (New York: 1874), 79–81; Bishop, *The Chamber of Commerce of the State of New York*, 269–72.

[95]Quote: Chamber of Commerce of the State of New York, *Proceedings, 1879*, 12–13; ibid., 3–5; Lee Benson, *Merchants, Farmers and Railroads: Railroad Regulation and New York Politics, 1850–1887* (Cambridge, Mass.: Harvard University Press, 1955), 78.

[96]Quotes: "annihilation," Chamber of Commerce of the State of New York, *Report on Pacific Ocean Telegraph in Connection with the Commerce of the World* (New York: 1871), 8; "gigantic," Chamber of Commerce of the State of New York, *Annual Banquet, 1873*, 3–14; "Rail competition," Benson, *Merchants, Farmers and Railroads*, 35; 22–32, 36.

[97]Quote: Benson, *Merchants, Farmers and Railroads*, 23; Chamber of Commerce of the State of New York, *Annual Report, 1869*, cxlii.

[98]Quote: Burrows and Wallace, *Gotham*, 1035; Mandelbaum, *Boss Tweed's New York*, 148–49.

[99]Chamber of Commerce of the State of New York, *Annual Report 1877*, 13, 75–76, 18; Benson, *Merchants, Farmers and Railroads*, 310.

[100]Quote: *New York Sun* in Hammack, *Power and Society*, 52, 230–31; Cheape, *Moving the Masses*, 29–31; Burrows and Wallace, *Gotham*, 1053–57.

[101]Hammack, *Power and Society*, 230–58.

[102]Mandelbaum, *Boss Tweed's New York*, 10.

[103]Chamber of Commerce of the State of New York, *Proceedings Annual Banquet 1877* (New York: 1878), 5–14.

[104]Quotes: "haunt," Charles Francis Adams Jr., "A Chapter of Erie," *North American Review* 109 (July 1869): 30–106, reprinted in Frederick Hicks, ed., *High Finance in the Sixties: Chapters from the Early History of the Erie Railway* (New Haven, Conn.: Yale University Press, 1929), 114; "It is but," ibid., 115; ibid., 63.

[105]Quotes: "we presume," *New York Times*, December 3, 1868; "one asylum," *New York Herald*, September 16, 1870; "Nowhere," *New York Times*, December 3, 1868.

[106]Calculation based on figures from Hacker, *Triumph of American Capitalism*, 403–4; Burrows and Wallace, *Gotham*, 1022; Fels, *American Business Cycles*, 108; Association for the Improvement of the Conditions of the Poor, *Annual Report, 1875* (New York: 1876), 33, in Leah H. Feder, *Unemployment Relief in Periods of Depression* (New York: Arno Press, 1971), 39; *New York Herald*, February 5, 1874.

[107]Fels, *American Business Cycles*, 109; *Historical Statistics*, Volume 1, 201; *Historical Statistics*, Volume 2, 940.

## CHAPTER 5: SHAPING MODERN CAPITALISM

[1]Charles A. Conant, *Wall Street and the Country: A Study of Recent Financial Tendencies* (New York: Greenwood Press, 1968 reprint of 1904 ed.), 64–65, 14.

[2]John A. Garraty, ed., *Labor and Capital in the Gilded Age* (Boston: Little Brown and Co., 1968), 132.

[3]Jean Strouse, *Morgan: American Financier* (New York: Random House, 1999), 244.

[4]Quotes: "define[s]," Ron Chernow, *The Death of the Banker: The Decline and Fall of the Great Financial Dynasties and the Triumph of the Small Investor* (New York: Vintage Books, 1999), 19; "[B]efore his sway," Sigmund Diamond, *The Reputation of the American Businessman* (Cambridge, Mass.: Harvard University Press, 1955), 84; "the embodiment," *New York Sun*, March 31, 1913, in Strouse, *Morgan*, 15; "the king," ibid., xiii.

[5]Quote: Ibid., xii; Ron Chernow, *The House of Morgan: An American Banking Dynasty and the Rise of Modern Finance* (New York: Simon & Schuster, 1990), 21; George Wheeler, *Pierpont Morgan and Friends: The Anatomy of Myth* (Englewood Cliffs, N.J.: Prentice Hall, 1973), 61; Chernow, *Death of the Banker*, 90.

[6]Quotes: "good enough," ibid., 5–6; "no other king," Martin J. Sklar, *The Corporate Reconstruction of American Capitalism, 1890–1916: The Market, the Law, and Politics* (New York: Cambridge University Press, 1988), 16.

[7]*Review of Reviews* in Diamond, *The Reputation of the American Businessman*, 97; ibid., 95.

[8]Jonathan Hughes, *The Vital Few: American Economic Progress and its Protagonists* (Boston: Houghton Mifflin, 1966), 406.

⁹Quote: Norman Scott Brien Gras and Henrietta M. Larson, *Casebook in American Business History* (New York: Appleton-Century-Crofts, 1939), 549; Strouse, *Morgan*, 207; Vincent Carosso, *The Morgans: Private International Bankers, 1854–1913* (Cambridge, Mass.: Harvard University Press, 1987), 60, 62, 83–85; Chernow, *House of Morgan*, 20; Chernow, *Death of the Banker*, 89.

¹⁰Quotes: "Slow and sure," Chernow, *House of Morgan*, 12; "remember," Carosso, *The Morgans*, 85, italics added; "shrewdly conceived," *New York Times*, October 12, 1863, in Strouse, *Morgan*, 111; ibid., 109; Chernow, *Death of the Banker*, 90; Carosso, *The Morgans*, 86, 90, 102.

¹¹Quote: Strouse, *Morgan*, 111–12; Chernow, *House of Morgan*, 23, Carosso, *The Morgans*, 107.

¹²Quote: Strouse, *Morgan*, 137; Gras and Larson, *Casebook in American Business History*, 550; Carosso, *The Morgans*, 115–22; Chernow, *Death of the Banker*, 95.

¹³Quote: Strouse, *Morgan*, 141, 142, 147–48; Wheeler, *Pierpont Morgan and Friends*, 84–86; Chernow, *House of Morgan*, 33; Carosso, *The Morgans*, 142–43.

¹⁴Ibid., 135–40; Strouse, *Morgan*, 142. In 1895, the firm dropped the Drexel name to become J. P. Morgan & Co.: Chernow, *Death of the Banker*, 93.

¹⁵Quote: Carosso, *The Morgans*, 142–44; Strouse, *Morgan*, 7.

¹⁶Chernow, *House of Morgan*, 33; Vincent Carosso, *Investment Banking in America: A History* (Cambridge, Mass.: Harvard University Press, 1970), 18, 25, 142–46; Carosso, *The Morgans*, 142–43.

¹⁷Quotes: "We had," ibid., 144–45; "can be recommended," Chernow, *House of Morgan*, 37; Carosso, *The Morgans*, 149, 171, 181; Strouse, *Morgan*, 157; Carosso, *Investment Banking in America*, 27, 181; Henrietta M. Larson, *Jay Cooke Private Banker* (Cambridge, Mass.: Harvard University Press, 1936), 433.

¹⁸Thomas Childs Cochran and William Miller, *The Age of Enterprise: A Social History of Industrial America* (New York: Harper, 1961), 137; Carosso, *The Morgans*, 162; Carosso, *Investment Banking in America*, 29, 175; Chernow, *House of Morgan*, 40.

¹⁹William Roy, *Socializing Capital: The Rise of the Large Industrial Corporation in America* (Princeton: Princeton University Press, 1997), 140; Carosso, *The Morgans*, 177–78.

²⁰Carosso, *The Morgans*, 175, 181, 201–19; Strouse, *Morgan*, 187.

²¹Carosso, *The Morgans*, 156.

²²Quotes: "Defeat," Carosso, *The Morgans*, 187; "advantageous," Strouse, *Morgan*, 165, italics added.

²³Quote: Strouse, *Morgan*, 180; Carosso, *The Morgans*, 184, 187–88, 193.

²⁴Burrows and Wallace, *Gotham: A History of New York City to 1898* (New York: Oxford University Press, 1999), 1059; Alfred Chandler, *Scale and Scope: The Dynamics of Industrial Capitalism* (Cambridge: Belknap Press, 1990), 64; Carosso, *The Morgans*, 271; Strouse, *Morgan*, 182–83, 231–34.

²⁵Carosso, *The Morgans*, 184–86; Strouse, *Morgan*, 186–87; Niall Ferguson, *The House of Rothschild: The World's Banker, 1849–1999* (New York: Viking, 2000), 348.

[26]Quote: Strouse, *Morgan*, 186; Carosso, *Investment Banking*, 29; Carosso, *The Morgans*, 196–97, 179–203.

[27]Carosso, *The Morgans*, 190.

[28]Quote: "the wealth," Wheeler, *Pierpont Morgan and Friends*, 156; Carosso, *The Morgans*, 219.

[29]Quotes: "plethora," and "Capital," Julius Grodinsky, *Transcontinental Railway Strategy* (Philadelphia: University of Pennsylvania Press, 1957), 178–180; ibid., 226–338; Margaret Myers, *The New York Money Market*, Volume 1 (New York: Columbia University Press, 1931–32, 4 vols.), 290–91; Alfred Dupont Chandler, *The Visible Hand: The Managerial Revolution in American Business* (Cambridge: Belknap Press, 1977), 170–171; Roy, *Socializing Capital*, 11, 180, 254; Chandler, *Scale and Scope*, 57; Gras and Larson, *Casebook in American Business History*, 52; Carosso, *The Morgans*, 244, 299.

[30]Quote: Carosso, *The Morgans*, 229; ibid, 229–30, 238–42; Strouse, *Morgan*, 196; Chandler, *Visible Hand*, 156.

[31]*Commercial and Financial Chronicle*, November 29, 1879, 554, in Carosso, *Investment Banking*, 37; Carosso, *The Morgans*, 231, Chandler, *Visible Hand*, 158.

[32]New York Chamber of Commerce, *Twentieth Annual Report* (January 1878), 106, in Lee Benson, *Merchants, Farmers & Railroads; Railroad Regulation and New York Politics, 1850–1887* (Cambridge, Mass.: Harvard University Press, 1955), 55; ibid., 30–55, 80–94, 106.

[33]Benson, *Merchants, Farmers & Railroads*, 15–16, 78–79, 120, 123, 135–136, 164.

[34]Benson, *Merchants, Farmers & Railroads*, 139–41; Strouse, *Morgan*, 197; Chernow, *House of Morgan*, 43; Carosso, *Investment Banking*, 37.

[35]Quote: *Commercial and Financial Chronicle*, November 29, 1879, 554, in Carosso, *Investment Banking*, 37; Chernow, *House of Morgan*, 43–44; Gras and Larson, *Casebook in American Business History*, 52; Carosso, *The Morgans*, 231.

[36]Quote: Strouse, *Morgan*, 181; Carosso, *The Morgans*, 250–51, 181; Gras and Larson, *Casebook in American Business History*, 52.

[37]Strouse, *Morgan*, 161; Chernow, *House of Morgan*, 44; Carosso, *Investment Banking*, 29; Carosso, *The Morgans*, 220, 246; Chernow, *The Death of the Banker*, 24; Roy, *Socializing Capital*, 133.

[38]Quotes: "paranoiac," Joseph Frazier Wall, *Andrew Carnegie* (New York: Oxford University Press, 1970), 506–8; "send a circular," ibid., 508–9; ibid., 472.

[39]Benson, *Merchants, Farmers & Railroads*, 243; Wall, *Andrew Carnegie*, 508–10, 514.

[40]Chandler, *Visible Hand*, 171; Gras and Larson, *Casebook in American Business History*, 553; Carosso, *The Morgans*, 254.

[41]Carosso, *The Morgans*, 554, 256.

[42]Wall, *Andrew Carnegie*, 514.

[43]Quotes: "binding," Grodinsky, *Transcontinental Railway Strategy*, 334; "open warfare," ibid., 314; *Railroad Journal*, February 26, 1886, 149, in ibid., 319; ibid., 271, 339–40; Carosso, *The Morgans*, 257; Benson, *Merchants, Farmers & Railroads*, 242.

[44]Chandler, *Visible Hand*, 170; Roy, *Socializing Capital*, 11, 108, 254; Gras and Lar-

son, *Casebook in American Business History*, 555; Chandler, *Scale and Scope*, 57; Carosso, *The Morgans*, 244–49.

45Quotes: "mind in a generation," Strouse, *Morgan*, 245; "absolute control," Carosso, *The Morgans*, 240; "watched," Gras and Larson, *Casebook in American Business History*, 555; Carosso, *The Morgans*, 261, 265–66; Carosso, *Investment Banking*, 37; Gras and Larson, *Casebook in American Business History*, 554–55.

46Quotes: "masters," Chernow, *House of Morgan*, 38; "thirty three," Carosso, *Investment Banking*, 167–68.

47Quotes: "buccaneering," Carosso, *Investment Banking*, 38; "reasonable," Carosso, *The Morgans*, 258; ibid., 237, 246–49, 262–64, 288; Grodinsky, *Transcontinental Railway Strategy*, 341, 344–45, 262–64, 288; Strouse, *Morgan*, 195; *Historical Statistics of the U.S.*, Volume 1, 224; Gras and Larson, *Casebook in American Business History*, 556–57.

48Carosso, *The Morgans*, 219–21.

49Ron Chernow, *Titan: The Life of John Rockefeller, Sr.* (New York: Random House, 1998), viii.

50Ibid., 337; Chandler, *Scale and Scope*, 73–74; David Freeman Hawke, *John D.: The Founding Father of the Rockefellers* (New York: Harper and Row, 1980), 163.

51*World Telegram* in Diamond, *The Reputation of the American Businessman*, 122.

52Quote: Ibid., 115; Chernow, *Titan*, 17–18, 87, 99–100; Chandler, *Scale and Scope*, 93.

53Quote: Chernow, *Titan*, 104, 102.

54Ibid., 117–19, 168–72; Chandler, *Scale and Scope*, 93; Chandler, *Visible Hand*, 321–22.

55Chernow, *Titan*, 184.

56Ibid., 136.

57Quotes: "We wanted," Hawke, *John D.*, 153–54; "selfish," ibid., 155; ibid., 168–72, 206–7; Allan Nevins, *John D. Rockefeller: The Heroic Age of American Enterprise*, Volume 2 (New York: C. Scribner's Sons, 1941, 2 vols.), 42; Chandler, *Visible Hand*, 321–22.

58Chandler, *Scale and Scope*, 93.

59Quotes: "clamorer" and "monstrous monopoly," Nevins, *John D. Rockefeller*, Volume 2, 41; "smarter," Wheeler, *Pierpont Morgan and Friends*, 144–45, italics added; "mysterious," Chernow, *Titan*, 214; ibid., 211–14; Hawke, *John D.*, 157.

60Chernow, *Titan*, 214.

61Quote: Hawke, *John D.*, 171–72; Glenn Porter, *The Rise of Big Business, 1860–1920* (Arlington Heights, Ill.: Harlan Davidson, 1992, 2nd ed.), 67–70.

62*Dictionary of American Biography*, Volume 5 (New York: C. Scribner's Sons, 1928–1958, 22 vols.), 341–42.

63Quote: Chernow, *Titan*, 266; ibid., 226–27, 257; Chandler, *Visible Hand*, 319, 323, 324, 418; Hawke, *John D.*, 163.

64Hawke, *John D.*, 161, 166–67; Chandler, *Visible Hand*, 418–19, 421; Nevins, *John D. Rockefeller*, Volume 2, 20.

[65]Hawke, *John D.*, 163.

[66]Nevins, *John D. Rockefeller*, Volume 1, 622.

[67]Cochran and Miller, *The Age of Enterprise*, 142; Chandler, *Scale and Scope*, 24–25, 92.

[68]Nevins, *John D. Rockefeller*, Volume 2, 19–26, 83, 160–61; Chernow, *Titan*, 217–18, 221–22.

[69]Nevins, *John D. Rockefeller*, Volume 2, 5, 26; Chandler, *Visible Hand*, 322–25; Hawke, *John D.*, 187.

[70]Chandler, *Visible Hand*, 325.

[71]Quotes: Nevins, *John D. Rockefeller*, Volume 2, 118–22.

[72]Quote: Ibid., Volume 2, 122–23; Hawke, *John D.*, 154–56; Chernow, *Titan*, 154.

[73]Margaret G. Myers, *A Financial History of the United States* (New York: Columbia University Press, 1970), 223–25.

[74]Chandler, *Visible Hand*, 290–91, 328; Burrows and Wallace, *Gotham*, 1045–46; Alfred Chandler, "The Beginnings of Big Business in American Industry," *Business History Review* 33 (Spring 1959): 1–31, reprinted in Thomas McCraw, *The Essential Alfred Chandler*, 54–67; Myers, *Financial History*, 223–25; Roy, *Socializing Capital*, 226–27.

[75]Quote: *New York Times*, October 12, 1878.

[76]Wall, *Andrew Carnegie*, 515, 517; David C. Hammack, *Power and Society: Greater New York at the Turn of the Century* (New York: Russell Sage Foundation, 1982), 47, 309.

[77]Junius Henri Browne, *The Great Metropolis: A Mirror for New York* (Hartford: American Pub. Co., 1869), 568–69.

[78]Hammack, *Power and Society*, 50.

[79]*United States Department of Interior, Census of Manufacturers* (1890), xxxv–vi.

[80]Hammack, *Power and Society*, 305, 308.

[81]Quote: John A. Garraty, ed., *Labor and Capital in the Gilded Age: Testimony Taken by the Senate Committee upon the Relations Between Labor and Capital* (Boston: Little, Brown, 1968), 133; Hammack, *Power and Society*, 306.

[82]Quote: *New York Times*, December 7, 1879, editorial; ibid., December 26, 1878.

[83]Daniel M. Fox, *Engines of Culture: Philanthropy and Art Museums* (Madison, Wis.: University of Wisconsin, 1963), 32–35.

[84]Ibid., 34.

[85]Quotes: Wall, *Andrew Carnegie*, 558–60; ibid., 523–25.

[86]John A. Garraty, *The New Commonwealth, 1877–1890* (New York: Harper and Row, 1968), 149; *New York Commercial Advertiser*, June 22, 1886.

[87]Quotes: "protest," Eric Arnesen, "American Workers and the Labor Movement in the Late Nineteenth Century," in Charles Calhoun, ed., *The Gilded Age: Essays in Modern America* (Wilmington, Del.: Scholarly Resources, 1996), 39; "tocsin," in David Omar Stowell, "The Struggle for City Streets: People, Railroads and the Great Strikes of 1877" (Ph. D. dissertation, SUNY Buffalo, 1992), 18; "oligarchy," Saul K. Padover, ed., *The Letters of Karl Marx* (Englewood Cliffs, N.J.: Book Sales, 1979), 317. The general account of the strike

relies on Robert V. Bruce, *1877: Year of Violence* (Chicago: I. R. Dee, 1989 reprint of 1959 ed.), and Paul Avrich, *The Haymarket Tragedy* (Princeton: Princeton University Press, 1984), 26–30.

[88]Bruce, *1877: Year of Violence*, concludes that the strike broke "old patterns of thought and crystallized new ones," 223, 312, 318; Eric Foner, *Reconstruction: America's Unfinished Revolution, 1863–1877* (New York: Harper, 1988), 583–86; Stowell: *The Struggle for City Streets*, 1–5, 12–13, 302; Melvyn Dubofsky, *Industrialism and the American Worker, 1865–1920* (Arlington Heights, Ill: AHM Pub. Corp., 1975), 44–45; Alan Trachtenberg, *Incorporation of America* (New York: Hill and Wang, 1982), 39; Nick Salvatore, "Railroad Workers and the Great Strike of 1877: The View from a Small Mid-West City," *Labor History* 21 (Fall 1980): 524–26, 531.

[89]Quotes: "Communistic," Avrich, *Haymarket Tragedy*, 27–28; Beecher in Burrows and Wallace, *Gotham*, 1036.

[90]Ibid., 1037.

[91]Edward O'Donnell, "Henry George and the 'New Political Forces': Ethnic Nationalism, Labor Radicalism and Politics in Gilded Age New York City" (Ph.D. dissertation, Columbia University, 1995), 327–28, 331.

[92]*Banker's Magazine* (September 1883), 171–73.

[93]Quote: Klein, *The Life and Legend of Jay Gould*, 314; O'Donnel, "Henry George," 337.

[94]Dubofsky, *Industrialism and the American Worker*, 55–59; Klein, *The Life and Legend of Jay Gould*, 357–58.

[95]Richard Schneirov, *Labor and Urban Politics: Class Conflict and the Origins of Modern Liberalism in Chicago, 1864–97* (Urbana, Ill.: University of Illinois Press, 1998), 183; Dubofsky, *Industrialism and the American Worker*, 60–62; Arnesen, "American Workers and the Labor Movement," 44; Klein, *The Life and Legend of Jay Gould*, 359.

[96]Quotes: "grim," Klein, *The Life and Legend of Jay Gould*, 359; "take him," ibid., 363; *Tribune* in ibid; *Banker's Magazine* (April 1886), 796; Garraty, *The New Commonwealth*, 166.

[97]Ibid., 363; Garraty, *The New Commonwealth*, 165–67; Schneirov, *Labor and Urban Politics*, 200–201; Paul Avrich, *Haymarket Tragedy*; Burrows and Wallace, *Gotham*, 1098.

[98]Dubofsky, *Industrialism and the American Worker*, 61–65; Garraty, *The New Commonwealth*, 168–69.

[99]O'Donnell, "Henry George," 168; Samuel Gompers, *Seventy Years of Life and Labour* (New York: E. P. Dutton, 1925), 60–62.

[100]Quotes: "very different," Theodore Dreiser, *Color of a Great City* (New York: Boni and Liveright Publishers, 1923), viii; "cash," Harold Livesay, *Samuel Gompers and Organized Labor in America* (Boston: Little, Brown, 1978), 17–18; *Dictionary of American Biography*, Volume 7, 369–71.

[101]Quotes: "vast quadrille," Livesay, *Samuel Gompers*, 18; "on labor," Gompers, *Seventy Years of Life and Labour*, 69; ibid, 46–62, 73–88.

[102]Ibid., 111–27; Livesay, *Samuel Gompers*, 25–26, 46–51.

[103]Garraty, ed., *Labor and Capital in the Gilded Age*, 8–20; Gompers, *Seventy Years*, 186–98; Livesay, *Samuel Gompers*, 52–53, 60.

[104]Garraty, *The New Commonwealth*, 170.

[105]Quote: Livesay, *Samuel Gompers*, 83; ibid., 29–31; Gompers, *Seventy Years*, 228–31; 264–72.

[106]*New York Herald*, April 22, 1873.

[107]*New York Times* in O'Donnel, "Henry George," 463–65; Ibid., 183, 203, 348–74; 405–13, 433–34, 457; Edmund Morris, *The Rise of Theodore Roosevelt* (New York: Coward, McCann and Geoghegan, 1979), 343; Charles Albro Barker, *Henry George* (New York: Oxford University Press, 1955), 460.

[108]Quote: Barker, *Henry George*, 121; O'Donnel, "Henry George," 36–37, 54–58.

[109]Quotes: "Where," Henry George, *Progress and Poverty: An Inquiry into the Cause of Industrial Depressions and of Increase of Want with Increase of Wealth* (New York: 1885), 6–8; "toll," "debases," ibid., 364–65; "great co-operative," Garraty, *The New Commonwealth*, 317; O'Donnel, "Henry George," 58, 75–99, 119; Morris, *The Rise of Theodore Roosevelt, 344*.

[110]Quote: Garraty, *The New Commonwealth*, 318; *New York Times*, September 25, 1886; Barker, *Henry George*, 465.

[111]Ibid., 464, 473.

[112]Quotes: "the gamblers," Hammack, *Power and Society*, 10; "the weary," *New York Times*, September 25, 1886; O'Donnel, "Henry George," 124, 494; Burrows and Wallace, *Gotham*, 1099–1100.

[113]Quote: *New York Times*, October 8, 1886; ibid., October 27, November 19, 1886; Barker, *Henry George*, 464, 473.

[114]Quote: "just," Morris, *The Rise of Theodore Roosevelt*, 346; Hammack, *Power and Society*, 101; Burrows and Wallace, *Gotham*, 1102; Barker, *Henry George*, 468; G. Wallace Chessman, *Governor Theodore Roosevelt: The Albany Apprenticeship, 1898–1900* (Boston: Little, Brown, 1969), 47.

[115]Quotes: "face," ibid., 29; "mouth," Morris, *The Rise of Theodore Roosevelt*, 162; "brute . . . corrupt," Chessman, *Governor Theodore Roosevelt*, 30; Morris, *The Rise of Theodore Roosevelt*, 172.

[116]Quote: Chessman, *Governor Theodore Roosevelt*, 29; ibid., 30–31; Morris, *The Rise of Theodore Roosevelt*, 173, 177.

[117]Quotes: "criminal class," Morris, *The Rise of Theodore Roosevelt*, 193; "[W]hen I voted," Chessman, *Governor Theodore Roosevelt*, 36; "professional agitators," ibid., 37; "*Sun,*" Ibid., 35.

[118]Quotes: "socialistic," Burrows and Wallace, *Gotham*, 1102; "first waked," Chessman, *Governor Theodore Roosevelt*, 38.

[119]Morris, *The Rise of Theodore Roosevelt*, 241.

[120]Ibid., 233–35; Chessman, *Governor Theodore Roosevelt*, 40.

[121]Quotes: "riflemen," ibid., 45; "emasculated," Morris, *The Rise of Theodore Roosevelt*, 346; "timid good," ibid., 354–55; ibid., 348–53; Burrows and Wallace, *Gotham*, 1103.

[122]Morris, *The Rise of Theodore Roosevelt*, 346; Hammack, *Power and Society*, 115, 129–40; Burrows and Wallace, *Gotham*, 1105–106.

[123]Hammack, *Power and Society*, 112–13; Morris, *The Rise of Theodore Roosevelt*, 355–57; Barker, *Henry George*, 468.

[124]Quotes: "never go out," Burrows and Wallace, *Gotham*, 1106; "Defeat," *New York Times*, October 30, 1886; "significant feature" and "stupid," *New York Times*, November 4, 1886; ibid., November 18, 1886.

[125]Hammack, *Power and Society*, 137–39; Burrows and Wallace, *Gotham*, 1107–8.

[126]Hammack, *Power and Society*, 306, 315–19; *New York Times*, November 28, 1886; Burrows and Wallace, *Gotham*, 1110.

[127]Martin Sklar, *The Corporate Reconstruction of American Capitalism*, 22–23, 31–33.

[128]Frank Luther Mott, *American Journalism: A History of Newspapers in the United States Through 250 Years, 1690–1940* (New York: The Macmillan Company, 1941), 412, 430–38; Burrows and Wallace, *Gotham*, 681–703, 1151–53; Rodgers, *Atlantic Crossings*, 20–158; W. A. Swanberg, *Pulitzer* (New York: Scribner, 1967), 73–174.

[129]The literature on populism is extensive. A sample: John D. Hicks, *The Populist Revolt: A History of the Farmers' Alliance and the People's Party* (Minneapolis: University of Minnesota Press, 1931); Richard Hofstadter, *The Age of Reform: From Bryan to F.D.R.* (New York: Alfred A. Knopf, 1955); Norman Pollack, *The Populist Response to Industrial America* (Cambridge, Mass.: Harvard University Press, 1962); Lawrence Goodwyn, *Democratic Promise: The Populist Moment in America* (New York: Oxford University Press, 1976); Elizabeth Sanders, *Roots of Reform.*

[130]Quotes: "amount to something," Chessman, *Governor Theodore Roosevelt*, 27; "like to speak," Morris, *The Rise of Theodore Roosevelt*, 353; ibid., 239.

[131]Quote: Ibid., 349; ibid., 227, 347.

[132]Quote: Kirkland, *Industry Comes of Age* (New York: Holt, Rinehart and Winston, 1961), 404.

[133]Sklar, *The Corporate Reconstruction of American Capitalism*, 1–40.

[134]Kirkland, *Industry Comes of Age*, 407–8.

[135]Mandelbaum, *Boss Tweed*, 43; Thomas Kessner, *The Golden Door: Italian and Jewish Immigrant Mobility in New York City, 1880–1915* (New York: Oxford University Press, 1977), 165.

## CHAPTER 6: THE AGE OF MORGAN

[1]Sigmund Diamond, *The Reputation of the American Businessman* (Cambridge, Mass.: Harvard University Press, 1955), 84.

[2]Ibid., 93.

[3]Vincent Carosso, *The Morgans: Private International Bankers, 1854–1913* (Cambridge, Mass.: Harvard University Press, 1987), 433–36.

⁴Carosso, *The Morgans*, 435–36.

⁵Quotes: *"thermopylae,"* Jean Strouse, *Morgan: American Financier* (New York: Random House, 1999), 224; "No nose" and "driving," Vincent Carosso, *The Morgans*, 433; Strouse, *Morgan*, 222–30; 293–94.

⁶Carosso, *The Morgans*, 433–34.

⁷Ibid., 435; Strouse, *Morgan*, 379–80.

⁸Quote: Carosso, *The Morgans*, 275.

⁹Ronald Chernow, *The House of Morgan: An American Banking Dynasty and the Rise of Modern Finance* (New York: Simon & Schuster, 1990), 80.

¹⁰Quote: *The Banker's Magazine and Statistical Register* 45 (December 1890): 407; ibid., 411; Ibid. (February 1891): 593; Anna R. Burr, *The Portrait of a Banker: James R. Stillman* (New York: Duffield and Company, 1927), 90–91; Carosso, *The Morgans*, 302.

¹¹Rendigs Fels, *American Business Cycles, 1865–1897* (Chapel Hill, N.C.: University of North Carolina Press, 1959), 167–68, 186; Charles Hoffman, *The Depression of the Nineties* (Westport, Conn.: Greenwood Pub. Corp., 1970), 127–32, 146; 153–54, 177; Vincent Carosso, *Investment Banking in America: A History* (Cambridge, Mass.: Harvard University Press, 1970), 302; *The Banker's Magazine and Statistical Register* 45 (December 1890): 56; Ibid., 47 (June 1893): 882–83; Ibid., (February 1893): 568–70.

¹²Quote: *The Banker's Magazine and Statistical Register* 47 (June 1893): 883; Fels, *American Business Cycles*, 115, 181.

¹³*New York Times*, June 30, 1893.

¹⁴*New York Times*, June 26, 1893; Edward Burrows and Michael Wallace, *Gotham: A History of New York City to 1898* (New York: Oxford University Press, 1999), 1185–90. Other estimates are in Leah H. Feder, *Unemployment Relief in Periods of Depression* (New York: Arno Press, 1971), 79–80; Carlos Closson Jr., "The Unemployed in American Cities," *Journal of Economics* 8 (January 1894): 257–58; Charles D. Kellog, "The Situation in New York City During the Winter of 1893–1894," *Proceedings of the National Conference of Charities and Correction*, in Feder, *Unemployment Relief*, 83.

¹⁵Quotes: "opulent," *New York Times*, January 22, 1894; "they take," Strouse, *Morgan*, 318; *New York Times*, March 12, 1894; Carosso, *The Morgans*, 302; Fels, *American Business Cycles*, 119, 190, 194–95; Hoffman, *Depression of the Nineties*, 248.

¹⁶Quote: *The Banker's Magazine and Statistical Register* 47 (August 1893): 129; Carosso, *The Morgans*, 304, 305, 396.

¹⁷Quote: Fels, *American Business Cycles*, 185–86; Carosso, *The Morgans*, 302, 311.

¹⁸Quote: Carosso, *The Morgans*, 313–15; *New York Times*, November 12, 1893.

¹⁹Quote: Carosso, *The Morgans*, 316; ibid., 317–18; Strouse, *Morgan*, 340.

²⁰Carosso, *The Morgans*, 321.

²¹Ibid., 323–25.

²²Ibid., 325.

²³Ibid., 326; Strouse, *Morgan*, 342–43.

²⁴Quote: Carosso, *The Morgans*, 328; ibid., 330; Fels, *American Business Cycles*, 202–3.

²⁵Carosso, *The Morgans*, 331–33.

[26]Ibid., 334.

[27]Quote: Ibid., 320–21; *New York Times* in Strouse, *Morgan*, 350–51.

[28]Carosso, *The Morgans*, 339.

[29]Strouse, *Morgan*, 351.

[30]Quote: Carosso, *The Morgans*, 337; ibid., 320.

[31]Quotes: "watched & followed," ibid., 333; "no middle ground," Ray Allen Billington, *Westward Expansion: A History of the American Frontier* (New York: Macmillan Co., 1949), 741.

[32]Hoffman, *The Depression of the Nineties*, 274.

[33]*New York Times*, February 28, 1892.

[34]Quote: *New York Times*, July 5, 1892; Strouse, *Morgan*, 349, 355–60; Burrows and Wallace, *Gotham*, 1204–206. While outdated in many ways, Richard Hofstadter's provocative and stylishly written *The Age of Reform: From Bryan to FDR* (New York: Alfred A. Knopf, 1955), especially 23–130, offers a fine insight into this aspect of the populist revolt against modern society. See also the other monographs on populism cited in chapter 5.

[35]*New York Times*, February 21, 1892, July 11, 1896.

[36]Quote: Carosso, *The Morgans*, 347; ibid., 276.

[37]Quote: Joseph F. Wall, *Andrew Carnegie* (New York: Oxford University Press, 1970), 467–68; Paul W. Glad, *McKinley, Bryan and the People* (Philadelphia: Lippincott, 1964), 23, 169; Strouse, *Morgan*, 355, 358; Chernow, *Titan: The Life of John D. Rockefeller, Sr.* (New York: Random House, 1998), 388; Burrows and Wallace, *Gotham*, 1205.

[38]Quote: Strouse, *Morgan*, 358; Glad, *McKinley, Bryan*, 189–95, 200–10.

[39]Carosso, *The Morgans*, 348–49; Strouse, *Morgan*, 359.

[40]N. S. B. Gras and Henrietta Larson, *Casebook in American Business History* (New York: Appleton-Century-Crofts, 1939), 556.

[41]Strouse, *Morgan*, 320; Carosso, *The Morgans*, 363.

[42]Quotes: "frankness," Gras and Larson, *Casebook*, 558, "your roads," ibid., 556; Carosso, *The Morgans*, 363, 367, 370–71; Strouse, *Morgan*, 320.

[43]Carosso, *The Morgans*, 365–66, 373–78.

[44]Ibid., 375–76.

[45]Quote: Ibid., 360; ibid., 364–67, 398; Gras and Larson, *Casebook*, 557; E. G. Campbell, *The Reorganization of the American Railroad System: 1893–1900* (New York: Columbia University Press, 1938); Strouse, *Morgan*, 322.

[46]Chandler, *Visible Hand*, 173–74; Carosso, *The Morgans*, 364–67; Chernow, *House of Morgan*, 58, 66, 68; Gras and Larson, *Casebook*, 559.

[47]Quote: Carosso, *The Morgans*, 396, ibid., 365–66.

[48]Quote: *New York Times* in ibid., 366.

[49]Quotes: "unwise," Strouse, *Morgan*, 336; "shudder," ibid., 335.

[50]Quotes: "demands," Carosso, *The Morgans*, 438; "gigantic," Strouse, *Morgan*, 367; ibid., 394.

[51]Strouse, *Morgan*, 394.

[52]Carosso, *The Morgans*, 352; Chandler, *The Visible Hand: The Managerial Revolution in American Business* (Cambridge: Belknap Press, 1977), 171.

[53]William Roy, *Socializing Capital: The Rise of the Large Industrial Corporation in America* (Princeton: Princeton University Press, 1997), 4; 198–99.

[54]Carosso, *The Morgans*, 43; Roy, *Socializing Capital*, 202–3.

[55]Quote: Alfred Eichner, *The Emergence of Oligopoly: Sugar Refining as a Case Study* (Baltimore: Johns Hopkins Press, 1969), 71; ibid., 69, 117; Roy, *Socializing Capital*, 208–10; *Dictionary of American Biography*, Volume 8 (New York: C. Scribner's Sons, 1928–1958), 404.

[56]Eichner, *Emergence of Oligopoly*, 149.

[57]Quote: *The Banker's Magazine and Statistical Register* 46 (August 1892): 81–82; Alfred Chandler, *Scale and Scope: The Dynamics of Industrial Capitalism* (Cambridge: Belknap Press, 1990), 73; Chandler, *Visible Hand*, 330–31; Eichner, *The Emergence of Oligopoly*, 149; Roy, *Socializing Capital*, 152, 165–66, 171, 200–203.

[58]Quotes: All, Eichner, *Emergence of Oligopoly*, 172–75; ibid., 75, 76, 150; Roy, *Socializing Capital*, 212–13.

[59]Eichner, *Emergence of Oligopoly*, 177–78; 186–87. See also Morton J. Horowitz, *The Transformation of American Law, 1780–1860* (Cambridge, Mass.: Harvard University Press, 1977); Donald Dewey, *Monopoly in Economics and Law* (Chicago: Rand McNally, 1959).

[60]Carosso, *The Morgans*, 42; Roy, *Socializing Capital*, 177, 251; Chandler, *Visible Hand*, 316; Chandler, *Scale and Scope*, 8.

[61]Glenn Porter, *The Rise of Big Business, 1860–1920* (Arlington Heights, Ill.: Harlan Davidson, 1992, 2nd ed.), 62; *Historical Statistics of the United States, Colonial Times to 1970*, Volume 1 (Washington, D.C.: U.S. Govt. Print. Off., 1975, 2 vols.), 200–201.

[62]Abraham Lincoln to William F. Elkins, November 21, 1864, Archer H. Shaw, *The Lincoln Encyclopedia* (New York: Macmillan, 1950), 40; Eichner, *Emergence of Oligopoly*, 17.

[63]Quotes: "tempted," Roy, *Socializing Capital*, 198; "rich," Carosso, *The Morgans*, 29; "big deals," ibid., 48; Chernow, *Titan*, 389; Chandler, *Scale and Scope*, 81–82; Eichner, *Emergence of Oligopoly*, 3; Chandler, *Visible Hand*, 334–35.

[64]Carosso, *The Morgans*, 29, 76–79, 432.

[65]Quote: Ibid., 59–60; ibid., 66, 171.

[66]Quote: Ibid., 89; Ibid., 66–78, 452; *New York Times*, March 4, 1902.

[67]Quote: Cyrus Adler, *Jacob Schiff: His Life and Letters*, Volume 1 (Garden City, N.Y.: Doubleday, Doran, 1928, 2 vols.), 4–5; Naomi Cohen, *Jacob Schiff: A Study in American Jewish Leadership* (Hanover, N.H.: Brandeis University Press; University Press of New England, 1999), 3; Ron Chernow, *The Warburgs: The Twentieth-Century Odyssey of a Remarkable Jewish Family* (New York: Random House, 1993), 46; Carosso, *The Morgans*, 81, 452.

[68]Quote: Cohen, *Jacob Schiff*, 5; ibid., 3–5; Adler, *Jacob Schiff*, 1, 4–9; Carosso, *The Morgans*, 19, 71.

[69]Chernow, *The Warburgs*, 48; Cohen, *Jacob Schiff*, 6, 9; Adler, *Jacob Schiff*, 11–12; Barry E. Supple, "A Business Elite: German-Jewish Financiers in Nineteenth Century New York," *Business History Review* 3 (Summer 1957): 143–78.

[70]Quote: Adler, *Jacob Schiff*, 13; Cohen, *Jacob Schiff*, 9.

[71]Quote: Cohen, *Jacob Schiff*, 9; Adler, *Jacob Schiff*, 25–26; 66–67.

[72]Quotes: "Friday evening," in Adler, *Jacob Schiff*, Volume 2, 322; "waste," ibid., 293; ibid., 343–45, 358–63, 383–85, 392–93; Chernow, *The Warburgs*, 49, 99–100.

[73]Quote: "spanked," Chernow, *The Warburgs*, 50; Adler, *Jacob Schiff*, 349–50; Cohen, *Jacob Schiff*, 12.

[74]Adler, *Jacob Schiff*, 71–73, 124; Cohen, *Jacob Schiff*, 9; Carosso, *The Morgans*, 31.

[75]Quote: "J. P. Morgan's affair," ibid., 387; ibid., 452; Adler, *Jacob Schiff*, 179.

[76]Quote: Adler, *Jacob Schiff*, 102–7; ibid., 177; Carosso, *The Morgans*, 100.

[77]Strouse, *Morgan*, 396, Eichner, *Emergence of Oligopoly*, 187.

[78]Carosso, *The Morgans*, 394.

[79]Strouse, *Morgan*, 311–12.

[80]Chandler, *Visible Hand*, 427; Carosso, *The Morgans*, 391; Strouse, *Morgan*, 312–15.

[81]Quote "exploded," Carosso, *The Morgans*, 533; "ideology," in Roy, *Socializing Capital*, 180.

[82]Quotes: "Reckafellow," Wall, *Andrew Carnegie*, 600; "It is," ibid., 589–90; Chernow, *Titan*, 383–84; Sven Beckert, *The Monied Metropolis: New York City and the Consolidation of the American Bourgeoisie, 1850–1896* (Cambridge: Cambridge University Press, 2001), 244; Wall, *Andrew Carnegie*, 589–90, 600.

[83]Quotes, "Messaba," Wall, *Andrew Carnegie*, 596; "All hail," ibid., 606–7; ibid., 591–98; David Freeman Hawke, *John D.: The Founding Father of the Rockefellers* (New York: Harper and Row, 1980), 245–56; Harold Livesay, *Andrew Carnegie and the Rise of Big Business* (Boston: Little, Brown, 1975), 152–54; Chernow, *Titan*, 383.

[84]Wall, *Andrew Carnegie*, 606–7; Livesay, *Andrew Carnegie*, 155; Chandler, *Scale and Scope*, 129; Hawke, *John D.*, 263.

[85]Quotes: "may be millions," Wall, *Andrew Carnegie*, 645–65; "Prodigious" and "where is there," Livesay, *Andrew Carnegie*, 184.

[86]Quotes: Ibid., 166, 182–83; Strouse, *Morgan*, 397–400; Carosso, *The Morgans*, 391–92.

[87]Gras and Larson, *Casebook*, 559; Strouse, *Morgan*, 397–99; Carosso, *The Morgans*, 391–92; Hawke, *John D.*, 263–64.

[88]Quotes: "fail sadly," Livesay, *Andrew Carnegie*, 183; "finished articles," Wall, *Andrew Carnegie*, 584; "railroad cars," Livesay, *Andrew Carnegie*, 169; "fittest," Strouse, *Morgan*, 400; ibid., 399; Wall, *Andrew Carnegie*, 606–10, 654; Livesay, *Andrew Carnegie*, 186–87.

[89]Hawke, *John D.*, 266.

[90]Quote: Carosso, *The Morgans*, 467; Livesay, *Andrew Carnegie*, 181; Strouse, *Morgan*, 396; Wall, *Andrew Carnegie*, 781–85.

[91]Strouse, *Morgan*, 401–2; Carosso, *The Morgans*, 468–69; *New York Times*, May 5, 1899; Wall, *Andrew Carnegie*, 784–85.

[92]Quote: Burr, *Portrait of a Banker*, 153; Wall, *Andrew Carnegie*, 780–81; Hawke; *John D.*, 263–66; Herbert Satterlee, *J. Pierpont Morgan: An Intimate Portrait* (New York: The Macmillan Company, 1939), 346.

[93]Quote: Ibid.; Carosso, *The Morgans*, 469; Strouse, *Morgan*, 403–4; Wall, *Andrew Carnegie*, 789; Hawke, *John D.*, 267–68.

[94]Quotes: "manly," Chernow, *Titan*, 390; "high and mighty," Hawke, *John D.*, 267–68; Chernow, *The House of Morgan*, 103–4; Chernow, *Titan*, 372–73.

[95]Quote: Hawke, *John D.*, 271; ibid., 208, 275; Chernow, *Titan*, 390–93.

[96]Chernow, *Death of the Banker*, 98–99; Carosso, *The Morgans*, 472–73.

[97]Quotes: "richest," Strouse, *Morgan*, 403–4; "It takes," Satterlee, *Morgan: An Intimate Portrait*, 348.

[98]Quotes: "sun," Strouse, *Morgan*, 404; Mr. Dooley, ibid., 405; Chernow, *Titan*, 393; Carosso, *The Morgans*, 470.

[99]Quote: Strouse, *Morgan*, 406; Eichner, *Emergence of Oligopoly*, Volume 1; Martin J. Sklar, *The Corporate Reconstruction of American Capitalism, 1890–1916: The Market, the Law, and Politics* (New York: Cambridge University Press, 1988), 46.

[100]Woodrow Wilson, *The Making of the Nation*, Volume 1 (New York: 1925), 328, in Sklar, *Corporate Reconstruction*, 11; Naomi Lamoreaux, *The Great Merger Movement in American Business: 1895–1904* (New York: Cambridge University Press, 1985), 187; Roy, *Socializing Capital*, 177; Chandler, *Visible Hand*, 316, 338–39.

[101]Lamoreaux, *Great Merger Movement*, 1, 10; Eichner, *Emergence of Oligopoly*, 99; T. R. Navin and M. V. Sears, "The Rise of a Market for Industrial Securities, 1877–1902," *Business History Review* 29 (June 1955): 114–16.

[102]Quote: *New York Times*, January 24, 1899; *The Banker's Magazine and Statistical Register* 51 (March 1897): 392; Carosso, *The Morgans*, 84–85; Eric Lampard, "The New York Metropolis in Transformation: History and Prospect, A Study in Historical Particularity," H. J. Ewers, J. B. Goddard, and H. Matzerath, eds., *The Future of the Metropolis* (Berlin: W. de Gruyter, 1986), 65–66.

[103]Quote: Daniel Bell, *The End of Ideology* (New York: Collier Books, 1962, rev. ed.), 42–43; Chandler, *Scale and Scope*, 12, 75–81.

[104]Quote: John Brisben Walker, "The World's Greatest Revolution," the *Cosmopolitan* 30 (April 1901): 677–80, in Wall, *Andrew Carnegie*, 798; Eric Lampard, *The New York Metropolis*, 65; Ronald Chernow, *Death of the Banker*, 28.

[105]Quotes: *New York Times*, January 29, 1899; "small, single function," Chandler, *Scale and Scope*, 252; ibid., 292–94.

[106]*New York Times*, January 29, 1899.

[107]Simon Kuznets, *Economic Growth of Nations: Total Output and Production Structure* (Cambridge, Mass.: Belknap Press of Harvard University Press, 1971), 144–47; Chandler, *Scale and Scope*, 5; Walt W. Rostow, *The World Economy: History and Prospects* (Austin, Tex.: University of Texas Press, 1978), 52–53.

[108]Chandler, *Visible Hand*, 205; Roy, *Socializing Capital*, 5; Lampard, *The New York Metropolis*, 65–67.

[109]Chandler, *Scale and Scope*, 63.

[110]Quotes: Strouse, *Morgan*, 434–35.

[111] Carosso, *Investment Banking*, 107.

[112] Edmund Morris, *The Rise of Theodore Roosevelt* (New York: Coward, McCann and Geoghegan, 1979), 704.

[113] Quotes: "horror," Carosso, *The Morgans*, 453; "corrupt wealth," Strouse, *Morgan*, 438.

[114] Quotes: "rigorous control," Morris, *Rise of Theodore Roosevelt*, 712; "little loose," Thomas C. Platt to Theodore Roosevelt, May 6, 1899, Elting E. Morison and John Blum, eds., *The Letters of Theodore Roosevelt*, Volume 7 (Cambridge: 1951–1954, 8 vols.), 1004; ibid., TR to J. B. Bishop, March 22, 1900, Volume 7, 1238.

[115] Quotes: "just balance," ibid., TR to T. C. Platt, May 8, 1899, Volume 7, 1004–9; "dangerous element," TR to J. B. Bishop, April 11, 1900, Volume 7, 1256–57.

[116] Quotes: "kick me upstairs," ibid., also TR to H. C. Lodge, April 9, 1900, ibid., 1253; "take the veil," TR to H. C. Lodge, February 3, 1900, ibid., 1166; TR to T. C. Platt, May 8, 1899, 1004–9, and TR to J. B. Bishop, April 11, 1900, 1256–57, ibid., demonstrates the complicated relationship between TR and Boss Platt; George Mowry, *The Era of Theodore Roosevelt and the Birth of Modern America: 1900–1912* (New York: Harper and Row, 1962), 109.

[117] Carosso, *The Morgans*, 454.

[118] Mowry, *Era of Theodore Roosevelt*, 106–7.

[119] Quote: "real and grave," G. Wallace Chessman, *Theodore Roosevelt and the Politics of Power* (Boston: Little, Brown, 1969), 84; Mowry, *Era of Theodore Roosevelt*, 121; Strouse, *Morgan*, 439.

[120] Quote: Mowry, *Era of Theodore Roosevelt*, 131; Strouse, *Morgan*, 433.

[121] Quotes: All, Strouse, *Morgan*, 440–41; Chessman, *Theodore Roosevelt*, 85; Mowry, *Era of Theodore Roosevelt*, 132–33.

[122] Mowry, *Era of Theodore Roosevelt*, 131.

[123] TR to C. A. S. Rice, May 29, 1897, Morison, *Letters of TR*, Volume 6, 620.

[124] Chessman, *Theodore Roosevelt*, 84; Mowry, *Era of Theodore Roosevelt*, 121; Strouse, *Morgan*, 433–34, 439.

[125] *New York Times*, December 12, 1890; Kenneth T. Jackson, ed., *The Encyclopedia of New York City* (New Haven, Conn.: Yale University Press, 1995), 921–23.

[126] Quotes: "it requires," Harold C. Syrett, *The City of Brooklyn, 1865–1898; A Political History* (New York: Columbia University, 1948), 246; "What the bridge," ibid., 247; George A. Mazeraki, "The Public Career of Andrew Haswell Green" (Ph.D. dissertation, New York University, 1966), 316; David C. Hammack, *Power and Society: Greater New York at the Turn of the Century* (New York: Russell Sage Foundation, 1982), 185; John Foord, *The Life and Public Services of Andrew Haswell Green* (Garden City, N.Y.: Doubleday, Page and Company, 1913), 178.

[127] Quote: "public sentiment," *New York Times*, May 15, 1894; Burrows and Wallace, *Gotham*, 1228.

[128] John C. Teaford, *The Unheralded Triumph: City Government in America, 1870–1900* (Baltimore: Johns Hopkins University Press, 1983), 188–214. In

an 1870 report, the Chamber of Commerce speaks of itself as "abstaining from all interference in the affairs of government, taking no part in political decisions." Chamber of Commerce of the State of New York, *Twelfth Annual Report, 1870;* Burrows and Wallace, *Gotham,* 1223.

[129]Quotes: "imperial destiny" and "municipal grandeur," Hammack, *Power and Society,* 192–93; "splendidly," ibid., 13.

[130]"It is not intended now," Green wrote in a planning document in 1868, "to do more than direct attention to the important subject of bringing the City of New York and the County of Kings, a part of Westchester County and a part of Queens and Richmond, including the various suburbs of the city, within a certain radial distance from the centre, under one common municipal government." Foord, *Life and Public Services of Andrew Haswell Green,* 188; Syrett, *The City of Brooklyn,* 255.

[131]Quote: *New York Times,* March 6, 1894; Jackson, *Encyclopedia of New York City,* 143.

[132]Burrows and Wallace, *Gotham,* 1223.

[133]Quote: *New York Times,* January 18, 1895; Albert Henschel, *Municipal Consolidation: Historical Sketch of Greater New York* (New York: Press of Stettiner, Labert and Co., 1895), 39; *New York Times,* October 30, 1894.

[134]*New York Times,* February 27, 1894.

[135]Memorial to the Lexow Hearings, *In the Matter of the Hearing in Relation to the "Greater New York" Held Before the Sub-Committee of the Joint Committee on the Affairs of Cities Transmitted to the Legislature, 25 February 1896* (Albany and New York: Wynkoop Hallenbeck Crawford Co., 1896), 538, 541–45. First delivered as a speech in 1894 and reported in *New York Times,* December 23, 1894.

[136]Quotes: "coming forces" and "the crowns," both in A. H. Green, "To Make a Greater City," in *New York Times,* December 12, 1890; "vapory dimensions," Foord, *Life and Public Services of Andrew Haswell Green,* 188; "attained their rank," Henschel, "Municipal Consolidation," 39; Foord, *Life and Public Services of Andrew Haswell Green,* 294; Syrett, *The City of Brooklyn,* 255.

[137]Ibid., 11–13, 19–20, 25–26; Syrett, *The City of Brooklyn,* 249; Foord, *Life and Public Services of Andrew Haswell Green,* 186–96; Mazeraki, "The Public Career of Andrew Haswell Green," 328–69.

[138]Quote: Albert E. Henschel, Municipal Program Conference Address on "Greater New York," (May 24, 1894), 67–68; "The Municipal Problem and Greater New York," *Atlantic Monthly* 79 (June 1897): 740; *New York Times,* January 2, 1895.

[139]Barry J. Kaplan, "A Study in the Politics of Metropolitanization: The Greater New York City Charter of 1897" (Ph.D. dissertation, State University of New York at Buffalo, 1975), 208–337.

[140]Quote: *New York Times,* March 23, 1898, June 16, 1897.

[141]The historian of the Chicago metropolis, William Cronon, writes, "At the highest level there really was just one financial hinterland in the country" every-

where outside of New York. *Nature's Metropolis: Chicago and the Great West* (New York: W. W. Norton, 1991), 453.

[142]Henry Adams, *The Education of Henry Adams* (New York: Modern Library, 1931), 463; John Steele Gordon, "The Magnitude of John Pierpont Morgan," *American Heritage* (July–August, 1989): 86.

[143]*The Banker's Magazine and Statistical Register* 45 (June 1891): 985.

[144]Adams, *The Education*, 462–63.

[145]*The Conservator* in Sigmund Diamond, *The Reputation of the American Businessman* (Cambridge, Mass.: Harvard University Press, 1955), 91, italics added.

[146]Diamond, *The Reputation of the American Businessman*, 88.

[147]Quotes "born in 1839," *New York World Telegram*, May 24, 1937, in Diamond, *The Reputation of the American Businessman*, 122; "Like Napoleon," ibid., 118.

[148]*Dartmouth College* v. *Woodward*, 1819.

[149]Adams, *The Education*, 462.

# INDEX